SPONTANEOUS SHELTER

International Perspectives and Prospects

Spontaneous Shelter

International Perspectives and Prospects

Edited by

Carl V. Patton

TEMPLE UNIVERSITY PRESS

Philadelphia

Temple University Press, Philadelphia 19122

Published 1988
Printed in the United States of America

The paper used in this publication meets the minimum requirements of American National Standard for Information Sciences—Permanence of Paper for Printed Library Materials, ANSI Z39.48-1984

Library of Congress Cataloging-in-Publication Data

Spontaneous shelter.

Bibliography: by chapter
Includes index.
1. Poor—Housing—Developing countries. 2. Poor—Housing—Government policy—Developing countries.
3. Housing policy—Developing countries. I. Patton, Carl V.
HD7287.96.D44S66 1988 363.5′8′091724 87-10002
ISBN 0-87722-507-9 (alk. paper)

Contents

Illustrations

Figure

Tables

Acknowledgments

Numerous people provided valuable assistance in the preparation of this book, which includes contributions from around the world by authors of diverse backgrounds. Kathleen Reed applied her outstanding editorial skills to help put the chapters into a consistent format and resolve style problems. She also provided critical, substantive comments that helped clarify numerous arguments. Janet Tibbetts and the School of Architecture and Urban Planning secretarial staff efficiently produced the final manuscript from incompatible computer disks and marked-up manuscripts. Mary Capouya, of Temple University Press, oversaw the production of the book with efficiency and good humor. Unless noted otherwise, the chapter authors took the photographs and prepared the sketches and maps for their chapters, and Steve McEnroe printed the photo illustrations. Insightful comments were received from several anonymous reviewers, but Barry Checkoway, Albert Guttenberg, Samuel Noe, Amos Rapoport, and Jane Patton went beyond the call of duty by providing detailed, critical comments. Jane Patton also took on the tasks of checking references, locating obscure sources, and proofreading numerous versions of draft chapters. I deeply appreciate the valuable contributions of each of these colleagues.

Introduction

Shelter is a fundamental human need. It is a form of protection from the elements, a means through which to express individual and cultural values, and a way to produce, consume, and accumulate capital. Nevertheless, in virtually all parts of the world, but particularly in the developing or Third World countries, millions of people are ill housed or not housed at all.[1] Debate continues over the extent and composition of the shelter problem and appropriate roles for individuals and government in solving it. But there is agreement that culturally responsive, environmentally sound, and economically feasible policy initiatives are needed.

What are the leading contemporary and emerging problems and issues facing people needing shelter in the developing countries of the world? What factors underlie these problems and issues? How do these factors differ by culture and governmental structure? What can be learned from attempts by individuals and governments to resolve the shelter problem? What are the viable policy options? What are the prospects for change? These are among the questions addressed in this book.

An important premise of *Spontaneous Shelter* is that if the people of the developing world are to be sheltered adequately, they will have to continue to play a major role in the provision of this shelter, but the nature and extent of supporting governmental actions may need to change substantially. Although government officials and international agencies acknowledge user-based shelter efforts as an approach to resolving housing needs, more attention should be given to what will and will not work. This book responds to this situation by drawing together a group of concerned and involved authors to examine shelter issues. It provides a comprehensive view of user involvement in the planning, design, economic, cultural, and technical aspects of shelter provision in today's developing world.

Various approaches have been taken to investigate shelter issues. A number of writers have addressed the issue of housing in the Third World, particularly the efforts of people to provide their own housing. Some authors have looked at the issue in a historical context, while others have focused on particular geographic areas or specific potential solutions. Still other authors have examined particular methods of inquiry, specific components of the problem, and the education of housing researchers.[2]

No matter the approach taken, the importance of the roles of individuals in providing their own shelter is in evidence. The scope of the shelter problem, the rate at which housing availability is falling behind demand, the inability of many governments to respond adequately, and the difference between what people desire and what has been provided by third parties call for emphasizing the roles of individuals in shelter provision—whether this be user construction of the most basic, perhaps illegal, shelter or more substantial construction of regulated units built in part by third parties on a government-supplied site with services.

The contributors to this volume understand *shelter* and *housing* to mean more than a structure on a site and reflect the relation of that structure to culture and the larger environment. The issue is not housing alone; it includes the many other aspects of shelter—location, land tenure, related support and community services, building codes and their restrictions, finance and credit mechanisms, and the capacity of governments to respond to citizen needs.

Experience with owner-based shelter efforts is now extensive, and these efforts are increasingly recognized as supportable activities in developing countries. In fact, squatting and unauthorized construction are also taking place in Great Britain, the Netherlands, Denmark, the United States, and many other developed countries (Anning, 1980; Bailey, 1973; Katz and Mayer, 1985). In the United States, for example, squatting is occurring in abandoned tenements in New York and other cities, under the freeways in Los Angeles, and in numerous rural areas, although not of the scale to be found in developing countries. Self-help construction and upgrading schemes have also been suggested as models for aiding the homeless in the United States (Burns, 1986), but our focus is primarily on the developing world where policies toward user provision of shelter continue to change.

Spontaneous Shelter is divided into four sections that address the history and context of the phenomenon, planning and environmental issues, contemporary cases, and policies and prospects. Part I analyzes basic concepts such as the evolution of the shelter situation in the Third World, examines geographic patterns and trends, and provides an overview of the shelter issue. Part II examines several important broad issues, including the design characteristics of spontaneous settlements, appropriate technologies for shelter construction, and environmental challenges. Part III contains case examples selected to illuminate general problems, possible solutions, and emerging trends in eight countries located in South America, the Pacific Rim, Africa, and the Mediterranean area. Part IV addresses economic policies in shelter provision, analyzes various roles that governments have played in addressing the shelter problem, and reviews prospects for the future.

Notes

1. The terms *Third World, underdeveloped,* and *developing* countries tend to be used as synonyms. McGee (1971) defined "Third World" as: "that group of nations frequently labelled 'underdeveloped' which contains almost two-thirds of the world's population. Geographically it includes virtually all the countries of Africa, the Middle East, Asia, and Latin America and omits 'developed' nations such as South Africa, Israel and Japan. [It also excludes] the Communist countries of China, North Vietnam, North Korea and Cuba for their problems of development are being tackled in a different manner from that occurring in the non-Communist Third World nations. . . . A politically neutral term, the 'Third World' . . . distinguishes its countries from those of the capitalist developed world or the Communist World" (p. 10).

2. General works include *Man's Struggle for Shelter in an Urbanizing World* by Charles Abrams (1964), *Freedom to Build: Dweller Control of the Housing Process* by John Turner and Robert Fichter (1972), *People and Housing in Third World Cities: Perspectives on the Problem of Spontaneous Settlements* by Denis Dwyer (1975), *Slums of Hope?: Shanty Towns of the Third World* by Peter C. Lloyd (1979), *People, Poverty and Shelter: Problems of Self-Help Housing in the Third World,* by R. J. Skinner and M. J. Rodell (1983), and *Self-Helf Housing: A Critique* by Peter M. Ward (1982).

Coverage of specific geographic areas includes *The Slums of Karachi: A Case Study* by Shafik Hashmi (1975), *George: The Development of a Squatter Settlement in Lusaka, Zambia* by Ann and Thomas Schlyter (1979), and *The "Young Towns" of Lima: Aspects of Urbanization in Peru* by Peter C. Lloyd (1980).

Works about specific potential solutions include the *Urban Projects Manual: A Guide to Preparing, Upgrading, and New Development Projects Accessible to Low-Income Groups* by Forbes Davidson and Geoffrey K. Payne (1983), *Basic Housing: Policies for Urban Sites, Services and Shelter in Developing Countries* by Aprodicio A. Laquian (1983), and *Adaptive Reuse: Integrating Traditional Areas into the Modern Urban Fabric* by the Aga Kahn Program for Islamic Architecture (1983).

For particular methods of inquiry, see *Transitions: A Photographic Documentary of Squatter Settlements* by Edward Popko (1978). For specific components of the problem, see *Shelter Provision in Developing Countries: The Influence of Standards and Criteria* by Mabogunje, Hardoy, and Misra (1978) and *The Third World Tomorrow: A Report from the Battlefront in the War Against Poverty* by Paul Harrison (1980). On the education of housing researchers, see *Urban Housing Strategies: Education and Realization* by Wakely, Schmetzer, Mumtaz, and Koenigsberger (1976).

References

Abrams, Charles. 1964. *Man's Struggle for Shelter in an Urbanizing World.* Cambridge: MIT Press.

Aga Kahn Program for Islamic Architecture. 1983. *Adaptive Reuse: Integrating Traditional Areas into the Modern Urban Fabric.* Cambridge: Harvard University and MIT Press.

Anning, Nick, et al. 1980. *Squatting: The Real Story.* London: Bay Leaf Books.

Bailey, Ron. 1973. *The Squatters.* Harmondsworth, Middlesex, England: Penguin.

Burns, Leland S. 1986. "Third-World Models for Helping U.S. Homeless." *Wall Street Journal,* January 2, p. 14.

Davidson, Forbes, and Geoffrey K. Payne. 1983. *Urban Projects Manual: A Guide to Preparing, Upgrading and New Development Projects Accessible to Low-Income Groups.* Liverpool: Liverpool University Press with Fairstead Press.

Dwyer, Denis John. 1975. *People and Housing in Third World Cities: Perspectives on the Problem of Spontaneous Settlements.* New York: Longman.

Harrison, Paul. 1980. *The Third World Tomorrow: A Report from the Battlefront in the War Against Poverty.* New York: Penguin.

Hashmi, Shafik H. 1975. *The Slums of Karachi: A Case Study.* Lahore: Aziz Publishers.

Katz, Steven, and Margit Mayer. 1985. "Gimme Shelter: Self-Help Housing Struggles Within and Against the State in New York City and West Berlin." *International Journal of Urban and Regional Research* 9(1), 15–46.

Laquian, Aprodicio A. 1983. *Basic Housing: Policies for Urban Sites, Services and Shelter in Developing Countries.* Ottawa: International Development Research Centre.

Lloyd, Peter C. 1979. *Slums of Hope?: Shanty Towns of the Third World.* New York: Penguin.

———. 1980. *The "Young Towns" of Lima: Aspects of Urbanization in Peru.* Cambridge: Cambridge University Press.

Mabogunje, A. L., J. E. Hardoy, and R. P. Misra. 1978. *Shelter Provision in Developing Countries: The Influence of Standards and Criteria.* New York: Wiley.

McGee, T. G. 1971. *The Urbanization Process in the Third World.* London: Bell and Hyman.

Popko, Edward S. 1978. *Transitions: A Photographic Documentary of Squatter Settlements.* Stroudsburg, Pa.: Dowden, Hutchinson and Ross.

Schlyter, Ann, and Thomas Schlyter. 1979. *George: The Development of a Squatter Settlement in Lusaka, Zambia.* Stockholm: Swedish Council for Building Research.

Skinner, Reinhard J., and Michael J. Rodell. 1983. *People, Poverty and Shelter: Problems of Self-Help Housing in the Third World.* New York: Methuen.

Turner, John F. C., and Robert Fichter, eds. 1972. *Freedom to Build: Dweller Control of the Housing Process.* New York: Macmillan.

Wakely, P. I., H. Schmetzer, B. K. Mumtaz, and O. Koenigsberger. 1976. *Urban Housing Strategies: Education and Realization.* London: Pitman.

Ward, Peter M., ed. 1982. *Self-Help Housing: A Critique.* London: Mansell.

I

History and Context

Chapter 1

Evolution of Third World Shelter Policies

ELIZABETH KUBALE PALMER AND
CARL V. PATTON

World shelter conditions have changed dramatically since the beginning of the twentieth century. People in developed areas are better housed now than they were at the turn of the century, although substantial numbers still remain without adequate shelter (Hartman, 1975, p. 9; Wynn, 1984, pp. 4–5). In contrast, people in developing countries are now living in poorer conditions than at the turn of the century, and conditions have worsened during the past two decades (United Nations, 1976a, p. 91; United Nations, 1976c, p. 40; United Nations Centre for Human Settlements [UNCHS], 1981).

In spite of a variety of definitions and inconsistent figures, experts estimate that from one-fifth to one-half of the inhabitants of developing countries live in makeshift shelters, shantytowns, and various forms of substandard housing (UNCHS, 1982, p. 2; United Nations, 1976c, p. 28, 1976d).

We recognize that defining and measuring housing deficit is fraught with problems because government and aid agency criteria often relate to middle-class values rather than cultural standards (Hardoy and Satterthwaite, 1981, p. 256; Mabogunje, Hardoy, and Misra, 1978; Noe, 1981; United Nations, 1976b, p. 65) and that even the poorest people manage to find some kind of shelter. Nonetheless, there is clearly a need for additional suitable shelter in developing countries. Extrapolating data prepared a decade ago, more than a half-billion units would have to be built between now and the year 2000 to house adequately the people of developing countries (United Nations, 1976a). In order to meet this goal, the housing construction rate in less developed regions would have to increase to eight to ten units per 1,000 people per year from the rate of two to five units per 1,000 people during the past decade (United Nations, 1976c, p. 44). Moreover, between one-third and two-thirds of Third

World urban households cannot afford the lowest-cost dwelling on the market (Ayres, 1983, p. 150; United Nations, 1976a). By the turn of the century, the situation is expected to be more acute (Ghosh, 1984).

The Shelter Shortage Issue

Most observers attribute the shelter shortage in developing countries to a combination of rapid population growth resulting from decreased mortality but sustained fertility (Dwyer, 1974, p. 11; Hauser and Gardner, 1982, p. 54), the migration of rural populations to urban centers in search of employment and better living conditions (Dwyer, 1975; Payne, 1977; Ross, 1973; Ward, 1982), and the low purchasing power of poor people.[1] The rapid population growth far outstripped the ability of governments to provide housing, community services, and even basic infrastructure (Hardoy and Satterthwaite, 1981, p. 203; Payne, 1984, p. xii), and low incomes prevented people from acquiring decent housing (McHale and McHale, 1978). The results in many locales included the creation and expansion of areas of unsanitary and unsafe housing, increased population densities, and various forms of poverty-related problems, including unemployment, poor health, and the lack of essential community services (Drakakis-Smith, 1981; Hardoy and Satterthwaite, 1981; Herbert, 1979; Mountjoy, 1978). While such population growth was taking place early in the twentieth century, it reached alarming proportions after World War II. Moreover, the impacted areas were becoming more numerous, larger, and more visible.

Areas with deteriorated housing, inadequate community services, and poor people have often been called *slums.* The implication is that housing in these areas does not provide adequate shelter, but this is not always true. Many so-called slum areas, although visually chaotic, contain serviceable structures that meet the needs of residents at a cost they can afford and in a location that has economic advantages (Collier, 1976). The common concept of a slum also overlooks the strong social and cultural networks that exist in these areas and the benefits they provide to migrants to the city. This is not meant to romanticize areas of low-quality housing but to note that the word slum, with its negative connotation, is not an appropriate description for many low-quality housing areas.

Much of the housing in developing countries is built outside the formal private and public housing production systems by the owners themselves, often with the assistance of family and friends and with various amounts of hired labor. In some instances this development takes place on appropriated land and is called *squatter housing* or *illegal development.* In other cases the builder may own the land but build a structure not permitted by local laws, and the term *unauthorized housing* is then applied.[2] We have subsumed these various forms of housing production under the general term *spontaneous shelter,*[3] recognizing that some commentators have viewed such shelter provision as a problem while others have viewed it as a solution.

To some observers, the problem in the post–World War II era was the spreading of slums with their social pathologies (Juppenlatz, 1970, p. 5). To others, the problem centered on stemming the influx of migrants (Bonilla, 1961; Matos Mar, 1961). To yet others, the issue was the lack of planning to regulate land and direct growth (Pearse, 1961, p. 145).[4]

While many professional planners and government officials viewed the trends of the 1950s and 1960s with alarm, others were able to see potential benefits in the squatter shelters, the illegal housing, and the user-built structures that had developed in spontaneous settlements in virtually all parts of the world. These actions were viewed as the results of justifiable efforts of the poor to meet legitimate housing needs (Turner and Fichter, 1972). The resulting settlements were called "slums of hope" rather than "slums of despair" (Lloyd, 1979, p. 209; Stokes, 1962; Turner, 1976, p. 18), and the new migrants were seen as beneficial to the urban economy rather than a drain on it (Leeds, 1969; Lloyd, 1979, pp. 141–62).

Yet even when these positive aspects of spontaneous settlements were accepted, many local, national, and international policymakers also recognized that these settlements were typically below minimal standards of health and safety (Dwyer, 1974, p. 212; Laquian, 1983). The recognition that efforts by poor people to house themselves could help to solve the housing shortage in developing countries, joined with the realization that many of these settlements needed to be improved, resulted in the embracing of the so-called self-help approach by local and international development agencies. We say "so-called" because important distinctions exist among owner-built or user-built and contractor-built housing, and among various definitions of squatter, informal, illegal, and unauthorized settlements.[5] Such distinctions are made later in this chapter and in subsequent chapters. The task now is to describe how current efforts for resolving the shelter dilemma in developing countries were derived, and to assess approaches for the future. In order to do this, we present an overview of attempts to house the urban poor in developing countries. We divide the post–World War II era into several major periods, and for each we discuss the thought, action, and reaction of the time. *Thought* is defined as the prevailing ideas, concepts, opinions, and theories regarding the shelter issue and ideas about what ought to be done. *Action* means the primary policies, plans, and solutions applied to respond to perceived problems. *Reaction* refers to the redefinition of the issue and new theories, policies, and solutions suggested by the results of earlier actions.

An analysis of time periods and movements requires the definition of breakpoints and watersheds. Consequently, we divide our discussion of shelter need and provision into several periods. The first is that following World War II until the mid-1960s, when the impact of rural–urban migration was recognized and spontaneous settlements were seen as undesirable invasions.[6] The second and third periods are two ten-year intervals, with the period of the mid-1960s to mid-1970s being characterized by the discovery of both sites and services programs and upgrading schemes, and the mid-1970s to mid-1980s being characterized by a more balanced look at the spontaneous settlement phenomenon. Since these activities appeared at different times around the world, only approximate beginning and ending points can be discerned.

Post–World War II to the Mid-1960s: Spontaneous Settlements as Undesirable Invasions

The rapid urbanization following World War II has been well documented (Dwyer, 1975; Hauser, 1979; Ward, 1982). The rural–urban migration resulted in growth rates of 5 to 7 percent in the urbanizing areas of the world, but the rates experienced in spontaneous settlements were double that average (Turner, 1970, p. 3). Many writers characterized the urban migrants, especially squatters, as marginally skilled people who were not adapting to the urban setting. The situation was well publicized beyond academe by such writers as Franz Fanon (1965), Pablo Friere (1970), Oscar Lewis (1959, 1961), and Gunnar Myrdal (1971). The new urban dwellers were often described in both the academic and popular literature as a burden to the existing social structure and a potential threat to social and political relations.

The *thought* among policymakers in developing areas in the 1950s was not directed as much at finding a solution to the housing problem of the migrants as it was to protecting the formally developed areas of cities and existing social institutions. A major social analyst of the time, Charles Abrams, saw the problem in a more comprehensive manner. Among his many proposals was that of providing land and security of tenure for the new as well as old urban poor (Abrams, 1939, 1964).

While Abrams was calling for basic reform, planners and public officials of the era viewed the rapid population growth with alarm. Officials in many countries were too busy with immediate problems to devise appropriate future-oriented solutions. The major *actions* of the time were aimed at discouraging urban migrants, preventing squatter settlements, providing high-rise alternative housing, and removing spontaneous settlements (Perlman, 1976, p. 15).

Bulldozing low-quality housing has been a common practice in the Third World. Some commentators have argued that instead of trying to eliminate poor housing conditions, this form of urban planning is aimed at removing the poor themselves (Lakshmanan, Chatterjee, and Roy, 1977; Lloyd, 1979, pp. 49–52; Mangin, 1967; Perlman, 1976). Even where adequate alternative housing is provided, clearance programs have rarely managed to rehouse more than a fraction of a city's low-income population (Drakakis-Smith, 1981). Such schemes are also typically extremely costly (Ward, 1982, pp. 5–6).

While successful removal of urban squalor was the exception to the rule, the *reaction* of the time was to continue to remove low-quality housing and to build more high-rise replacement apartments. This approach appealed to Third World political leaders who saw the high-rise structures as evidence of modernity and recognized the political mileage they could gain from such visible projects. Consequently, the urban renewal and dislocation patterns familiar in the United States and Europe appeared in similar forms in Third World cities. As the mid-1960s approached, however, it was becoming clear that policies aimed at replacing poor-quality housing were not working (Abrams, 1964; Mangin, 1967); public housing was not an appropriate way, either culturally or economically, to house the poor (Linn, 1983); and spontaneous settlements were appearing faster than they could be eradicated (Laquian, 1983, p. 7).

Mid-1960s to Mid-1970s: Discovery of Sites and Services and Upgrading Schemes

A cynic might characterize the *thought* of this period as romanticism, but others might view it as realism. Observers began to argue that squatter settlements were not necessarily hopeless environments, rings of misery, or creeping cancers, like the older deteriorated urban environments, in which residents had little hope for advancement (Mangin, 1967; Ward, 1976, 1982). Instead, these evolving communities provided a foothold in the city for new residents and a way for them to adapt to the urban environment (Abrams, 1964). The major school of thought during this period argued that the needs of the user should be at the heart of housing policies for Third World residents, and that users should decide what they need and how it should be provided. The argument is well known now, its central features being that user-built shelter is a more economical alternative than state-provided housing and that the government has a role in assisting the poor in obtaining that shelter. Essentially the government was to be a facilitator of self-help housing (Davidson and Payne, 1983). Turner's phrase "freedom to build" asserted that, if left alone, but provided with government assistance in acquiring materials and security of tenure, the poor could house themselves. The poor would become homeowners, would have a source of capital, and would gradually improve their living conditions. Squatter settlements and shantytowns were seen, not as housing in deterioration, but as housing in the process of improvement (Mangin, 1967; Turner, 1968, 1976).

Other Third World experts also began to paint a new picture of the people living in poor urban conditions (Peattie, 1968). The sociologist Janice Perlman (1976), as a result of her work in a Rio de Janeiro *favela,* challenged the assertion that Latin American squatter settlements lacked internal social cohesion. She found a high rate of participation in clubs and voluntary associations, as well as extensive informal friendship and kinship networks, among neighborhood residents. She also challenged earlier descriptions of crime-laden *favelas,* citing the fact that residents had formed their own security committees and developed strong norms of in-group cooperation and mutual security (1976, p. 135).

In contrast, Anthony Seymour criticized those who believed that spontaneous settlements presented a solution to the housing problem of low-income groups. He disliked the optimistic and romantic overtones characteristic of the approach of Turner, Mangin, and their school of thought. Seymour did not accept the argument that squatter settlements are inhabited by people who are moving upward socially and economically, and that housing policies should aim at helping this process. Instead, he called for a more scientific analysis of the squatter phenomenon (Seymour, 1976, in Agarwal, 1981). Although the issue was never resolved, squatter settlements continue to provide a major source of affordable shelter to poor households.

Third World governments may have failed to provide people with houses, but shelter was nonetheless built, both in villages and in urban areas, by residents themselves with locally available materials. According to numerous observers, the desire of the homeless to house themselves could be the basis for resolving the shelter dilemma. Governments, the thought was, should concentrate their efforts on helping people to help themselves. The poor could be provided with a low-cost core house, consisting perhaps of one room and sanitary facilities, on a secure plot of land. The family could build more room when it could afford to do so. Even simpler, the government could provide families with a site and with services such as water supply, drainage, roads, and street lighting. It could also provide low-interest loans and building materials. Families could then build shelter at their own pace. These sites and services concepts could also be applied to existing areas. The government could legalize squatters' landholdings, provide the locale with essential services, and help residents upgrade their dwellings into permanent structures.

The major *actions* during this period included provision of shelter for the poorest through sites and services programs and upgrading projects, as well as through subsidies and public housing provision, which continued from the previous decade. Sites and services and upgrading schemes were advocated by the World Bank and were adopted by a large number of Third World governments. Upgrading projects were supported in Kenya, Tanzania, Upper Volta, India, Morocco, El Salvador, Bolivia, Egypt, Indonesia, and the Philippines, among many other countries. Yet even during this period of government assistance, unauthorized housing construction outpaced authorized dwelling construction in many locales. In Lusaka, for example, 22,000 houses were constructed between 1969 and 1972, but only 4,000 of these were dwellings built through the formal housing production system (United Nations, 1976a, p. 11).

During this period, some Third World governments also established housing corporations to build or finance houses, especially for the urban poor. Unfortunately, even the lowest-cost houses built or funded by these corporations were too expensive for most of the urban poor. As a result, these institutions came to serve the housing needs of middle-income groups (Strassman, 1977).

Of the possible housing strategies available in the early 1970s, the self-help approach was perhaps the most attractive. Governments around the world were strapped for funds, and the self-help approach was appealing as a low-cost, low-tech approach that responded to the criticism of the high-cost, high-tech, high-rise solutions of the earlier period. The self-help solution also responded to the problem of extensive unemployment among the urban poor. This approach theoretically would convert idle time to productive time, and the poor could build up capital in their housing units. Moreover, Turner and Fichter (1972) argued that housing should be viewed not as a consumer commodity, but as an employment opportunity and a force that would generate other economic activity. While few housing experts would deny the usefulness of the self-help model, including its present value, it seems overly optimistic to rely on any one approach to solve a large, multidimensional problem.

During this decade, self-help did not stop with housing but extended to other social and community services. The World Bank, the United States Agency for International Development (U.S. AID), and other international and bilateral agencies (e.g., the European Development Fund, the Canadian International Development Agency, and the Asian Development Bank) directed their efforts and funding primarily toward self-help projects, sites and services programs, and community upgrading schemes (Laquian, 1983, p. 8), but these projects also addressed water and sewerage services, transportation, and land acquisition.

This interest in self-help activities and family involvement caused some observers to address the important role of women in shelter provision. A considerable amount of research has been conducted on the topic (Charlton, 1984; Rogers, 1981; Tinker and Bramsen, 1976) but only recently have efforts been taken to assess women's roles in relation to the potential impact of development projects (Rogers, 1981). Most authors point to the fact that women perform essential, although usually unacknowledged, social, cultural, and economic activities that include food production and processing, fuel and water collection, the production and marketing of art and craft work, as well as family and household maintenance (Stitzel, Pytlik, and Curtis, 1985). In 1982 Vina Mazumdar pointed out in an opening address for the National Women's Studies Association Conference that women are left out of planning, implementation, and evaluation of development efforts. In short, they have little access to the thought, action, and reaction networks discussed in this chapter.

Reaction to the self-help approach came from many quarters, most notably from Marxist writers who saw in the approach not romanticism but capitalist exploitation (Burgess, 1977, p. 53). Marxist critics and others argued that the poor, in being forced to provide their own shelter, were continuing to be dominated by capitalists (Ward, 1982), and that the capitalist system would benefit from the cheap labor supply in the self-help settlements. The self-help approach, the argument went, would doom the poor to a dominated status. This criticism has not resulted in alternative housing, however, and user-built housing remains an important source of shelter for low-income citizens of the Third World. While providing basic shelter, the self-help approach often leaves unaddressed such issues as the provision of community services, security of land tenure, improvement of sanitary conditions, and the social isolation of the poor.

By the mid-1970s a body of knowledge had been assembled about housing problems and potential solutions, and international aid agencies were providing substantial levels of assistance to developing countries.[7] Much of this information was drawn together at the 1976 United Nations Habitat Conference on Human Settlements (UNCHS, 1982). But the conference has been criticized for producing little of substance, beyond calling for a recognition that squatter settlements could no longer be considered an isolated and temporary phenomenon and calling on governments to upgrade spontaneous settlements and integrate their residents into the national fabric (Hardoy and Satterthwaite, 1981).

By this time it had also become clear that the funds allocated for housing improvement efforts were inadequate, compared to the size of the problem. In 1976 an estimated one-third to two-thirds of urban inhabitants were still unable to afford the cheapest new standard housing unit (Grimes, 1976, p. 9). Land tenure and the rising value of land were also beginning to present problems by the mid-1970s. Rising land values generated individual wealth, with much of this wealth going to land speculators when it could have been recovered to finance housing and services for the poor. Inflation in the cost of land and building materials devalued loan repayments from participants in sites and services programs and upgrading efforts. Thus funds were not always effectively recycled, and new money was continually needed to respond to the growing demand.

These problems notwithstanding, a *major reaction* to the experience of the 1965 to 1975 period was to expand sites and services and upgrading schemes to new locations in the Third World as potentially viable ways to address the tremendous shelter shortage. Nevertheless, the lack of recognition of differences among places and the application of techniques without modification for social and cultural differences prevented effective transfer of potential solutions.

Mid-1970s to Mid-1980s: A More Balanced View of Potential Solutions

These ten years might well be termed the decade of experimentation and evaluation. The *thought* during this period focused on widespread application and analysis of the sites and services model, squatter upgrading, and other gradual improvement efforts. The reasoning was that governments alone could not solve the housing problem, but with government and professional assistance, people could upgrade their own living conditions (Saini, 1984), and homeownership for the poor was an achievable goal. These years witnessed an outpouring of studies of projects financed by the World Bank, the United Nations, and the Agency for International Development.

The major ameliorative *actions* of this period included sites and services projects, settlement upgrading schemes, and progressive development projects. Evaluations of these projects also became available (Bamberger, González-Polio, and Sae-Hau, 1982; Bamberger, Sanyal, and Valverde, 1982; Keare and Parris, 1982; and Mayo and Gross, 1985). It is too early to judge the long-term results of these efforts, although their evaluators generally call them positive—to the extent that the goal was to upgrade the quality of housing for squatters and to improve environmental conditions through sites and services projects.

Although the sites and services concept has been generally accepted as a useful approach, many such schemes supported by the World Bank in the 1970s were less than completely successful. To minimize costs, governments bought land relatively far from city centers, but this land was also removed from potential jobs. Some rehoused urban dwellers sublet or sold their units and returned to their original homes to be nearer employment opportunities. Recognizing this, the World Bank now places a greater emphasis on upgrading existing housing, although many bank-supported urban projects are a combination of upgrading and sites and services.

William Doebele and Lisa Peattie warned that sites and services projects could destroy small-scale pirate developers and lead to undesirable uniformity and a loss of autonomy on the part of settlers. With government-provisioned lots available at nonprofit prices, small entrepreneurial developers would be driven out of business (Doebele, 1975). Typically, owner–builders have supplied much of the unskilled labor and hired local carpenters, plumbers, roofers, and other technicians. Construction materials, too, have often been purchased from small-scale dealers. If sites and services projects supplied these skills and materials, local marginal entrepreneurs could be forced out of business. Larger-scale projects would also enable large suppliers, who normally have difficulty selling in low-income areas, to enter this market and eliminate small-scale competitors (Peattie, 1982, p. 135).

Selected World Bank sites and services projects try to work as much as possible with small suppliers. But financial deals with large suppliers are easy to justify in terms of administrative efficiency and hard to resist politically. The World Bank admits that its sites and services projects, which attract the relatively better-off among the poor, are affordable only to those above the 20th percentile in income. Various methods of differential pricing have had to be used to reach households below this income level (Keare and Parris, 1982, p. viii).

Some observers and governments believe that the only way to reach the very poor is to relax the concept of cost recovery, and with it the idea of recycling project funds. Upgrading projects then require continuing subsidies, which are not available on the scale needed. The Indonesian Kampung Improvement Program (KIP), for example, which the World Bank claims has reached some of the bottom 20 percent of the urban poor, has started to abandon the strict requirement of cost recovery (World Bank, 1983, p. 40). Such recovery has proven difficult because it requires that project residents make regular cash payments. Although the sum can be kept minimal by reducing the kinds and amount of services provided, a regular payment, however small, can be difficult for households that do not have secure employment and whose incomes fluctuate widely (casual laborers, street vendors, etc.). Some governments take strict measures to recover the loans, often creating problems for the poorest households. On the one hand, rigidly enforced repayments can exclude many poor families from a project entirely. On the other hand, little can be more disastrous for cost recovery than the belief that the housing agency is not serious about collecting payments.

Upgrading schemes have also had the paradoxical effect of harming renters living in the areas (Grimes, 1976). An upgraded environment can attract people with the capacity to pay a higher rent, and landlords therefore sometimes evict the poorer tenants. It also happens that the beneficiaries of housing improvement and new construction projects are sometimes the middle class, who buy improved or new units from the poor either directly or through agents.

Housing experts have identified other problems with upgrading schemes. Upgrading of densely populated areas has meant that some dwellers have to move to new sites (United Nations, 1976a, p. 80). Securing land tenure, to encourage settlers to put labor and savings toward upgrading, can be a complex process (Whittemore, 1981). And settlements situated on poor land, in ravines, or in easily flooded areas are difficult to upgrade (Grimes, 1976, p. 11; Wijkman and Timberlake, 1984). Moreover, community participation is essential for making decisions about relocation, self-help efforts, tax collection, compensation, and the like. Many governments mistrust any leadership from the poor, however, and conflicting priorities of landlords and tenants can also make local decision making difficult (Skinner and Rodell, 1983, p. 135).

In addition to these problems, some Third World officials dislike the idea of upgrading poor areas. They argue that an upgraded area still looks like a slum, even though life may have become a little better for the people living there. Other critics of upgrading see it as an attempt to curb social unrest without making an effort to restructure the economic pattern of society, which they believe is the essential cause of poverty and homelessness (Burgess, 1977, p. 56).

Even with the large amounts of money spent on sites and services and upgrading projects, only the surface of the problem has been scratched. For example, between 1975 and 1980 the World Bank provided $1.3 billion for urban projects that benefited 10 million people (Churchill, 1980), and from 1980 to 1983 the World Bank allocated $1.8 billion in loans to twenty-eight countries for urban projects (World Bank, 1980–83). Sites and services, settlement upgrading, and integrated development projects absorb the major portion of such loans (Blitzer, Hardoy, and Satterthwaite, 1983, p. 110). Working with the estimates of $1 billion in total urban assistance from all bilateral donors and development banks for 1980 (United States Agency for International Development, 1986), and 200 million urban people living in poverty in developing countries in that year (Churchill, 1980), we arrive at an expenditure of $5 per person. Because all urban loans were not made for housing improvement, the $5 per year per person figure may be too high. In any event, the amount is obviously inadequate to resolve the existing shelter shortage, much less the housing deficit expected by the year 2000 (Churchill, 1980).

Lack of availability of urban land for low-cost housing in developing countries is yet another related problem (Grimes, 1976; Linn, 1983). Dennis Conway argues, in fact, that the issue of land was virtually ignored during the development of policies to address the housing needs of the urban poor (1985, pp. 183–85). He identifies 1980 as the point when the problem of land price and availability began to be more widely recognized (1985, p. 186). In that year there was a "benchmark" World Congress on Land Policy in which empirical studies and theoretical papers pointed out the rapid escalation of land prices and the inevitability of this increase due to the capitalistic character of land development in Third World cities (Cullen and Woolery, 1982, in Conway, 1985, p. 186).

The United Nations Commission on Human Settlement also recognized the issue in 1982 when a position paper called for the creation of means for low-income and disadvantaged people to gain access to an adequate share of land on which they could house themselves and participate in the full life of the community (UNCHS, 1982).

Conway summarized the UNCHS position about current constraints on the supply of land, which he called "alarming," as including the following factors (1985, pp. 186–87):

1. The commercialization of land markets and institutionalization of land development reduces the availability of informal land supply to the poor.
2. Land supply through squatting and invading is disappearing in developing cities.
3. Land prices are increasing more rapidly than the cost of living, and land densities are increasing in existing spontaneous settlements.
4. Urbanized land is being held vacant and off the market because of a lack of development resources or as a hedge against inflation.
5. Land and housing markets are becoming integrated and monopolized by large corporations.
6. As built-up areas of cities have expanded, there has developed a shortage of appropriate land for housing the poor and an increase in transportation costs.

An issue related to land scarcity has emerged since the mid-1970s, namely the increase in unauthorized land development by middle- and upper-income individuals. In less developed Third World countries and in more developed countries such as Greece, Italy, and Spain, people above the level of the poor, including the former poor who have upgraded themselves by means of unauthorized building activities, have increasingly captured public land on which they are building their housing. The rationale of these unauthorized builders is similar to that of the poor—to maximize resources, to acquire housing in a desirable location not available through other means, and to acquire capital.

These illegal efforts are having a number of side effects, including the thwarting of city plans, increasing the burden on public infrastructure, and destroying sensitive lands. At the same time, the new middle-class squatters are taking away some of the land on which the poor would have built spontaneous shelters. The potential impact of this movement has yet to be judged fully, but in some locales where land is scarce, it works against the interests of the poor who are in need of housing but who cannot afford the land on which to build it and for whom other options are limited.

The *reaction* to efforts from 1975 to 1985 is only now being experienced but will certainly be affected by increased densities, population growth, the scarcity of accessible and suitable urban building sites, greater amounts of rental housing, more unauthorized development by middle- and upper-income households, a trend toward localized responses, and a strengthened political will of the poor to obtain the shelter they believe they deserve.

Beyond the 1980s: Continuing Urbanization, New Actors, and New Issues

A number of the factors contributing to the shelter problem in developing countries are expected to continue into the 1990s and beyond. For example, urban populations are expected to continue to grow rapidly and place increasing pressures on political, social, and economic systems (McNamara, 1985). At the beginning of the nineteenth century, only about 2.4 percent of the world's population lived in towns and cities. One hundred years later, the figure had increased to 20 percent (Abrams, 1964, p. 2). By 1980 it was 40 percent, with 70 percent of the population in the developed countries and 29 percent in the less developed countries living in urbanized areas (Jones and Shepherd, 1986). By the year 2000 the overall urbanization level will likely exceed 50 percent (United Nations, 1982, p. 39) and perhaps be as high as 65 percent (Ghosh, 1984, p. 7). Also, by the year 2000 two out of three urban dwellers will live in a less developed country (Prakash, 1985, p. 10).

This population growth will certainly place a heightened demand on land for housing the poor, with disproportionate increases by region. Between 1980 and 2000, the urban population is expected to increase 25 percent in Europe, 30 percent in Northern America, 40 percent in the Soviet Union, and 50 percent in Oceania. But the number of urban dwellers will increase 75 percent in East Asia, 95 percent in Latin America, 130 percent in South Asia, and 150 percent in Africa (United Nations, 1976c, p. 143, 1985a).

The urban population, both in the developed countries and in the Third World, is not only increasing, it is concentrating in larger cities. Between 1950 and 1985, the number of cities with over a million inhabitants rose from 75 to 273. While the number of these megacities doubled (from 51 to 108) in the developed countries, it increased six times (from 24 to 147) in the Third World (United Nations, 1976c, p. 148). In 1950 Buenos Aires, with a population of 4.5 million, was the largest Third World city, whereas 6 cities in the noncommunist industrialized world had already reached that size (United Nations, 1976c, p. 27). Between 1980 and 2000, the number of Third World cities of 10 million or more will grow from 3 to 16, while in the noncommunist industrialized countries the number will remain unchanged at 3 (Jones and Shepherd, 1986, p. 10). By the turn of the century Mexico City will be the world's largest city, with 30 million people. Of the 10 largest cities in the year 2000, only

1 (the New York metropolitan area) will be in the developed Western world (Hauser and Gardner, 1982, p. 36).

The population living in megacities of a million persons or more is one measure of urban concentration. Between 1970 and 1985, this figure rose from 224 million to 340 million in the developed regions, and from 193 million to 465 million in the developing regions. By the year 2000 these numbers will grow to 440 million in the developed regions (a 29 percent increase) and 956 million in the developing regions (a 105 percent increase) (United Nations, 1976c, pp. 26, 149). Overall population forecasts indicate an *annual* growth rate between 1985 and 2000 of almost .6 percent in the developed world and nearly 2 percent in the developing world (United Nations, 1985a, 1985b, p. 13).

These intense accumulations of people generate enormous demands for housing and public services such as streets, water and sewer systems, crime prevention, disease control, electricity, telephones, transportation, and human services (Laconte, 1976; Tinker and Buvinic, 1977). Where and under what conditions these additional urban dwellers of the Third World will live and how their shelter needs will be met will be critical issues between now and the year 2000.

The continued population growth and higher densities will result in increased demand for housing and urban services; competition for the better urban sites; and the increasing use of steep slopes, hazardous areas, and other environmentally sensitive sites. Affordable urban sites are growing scarce, especially those located near employment centers and transportation routes. The location of the dwelling is critical, as a remote site can spell economic disaster for its inhabitants (Tym, 1984). As the price of these urban building sites is increasing, some existing sites are being subdivided. People are selling or renting part of their already small plots to others who wish to build cheaply. More and more homeowners in some cities are renting or sharing portions of their homes, both as a way to help relatives, friends, and other new migrants and as a way to accumulate capital.

Middle-income and relatively well-housed people in developing and even developed countries have come to realize that building on marginal land or not adhering to building codes provides more house for their money. This means not only that higher-quality spontaneous housing is being built in some areas but also that these new settlers are able to outbid the low-income migrants for building sites. Consequently, land prices are increasing and making it even more difficult for the urban poor to own housing. The growing rental market in Third World cities is one response to this trend, and a response that is expected to increase.[8]

As larger numbers of middle-class residents in Third World countries begin to provide their own housing through various forms of squatting and unauthorized development, an effect on shelter provision policy should result. Because of their higher levels of literacy, influence, and power, the middle classes involved in shelter provision are more likely to cause governments to reassess their housing policies. It is too early to know what the direction of change will be, but it is not out of the question to expect the response to include increased subsidies, loans, and funding for infrastructure improvements. At the same time, because of a stronger political position, it would not be surprising to see the middle class acquire a larger portion of shelter provision funds at the expense of the poor.

International aid agencies are expected to continue to provide housing assistance to developing countries, but many observers wonder about the wisdom of continuing such assistance. Questions of affordability, cost recovery, and the relevance of particular approaches suggest to some that a better option might be found in localized solutions that include more comprehensive approaches with health care, agricultural and economic development, and literacy enhancement components intended to improve the competitive position of the poor.

While these additional components may be well conceived, the overriding question is where the funds to support the efforts will be obtained and how loans and other forms of assistance can be repaid. As suggested by other contributors to this book in regard to their individual countries, worldwide shelter improvement depends to a great degree on economic improvement and the sharing in this improvement by all citizens.

Acknowledgments

Useful comments on earlier drafts of this chapter were provided by Barry Checkoway, Albert Guttenberg, Amos Rapoport, and Samuel Noe.

Notes

1. Buick (1975) provides an overview of earlier literature on shelter in developing countries.
2. The names for such housing and settlements vary, and include the following terms in selected countries:

Argentina: *villas miserias*
Brazil: *favelas, alagados, villas de malocas, corticos, invasões,* and *mocambos*
Chile: *callampas, campamentos,* and *poblaciones*
Colombia: *invasiones, barriadas, barrios piratas, urbanizaciones piratas, barrios clandestinos,* and *tugurios*

Ecuador: *barrios, urbanizaciones,* and *ranchos*
Ethiopia: *chica*
India and Pakistan: *bustees, jhuggis, jhopris, chawls, ahatas, cheris,* and *katras*
Italy: *abusivismo, baracche,* and *borghetti*
Indonesia: *kampung*
Korea: *panjachon*
Mexico: *asentamientos irregulares, colonias populares, colonias paracaidistas, jacales,* and *ciudades perdidas*
Morocco: *bidonvilles*
Panama: *barriadas de emergencia*
Peru: *pueblos jóvenes, barriadas,* and *barrios marginales*
Philippines: *barong-barongs*
El Salvador: *colonias ilegales* and *tugurios*
Tunisia: *gourbivilles* and *bidonvilles*
Turkey: *gecekondus* and *hisseli tapu*
Venezuela: *ranchos* and *barrios*
Yugoslavia: *crne gradnje*

3. No term describes completely the many dimensions of this shelter production phenomenon. We have elected to use the phrase *spontaneous shelter* to capture the idea of various kinds of shelter that are brought about by personal action without significant external stimulus. Dwyer (1975) used the term *spontaneous settlements* in a similar sense, but since this book focuses on shelter production, we use *spontaneous shelter.*
4. For an overview of these issues, see Eke (1982).
5. *Squatting* usually implies the rapid construction of a shelter in some instances associated with a large-scale invasion of land. But sometimes these units are built on land that is purchased, albeit often of uncertain title. Furthermore, instead of being erected overnight, these units may be built over a long time by the users as materials can be acquired. Thus the term *user-built* housing has been employed. But often the owner will contract with others for construction of major portions of the house or even for an entire unit. Furthermore, use of this term tends to overlook the substantial commercial rental market that exists among this type of housing.

The terms *unauthorized* or *clandestine* have also been used, with the idea that they would imply a semilegal process of home construction, where the land may be purchased but the house is built without necessary permits or violates some aspect of the formal city plan or building code. This term, however, is limited by its focus on the structure and legal issues.

Informal development has been proposed as a term, in that it depicts the process by which deals are made, land is obtained, and structures are built. Again the terminology is accurate in part but misses the fact that formal land acquisition and building construction might be a feature of this shelter provision process.

None of the above phrases is entirely appropriate, since the production of shelter in developing countries is a multidimensional problem that involves questions of land tenure, construction practices, ownership, and other factors that change over time. For example, appropriated land eventually may be purchased. Structures that violate building and zoning codes may be brought into compliance. Renters may purchase their units. Owners may build an addition to rent, and so on.

6. Self-help efforts could be traced back to ancient times, but that would be beyond the scope of this inquiry.

7. One limitation to the experience of this decade is the heavy reliance on work from one region and the lack of recognition of differences among places. Turner, Mangin, and Perlman, for example, all worked in Latin America, and as we now know, experiences in other parts of the world were somewhat different.

8. Rental housing has been available in many countries for centuries. The emerging practice is the commercialization of unauthorized rental housing in spontaneous settlements.

References

Abrams, Charles. 1939. *Revolution in Land.* New York: Harper & Bros.

———. 1964. *Man's Struggle for Shelter in an Urbanizing World.* Cambridge: MIT Press.

Agarwal, Anil. 1981. *Mud, Mud.* London: Earthscan Publications, International Institute for Environment and Development.

Ayres, Robert L. 1983. *The World Bank and World Poverty, Banking on the Poor.* Cambridge: MIT Press.

Bamberger, Michael, Edgardo González-Polio, and Umnuay Sae-Hau. 1982. *Evaluation of Sites and Services Projects: The Evidence from El Salvador.* Working Paper no. 549. Washington, D.C.: World Bank.

Bamberger, Michael, Bishwapura Sanyal, and Nelson Valverde. 1982. *Evaluation of Sites and Services Projects: The Experience from Lusaka, Zambia.* Working Paper no. 548. Washington, D.C.: World Bank.

Blitzer, S., J. E. Hardoy, and D. Satterthwaite. 1983. "The Sectoral and Spatial Distribution of Multi-lateral Aid for Human Settlements." *Habitat International* 7, 103–27.

Bonilla, Frank. 1961. "Rio's *Favelas:* The Rural Slum within the City." *AUFS Reports* (East Coast South America Series) 8(3).

Buick, Barbara, ed. 1975. *Squatter Settlements in Developing Countries: A Bibliography.* Research School of Pacific Studies Aids to Research Series no. A/3. Canberra: Australian National University Press.

Burgess, Rod. 1977. "Self Help Housing: A New Imperialist Strategy? A Critique of the Turner School." *Antipode,* no. 2 (September 9), 50–59.

Charlton, Sue Ellen M. 1984. *Women in Third World Development.* Boulder, Colo.: Westview Press.

Churchill, Anthony A. 1980. *Shelter.* Washington, D.C.: World Bank.

Collier, David. 1976. *Squatter Settlements and the Incorporation of Migrants into Urban Life: The Case of Lima.* Cambridge: MIT, Migration and Development Study Group, Center for International Studies.

Conway, Dennis. 1985. "Changing Perspectives on Squatter Settlements, Intraurban Mobility, and Constraints on Housing Choice of the Third World Urban Poor." *Urban Geography* 6, 170–92.

Cullen, M., and S. Wollery, eds. 1982. *World Congress on Land Policy: 1980.* Lexington, Mass.: Lexington. Cited in Dennis Conway, "Changing Perspectives on Squatter Settlements." *Urban Geography* 6 (1985), 170–92.

Davidson, Forbes, and Geoffrey K. Payne. 1983. *Urban Projects Manual: A Guide to Preparing, Upgrading and New Development Projects Accessible to Low Income Groups.* Liverpool: Liverpool University Press with Fairstead Press.

Doebele, William A. 1975. "The Private Market and Low Income Urbanization in Developing Countries: The 'Pirate' Subdivisions of Bogotá." Discussion Paper no. D75-11. Cambridge: Department of City and Regional Planning, Harvard University.

Drakakis-Smith, David. 1981. *Urbanization, Housing and the Development Process.* New York: St. Martin's Press.

Dwyer, Denis John. 1975. *People and Housing in Third World Cities: Perspectives on the Problem of Spontaneous Settlements.* New York: Longman.

———, ed. 1974. *The City in the Third World.* London: Macmillan.

Eke, E. Feral. 1982. "Changing Views on Urbanisation, Migration and Squatters." *Habitat International* 6(1/2), 143–63.

Fanon, Franz. 1965. *The Wretched of the Earth.* New York: Grove Press.

Friere, Pablo. 1970. *Pedagogy of the Oppressed.* New York: Seabury Press.

Ghosh, Pradip K., ed. 1984. *Urban Development in the Third World.* Westport, Conn.: Greenwood Press.

Grimes, Orville F., Jr. 1976. *Housing for Low-Income Urban Families: Economics and Policy in the Developing World.* Baltimore: Johns Hopkins University Press.

Hardoy, Jorge E., and David Satterthwaite. 1981. *Shelter, Need and Response: Housing, Land and Settlement Policies in Seventeen Third World Nations.* New York: Wiley.

Hartman, Chester W. 1975. *Housing and Social Policy.* Englewood Cliffs, N.J.: Prentice-Hall.

Hauser, Phillip M., ed. 1979. *World Population and Development: Challenges and Prospects.* Syracuse: Syracuse University Press.

Hauser, Phillip M., and Robert W. Gardner. 1982. "Urban Future: Trends and Prospects." In *Population and the Urban Future,* ed. Phillip M. Hauser et al., pp. 1–58. Albany: State University of New York Press.

Herbert, John D. 1979. *Urban Development in the Third World: Policy Guidelines.* New York: Praeger.

Jones, Barclay, and William F. Shepherd. 1986. "Cities of the Future: Implications of the Rise and Relative Decline of the Cities of the West." Paper prepared for the Wingspread Conference on the World Cities of the Future International Planning and Design Competition, Racine, Wisconsin, April 13–15.

Juppenlatz, Morris. 1970. *Cities in Transformation: The Urban Squatter Problem of the Developing World.* Brisbane: University of Queensland Press.

Keare, Douglas H., and Scott Parris. 1982. *Evaluation of Shelter Programs for the Urban Poor: Principal Findings.* Working Paper no. 547. Washington, D.C.: World Bank.

Lakshmanan, T. R., Lata Chatterjee, and P. Roy. 1977. "Housing Requirements and National Resources: Implications of the U.N. World Model." In *The Many Facets of Human Settlements: Science and Society,* ed. Irene Tinker and Mayra Buvinic, pp. 277–90. Oxford: Pergamon Press.

Laconte, Pierre. 1976. *The Environments of Human Settlements: Human Wellbeing in Cities.* New York: Pergamon.

Laquian, Aprodicio A. 1983. *Basic Housing: Policies for Urban Sites, Services and Shelter in Developing Countries.* Ottawa: International Development Research Centre.

Leeds, Anthony. 1969. "The Significant Variable Determining the Character of Squatter Settlements." *America Latina* 12(3), 44–86.

Lewis, Oscar. 1959. *Five Families: Mexican Case Studies in the Culture of Poverty.* New York: Basic Books.

———. 1961. *The Children of Sanchez.* New York: Random House.

Linn, Johannis. 1983. *Cities in the Developing World: Policies for Their Equitable and Efficient Growth.* New York: Oxford University Press.

Lloyd, Peter C. 1979. *Slums of Hope?: Shanty Towns of the Third World.* New York: Penguin.

Mabogunje, A. L., J. E. Hardoy, and R. P. Misra. 1978. *Shelter Provision in Developing Countries.* Chichester: Wiley.

Mangin, W. 1967. "Latin American Squatter Settlements: A Problem and a Solution." *Latin American Research Review* 2(3), 65–99.

———. 1970. *Peasants in Cities: Readings in the Anthropology of Urbanisation.* Boston: Houghton Mifflin.

Matos Mar, J. 1961. "Migration and Urbanization: Urbanization and the Barriades of Lima." In *Urbanisation in Latin America,* ed. Phillip Hauser, pp. 170–90. Paris: UNESCO.

Mayo, Stephen K., and David J. Gross. 1985. *Sites and Services—and Subsidies: The Economics of Low-Cost Housing in Development Countries.* Washington, D.C.: World Bank.

McHale, John, and Magda Cordell McHale. 1978. *Basic Human Needs: A Framework for Action.* Center for Integrative Studies, University of Houston, Report to the United Nations Environment Programme (UNEP).

McNamara, Robert S. 1985. "The Population Problem: Time Bomb or Myth." *Asian and Pacific Quarterly of Cultural and Social Affairs* 17(1), 1–25.

Mountjoy, Alan B., ed. 1978. *The Third World: Problem and Perspectives.* London: Macmillan.

Myrdal, Gunnar. 1971. *Asian Drama: An Inquiry into the Poverty of Nations.* (An abridgement of his 1968 three-volume study.) New York: Pantheon.

Noe, Samuel V. 1981. "Urban Development and Redevelopment in the Third World: The Collision of Western Approaches and Traditional Form." *Studies in Comparative International Redevelopment* 16(2), 3–22.

Payne, Geoffrey, K. 1977. *Urban Housing in the Third World.* London: Leonard Hill.

———, ed. 1984. *Low-Income Housing in the Developing World: The Role of Sites and Services and Settlement Upgrading.* New York: Wiley.

Peattie, Lisa R. 1968. *The View from the Barrio.* Ann Arbor: University of Michigan Press.

———. 1982. "Some Second Thoughts on Site-and-Services." *Habitat International* 6(1/2), 131–39.

Pearse, Andrew. 1961. "Some Characteristics of Urbanization in Rio de Janeiro." In *Urbanisation in Latin America,* ed. Phillip Hauser, pp. 191–205. Paris: UNESCO.

Perlman, Janice. 1976. *The Myth of Marginality: Urban Politics and Poverty in Rio de Janeiro.* Berkeley: University of California Press.

Prakash, Ved. 1985. "Affordability and Cost Recovery of Urban Services for the Poor." *Regional Development Dialogue* 6(2) (Autumn), 1–39.

Rogers, Barbara. 1981. *The Domestication of Women: Discrimination in Developing Societies.* London and New York: Tavistock.

Ross, Marc Howard. 1973. *The Political Integration of Urban Squatters.* Evanston: Northwestern University Press.

Saini, B. S. 1984. "Barefoot Architects—A Proposal for the Third World." *Ekistics* 51(304), 34–36.

Seymour, Anthony. 1976. *The Causes of Squatter Settlements: Zambia.* Institute of African Studies, University of Zambia, Lusaka Communication no. 12. Cited in Anil Agarwal, *Mud, Mud.* London: Earthscan Publications, 1981.

Skinner, Reinhard J., and Michael J. Rodell, eds. 1983. *People, Poverty and Shelter: Problems of Self-Help Housing in the Third World.* London: Methuen.

Stitzel, Judith, Ed Pytlik, and Kate Curtis. 1985. "'Only Connect': Developing a Course on Women in International Development." *Women's Studies Quarterly* 13(2), (Summer), 33–35.

Stokes, C. 1962. "A Theory of Slums." *Land Economics* 38(3), 187–97.

Strassman, W. P. 1977. "Housing Priorities in Developing Countries: A Planning Model." *Land Economics* 53, 310–27.

Tinker, Irene, and Bo Bramsen. 1976. *Women and World Development.* Washington, D.C.: Overseas Development Council (WWD).

Tinker, Irene, and Mayra Buvinic. 1977. *The Many Facets of Human Settlements: Science and Society.* New York: Pergamon Press.

Turner, John F. C. 1968. "The Squatter Settlement That Works." *Architectural Digest* 38, 355–60.

———. 1970. "Barriers and Channels for Housing Developments in Modernizing Cities." In *Peasants in Cities,* ed. W. Mangin, pp. 1–14. Boston: Houghton Mifflin.

———. 1976. *Housing by People: Towards Autonomy in Building Environments.* New York: Pantheon.

Turner, John F. C., and Robert Fichter, eds. 1972. *Freedom to Build: Dweller Control of the Housing Process.* New York: Macmillan.

Tym, Roger. 1984. "Finance and Affordability." In *Low-Income Housing in the Developing World,* ed. Geoffrey K. Payne, pp. 209–20. New York: Wiley.

United Nations Centre for Human Settlements (UNCHS) (Habitat). 1981. *The Residential Circumstances of the Urban Poor in Developing Countries.* New York: Praeger.

———. 1982. *Survey of Slum and Squatter Settlements.* Dublin: Tycooly International.

United Nations. 1976a. *Global Review of Human Settlements—A Support Paper for HABITAT: United Nations Conference on Human Settlements.* Document A/CONF.70/A/1. Oxford, England: Pergamon Press.

———. 1976b. *Housing Policy Guidelines for Developing Countries.* Document ST/ESA/50. New York: United Nations, Department of Economic and Social Affairs.

———. 1976c. *World Housing Survey: 1974—An Overview of the State of Housing, Building and Planning Within Human Settlements.* Document ST/ESA/30. New York: United Nations.

———. 1976d. *Community Programmes for Low-Income Populations in Urban Settlements of Developing Countries.* Document ST/ESA/52. New York: United Nations, Department of Economic and Social Affairs.

———. 1982. *Demographic Indicators of Countries: Estimates and Projections as Assessed in 1980.* New York: United Nations.

———. 1985a. *Estimates and Projections of Urban, Rural, and City Populations, 1950–2025: The 1982 Assessment.* New York: United Nations, Department of International Economic and Social Affairs.

———. 1985b. *World Population Prospects: Estimates and Projections as As-*

sessed in 1982. Population Studies no. 86, ST/ESA/SER.A/86. New York: United Nations.

United States Agency for International Development (U.S. AID). 1986. *Development Cooperation and Urban Development.* Washington, D.C.: U.S. AID, Office of Housing and Urban Programs.

Ward, Peter M. 1976. "The Squatter Settlement as Slum or Housing Solution: Evidence from Mexico City." *Land Economics* 52(3), 330–46.

———, ed. 1982. *Self Help Housing: A Critique.* London: Mansell.

Whittemore, Claire. 1981. *Land for People: Land Tenure and the Very Poor.* Oxford: Oxfam.

Wijkman, Anders, and Lloyd Timberlake. 1984. *Natural Disasters: Acts of God or Acts of Man?* Washington, D.C.: Earthscan Publications.

World Bank. 1980–83. *The World Bank Annual Report.* 4 vol. Personal communication of selected data by World Bank staff, June 1986. Washington, D.C.: World Bank.

———. 1983. *Learning by Doing: World Bank Lending for Urban Development, 1972–1982.* Washington, D.C.: World Bank.

Wynn, Martin. 1984. *Housing in Europe.* London: Croom-Helm.

Chapter 2

Geographic Perspectives on Spontaneous Shelter

W. DONALD McTAGGART

Spontaneous shelter is an obvious characteristic of the rapidly expanding cities that have emerged in the Third World over the past several decades. A large proportion of the urban landscape consists of buildings erected by the inhabitants with whatever materials were readily available. Thus it is surprising that in all the literature dealing with shelter for the poor so little has focused specifically on its spontaneous nature.

Leeds (1981) provides a comprehensive review of housing situations among the urban poor, distinguishing mainly between squatter settlements, titled plots without services, emergency housing, and inner-city slums. But the idea of spontaneous shelter cuts across several of these categories. By *squatter settlements,* he means those built on land not belonging to the inhabitants but invaded and taken over by them. Insecurity of tenure provides a strong impulse to spontaneous shelter because the residents are not encouraged to invest heavily in improvements. *Titled plots* imply some security of tenure and normally some ordered spatial arrangement; residents therefore may be encouraged to build a higher quality of housing, depending on their means. Emergency housing usually has a firmer jural status than squatting, since it is frequently established under the guise of some government authority; but it may be of limited duration and consequently does not offer its inhabitants the opportunity for an indefinite, guaranteed period of occupancy. *Inner-city slums* represent deteriorated housing that at one time may have been of high quality.

The primary characteristic of spontaneous shelter is its construction essentially by the residents. They do not depend on builders or contractors but use their own labor and skills to put together whatever kind of lodging they see fit to erect. The primary characteristic, then, is that of "disintermediation," to use the term employed by Hawken (1982). By this I mean the avoidance of professionalized services and a reliance on one's own abilities and energies. "Intermediation" is characteristic of strongly service-oriented economies, especially those of the so-called postindustrial states. But even in these countries a considerable amount of disintermediation is readily observable as individuals seek survival strategies in the face of economic change, stagnation, or decline.

This chapter provides a brief overview of the conditions in which spontaneous shelter seems to occur. I consider some of the major contours of the phenomenon and argue that it is an expected response to conditions encountered in many Third World cities.

How Extensive a Phenomenon?

It is very difficult to arrive at an accurate measurement of the magnitude of the phenomenon of spontaneous shelter. If we lump together the occurrence of slums and squatter housing in a major Third World city, we find that estimates of its extent range between 40 and 60 percent of the total population of the agglomeration (Akom, 1984, for Lagos; Steinberg, 1984, for Colombo). Table 2.1 provides estimates for a number of cities of the percentage of population residing in slums and squatter settlements (Ghosh, 1984, pp. 398–99). In most instances, the figures

Table 2.1. Estimates of the Proportion of Population Housed in Slums and Squatter Areas, Selected Cities

Country	*City*	*Date*	*Percentage of Population in Slums and Squatter Areas*
Relatively High-Income			
Venezuela	Caracas	1969	40
Chile	Santiago	1964	25
Mexico	Mexico City	1970	46
Singapore	Singapore	1970	15
Middle-Income			
Korea	Seoul	1970	30
Malaysia	Kuala Lumpur	1971	37
Brazil	Rio de Janeiro	1970	30
Senegal	Dakar	1971	60
Morocco	Casablanca	1971	70
Poorer			
Sri Lanka	Colombo	1968	43
India	Calcutta	1971	33
Indonesia	Jakarta	1972	26
Nigeria	Ibadan	1971	75
Tanzania	Dar es Salaam	1970	50
Somalia	Mogadishu	1967	77
Ethiopia	Addis Ababa	1968	90

Source: Ghosh (1984, pp. 398–99).

cover 1968 to 1972, but substantial changes have not intervened since then.

The countries have been grouped in terms of income—relatively high income, middle income, and poorest. There appears to be a tendency for the poorest countries to have higher figures than those countries that are better-off, but there are clearly exceptions. Very few cities had fewer than 15 percent of their residents housed in these circumstances; in some cities the proportion was as high as 80 or 90 percent.

Most of the countries cited in Table 2.1 are in equatorial or subtropical regions. But spontaneous shelter is by no means absent from temperate and higher-latitude countries; Korea offers one example, and various studies have dealt with the phenomenon in European countries (Marcussen, 1978; and Albert Guttenberg and Boris Pleskovic in Chapters 12 and 13 of this book). That such housing occurs more frequently in tropical and subtropical regions is related, first, to the fact that underdevelopment is characteristic of countries in that part of the globe, for reasons that in no way need include climatic factors. Yet climate does play a role. A warm climate greatly eases the problem of attaining basic minimum survival standards of housing, enabling units to be constructed in a simple manner, often using locally available materials. Nevertheless, the argument should not be carried too far. Self-help housing is striking as a phenomenon only insofar as it diverges from some norm, and the norm in this case is clearly the expectation that a city will be built in some conventional way. The Western model of a city as a place of business and commerce, with a central business district surrounded by spreading suburbs, is scarcely appropriate for conditions in Third World countries. User-built housing has long been the rule in many of the countries we are considering, and there is no reason to suppose that it will not continue to be so (Misra and Tri Dung, 1983).

The primary environmental characteristic of Third World self-help housing areas is neither meteorological nor biological, but societal. It is the environment of poverty. Residents of such areas have neither the technical nor political means to protect themselves and their living areas from potential hazards, both natural and human. Lack of drainage exacerbates flood damage; stripping of vegetation causes or aggravates dust problems. Lack of safe water supplies and sewerage systems causes health problems. Poor control over garbage disposal, and over the polluting activities of nearby industries, poses serious threats to the health and well-being of inhabitants (Hardoy and Satterthwaite, 1984). The more conventional parts of the city have grown up with a framework of political support and a power base that leaves them better able to fend for themselves in the struggle for environmental quality than the areas of informal or illegal settlement.

There has long been a tendency to regard slums and shantytowns as places of social dislocation—as areas of crime and rootlessness in which migrants to the city first install themselves, but from which they extricate themselves as soon as their means allow. But, as McGee (1967) showed in his early work on squatters in Kuala Lumpur, there was remarkable stability among residents of these areas. Many of them had resided there for years and evinced no particular desire to leave. Explanations were sought as to why urbanites in these Third World cities might prefer to remain in the environment of a shantytown rather than relocate to areas more compatible with the higher material standards that some of them were able to afford. Gradually a realization emerged that shantytowns were not altogether regions of social distress and dislocation; they formed an integral part of the city structure and should therefore be incorporated into plans for the future of the urban region.[1]

Urbanization, as we know it today in Third World countries, sprang from the incorporation of such territories into the global economy, largely through a process of colonization in the eighteenth and nineteenth centuries.[2] European powers required urban centers in their colonial territories in order to facilitate their administration and economic development, processes that necessitated a radical reordering of previously existing social and spatial structures.

A number of different patterns can be discerned. In some places, such as the Indian subcontinent, colonizers were brought into contact with a sophisticated indigenous social system. In most instances, a wholly new segment of urban landscape was grafted into the indigenous city. Throughout much of Latin America, new cities were founded during the period of Spanish rule; some, such as Guadalajara, were completely new foundations; others, such as Mexico City, set on the remains of Tenochtitlán, were implanted on the sites of former centers. Urban areas developed as centers for colonial and then postcolonial elites. They were not initially magnets for the in-migration of indigenous people.

Most contemporary African and Southeast Asian countries fell into the category of classic nineteenth-century colonies. Given prevailing views as to the nature of a colonial economy, it was not anticipated that large numbers of natives of these territories would need to be accommodated in towns. In most colonial administrations, indigenous forms of social organization were utilized.[3] This implied some degree of concern for the conservation of indigenous societies, and therefore for their maintenance, at least in the rural areas where they were predominantly located.

Consequently, the typical nineteenth-century colonial or ex-colonial city was the domain of the new national elite, and the structures and functions set in place were those required to provide for the needs and comfort of this group. To some extent it was natural to expect that there would be an indigenous presence in the city, although many colonial regimes specifically sought other foreign elements to perform these functions. Immigrants from China or India provided small-scale commercial services in a number of colonial territories elsewhere in Asia and in Africa. In general there was little expectation of any need to provide urban services of a relatively sophisticated kind—utilities, urban transport, and the like—for a population of indigenous immigrants whose presence in the city, even if not specifically forbidden, was not planned for in any meaningful sense.

Nonetheless, the indigenous populations did make their presence felt in all of what are now the Third World's major cities. In certain instances, employers brought them to the city and utilized their labor in the raw materials processing industries that often constituted an important part of the economy of these territories. The employers often provided housing and considered the natives' stay in the city would be one of relatively short duration. But native populations saw the cities as places where they might be able to break out of the confines of restrictive social structures and began to make their way there for the purpose of indefinite settlement. In considering Javanese cities under the Dutch, Cobban (1970) has described how the indigenous urban *kampung*, or settlement, sprang up. Municipal authorities somehow had to cope with this intrusion into the urban landscape, although they had considerable difficulty in doing so. Natives and nonnatives fell under completely different legal codes for administrative purposes. Municipalities did not wield administrative authority over the natives, since their jurisdiction was limited to the nonnative population.

As native people moved into the cities, they brought with them their techniques of settlement and housing design. They created partly traditional villages in an urban setting, building houses on their own, using designs and materials that, if they did not actually match those of the rural areas from which the natives came, were as close an approximation as they could reasonably achieve.[4]

It is therefore not appropriate to regard the phenomenon of spontaneous shelter as a recent occurrence in Third World cities. It is a feature that emerged along with the cities' rapid growth as centers of population. It is also a very understandable phenomenon, given the technical and financial means at the disposal of urban dwellers and rural migrants. Nonetheless, this in no way lessens the sharpness of contrast and contradiction that appears in cities where spontaneous settlements have to share geographic and social space with more formal elements of the urban landscape. The modern city in the Third World reflects the intrusion of external influences—colonial administration in many instances, and in others simply participation in international trading and commercial circuits—and spontaneous shelter is the means whereby indigenous populations can accommodate the demands of the city and at the same time enjoy some of its benefits.

Spontaneous Shelter and the Landscape of the City

Third World cities characteristically have a dual economy (Castells, 1977; Santos, 1977). On the one hand, there is the so-called formal sector, containing the large business enterprises that function in the international economic arena. On the other hand, there is an informal sector, comprising the great mass of small-scale urban activities—petty trading, hawking, and transport, to mention only a few (Hart, 1973; Leys, 1973). The formal sector represents a modernized sector that is frequently owned, directed, or controlled by foreign centers of economic power and responds to the needs of the international economy. It is usually highly capitalized, and its activities are structured in familiar, global institutional forms. It is essentially a corporate economic sector in which business and personal contacts follow the logic of corporate relationships. The informal sector is not quite the counterpart of the small-business segment of Western economic society. Although it contains a vast number of small businesses, these seldom have a Western formal structure. Capital needs may be very small (and are seldom satisfied by reliance on the banking industry), enabling such enterprises to withstand considerable fluctuations. Individuals may move from one activity to another, or cultivate several activities at one time. Use of family labor is common, and thus regular wage-paying mechanisms are bypassed. Generally the informal-sector business is not geared for interregional or international dealings; the focus is on a clientele within the city or, more probably, within the neighborhood.

It is broadly accepted that a symbiotic relationship exists between the two sectors. On occasion they compete, but in many instances they function in a complementary fashion.[5] Some would go further and suggest that the formal sector achieves its success because of its ability to work with, indeed exploit, the informal sector, particularly in the matter of wage levels. The informal sector, then, may be viewed as an essential device permitting the migration of rural dwellers to the city, which maintains them at a level of poverty until such time as they may be fortunate enough to break into a higher level of earnings. Nevertheless, as long as people remain in informal-sector economic activities, it is not normally conceivable for them to have sufficient reliable or regular financial resources to undertake a long-term commitment, such as the purchase of a house.

Cities in the Third World are overwhelmed primarily because they have been the target for a massive in-migration of population from rural areas. Misra and Tri Dung (1983) estimate that in the 1950s in-migration contributed 60 percent of the population growth in the large cities of the Third World. In the 1980s this is expected to decline to about 42 percent, but it still implies a high level of migration from rural to urban areas. This massive flow of migrants has been implicated in the emergence of slums, squatter areas, and in the phenomenon of spontaneous shelter. City governments have been unable to keep up with the growth of their populations, and settlements that sprang up and housed these migrants have been left largely to their own devices when it comes to providing urban services.

The migrants are said to be poor, without significant resources, and largely uneducated. Often this is true, but as indicated previously, even after long years of residence in the city, many erstwhile migrants continue to live in spontaneous shelter. Why do they not enter the more formal housing market, which cannot only provide them with a higher quality of house but also give them more certain assurance of security of title? One answer is provided by Benjamin et al. (1985), reporting on a survey of building procedures and costs carried out in Bandung, West Java. He and his co-workers report that the costs of using informal construction avenues (either building the house oneself or contracting with building specialists who work largely in the informal sector) are substantially lower than building costs in the formal sector, lower by as much as 75 percent.[6]

The notion that a functional relationship exists between spontaneous shelter and the formal and informal sectors of the economy has been made explicit by Johnstone (1984). Figure 2.1, from his analysis, proposes dividing all new housing construction into two categories: conventional, which represents housing that is universal in character and quality, similar to that which can be found in any of the world's major cities; and unconventional, which in terms of either design or materials is a local product. The former is characteristically the product of formal-sector construction enterprises, and the latter of the informal sector. Unconventional or indigenous housing is further subdivided into two categories: vernacular and squatter. Vernacular housing reflects the fact that many urban dwellers do try to build traditional styles of housing in their new city environment, usually inspired by the design of rural houses that the formal construction industry of the city normally has very little competence to achieve. Indigenous squatter housing includes what is referred to here as spontaneous shelter. According to Johnstone's formulation, squatter housing derives partly from the petty capitalist mode of production and partly from the quasi-capitalist informal sector. The entrepreneurs, where they are not the inhabitants, are local and private. They also operate on a small scale; the dwellings are of low quality and temporary in nature, and costs are relatively low.

The picture presented is broadly accurate. Although based on the major sectors of the housing production industry in Malaysian cities, it is applicable elsewhere. The housing industry in such instances is clearly stratified, and the powerful linkages tend to be the horizontal ones. The modern building sector is preoccupied with the construction of higher-cost, high-amenity housing; the informal sector provides lower-quality

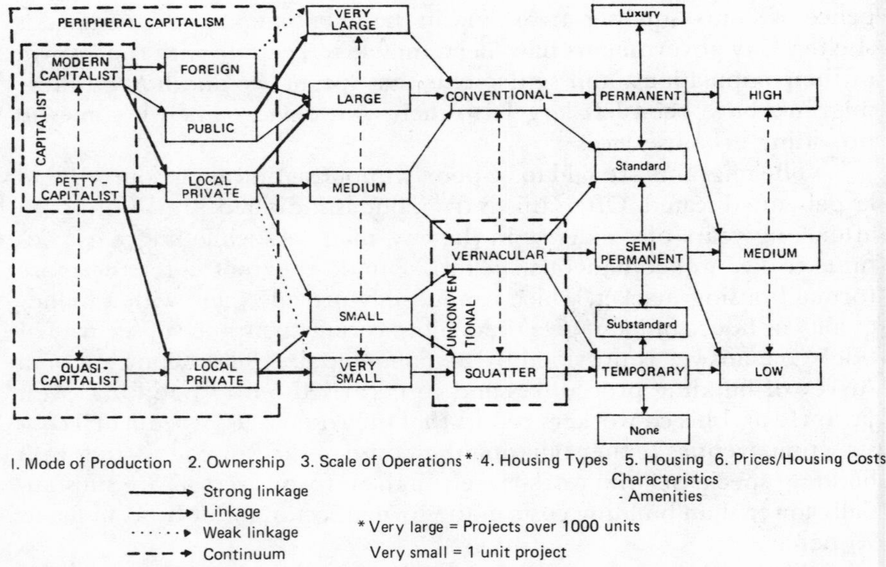

Figure 2.1 A model of urban housing in Malaysian cities. Reprinted with the permission of Edward Arnold Publishers from Michael Johnstone, "Urban Housing and Housing Policy in Peninsular Malaysia," *International Journal of Urban and Regional Research* 8 (1984), 501.

housing or at least the inputs required by residents who build their own low-quality housing.

Considerable evidence suggests that governmental authorities have come to recognize that spontaneous shelter is not altogether unacceptable. The writings of Turner (1969) concerned with such housing have had a profound influence on debates relating to policy on residential land use. As a result, instead of pursuing policies of slum clearance in areas where spontaneous shelter has been shown to exist, many countries have sought to find ways to upgrade such areas and occasionally even to legitimize them.[7] Steinberg (1982) indicates that Colombo seems to be imitating Singapore (Lim, 1979) in trying to upgrade and thus by implication eradicate all the slums in the city. Both clearance and improvements are projected in the plans adopted; nonetheless, given the costs of the operations, it is unlikely that Colombo will be able to accomplish the complete elimination of spontaneous settlements.

Upgrading has also become a regular part of the policies of a number of Latin American governments. Riofrío (1980) has outlined the complexity of the situation in Lima, Peru. There the settlers, instead of being the object of hostile attention (Riofrío, 1978), are wooed by a series of agencies—some local, others foreign—with a view to the settlers' betterment. Hollensteiner (1975) has documented for part of Manila the process whereby a squatter settlement has gradually evolved, partly as a result of persistence, into a recognized entity within the overall urban region. In Indonesia the government established a national housing agency in 1975, called PERUMNAS, intended to provide public housing for urban dwellers who live in substandard conditions (Radinal Mochtar, 1979; Rosser, 1983; for Pakistan, see Schoorl, 1983).

A Spatially Stable Pattern?

Although much attention has been devoted to questions of land for urban slum housing and spontaneous settlements in the Third World, there is no consensus as to the broad spatial contours of such cities. Much of the literature recognizes that there is intense conflict over land, but most authors who have studied this aspect view the conflict as one between differing social and political elements, with land, the urban spatial resource, as the prize awaiting the emergence of a winner (Babcock, 1984; Geisse, 1982; Lloyd, 1979; Losada, 1976; Rogers and Williamson, 1982; Scott, 1982; Smith, 1984; White, 1975). It is, however, possible to sketch the main outlines of a model of urban land use that will reflect the dynamics of the relationship between the formal and informal sectors and the impact of a development that, although long observable in some Third World cities, is comparatively new in others. That development is the emergence of a substantial middle class.

The dominant forces at work in the cities of the Third World at the present time are those of the international economy. It is not simply that the elements of this economy—banks, trading companies, multinational manufacturing companies, airlines, plantation companies, and shipping agencies, to mention only some—need office or factory space and are capable of financing their needs more readily than other segments of the economy. The presence of any formal-sector activity implies a whole series of ancillary needs and related purposes. Personnel must be housed, and in the circumstances of ease and relative comfort appropriate for employees of a prestigious corporation. Highly paid executives and employees have come to expect a whole range of services. These include restaurants, travel agencies, shopping facilities, tailors, launderers, and so on. To be sure, many of these services have also to be available for the whole population, but most of the population cannot match the buying power of the elite for whom these services will be provided as a sign of the willingness of a locale to enter the world economy.

While some persons who constitute the elite may be foreigners, others are members of the local population. They may be independent practitioners such as doctors, dentists, or lawyers; they may be senior members of the military or of governmental agencies. They quickly come to accept the comforts and conveniences of this international living style and are among its staunchest defenders (Friedmann and Wolff, 1982). The importance of the formal-sector city landscape is therefore enhanced by the participation of significant segments of the local elite.

Formal-Sector Activities

The city landscape is more than just the stage on which events and developments unfold. It is part of the drama. Formal-sector entrepreneurs regard urban property as important for a variety of reasons, not all of them strictly related to the functional aspects of their businesses. In many instances the prestige of location, or of imposing construction, is part of the appeal and is therefore an essential element in the conduct of business. Urban real estate becomes an important form of investment; it may in the end come to be as important, if not more important, than the ostensible purpose for which a business was first established. The formal sector therefore has a powerful interest in the land of the city, and it is vital to its prosperity that it be able to control adequately the development and use of this land. The mechanisms at its disposal are usually sufficiently strong to achieve this end. Formal-sector businesses exert a disproportionate influence on the political process, and regardless of their frequently voiced concerns for minimal government control, are generally strong supporters of city planning procedures in the Third World.

The following constitute the major landscape elements of the formal sector:

- Major business district offices
- Government agencies, including legislature if appropriate
- Embassies
- Commercial premises
- International hotels
- Warehousing and wholesaling areas
- Airports
- Industrial estates
- High-grade housing

Permanent construction is invariably preferred by the formal sector, and consequently a tendency exists toward locational stability. Pressures are strong to have such landscape entities enshrined in a master plan and zoning scheme that will guarantee reasonable stability of land-use activities in their vicinity. Other than this, specific locational criteria are not invariably followed. It is not considered obligatory for businesses to locate in the center of the city, however that term is defined. If there is a prestigious central business district, as in Singapore, many businesses do try to locate there. But outlying centers may be equally satisfactory as long as they exhibit a certain preponderance of business and economic activities and are suitably accessible. If possible, such concentrations of business activities should be linked to one another, and to other important components of formal-sector activities, by arterial roads that are not intrinsically part of any informal-sector areas.

Government buildings tend to be relatively stable in their configuration, and their spatial patterns often reflect decisions taken many years in the past. They reach monumental scale in many Third World countries, and perform an important role in establishing the symbolic role of the city. They do not, as a rule, exhibit any strong tendency to locate in relation to the business clusters.

Embassies, where they are present, form part of the governmental network in a functional sense, but their spatial affiliation is strongly toward the high-quality residential zones. Although a number of embassies maintain customized buildings, the majority opt for a large residence, adapted to become an office, and therefore tend to concentrate in residential areas.

Commercial premises of the formal sector cover a wide spectrum from large scale to small scale, with a variety of locational needs and constraints. Originally the classic department stores sought a location in the main business district, but as business districts have evolved into financial centers (like some of their counterparts in developed countries), such stores have found it difficult to continue at this location. The decisions made tend to reflect a prognosis as to the importance of automobiles to the clientele they serve. If automobiles are deemed important, locations are sought analagous to those of Western shopping centers, with adequate parking and good access. Otherwise a more restricted space is sought in a shopping complex, where vehicle access may be difficult and parking a problem. For smaller businesses, however, the shopping complex is an ideal solution, since it obviates some of the problems associated with the initial attraction of customers.

International-class hotels are a rapidly expanding component of the formal-sector landscape, reflecting both the growth of tourism and the rise in the number of business travelers. Major international hotels have become the focal point for a range of social, cultural, and political activities; their role in setting the tone for the city's life is increasingly important.

Warehousing and wholesaling arise as formal-sector activities because neither formal- nor informal-sector retail and distribution businesses have the capital to carry extensive inventories. As in developed countries, warehousing and wholesaling require large blocks of land and may utilize attractive locations in the vicinity of port or railroad facilities.

Airports, like their counterparts in Western cities, are located well outside the city. Cities that had airports within their confines, such as Jakarta or Kuala Lumpur, have built new ones at some distance, although some cities, such as Hong Kong, have had no choice but to continue with existing airports. Once a decision is taken to locate an airport on a specific site, other spatial and locational consequences follow. Upgrading the highway from city to airport is almost universal, presumably with a view to creating good first impressions for new arrivals. As such, the highway becomes an integral part of the accessibility system so essential to formal-sector businesses and may quickly attract major elements of the formal sector.

The planned industrial estate has been one of the major inducements offered to industrialists for investment in Third World countries. Such estates offer many advantages, as they are usually planned and set up by governmental agencies and therefore are assured of government approbation.[8] Important infrastructural questions, such as the availability of water, power, and transport, are taken care of at the planning stages; matters such as waste disposal, even if not dealt with in a manner universally agreed upon, are usually provided for at a level acceptable to the authorities. Although work sites are often located far from areas of residence, the transport of workers is not necessarily the responsibility of the corporation and is sometimes organized by the municipality. As far as these industrial estates are concerned, location on the periphery of the built-up area is virtually obligatory, given the need for sizable building parcels.

High-quality housing areas tend to be somewhat exclusive as a land use in Third World cities; that is, other uses, such as self-help housing or commercial activities, tend to be absent from the immediate area. These exclusive residential zones are both legacies and recent developments. In many Third World cities the affluent suburbs have been inherited from a colonial past, during which the housing needs of government officials or expatriate commercial personnel were provided for. The military cantonments in Indian cities typify such arrangements, as do the European-style quarters established in many Indonesian cities and towns by the Dutch during the colonial period (McTaggart, 1982). In these situations the existence of substantial tracts of higher-quality housing may be regarded as the persistence of a landscape element from one phase of a city's history to another. In contrast, the combination of an emerging real estate market and the establishment of zoning practices has helped create and define new exclusive areas of high-quality housing.

The international population in Third World cities is transient; it is also generously supported in terms of rental subsidy by the commercial and diplomatic agencies. Construction of high-quality rental housing has therefore become a lucrative investment for the local elites, especially those who happen to be well placed to manipulate the local political and financial machinery. It is difficult to generalize about the location of these high-quality areas. The existence of sufficiently large tracts of land with a potential for development as residential zones, either under ownership of or available to an appropriate entrepreneur, seems to be the determining factor rather than specific locational requirements.[9]

Informal-Sector Activities

Informal-sector requirements and dynamics are different from those of the formal sector. Many activities that take place in the informal sector do not have or need established places of business. They do not seek the prestige of location or the eventual windfall from a real estate investment that may be as important to a formal-sector enterprise as its ostensible business. The main informal-sector uses may be subsumed as follows:

- Markets
- Other small-scale commerce
- Workshops
- Streets
- Transport functions
- Low-grade housing

Markets form an important commercial outlet for informal-sector retailing. Typically a market is owned and operated by the municipality, which leases out stall space to individuals who operate their businesses as family concerns. Markets thus have important links to the wholesaling segment of the formal sector, especially the part that deals in the movement of foodstuffs and produce. The municipality tends to seek a service-oriented location for a market, placing it where it will be of maximum benefit to the largest number of consumers. There may be a central market in the overall city "center of gravity," offering the largest amount of produce for sale. Other markets may be scattered throughout the urban area, following whatever formula the city administration has decided to adopt.

Other small-scale commerce includes a vast array of small shops that, unlike the market stalls, demand some, perhaps considerable, capital investment. Indeed, many smaller regular retail outlets could be placed in the formal sector, especially if the scale of the business and the degree of formalism in its management warranted it. Nevertheless, the great majority of these small retail shops should be considered part of the informal sector, depending heavily as they do on family labor for their operation. They are also usually heavily dependent on formal-sector businesses, especially wholesalers, both for their stock and for the various forms of credit under which it is provided. Clusters of shops line the streets in older parts of the cities and form nuclei in many newer areas. Frequently these shops are operated predominantly by nonindigenous population groups; Indians have played this role in several

African countries, and the Chinese in Southeast Asia. The locational orientation, however, is strongly toward areas of population concentration, since the clientele is heavily dependent on foot, bicycle, or public transportation.

Workshops are seldom separate entities and are found throughout areas of residential land use; indeed they are often part of the residence. Clearly this poses certain dangers for the inhabitants, depending on the nature of the activities concerned. But the advantages are those of proximity of place of work and residence.

The streets are an important part of the space of the informal sector. A distinction must be made between streets that function primarily as transport arteries and those that constitute part of the "people-occupied space." The latter function in a multiplicity of ways. Their space is an extension of the adjacent businesses, whether these are workshops, municipal markets, retail shops, or services. In addition they constitute the major business space for a host of ambulatory businesses—hawkers, traders, mobile restaurants, knife sharpeners, shoe repairers, and the like. The existence of public space is vital in reducing the need for the costly overheads of premises, and it is understandable that the use of streets for business is a constant bone of contention between government and the businesses concerned.

Intraurban transport is often an important part of the informal sector (Forbes, 1981). Typically, traditional forms of transport are provided on demand, using either human power (e.g., the trishaw) or animal power. Such forms of transport have an advantage in that they may be able to approach the poorer housing areas, not always accessible by motor transport.

Areas of low-grade housing are those in which spontaneous shelter normally occurs. Occupants of these areas have very little say in their location, since people in search of inexpensive land to build on can find it only where it exists. It is advantageous to be able to establish a large colony, rather than a series of small ones, since the authorities may be slow to move against a community of thousands, whereas they may well move quickly to evict smaller entities. A location that minimizes the journey to possible places of employment is also desirable; consequently, many such settlements have appeared in the central zones of major cities.

Dependency is a striking characteristic of spontaneous shelter areas, and it applies particularly to location. The inhabitants have neither political nor financial power. Their act of settlement is an act of seizure—a violent and defiant act that challenges established authority and invites forceful repression. But repression, other than its value as a symbolic act of maintenance of authority, serves no real purpose because the impoverished inhabitants of zones of spontaneous shelter are essential to the city system of which they form a part. Unless removal is accompanied by a realistic rehousing program, it merely shifts the phenomenon elsewhere. For the would-be settlers, the strategy is to find some available land on which to build, land where seizure will not be so dramatically challenging to authorities that removal becomes inevitable. Consequently, the formal sector, acting through its political mechanisms, has in each instance of spontaneous settlement the power to determine whether to leave it alone to survive or try to remove it. The formal sector, in short, functions as the dominant plant species of the community; the informal sector adapts as best it can to the niches.

Spontaneous shelter is a reasonable response to such a spatial structure and its underlying dynamics. For the most part, its builders have no security of tenure, although usage has tended to create all manner of "titles" within the context of informal relationships. The builders have low and irregular incomes, and cannot therefore commit themselves to long-term regular payments. Their time and energies may be devoted to working on their own houses—with no employment available, they may have zero opportunity costs—and in due course they may indeed create a valuable asset.

Figure 2.2 illustrates a number of these spatial characteristics as they are revealed in Surabaya, a medium-size Indonesian city situated on the northern coast of East Java, immediately opposite the island of Madura. The eastward flowing Brantas River crosses the plains just to the south of the city, building up extensive coastal marshes in the vicinity. The city itself occupies a spit running north from the river, but no part of the urban area is much above sea level. The city was developed as a port during the Dutch colonial period, and it continues to function as the most important transport center in eastern Indonesia. In the post–World War II period it has also become a significant manufacturing center with a domestic market covering virtually all the provinces of the eastern part of the country.

The spatial structure of the city has been determined by the growth of *formal-sector* activities. In the north lies the port zone, with quays, a ferry terminal, extensive warehousing, and a growing number of industrial establishments. Since Surabaya was developed as one of the Indonesian Navy's main bases, extensive military zones flank the port facilities on either side. To the immediate south lies the city center. Originally it focused on government and commerical buildings, and these continue as important elements in this part of the city. The layout is spacious, and in some parts almost ornamental. Extensive development of formal-sector commercial activities has also taken place over the past several years, and there has been a considerable amount of reconstruction. Several of the city's newest hotels have appeared in this area.

To the south, east, and west, main roads leave the town, and these arteries are followed closely by formal-sector development. Several industrial parks have been started along them, and elsewhere clusters of

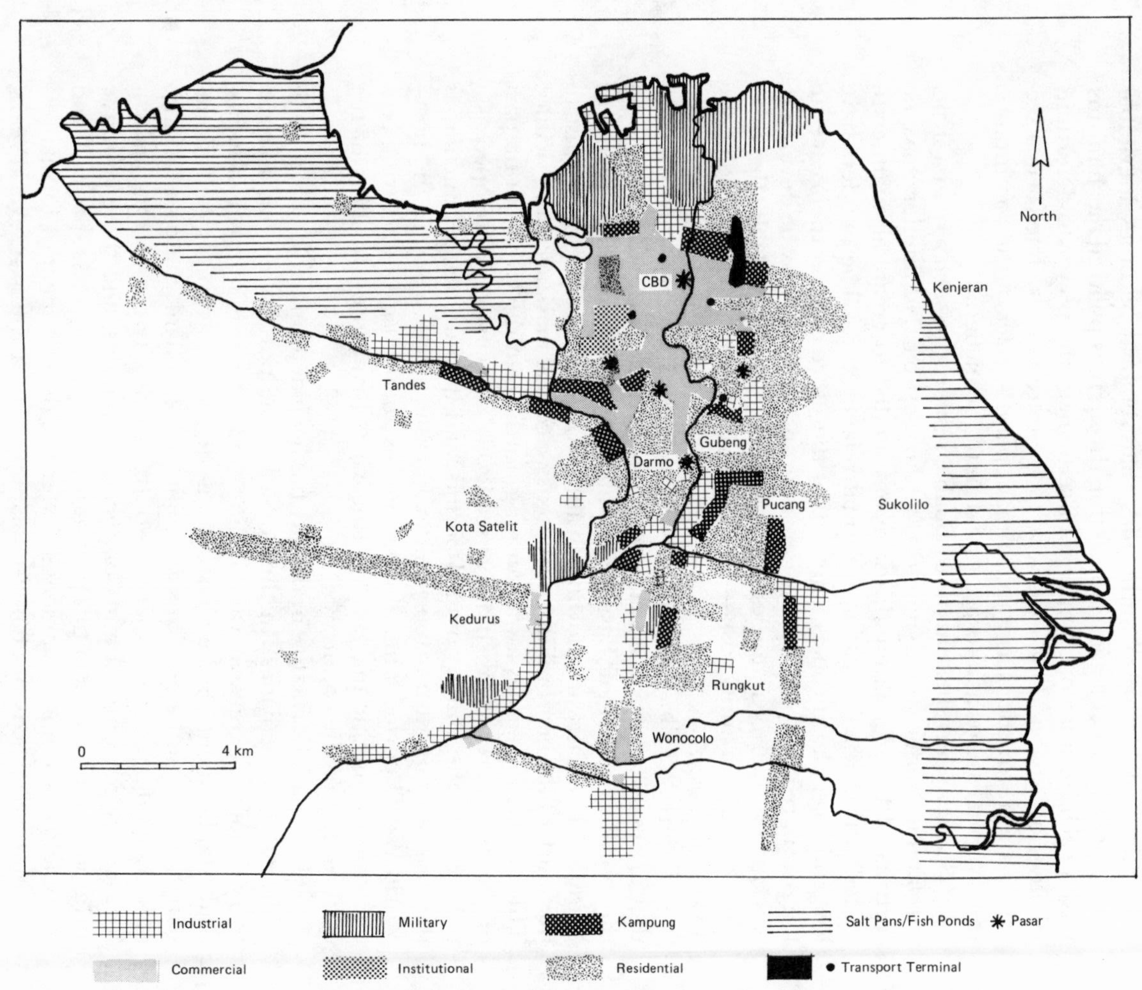
North
Kenjeran
CBD
Tandes
Gubeng
Darmo
Sukolilo
Pucang
Kota Satelit
Kedurus
Rungkut
Wonocolo
0
4 km
Industrial
Military
Kampung
Salt Pans/Fish Ponds
Pasar
Commercial
Institutional
Residential
Transport Terminal

industry and formal-sector commerce are strung out in the form of ribbon developments. Residential uses (moderate to high-quality residences) cover substantial areas both in the older parts of the town and in the expanding surrounding tracts.

In terms of *informal-sector* land uses, two types stand out: *kampung* (residential) and *pasar* (market). Of course, many informal-sector activities, especially commercial activities, are carried on in the streets and therefore do not generate any specific land-use type. The *kampung* are spread throughout the city in heavy clusters. There is no evident spatial pattern in the arrangement of these settlements; some are close to the city center or the docks, others have located close to major highways. The greatest amount of spontaneous shelter occurs in these areas. The *pasar,* unlike *kampung,* tend to be located almost exclusively in central areas. The main *pasar* is in the central part of the city, and this continues to draw customers from other parts of the city. In addition there are several other markets, some of them more recently established. They are, for the most part, in or near the well-established city center, which continues to contain a large proportion of the city's population.

Functional spatial differentiation is a characteristic of formal-sector activities. Central district, port zone, industrial area, residential zones; these all fit into a coherent pattern. Informal-sector areas, however, like the phenomenon of spontaneous shelter they contain, are not in a position to determine the form of land use. They are activities and uses that respond to perceived opportunities rather than create their own preferred land-use patterns. Their spatial patterns arise, not from the internal logic of the activities, but as a result of having to occupy whatever sites are available or whatever sites can be seized with the least amount of difficulty.

The Role of the Middle Class

The picture presented above has focused primarily on the interaction of two sectors, the formal and the informal. It is readily granted that neither of these sectors is watertight. In fact, the rather simple outline I have sketched has to be modified somewhat to take account of the existence of another important element on the urban scene: the growing middle class.

The middle class has been described as a group with an income comparable to that of the better-off among the informal-sector members, but with aspirations to a consumption pattern and a life style typical of lower segments of the elite (Durand-Lasserve, 1985; Kayser, 1985). The growth of this class reflects the growth of job opportunities in vari-

---

Figure 2.2 Surabaya, Indonesia, as an example of spatial structure in Third World cities. (Illustration adapted by David Loehr)

ous branches of government, commerce, and industry; expansion of educational opportunities; and the fact that more modern industries require a larger number of employees with technical and educational skills.

The middle class does not wish to live in a squatter area. Its members are prepared to assign a substantial proportion of earnings to shelter in order to occupy housing of reasonable quality located in a neighborhood characterized by such housing. They have regular earnings and can therefore qualify, under formal-sector rules, for long-term loans. Consequently they are prospective clients for speculative tract-house builders.

The appearance of the middle class may be dated differently in various countries. It has long been a feature of the urban scene in Mexico, for example. In Malaysia the middle class has been evolving rapidly since independence in 1957. In Indonesia it is a very recent phenomenon, dating from the late 1970s (Raillon, 1985).

The effect of the middle class on the development of the urban landscape has often been dramatic. Entire new suburbs and even towns have appeared that cater especially to this group. In other instances, the rules and regulations of formal-sector government have been manipulated to create an urban environment that, while much better hygienically than that of the slums, is still far from conforming to all established urban codes (Ameur and Naciri, 1985). Nevertheless, even though the phenomenon of middle-class spontaneous shelter is significant, its dynamics are different from those of the settlements referred to previously. The middle class aspires to formal-sector participation, with its security of employment and regularity of income. Even if members of this group construct their own housing, they are strongly motivated to consolidate their tenure and upgrade housing and environmental quality.

This middle class is a strong competitor for space and is having a profound impact on the availability of land. There have been relatively few studies of land tenure in Third World cities, but some that have been carried out (Durand-Lasserve, 1980; Evers, 1984) strongly suggest that tract-house development for this new middle class is causing waves of land speculation. Typically these seem to have affected parts of the inner-city suburbs first, then parts of the center, finally sweeping out to areas on the periphery and beyond. These developments place great pressure on the existing urban residents, whether they are middle class or urban poor. Pressure for removal of illegal occupants grows during phases of speculation, and speculation increases the cost and difficulty of relocating illegal settlers at any reasonable distance from the city. Earlier I suggested that in terms of spatial structures the illegal settlers were essentially at the mercy of the elite and the formal sector. I must now add that they are equally at the mercy of the emerging middle class, which is likely to be an ever-more-avid consumer of urban space.

Noncapitalist Cities

In what was set out above, it has been assumed that we are dealing with a city whose economy responds to market forces. The concept of formal and informal sectors implies some ability on the part of economic entities to formulate their own policies and practices. But a number of Third World countries with significant urban experiences have economies that are socialist. It is therefore interesting to ask whether the same or similar patterns seem to occur in them. Unfortunately only a rather limited literature deals with the landscapes of such cities, and much of what I have to say must therefore be considered tentative.

In socialist developing countries, urban centers, often a relic from a prerevolutionary period, were considered to be parasitic. Murray and Szelenyi (1984) have put forward a set of stages through which, they suggest, socialist countries have passed in their handling of urban problems. They label these as *deurbanization, zero urban growth, underurbanization,* and *socialist intensive urbanization.* Some degree of deurbanization was clearly evident in Kampuchea and South Vietnam, North Vietnam having been somewhat forcibly deurbanized as a result of aerial bombing (see Forbes and Thrift, 1983). China sent many urban youths out to the countryside (Cell, 1980), and to this extent did try to control urban population. Almost all socialist countries (and many nonsocialist ones) have tried to use identity-card systems and food rationing to prevent migrants from flowing toward the cities.

The rather different forms of economic organization (Musil, 1980) have not been conducive to a large growth of an illegal squatter population in the cities. Workers have been assigned to various economic activities, and there has been little hesitation in sending people out to new agricultural development areas, instead of encouraging them to remain in the city in some clandestine fashion (Barkin, 1978). In general terms, the phenomena of illegal settlement and spontaneous housing, although not absent from socialist cities, assume smaller significance. For an exception to this statement, however, see Chapter 13 in this book, which discusses spontaneous shelter in Yugoslavia.

Conclusion

Spontaneous shelter seems to be primarily a phenomenon of Third World countries that have adopted a market economy and it is clearly related to the overall structure of the urban economy in such circumstances. It largely reflects the differences between the formal and informal sectors and their spatial structures as expressed in the city landscape. These two sectors have different mechanisms at work that create their respective landscapes, and while the formal sector seems to create a landscape at least recognizable in terms of Western urban forms and structures, the informal sector develops its distinctive forms in accordance with its own needs and abilities. Spontaneous shelter is thus to be considered a normal product of the informal sector, acting on the urban environment.

The informal sector is subservient to the formal sector. Consequently, the spatial arrangements that appear in individual cities are not so much the result of the working out of a set of generalized locational or structural principles, but reflect the actual accommodations arrived at in each instance by the poor on the one hand and the ruling elite on the other.

Recent developments that are sharply influencing these trends include the emergence of a large middle class with greater purchasing power than the urban poor. One effect of this development is to provoke massive land speculation, thus increasing the pressure against spontaneous settlements. It is too soon to say what the ultimate effect of this trend will be, but it is not calculated to make life easier for the city's underprivileged.

Notes

1. For a clear picture of the changing attitudes of governments and researchers toward the urban poor, see Eke (1982).
2. There are exceptions to this rather broad generalization. One particularly significant exception is that of the city tradition in the Middle East. Throughout much of its history the Middle East has been a pivotal trading region, and many of its cities functioned as commercial centers in an international network, rather than as organizing centers for a rural peasant population.
3. This is not to suggest that there are no instances where indigenous social structures were totally disregarded. However, the most flagrant cases were those in which an implicit policy of elimination was followed, as, for example, in Australia or New Caledonia.
4. See Lasserre (1958) for a study of Libreville, showing how indigenous people adapted to the new conditions imposed by urban living.
5. One notable area of competition has been that of urban transport. Informal-sector enterprises cannot finance the equipment needed to run bus or taxi operations, and there has been a steady erosion of the legality and permitted area of operation of human-powered urban transport services. This is done usually on the pretext of improving traffic flow.
6. For a contrary view of building costs in Mexico City, see Connolly (1982).

7. For an interesting discussion of the use of Islamic law to enable squatters to legitimize their presence and possession, see Saleem Bukhari (1982).
8. The Indian government's involvement with Union Carbide at Bhopal was a good example of the degree of protection accorded to industry that functions in some way in association with government policy.
9. Bangkok (never actually a colonial city) is an exception in that it exhibits a great deal of heterogeneity in its residential areas. High-quality housing and squatter-type settlements frequently coexist in close proximity.

References

Akom, A. A. 1984. "Development Strategies for the Slums of Lagos." *Habitat International* 8, 159–71.

Ameur, M., and M. Naciri. 1985. "L'urbanisation Clandestine au Moroc; Un Champ d'Action pour Les Classes Moyennes." *Tiers Monde* 26(101), 79–92.

Babcock, B. 1984. *Unfairly Structured Cities*. Oxford: Blackwell.

Barkin, David. 1978. "Confronting the Separation of Town and Country in Cuba." In *Marxism and the Metropolis*, ed. L. Sawers and W. Tabbs, pp. 317–37. New York: Oxford University Press.

Benjamin, S., et al. 1985. "The Housing Costs of Low Income Kampung Dwellers: A Study of Product and Process in Indonesian Cities." *Habitat International* 9, 91–110.

Castells, Manuel. 1977. *The Urban Question*. London: Arnold.

Cell, Charles P. 1980. "The Urban–Rural Contradiction in the Maoist Era: The Matter of De-urbanization in China." *Comparative Urban Research* 21, 48–62.

Cobban, James L. 1970. "The City of Java: An Essay in Historical Geography." Doctoral dissertation, Department of Geography, University of California, Berkeley.

Connolly, Priscilla. 1982. "Uncontrolled Settlements and 'Self-Build': What Kind of Solution?" In *Self-Help Housing: A Critique*, ed. Peter M. Ward, pp. 141–74. London: Mansell.

Durand-Lasserve, Alain. 1980. "Speculation in Urban Land, Land Development, and Housing Development in Bangkok: Historical Process and Social Function." Paper prepared for the Thai-European Seminar on Contemporary Social Change in Thailand, Amsterdam.

———. 1985. "Paraître et Gérer: La Résistible Ascension des Classes Moyennes Urbaines dans les Pays du Tiers Monde." *Tiers Monde* 26(101), 41–53.

Eke, E. Feral. 1982. "Changing Views on Urbanisation, Migration, and Squatters," *Habitat International* 6(1/2), 143–63.

Evers, Hans-Dieter. 1984. "Urban Landownership, Ethnicity, and Class in Southeast Asian Cities." *International Journal of Urban and Regional Research* 8, 481–96.

Forbes, Dean. 1981. "Production, Reproduction, and Underdevelopment: Petty Commodity Producers in Ujung Pandang, Indonesia." *Environment and Planning* 13, 841–56.

Forbes, Dean, and Nigel Thrift. 1983. "The Geography of the non-Capitalist 'Developing' Countries: The Case of Urbanisation in Vietnam." Geography Seminar Paper, Australian National University, Canberra.

Friedmann, John, and Goetz Wolff. 1982. "World City Formation; an Agenda for Research and Action." *International Journal of Urban and Regional Research* 6, 309–44.

Geisse, Guillermo. 1982. "El Acceso de Los Pobres a la Tierra Urbana: Tres Problemas Críticos de Políticas." *Revista Latino-Americana de Estudios Urbano-Regionales* 9, 2.

Ghosh, Pradip K., ed. 1984. *Urban Development in the Third World.* Westport, Conn.: Greenwood Press.

Hardoy, Jorge, and David Satterthwaite. 1984. "Third World Cities and the Environment of Poverty." *Geoforum* 15, 307–33.

Hart, Keith. 1973. "Informal Income Opportunities and Urban Employment in Ghana." *Journal of Modern African Studies* 11, 61–89.

Hawken, Paul. 1982. *The Next Economy.* Baltimore: Ballantine.

Hollensteiner, M. R. 1975. "Metamorphosis from Tondo Squatter to Tondo Settler." *Ekistics* 40(238), 211–15.

Johnstone, Michael. 1984. "Urban Housing and Housing Policy in Peninsular Malaysia." *International Journal of Urban and Regional Research* 8, 497–529.

Kayser, Bernard. 1985. "Pour une Analyse de la Classe Moyenne dans les Pays du Tiers Monde." *Tiers Monde* 26(101), 7–30.

Lasserre, Guy. 1958. *Libreville: La Ville et Sa Région: Etude de Géographie Humaine.* Paris. Cahiers de la Fondation Nationale des Sciences Politiques.

Leeds, Anthony. 1981. "Lower Income Settlement Types: Processes, Structures, Policies." In *The Residential Circumstances of the Urban Poor in Developing Countries,* United Nations Centre for Human Settlements (HABITAT), pp. 21–61. New York: Praeger.

Leys, Colin. 1973. "Interpreting African Underdevelopment: Reflections on the ILO Report on Employment, Incomes and Equality in Kenya." *African Affairs* 72, 419–29.

Lim, William. 1979. "Low Income Housing in Third World Countries: An Overview and Some Policy Guidelines." *Habitat International* 4, 265–72.

Lloyd, Peter C. 1979. *Slums of Hope?: Shanty Towns of the Third World*. New York: Penguin.

Losada, Rodrigo. 1976. *La Tierra en el Mercado Pirata de Bogotá*. Bogotá: Fundación para la Educación Superior y el Desarrollo.

Marcussen, Lars. 1978. *Settlement in Greece: A Report on the Politics of Housing and Urbanization*. Copenhagen: Royal Danish Academy of Art.

McGee, Terry G. 1967. *Southeast Asian City*. London: Bell.

McTaggart, W. Donald. 1982. "Land Use in Sukabumi, West Java: Persistence and Change." *Bijdragen tot de Taal-, Land-, en Volkenkunde* 138, 295–316.

Misra, R. P., and Nguyen Tri Dung. 1983. "Large Cities: Growth Dynamics and Emerging Problems." *Habitat International* 7, 47–65.

Murray, Pearse, and Ivan Szelenyi. 1984. "The City in the Transition to Socialism." *International Journal of Urban and Regional Research* 8, 90–107.

Musil, J. 1980. *Urbanization in Socialist Countries*. White Plains, N.Y.: Sharpe.

Radinal Mochtar. 1979. "Urban Housing in Indonesia." *Habitat International* 4, 325–28.

Raillon, Francois. 1985. "Les Classes Moyennes en Indonésie: Opacités Culturelles et Réalites Economiques." *Tiers Monde* 26(101), 207–18.

Riofrío, Gustavo. 1978. *Se Busca Terreno Para Proxima Barriada: Espacios Disponibles en Lima, 1940–1978–1990*. Lima: DESCO.

———. 1980. *De Invasores a Invadidos: Diez Años de Autodesarrollo en Una Barriada*. Lima: Centro de Estudios y Promoción de Desarrollo.

Rogers, A., and J. G. Williamson. 1982. "Migration, Urbanization, and Third World Development: An Overview." *Economic Development and Cultural Change* 30(3), 463–82.

Rosser, Colin. 1983. "The Evolving Role of a National Agency for Housing and Urban Development in Indonesia." *Habitat International* 7, 137–50.

Saleem Bukhari, M. 1982. "Squatting and the Use of Islamic Law." *Habitat International* 6, 555–63.

Santos, Milton. 1977. "Spatial Dialectics: Two Circuits of the Urban Economy in Underdeveloped Countries." *Antipode* 9, 49–59.

Schoorl, J. W. 1983. *Between Basti Dwellers and Bureaucrats: Lessons in Settlement Upgrading in Karachi*. New York: Pergamon Press.

Scott, Ian. 1982. *Urban and Spatial Development in Mexico*. Baltimore: Johns Hopkins University Press.

Smith, Michael P. 1984. *Cities in Transformation: Class, Capital, and the State*. Beverly Hills: Sage Urban Affairs Annual Review.

Steinberg, Florian. 1982. "Slum and Shanty Upgrading in Colombo: A Help for the Urban Poor?" *International Journal of Urban and Regional Research* 6, 372–92.

———. 1984. "Town Planning and the Neocolonial Modernization of

Colombo." *International Journal of Urban and Regional Research* 8, 530–48.

Turner, John F. C. 1969. "Uncontrolled Urban Settlements: Problems and Policies." In *The City in Newly Developing Countries,* ed. G. Breese, pp. 507–34. Englewood Cliffs, N.J.: Prentice-Hall.

White, Alastair, 1975. *Squatter Settlements, Politics, and Class Conflict.* Glasgow: University of Glasgow Press.

II

Planning and Environmental Issues

Chapter 3

Spontaneous Settlements as Vernacular Design

AMOS RAPOPORT

As one reads the voluminous literature on spontaneous settlements, several things become apparent. First, the emphasis is on process rather than product; much more is written about the ways in which such settlements come about than on the characteristics of the resulting built environments. Second, the emphasis has been almost exclusively on economic, political, and social aspects; the relation of the built environment to culture has been discussed very little. Third, no clear-cut conceptual framework has been developed that could help integrate different aspects of the topic, for example, process and product characteristics, and within which a variety of findings could be considered and understood.

In this chapter I try to address and redress all three of these lacunae. In previous work I have dealt to a limited extent with some of the characteristics of spontaneous settlements as product—more particularly with their congruence with culture and their resultant supportiveness of culture (Rapoport, 1973, 1977, 1979a,b, 1980a, 1982a, 1983a, b). This is also elaborated in this chapter. At the same time I wish to initiate a discussion of the "design quality" of spontaneous settlements. It seems most important to draw attention to the often remarkable aesthetic or perceptual and formal environmental quality components of spontaneous settlements. The nature of these qualities, and how they come to be achieved, can potentially provide many lessons for improving shelter conditions. The specific question posed here is: how successfully do spontaneous settlements respond to the cultural and aesthetic needs of their inhabitants?[1]

Finally, I propose a conceptual framework within which the consideration of cultural and formal qualities of spontaneous settlements can best be achieved; that is, to consider them as *vernacular environments,* a term commonly applied to such traditional settlements as Greek island communities, Italian hill towns, and Indian villages. The economic and social qualities of these environments also fit into that framework.

Spontaneous Settlements as Cultural Landscapes

I use *spontaneous* rather than *squatter* because the latter is essentially a legal term, referring to land tenure rather than to the nature of the built environment. Moreover, not all spontaneous settlements are built illegally on land that has been appropriated. Note also that one could speak of spontaneous environments, some of which may be nonresidential (e.g., outdoor markets).

The word "spontaneous" introduces its own difficulties, however. In an important sense the term is incorrect because it implies self-generation and absence of design. That, of course, is impossible. Spontaneous settlements, like all human environments, do not just happen; they are designed in the sense that purposeful changes are made to the physical environment through a series of choices among the alternatives available. I have described this as the "choice model of design" (Rapoport, 1976, 1977, 1985b). In spontaneous settlements, the alternatives, the constraints, and the choices made are informal and are not based on explicitly stated models or theories. In this way they are like most environments, for example, cultural landscapes, which are hardly ever designed by a single person or team working with explicit models. Typically, cultural landscapes are the outcome of many decisions by many individuals over long periods of time. What makes them of general interest is that they add up to recognizable wholes. There must, therefore, be an implicit model or cognitive scheme shared by all the individuals making apparently independent decisions (Rapoport, 1972, 1976, 1980b, 1984a).

As a particular type of cultural landscape, spontaneous settlements are characterized by specific qualities that can be discussed and studied. Some constraints to the creation of such settlements, (e.g., those of knowledge and resources) are severe, but those of regulations, codes, and formal professional ideologies tend to be very weak. In environments created by the users, resource constraints may often be less harmful than those of regulations or professional ideology. This is because wrong planning decisions on the larger scale (e.g., road frameworks or infrastructure) may make the creation of user-built dwellings or groupings of dwellings on the smaller scale impossible (Rapoport, 1979b, 1980a, 1983b).

Another characteristic of spontaneous settlements is that their underlying schemata are in a state of flux and include both traditional culture core elements and newly introduced elements highly desired by the builders and users. These latter elements have a great influence and may include certain forms, materials, or services (Rapoport, 1969a,

1983a, b). One example is provided by Bedouin settlements in the Sinai and elsewhere; their form and spatial organization are traditional, but they contain dwellings built of modern materials. In one settlement I visited, dwellings were supplied with wall switches and chandeliers, although the dwellings were far from the nearest power line. A similar combination of traditional and modern components can be seen in new spatial organizations of settlements composed of traditional dwellings (Rapoport, 1983b; cf. Martin, 1984).

It is instructive to compare spontaneous settlements around the world to see how widely they vary—much more widely than indicated by the illustrations in Caminos and Goethert (1978, pp. 199–309). Such settlements also vary greatly in a single region (Southeast Asia, southern Africa, etc.), country (India or Brazil), or even in a single city.

A Framework for Analysis

A framework may be helpful in looking at spontaneous settlements as product while also allowing process and economic and social characteristics to be considered. Vernacular design provides such a framework. If vernacular design is defined properly, spontaneous settlements can be shown to be its closest contemporary equivalent.

I have recently proposed a redefinition of vernacular design (Rapoport, 1982b, 1983g) that hinges on moving away from ideal-type definitions based on a single characteristic or a small set of characteristics. Instead, the definition is based on a large number of characteristics, and not every member of a type must have all the qualifying attributes. As a result, one finds a range of variations within defined limits, so that each member of the type possesses many of its characteristics, and each variable is shared by many members of the type. Thus, *no single characteristic or attribute is both sufficient and necessary for membership in the type.*[2] It follows that environments also need to be defined by a large number of attributes or characteristics, not all of which will necessarily be present in any given case.

For my purposes, characteristics of environments are first divided into *process* and *product* characteristics. The former refer to the ways in which the environment in question is created; the latter describe what the environment is—its nature, qualities, and attributes. Both process and product are then described in terms of multiple characteristics.

In this chapter I use a preliminary list of characteristics of traditional vernacular environments (Rapoport, 1983g) (Table 3.1). These are neither exhaustive nor ranked in order of importance. Their role in discriminating among environments is not necessarily a matter of the given characteristic being present or absent. Instead, for most, it is a matter of degree and scale.

Table 3.1. Process and Product Characteristics of Spontaneous Settlements

Process Characteristics	*Product Characteristics*
1. Identity of designers	1. Degree of cultural and place specificity
2. Intentions of designers	2. Specific models, plan forms, and morphologies
3. Anonymity of designers	3. Nature of relationships among elements and the underlying rules
4. Reliance on a model with variations	4. Presence of specific formal qualities
5. Presence of a single model	5. Use of specific materials, textures, and colors
6. Extent of sharing of model	6. Nature of relation to landscape
7. Nature of underlying schemata	7. Effectiveness of response to climate
8. Consistency of use of a single model for different parts of the house-settlement system	8. Efficiency in use of resources
9. Relationships among models used in different environments	9. Complexity due to place specificity
10. Specifics of the choice model of design	10. Complexity due to the use of a single model with variations
11. Congruence of the choice model with ideals of users	11. Clarity of the environment due to the order expressed by the model used
12. Degree of congruence between environment and culture–life style	12. Open-endedness allowing changes
13. Use of implicit vs. explicit design criteria	13. Presence of "stable equilibrium" vs. the "unstable equilibrium" of high style
14. Degree of self-consciousness of the design process	14. Complexity due to variations over time
15. Degree of constancy vs. change of the basic model	15. Open-endedness regarding activities
16. Form of temporal change	16. Degree of multisensory qualities of environment
17. Extent of sharing of knowledge about design and construction	17. Degree of differentiation of settings
	18. Effectiveness of environment as a setting for life style and activity systems
	19. Ability of settings to communicate effectively to users
	20. Relative importance of semifixed features vs. fixed feature elements

Spontaneous Settlements as Vernacular Design

In order to classify spontaneous settlements formally, each characteristic would need to be discussed in detail. A large number of settlements would then need to be analyzed, using these attributes, and compared to similar analyses of preliterate (so-called primitive), traditional vernacular, popular (e.g., roadside strips, drive-ins, and suburbia), and other environments. Instead, I ask the reader mentally to compare traditional vernacular environments, spontaneous settlements, and professionally designed environments (and, possibly, popular environments), and to apply the attributes to them. I would suggest that for both process and product characteristics this exercise would place spontaneous settlements closer to traditional vernacular than to any other type of environment and farthest from professionally designed, or "high-style," environments.

The positioning of spontaneous settlements on a continuum of environments becomes clear if one discusses such environments in terms of the list proposed. When dealing with *process characteristics,* I do this largely in words; for *product characteristics,* I also use visual examples.

Process Characteristics of Spontaneous Settlements

Consider the characteristics of designers. If the *identity of designers* (characteristic 1) is examined, one finds that in both traditional vernacular and spontaneous settlements these are users and part-time specialists. A major similarity between spontaneous and vernacular settlements is that, as during most of human history, people in both settings obtain shelter by designing and building it. This plus the attendant sense of mastery and control may help explain the relative satisfaction with, and pride in, spontaneous settlements. In most present-day environments other than spontaneous settlements, settings are at best chosen from among the existing environments and then modified (Rapoport, 1985b).

In terms of the *intentions and purposes of designers* (characteristic 2), in both vernacular and spontaneous settlements, use, pleasure, and identity are primary. One difference is that individual identity tends to become more important in spontaneous settlements (cf. Rapoport, 1981). The *degree of anonymity of designers* (characteristic 3) in both spontaneous and vernacular settlements tends to be rather high, at least to outside observers.

Consider the models used in design (characteristics 4–9). In preliterate and traditional vernacular settlements there is a great *reliance on a model with variations* (characteristic 4). In spontaneous settlements the strength of the rule system, which leads to the use of a particular model, while lower, is still very high. But with regard to that model, in traditional vernacular settlements one typically finds the *presence of a single model or image* (characteristic 5). In spontaneous settlements there is a choice among a multiplicity of images from various sources, although in any one place the choices tend to be fairly systematic, which leads to place- and culture-specificity (cf. Rapoport, 1984a). The *extent of sharing of the model* (characteristic 6) tends to be very high in both traditional vernacular and spontaneous settlements, although it often weakens over time in the latter. Turning to the *nature of schemata underlying the model* (characteristic 7), in vernacular design folk schemata tend to be used. In spontaneous settlements these are combined with newly acquired schemata—often through the media—which are transformed in a popular manner.

A *consistent use of a single model for different parts of the house-settlement system* (characteristic 8) is found in both traditional vernacular and spontaneous settlements. Although the consistency of use is lower in the latter, it is much higher than in professionally designed environments. It is also useful to consider the form of *relationships among the models* used in different types of environments (characteristic 9), for example, in the high-style elements and the vernacular matrix in a given settlement. In traditional vernacular settlements similar models are frequently used but elaborated differently. For example, high-style elements such as religious buildings may employ the same model as dwellings but differ in size, relative prominence, location, materials, colors, degree of decoration, and the like. There seems to be no information available that would make it possible to specify the relationship among models used for spontaneous settlements.

It is possible to think of all design in terms of a "choice model of design" (Rapoport, 1976, 1977). What varies is the initial set of alternatives, the nature of the criteria, who applies them, and over what length of time—the *specifics of the choice model of design* (characteristic 10). It follows from characteristics 1 and 2 that the specifics in dealing with spontaneous settlements are closer to those found in traditional vernacular settlements: a relatively small initial set of alternatives, and group criteria not based on explicit theories and applied over longer periods of time. In terms of this characteristic, spontaneous settlements are intermediate between vernacular and high-style design but are closer to the former. The choice criteria are used to approach some ideal. In terms of characteristic 11, the *congruence of the choice model and its criteria with shared ideals of users,* spontaneous settlements are very similar to vernacular ones and very different from high-style equivalents or professionally designed settlements.

The *degree of congruence and the nature of the relation between environment and culture–life style* (characteristic 12) place spontaneous settlements particularly close to vernacular in their close fit to lifestyle, activity systems, institutions, and the like, largely because they are shaped by users. It follows that they are highly effective as settings for the life styles (and hence cultures) of particular groups. As we see later, this has product characteristic consequences, such as the effective communication of meaning (Rapoport, 1982c).

In terms of the *use of implicit/unwritten versus explicit/legalistic design criteria* (characteristic 13), spontaneous settlements are similar to vernacular and different from both high-style and popular environments. Upgrading schemes tend to move them closer to the latter through the imposition of explicit legal codes and regulations. Furthermore, the *degree of self-consciousness* of the design process (characteristic 14) tends to be lower in both vernacular and spontaneous environments than in professional design, although it is possibly higher in traditional situations than had been assumed (Rapoport, 1984b).

Two characteristics refer to temporal aspects. Characteristic 15 concerns the *degree of constancy/invariance versus change/originality (and speed of change over time) of the basic model.* In this respect there is a difference between vernacular settlements, which tend to have very slow rates of change in basic form, and spontaneous settlements, where rates of change can be rather rapid. Although hypotheses can be stated about the *form of temporal change* (characteristic 16), this has not been studied for either traditional vernacular or spontaneous settlements, and no comparison can be made at present.

Finally, the *extent of sharing of knowledge about design and construction* (characteristic 17) is highest in preliterate situations and very high in both vernacular and spontaneous environments. It possibly may be decreasing rapidly in spontaneous settlements as a result of urbanization, outside employment, and increasing specialization.

On the basis of this comparison of process characteristics, spontaneous settlements seem to be located close indeed to traditional vernacular settlements on any scale—and very far from professionally designed environments.

Spontaneous Settlements as Product

I now turn to the product characteristics of spontaneous settlements, among which I particularly wish to emphasize two aspects: the congruence of such settlements with, and supportiveness of, cultural characteristics of users, and the frequent success of such settlements in terms of formal, perceptual qualities.

In terms of these two criteria, spontaneous settlements are particularly similar to vernacular design, not the least because they meet the needs of their users extremely effectively. Moreover, these two criteria are intimately related directly: some formal qualities have cultural significance, for example, as signs of ethnic identity (Rapoport, 1981, 1982c). They are also related indirectly in that both are components of environmental quality, the improvement of which is the main purpose of the design and construction of all environments.

Relationship to Culture. I have argued for some time that, like vernacular environments, spontaneous settlements are much more culturally responsive than professionally designed environments as settings for life style; they often communicate meaning more effectively in terms of identity, appropriate behavior, and so on. My starting point is the concept of supportiveness, about which several points need to be made. First, the major effect of environment on people is through choice; the same environments work better when selected than when imposed (Rapoport, 1980c, 1983c, 1985b). Second, environments do not determine behavior but are either inhibiting or supportive. Regarding supportiveness, it is useful to ask three questions (Rapoport, 1979a, 1983b):

- What is being supported?
- By what environmental elements is it being supported?
- How is it being supported?

For our discussion of cultural variables, the specifics of what is being supported are important: by what elements in the environment and by what mechanisms? To design supportive environments one needs to know the relevant group, describe and analyze its important characteristics, and understand how these interact with the various elements of the built environment and through what mechanisms. Generally what is supported are, among other things, kinship groups and other social structures, a variety of intermediate institutions, rituals and festivals, language, food habits, and a wide range of activity systems. These are supported by various physical elements and settings at different scales (Rapoport, 1983b, pp. 256–57). For example, particular forms of residential organization may support important family or kinship structures. Particular forms of clustering may reinforce group identity and preserve core cultural patterns such as institutions and language, food shops, baths, and other elements that may be essential to rituals. Various mechanisms—meaning, perception, cognition, choice, and so on—can also be specified (Rapoport, 1983f).

In spontaneous settlements, as in traditional vernacular settlements, the group of settlers is self-selected and generally attempts to create settings and elements that support components of culture regarded as important. I say "attempt" because, at times, constraints are so severe that they become dominant; in those instances the environment may be inhibiting rather than supportive. At other times, the imposition of the wrong frameworks from outside, such as a grid layout of roads with individual lots, blocks the development of supportive elements such as compounds for extended family or kin groups (Rapoport, 1980a, 1982a, 1983b).

It is useful to begin the discussion of the relation of built environments to culture with basic concepts. Among these I have emphasized life style and activity systems. If one includes their latent aspects, activity systems incorporate a wide spectrum of important components of culture. In addition I have emphasized the importance of social groups and other intermediate institutions or structures, and their congruence with physical units and units of integration such as neutral places where different groups can meet. This congruence is frequently achieved through the ability to cluster by perceived homogeneity. Also important is the ability to express this through the physical environment and its components. This expression, in turn, has important consequences for the culturally effective functioning of the environment.[3] I have already discussed the importance of settings that support kinship and other social structures, intermediate institutions, rituals and festivals, language, food habits, and a wide range of activity systems. Also highly significant are appropriate patterns of economic activities, work, shopping, and health, and their associated settings. All of this also presupposes effective communication and easy comprehension of environmental cues, the proper blending of modern and traditional elements, and high open-endedness and adaptability to changing characteristics.

If we analyze spontaneous settlements in terms of these more specific components of culture, we find that they are next only to preliterate and traditional vernacular settlements in their supportiveness of culture.

Formal, Perceptual Environmental-Quality Aspects. Spontaneous settlements are also often extremely successful in formal and perceptual (aesthetic) terms, much more successful than most present-day professionally designed environments. In this respect spontaneous settlements resemble traditional vernacular settlements. I have felt for some time that spontaneous settlements often have great perceptual quality, and this was reinforced when I served on a jury for a competition to redesign the La Perla settlement in San Juan, Puerto Rico. I was struck by how much less successful all entries seemed in purely urban design terms than what existed (Photo 3.1). At least part of the failure seemed to be related to process: the need to illustrate concepts through architectural drawings made levels of complexity like those of the existing settlement impossible to achieve.

Many spontaneous settlements are outstandingly successful as designs in the most traditional sense of the word.[4] Clearly, discussing formal qualities in isolation presents problems; one inevitably neglects the importance of the intimate links between settings, their perceptual qualities, culture, and behavior (Rapoport, 1983f, 1984c). Yet, when considered in this way, one finds among spontaneous settlements some of

Photo 3.1 La Perla, San Juan, Puerto Rico. Note the use of site, complexity, distinctions between public and semipublic space, culture-specific settings (e.g., table for cards, chess, checkers), fine grain.

the most effective environments in terms of formal qualities. This is particularly surprising not only because of the limited resources of the builders but also because the creators and users of these settlements tend to emphasize nonphysical aspects of the environmental-quality profile; they emphasize even more the many variables completely outside the profile—for example, education for their children (Rapoport, 1983b, 1985b).

Many such environments, however, have been and are being destroyed by so-called improvements (Rapoport, 1983b). In Brazil (Salvador, Bahia and Rio de Janeiro), in India (Jamshedpur), and elsewhere, many settlements of great design quality are being replaced by ones less successful in such terms (Photo 3.2). These environments are threatened by planners who seem aware only of problems such as smoke, lack of ventilation and light, and drainage. Some of these problems are, in fact, being solved by improvements introduced by the residents. The plan in Jamshedpur, however, was to replace these settings with apartments; those already built were remarkably unsuccessful in design terms. Nothing I could say, nor appeals to Patrick Geddes's "conservative surgery" (Goodfriend, 1979), seemed to have any effect.

In dealing with perceptual qualities I will not explicitly contrast spontaneous settlements with the adjacent constructed or proposed projects that are less than satisfactory. Such examples are plentiful, and include São Paulo, Brazil; Rosario, Argentina; and Kharagpur, India; in addition to Jamshedpur mentioned above. In each case, adjacent to each other can be found spontaneous settlements and government-sponsored architectural attempts to replace them. The contrast is not only striking but poignant.

There is a major problem of how to illustrate the perceptual points being made. Some of the most successful examples cannot be photographed adequately. Drawings may also prove impossible where environments are complex. Often even a plan and sections cannot be drawn successfully in the time available.

It is also generally true that discussing perceptual qualities in writing and using black-and-white illustrations is inadequate. Even colored slides, photographs, or films are not sufficient. Environmental perception is multisensory, and spontaneous settlements (like vernacular environments) are particularly rich. They are extremely complex not only visually but in terms of smells, sounds, temperature variations, air movement, textures, types of people, types of behavior, types of activity, tempos, and many other variables. Environments are also perceived by active individuals in a dynamic and sequential process and are thus virtually impossible to capture or describe (Rapoport, 1977).

In view of the above, I urge readers to visit as many spontaneous settlements as possible and to perceive them with an open mind and senses. Often one needs to learn to ignore building materials, garbage in spaces, and the like; one needs to become aware of relationships rather than only elements. Since the former are the more important, high-quality environments can be created from torn sacking, cardboard, rusty metal, bits of wood, and other such materials (cf. Rapoport, 1969b).

I would even make the stronger case that the designs of architects

Photo 3.2 Jamshedpur, India. Interior spaces of spontaneous clusters. Note the space articulation, enclosure, altars.

photograph better than they are experienced. They may well be designed to be photographed. In contrast, the spontaneous environments with which we are concerned are often outstanding when experienced but photograph very badly indeed. Even the best colored slides capture only a small fraction of the *visual* quality of spontaneous settlements and neglect all the other senses and feelings of cultural fit.

Even worse, in selecting formal qualities and examples, I am doing what I usually criticize: perpetuating designers' visual and aesthetic biases as adequate criteria for evaluation (which they are not) and arguing on the basis of personal likes (which are irrelevant). Since that is the way most designed environments are still evaluated, however, this makes my point another way: spontaneous settlements are as worthy as traditional vernacular settlements of being evaluated on aesthetic grounds by designers.

I will go further. When I travel, I hardly ever visit, or wish to visit, the work of designers; increasingly I wish to visit only traditional vernacular and spontaneous environments. When there is no traditional vernacular to be found, I tend to look only at spontaneous settlements, which, as this chapter argues, may well be the closest thing to vernacular we have today. This point is emphasized by the fact that one is frequently liable to take fairly recent spontaneous forms to be traditional, as has been the case with Jamshedpur. Another example is the settlement of Bantwane, South Africa (Photo 3.3), which was thought to be a tradi-

Photo 3.3 Bantwane, Kwarrielaagte, South Africa. View of a courtyard. Note the combination of traditional and new forms and materials, decorations, space articulation, and penetration gradients.

tional form but is indeed a spontaneous settlement (cf. Rich, 1983). Similarly, the N'Debele decorations in southern Africa, generally considered traditional, also are rather recent.

I now discuss and illustrate spontaneous settlements in terms of the product characteristics listed in Table 3.1. I concentrate on cultural fit and on those perceptual qualities often praised in discussions of traditional vernacular environments. Examples used are from places that I have visited and recorded.[5]

Product Characteristics of Spontaneous Settlements

Vernacular environments commonly have been described as highly place specific. This is also true of spontaneous settlements. To illustrate this *degree of cultural and place specificity* (characteristic 1) would require a large number of photographs from many locales. Most of the specificity results from congruence with culture and has particular implications such as ease of communication, maintenance of cultural identity, and ability to support culture-specific patterns of all kinds. This specificity is expressed perceptually through a great variety of formal qualities, some of which constitute the list of product characteristics. This variety is also typical of traditional vernacular design, and both types show a much greater range of variation than their high-style equivalents.

Particular models, plan forms, morphologies, and the like (characteristic 2) can be seen as specific manifestations of product characteristic 1. Their use makes the task of the designers and builders of such environments much easier by providing clear guidelines. Such models and forms tend to be clearest in preliterate environments and are very strong in traditional vernacular settings. Among present-day environments they operate most effectively in spontaneous settlements by enabling cultural supportiveness and specificity to develop at a smaller scale. These models and forms provide a potential lexicon of formal elements.

I have already emphasized the importance of studying relationships among elements rather than only the elements (Rapoport, 1969b, 1977). Examining *the nature of relationships among elements and the nature of the underlying rules* (characteristic 3) allows one to become aware of the structure of the environment behind "tatty" materials. Looking at such environments draws attention to design as the result of choices based on consistent rule systems, and the study of such rule systems can greatly strengthen one's understanding of the nature of design generally. As we saw when discussing process, the rules used in both traditional vernacular and spontaneous settlements are not based on explicit theory and are much freer and less self-conscious than in professional design. The result is an extremely rich environment with a wide range of often unexpected relationships (Photos 3.4 and 3.5). One consequence is the complexity of scale discussed in characteristic 10 below.

Photo 3.4 *Favela* in Rio de Janeiro, Brazil. Note the use of sites, formal qualities, potential open-endedness.

Photo 3.5 Overwater settlement (Alagado) in Salvador, Bahia, Brazil. Note the response to a specific site, potential open-endedness, and possibility of relating morphology to cultural variables.

A large list of *formal qualities* (characteristic 4) can be generated as the specific consequences of characteristic 3. What is striking about spontaneous settlements is the extraordinary range of such formal devices, which are very similar to, if not even more varied than, those in traditional vernacular design (Photo 3.6). The range of devices emphasized by the "townscape" approach to urban design in Britain (and based on analyses of traditional vernacular designs) may be even greater in spontaneous settlements.

The *use of specific materials, textures, and colors* (characteristic 5) is an even more specific subset of several of the above points. These characteristics are emphasized separately because the ingenious and daring use of materials in new ways, textural combinations, and above all the use of *color,* open a new domain of perceptual qualities. In both traditional vernacular and spontaneous settlements many more possibilities are found than in other environments; the vocabulary is much richer. In addition, color is often used to indicate ethnic, religious, regional, and other forms of identity (as in India, southern Africa, Brazil, and so on). Colors can also serve as indicators of modernization and levels of acculturation (as

Photo 3.6 *Gecekondus* in Ankara, Turkey. Note the use of site, formal qualities, landscaping, and general environmental qualities.

an example of the latter among Mexican-Americans in the United States, see Arreola, 1984).

The *nature of relation to landscape* (characteristic 6) is important because spontaneous settlements are often built on land that no one else wants, including extremely steep slopes (e.g., Puerto Rico, Brazil, Turkey), mud flats (e.g., Brazil, Southeast Asia), or narrow strips of land (e.g., India, Indonesia, Brazil). The ways in which builders cope with these relationships are most striking and enlightening. The solutions to difficult sites one can find among spontaneous settlements far surpass the simplistic approaches of professional designers. They also more than equal the greatly admired traditional vernacular equivalents such as Greek islands, Italian hill towns, and the *villages perchés* of Southeast France.

There is little information on the *effectiveness in response to climate* (characteristic 7). Informal observation suggests that spontaneous settlements, while possibly more effective than the equivalent professional solutions, are not as effective as traditional vernacular solutions, which may also not always respond effectively to climate (Rapoport, 1969a). This is the result of changes, such as the loss of some traditional devices (e.g., thatched roofs, windowless walls of high heat capacity, and mutual shading in very dense groupings); changes in life style; the importance of meaning in the choice of materials, which leads to the use of climatically less effective but higher-status materials (Rapoport, 1979a, 1983b); and the severity of constraints, such as the imposition of codes and regulations.

The *efficiency in use of resources* (characteristic 8) in spontaneous settlements has been studied, but most of this work has emphasized the use of materials. Space use has received less attention, although it clearly is a major resource. Correa (1976) and Payne (1979) recognize space use, and it is also mentioned in passing in Lakshmanan and Rotner (1985, p. 80) where twenty-two spontaneous houses use the same space as one typical villa. In the case of an Indian spontaneous settlement studied in some detail, space use is so efficient that the resulting effective space is many times the actual space (Payne, 1979). This efficiency is a result of the way activities occur (see characteristic 15 below) and the very fine grain of activities (Photos 3.7 and 3.8).

Complexity, an important perceptual quality, can be examined at several scales. For example, *complexity at the largest scale due to place specificity* (characteristic 9) results from movement among places that differ markedly one from another. In that event the highly noticeable transitions create the complexity (e.g., Rapoport, 1977). Complexity is also a major factor in the effectiveness of traditional vernacular cultural landscapes, and its absence plays a role in the corresponding criticism of present-day "placelessness."[6] *Complexity at other scales due to the use of a*

Photo 3.7 Barrio Rafineria, Rosario, Argentina. A courtyard interior. Note the use of space, decorations—plants, birdcages, paintings, and so on.

Photo 3.8 Timbal area of do Marro settlement, Rio de Janeiro, Brazil. Note the fine grain, multiple uses, climatic response, general environmental quality.

single model with variations (characteristic 10) is one of the major reasons that traditional vernacular environments are enjoyed (Rapoport, 1977). Spontaneous settlements also share this attribute.

As already argued, *clarity, legibility, and comprehensibility of the environment due to the order expressed by the model used* (characteristic 11) leads, among other things, to effective use of the environment and to cultural supportiveness. It also has implications for perceptual qualities through the presence of an easily legible order. Traditional vernacular and spontaneous settlements are very similar in this respect.

Both vernacular and spontaneous environments are extremely open-ended. *Open-endedness, allowing additive, subtractive, and other changes* (characteristic 12), has important social and economic consequences. It leads to cultural supportiveness: environments can change to accommodate changes in life cycle, life style, income, acculturation, and the like. This open-endedness, related to the flexible rule system discussed in characteristic 3, also leads to many unique perceptual qualities in both traditional vernacular and spontaneous settlements, as well as much higher levels of complexity. Moreover, open-endedness leads to the *presence of the "stable equilibrium" vs. the "unstable equilibrium" of high-style design* (characteristic 13). The spaces, buildings, relationships, fenestration, and other characteristics of both traditional vernacular and spontaneous settlements can change often, and in many ways, without losing their essential character or quality. High-style environments tend to be perceptually very unstable, often a single change can destroy a composition (see Rapoport, 1977, p. 358, for an example).

Complexity due to variations over time (characteristic 14) refers to changes *to* the model, not *of* the model, as discussed under process characteristic 16. This is a result of open-endedness and the presence of stability, among other characteristics. Since the environment is always changing, although within a clear order, it becomes extremely rich and complex. In this respect vernacular and spontaneous environments are much alike.

Open-endedness regarding activities—their types, numbers, and overlaps (characteristic 15)—is important for efficient and effective use of space (see characteristic 8; Payne, 1979). This open-endedness allows the residents to act in culturally appropriate ways and is critical in economic terms, allowing for many informal businesses and workshops and combinations of work with childrearing. A good example is street food vendors (Rapoport, 1977, 1983a), who are important for culturally appropriate activities, provide food where and when needed, and are of great economic significance (Rapoport, 1977, 1979a, 1983a, b; *Urban Edge*, 1985, pp. 5–6.) In spontaneous settlements, as well as traditional vernacular, this attribute also leads to complexity related to activities, their overlaps, changes over time, and so on.

Characteristic 16, *degree of multisensory character of the environment—large range of nonvisual sensory qualities*—follows directly from characteristic 15. Whether such multisensory complexity is liked or not is both a cultural and a personal matter. The presence of this multisensory character is, however, clearly very much higher in both traditional vernacular and spontaneous settlements than in high-style ones, although lower in some cultures than others (Rapoport, 1969a, 1977, 1983f).

In general, the *degree of differentiation of settings and the number, type, and specialization of settings* (characteristic 17) increases as one moves from preliterate through vernacular to high-style (especially modern) environments. I have seen no studies on this, but it seems that spontaneous settlements tend to be closer to vernacular environments in the number of specialized types of settings, although in the number of activities they tend to be closer to modern environments (this relates to characteristic 15 above).

The *effectiveness of the environment as a setting for life style and activity systems* is characteristic 18. I have already suggested that, like traditional vernacular settings, spontaneous settlements tend to be effective settings for the activities characteristic of different life styles. In some instances the severity of outside constraints may make them less effective than vernacular settings, but spontaneous settlements are still significantly more effective than their professionally designed equivalents. This does *not* mean that these environments are like traditional vernacular ones. They are not. The new values of modernity often lead to a rejection of traditional spatial organizations, house types, and so forth (Martin, 1984; Rapoport, 1983b). This suggests the need to emphasize the values of traditional environments and communicate them effectively to users and decision makers (Rapoport, 1973, 1983a). The effectiveness of environments as settings for life styles is intimately related to characteristic 19, the *ability of setting to communicate effectively to users,* as discussed above.

The last product characteristic is the *relative importance of semifixed features as opposed to fixed-feature elements.* In vernacular settlements the latter tend to be more dominant. In spontaneous settlements semifixed elements and nonfixed elements (i.e., people) are also prominent features of the cultural landscape. Both vernacular environments and spontaneous settlements tend to have more people visible than do other environments; urban space is an important setting rather than merely a transitional domain (Rapoport, 1969a, p. 71, 1977, p. 92, 1983f).

Cultural and Formal Qualities Combined

Cultural qualities were separated from formal ones in the preceding discussion for analytic convenience. Nevertheless, both form part of the environmental-quality profile, which links them indirectly, and they are also linked directly. One example of the latter link is the domain of cultural identity. In situations of rapid change, the maintenance of cultural identity becomes an important role of the culture core. It is achieved through many nonenvironmental means (which may, however, require appropriate settings). It is also achieved through the use of certain environmental qualities. These may include color, as in São Paulo, Brazil, throughout India, and even in the United States (Arreola, 1984); spatial organization, as in India and Africa, among the Bedouin and Navaho, and elsewhere; or specific elements, such as crosses among the Mayo Indians or the Marae in the case of the New Zealand Maori (Rapoport,

1981). Elements such as these are among product characteristics used for cultural purposes and in support of culture (Rapoport, 1983b,d).

In *House Form and Culture* (Rapoport, 1969a, p. 129), I proposed four objectives that need to be met by the residential environment (in the sense of the house-settlement system) for it to be successful.

1. It needs to be socially and culturally valid.
2. It should be sufficiently economical to ensure that the greatest number can afford it.
3. It should ensure the maintenance of the health of the occupants.
4. It should require a minimum of maintenance.

I would now add a fifth:

5. It needs to be successful in perceptual, formal terms.

In the past I argued that traditional vernacular design worked best for 1, worked well for 2, was frequently successful climatically but unsuccessful in relation to sanitation, parasites, and the like for 3, and that the evidence was equivocal for 4. I would now add that it also works best for 5. I would also conclude that spontaneous settlements lead to a very similar, if not identical, evaluation, although more studies addressing these issues are needed.

Conclusion

I began with the rhetorical question whether spontaneous settlements work well culturally and aesthetically, that is, in terms of some components of environmental quality. Having answered that question affirmatively, I conclude with another question, which seems to me more critical. How is it that people who are often illiterate, with very limited resources and power, and hence operating under stringent constraints—economic, informational, political, and so on—are able to produce settings and environments that I at least judge to be vastly superior, in terms of cultural supportiveness and perceptual quality, than designers working in the same places. I would go further—these environments are frequently even of higher quality than those of designers working in much more developed and wealthier places. The environments of spontaneous settlements are frequently comparable in quality to those of traditional vernacular, many of which professional designers admire.[7]

An answer to this very troubling question would take us far from the present topic and into an analysis of the state of designers' values; the state of their knowledge, beliefs, and "theory"; and the state of the profession and its institutions (Rapoport, 1983d,e). An interim conclusion, however, is that these spontaneous settlements, no less than the more widely admired traditional vernacular ones, can teach designers much. This is what I have called their *extrinsic* as opposed to their *intrinsic* importance.

I have argued elsewhere (Rapoport, 1982b, 1983b) that four attitudes are possible with regard to vernacular design; these also apply to spontaneous settlements.

1. They can be ignored.
2. Their existence can be acknowledged, but any relevance can be denied.
3. They can be copied (that has not yet happened regarding spontaneous settlements!).
4. One can learn by analyzing them.

It is point 4 that I regard as the only valid approach. The interim question then becomes how planners and designers can learn by analyzing spontaneous settlements. The answer is similar to the one that I have given to the same question relative to vernacular design: one derives principles and lessons by applying concepts, models, and theories to the evidence and then applies the principles and lessons (Rapoport, 1982b, 1983b).

There is a more general issue. One problem with design and designers is the lack of any real theory. Such a theory can emerge only from research, from a rigorous analysis of environment–behavior relations; that, in turn, can happen only if one considers the broadest possible body of evidence. This, I have repeatedly emphasized, means looking at the full span of history, at the full range of cultures, and at all types of environments. Spontaneous settlements, being contemporaneous, preclude a historical approach, although certainly not longitudinal studies (Rapoport, 1984b). They satisfy the other two of these necessary conditions. Moreover, in many places they represent most of the environment. Also, everywhere the cultural landscape—which is what we all live in—is spontaneous in the sense that most of its elements and an even higher proportion of relationships among elements are not professionally designed.

It therefore follows that spontaneous settlements are an essential part of the built environment, of the body of evidence on the basis of which generalizations are made. No theory of the built environment that ignores spontaneous settlements, as most so-called architectural, urban design, and landscape "theory" does, is worthy of the name.

Notes

1. At this point, the success of spontaneous settlements for their inhabitants cannot be evaluated since little work has been done on cultural

variables and environmental quality. My conclusion, in addition to subjective evaluation (which is most suspect), is based on inferences made from observation and informal comments and answers to questions of inhabitants (through interpreters). It is also based on my interpretation of the literature. In this discussion most references are to my own work. What follows is a continuation of a body of work that has been in progress for some time and that has, by and large, not been addressed by others.

2. Slightly more technically, this is equivalent to moving from a monothetic definition to a polythetic approach. The former is based on the possession of a unique set of attributes that is both necessary and sufficient to assign a "thing" (in this instance, a type of environment) to a class. It is frequently an ideal-type definition in which every member of the class must have all the qualifying attributes. A polythetic approach uses a larger set of characteristics so that "things" fit into groups by the range of variation between defined limits, a high proportion of the attributes being shared among individual members of the class. Thus no single attribute is both sufficient and necessary for membership in the class. (This formulation is based on Clarke, 1978, pp. 35–37.)

3. Regarding the congruence of life-style profiles and environmental-quality profiles, see Rapoport, 1976, 1977, 1980b, c, 1983b, 1985b; on activity systems and their latent aspects see Rapoport, 1977, 1982c, 1983b; on social groups and intermediate institutions, physical units, units of integration, and neutral places, see Rapoport, 1979b, 1980a, 1983b; on the relationship of such congruence to perceived homogeneity, see Rapoport 1977, 1979a, 1980a, b, 1980/81, 1983b, 1985b; on the role of expression in culturally effective functioning of settings, see Rapoport, 1977, 1980/81, 1982d.

4. There is a real danger of romanticizing spontaneous settlements. There are extremely unsuccessful and environmentally disastrous spontaneous settlements (as their variety would suggest). My point is that there are proportionately more successes among spontaneous settlements than among professionally designed environments.

5. These include various locations in Puerto Rico, India, Argentina, Brazil, Mexico, Costa Rica, Peru, South Africa, Botswana, Zimbabwe, Turkey, New Guinea, Israel, the Sinai, and Spain (Barcelona).

6. I do not accept this term, which I have criticized elsewhere (Rapoport, 1985a).

7. It is essential to avoid romanticizing both kinds of environments. In emphasizing their positive qualities for the sake of my argument, I have tended to underemphasize their failings. Analyzing them along the lines described in this chapter should lead to more balanced judgments. Note also that, by and large, I have neglected social, economic, and political issues, which may make *overall* success or failure quite a different matter.

References

Arreola, Daniel D. 1984. "House Color in Mexican-American Barrios." Paper presented at the Conference on Built Form and Culture Research, Lawrence, Kansas, October 18–20.

Caminos, Horacio, and Reinhard Goethert. 1978. *Urbanization Primer.* Cambridge: MIT Press.

Clarke, David L. 1978. *Analytical Archaeology.* London: Methuen.

Correa, Charles M. 1976. "Third World Housing: Space as a Resource." *Ekistics* 41(242), 33–38.

Goodfriend, Douglas E. 1979. "Nagar Yoga: The Culturally Informed Town Planning of Patrick Geddes in India, 1914–1924." *Human Organization* 38(4), (Winter), 343–55.

Lakshmanan, A., and E. Rotner. 1985. "Madras, India: Low-Cost Approaches to Managing Development." In *Cities in Conflict, Studies in the Planning and Management of Asian Cities,* ed. J. P. Lea and J. M. Courtney, pp. 81–94. Washington, D.C.: World Bank.

Martin, Richard. 1984. "Poverty and Professionals: The Role of Architects in Low Income Housing in Developing Countries." *RIBA Journal* 91(7) (July), 17–28.

Payne, Geoffrey K. 1979. *Urban Housing in the Third World.* Boston: Routledge & Kegan Paul.

Rapoport, Amos. 1969a. *House Form and Culture.* Englewood Cliffs, N.J.: Prentice-Hall.

———. 1969b. "The Notion of Urban Relationships." *Area* (Journal of the Institute of British Geographers) 3, 17–26.

———. 1972. "People and Environments." In *Australia as Human Setting,* ed. A. Rapoport, pp. 3–21. Sydney, Australia: Angus and Robertson.

———. 1973. "The City of Tomorrow, the Problems of Today and the Lessons of the Past." *DMG-DRS Journal* 7(3) (July–September), 256–59.

———. 1976. "Sociocultural Aspects of Man–Environment Studies." In *The Mutual Interaction of People and Their Built Environment,* ed. A. Rapoport, pp. 7–35. The Hague: Mouton.

———. 1977. *Human Aspects of Urban Form.* Oxford: Pergamon Press.

———. 1979a. "An Approach to Designing Third World Environments." *Third World Planning Review* 1(1), 23–40.

———. 1979b. Review of Horacio Caminos and Reinhard Goethert, *Urbanization Primer* (Cambridge: MIT Press, 1978). In *Journal of Architectural Historians* 30(4) (December), 402–3.

———. 1980a. "Culture, Site Layout and Housing." *Architectural Association Quarterly* 12(1), 4–7.

———. 1980b. "Cross-Cultural Aspects of Environmental Design." In

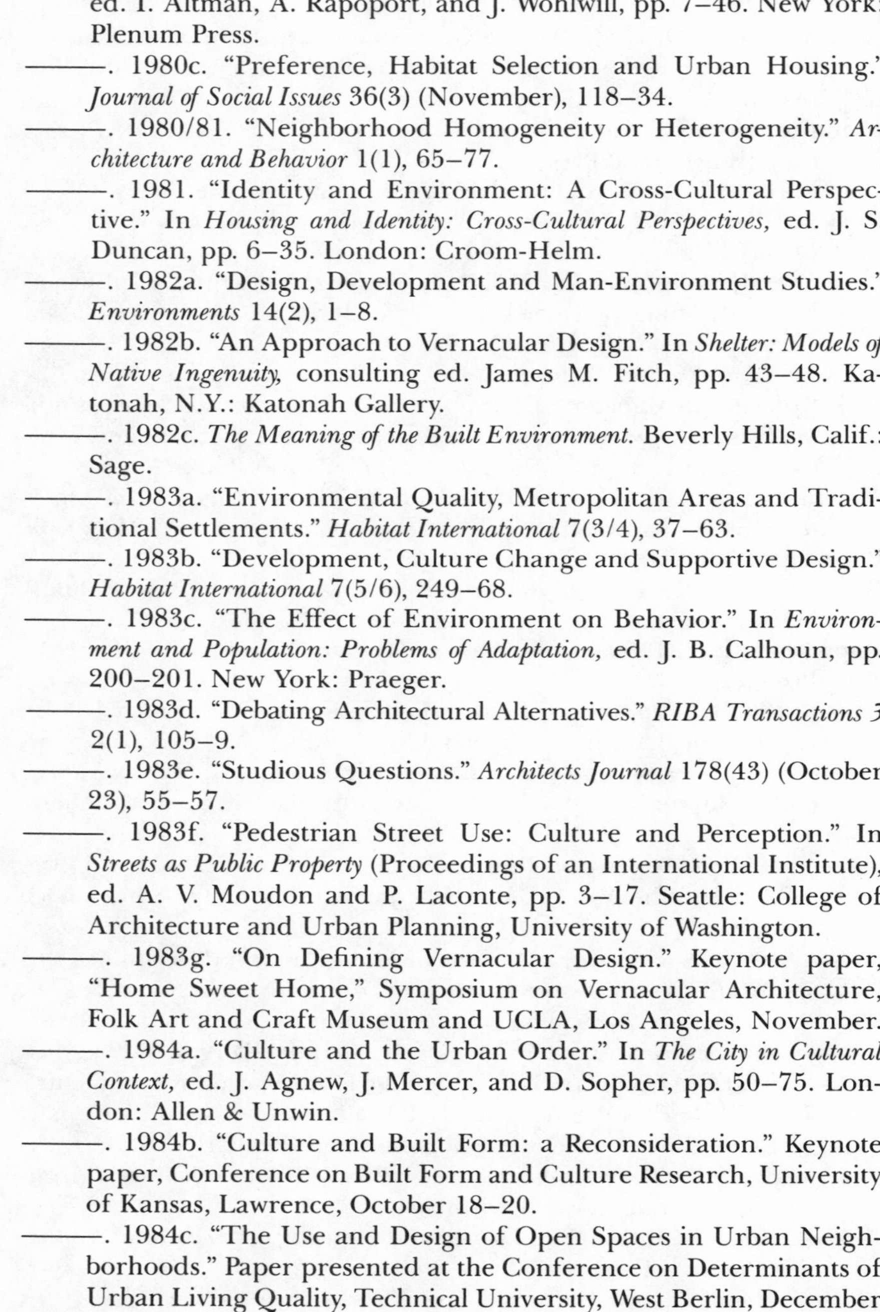

Culture and Environment: Human Behavior and the Environment, vol. 4, ed. I. Altman, A. Rapoport, and J. Wohlwill, pp. 7–46. New York: Plenum Press.

———. 1980c. "Preference, Habitat Selection and Urban Housing." *Journal of Social Issues* 36(3) (November), 118–34.

———. 1980/81. "Neighborhood Homogeneity or Heterogeneity." *Architecture and Behavior* 1(1), 65–77.

———. 1981. "Identity and Environment: A Cross-Cultural Perspective." In *Housing and Identity: Cross-Cultural Perspectives,* ed. J. S. Duncan, pp. 6–35. London: Croom-Helm.

———. 1982a. "Design, Development and Man-Environment Studies." *Environments* 14(2), 1–8.

———. 1982b. "An Approach to Vernacular Design." In *Shelter: Models of Native Ingenuity,* consulting ed. James M. Fitch, pp. 43–48. Katonah, N.Y.: Katonah Gallery.

———. 1982c. *The Meaning of the Built Environment.* Beverly Hills, Calif.: Sage.

———. 1983a. "Environmental Quality, Metropolitan Areas and Traditional Settlements." *Habitat International* 7(3/4), 37–63.

———. 1983b. "Development, Culture Change and Supportive Design." *Habitat International* 7(5/6), 249–68.

———. 1983c. "The Effect of Environment on Behavior." In *Environment and Population: Problems of Adaptation,* ed. J. B. Calhoun, pp. 200–201. New York: Praeger.

———. 1983d. "Debating Architectural Alternatives." *RIBA Transactions 3* 2(1), 105–9.

———. 1983e. "Studious Questions." *Architects Journal* 178(43) (October 23), 55–57.

———. 1983f. "Pedestrian Street Use: Culture and Perception." In *Streets as Public Property* (Proceedings of an International Institute), ed. A. V. Moudon and P. Laconte, pp. 3–17. Seattle: College of Architecture and Urban Planning, University of Washington.

———. 1983g. "On Defining Vernacular Design." Keynote paper, "Home Sweet Home," Symposium on Vernacular Architecture, Folk Art and Craft Museum and UCLA, Los Angeles, November.

———. 1984a. "Culture and the Urban Order." In *The City in Cultural Context,* ed. J. Agnew, J. Mercer, and D. Sopher, pp. 50–75. London: Allen & Unwin.

———. 1984b. "Culture and Built Form: a Reconsideration." Keynote paper, Conference on Built Form and Culture Research, University of Kansas, Lawrence, October 18–20.

———. 1984c. "The Use and Design of Open Spaces in Urban Neighborhoods." Paper presented at the Conference on Determinants of Urban Living Quality, Technical University, West Berlin, December 5–7.

———. 1985a. "Place, Image and Placemaking." Keynote paper, Conference on Place and Placemaking, Melbourne, Australia, June.

———. 1985b. "Thinking About Home Environments: a Conceptual Framework." In *Home Environments: Human Behavior and the Environment,* vol. 8, ed. I. Altman and C. Werner, pp. 255–86. New York: Plenum Press.

Rich, Peter. 1983. "The Bantwane Settlement at Kwarrielaagte." *ITCC Review* 12(2), 12–19.

Urban Edge. 1985. "Street Foods: A Source of Food, Jobs for Urban Poor." *Urban Edge* 9(8) (September/October), 5–6.

Chapter 4

Self-Help Housing Technology

DAVID EVAN GLASSER

Owner-built housing is not a recent phenomenon. Until the rise of capitalism, most dwellings were built by their occupants. The use of contracting firms, specialized labor forces, and industrialized components for buildings began only in the nineteenth century. Before then, dwellings were built using local materials, resources, and local technology in much the same way that many Third World residents build dwellings today.

The term *self-help technology,* however, used in relation to housing construction in developing nations, has additional significance. Third World residents, having limited resources, are obliged to develop their own housing out of necessity rather than choice. The methods and materials selected constitute their technology, one that reflects the social and political realities of their environment and the economic constraints within which they undertake to construct shelter.

This chapter describes the nature and extent of technological resources available to low-income residents and examines the implications of global industrialization for appropriate technological approaches to Third World housing construction.[1] An initial distinction must be drawn between squatter and self-help technology. In the first type, the owner is building on illegally held land, or on a site whose tenure is in question, and is obliged to construct a house as rapidly as possible in order to consolidate de facto occupancy. In the second type, the owner has tenure but has limited resources and must proceed with house construction in stages, often over many years. The emergency nature of squatter housing often generates ad hoc construction consisting of found objects, which causes the housing to be characterized, often uncritically, as slums or shantytowns. Residents are understandably reluctant to make investments in labor or scarce resources in uncertain circumstances (Abrams,

1966, p. 21). Once land title is established, however, residents will initiate the long-term process of gradual improvement associated with self-help housing.

There is also a substantial difference between owner-built dwellings in rural and urban areas. Village land is likely to be inexpensive and accessible, labor is plentiful and cheap, and local building materials (e.g., mud, adobe, and thatch) are available at little or no cost (Karachi Development Authority, 1966, p. 47). In contrast, the urban house builder faces a bewildering array of complex issues to resolve: tight building sites, relative inaccessibility of local materials, expensive transportation requirements, lack of urban infrastructure, and unachievable building regulations, to mention only a few. The pattern of Third World development has been one of urbanization fueled by the search for employment opportunities. For this reason, and because urban housing is by far the most significant area of owner-built construction activity, I limit this discussion of self-help technology to the urban sector, although occasional references to rural construction typologies are made when pertinent.

An additional distinction is made between primary and ancillary construction systems. This chapter deals principally with the former, that is, with methods and materials used for structural support and enclosure of dwelling units, and treats the latter, including electrical, water, plumbing and sewerage systems, to a lesser extent. In the overwhelming number of cases, houses are built on sites totally unprovided with infrastructure, which is treated ad hoc or postponed for years. Furthermore, the significant financial and technological challenges faced by owner–builders have to do with wall and roof construction. The narrow spectrum of technological alternatives notwithstanding, owner–builders throughout the world have demonstrated extraordinary imagination and skill in house construction.

The Appropriate Technology Debate

Today it is generally agreed that efforts to produce large numbers of low-cost housing units by means of industrialized technology have been ineffective in developing nations or, for that matter, in the United States, as the failure of Operation Breakthrough has clearly demonstrated (Terner, 1978, pp. 107–8). Moreover, there is probably universal agreement about the relative effectiveness of self-help approaches to low-cost housing, evidence for which is provided by the many government programs for sites and services and low-interest loan programs for owner–builders.

Policies encouraging massive investment in advanced housing technology production, often promulgated by Western-educated local officials, necessarily divert scarce resources from other social projects: education, health, job training, and the like. Instead of providing work for a broad number of underemployed citizens, high-technology programs benefit only a few highly skilled technicians and workers. These methodologies, moreover, rely heavily on large imports of basic construction elements such as reinforcing rods, cement, and even stone aggregate, all of which require substantial energy in their production. Dependency on imports of required construction materials has had increasingly negative consequences for owner–builders in recent years. The international market, not the end user's ability to pay, determines the cost of steel and concrete. In many developing nations monopolies have been set in place that virtually ensure the maintenance of artificially high prices for basic building materials (Connolly, 1982, p. 158; Ward, 1982, p. 177).

Aside from the questionable economics involved in intensive technology methods, there are issues relating to cultural values and traditions that are seldom considered. The regional character of many countries, the results of centuries of traditional building activity, is now being threatened by the massive influx of imported building materials and techniques. Reinforced concrete, concrete block and corrugated steel construction continue to replace mud brick and thatch throughout most of the developing nations, often with the eager concurrence of both owner–builders and government agencies (Photo 4.1). One of the persistent concerns of housing consultants and advisers is how to diminish the luster of inappropriate, but prestigious, imported building products and develop an appreciation for traditional methods and materials (Hardoy and Satterthwaite, 1981, p. 177; Taper, 1980, p. 52).

The ubiquitous presence of concrete and concrete products in the Third World provides the mistaken impression that their use derives from a scarcity of domestic building materials. Although this may be true in a nation like Bangladesh, which is provided with few construction materials other than clay or reeds, many countries have local natural resources that are underutilized. In some nations, like Sudan, plentiful supplies of aggregate, stone, and sand exist, but inadequate internal transportation makes distribution difficult and costly (Hardoy and Satterthwaite, 1981, pp. 4, 47). In other countries, the use of certain materials, such as timber in Brazil, is reserved for the poorest of squatters because of its low status (Epstein, 1973, pp. 109, 110). Motivated by a desire to appear modern, Jordan has chosen to replace its long tradition of beautiful native limestone construction with reinforced concrete technology (Hardoy and Satterthwaite, 1981, p. 45).

A dichotomy exists between governmental regulatory policies and activities of owner–builders, who are highly pragmatic and motivated to make prudent choices from available alternatives. Since building products account for as much as 60 to 70 percent of nonland construction costs, self-help owners, particularly squatters, are anxious to reduce material costs as much as possible (Hardoy and Satterthwaite, 1981, p. 91;

Photo 4.1 Squatter housing in Manizales, Colombia. The use of concrete block and corrugated steel, which has become synonymous with self-help housing in all parts of the world, has effectively supplanted regional methods and materials in low-cost housing construction.

United Nations, 1962, p. 31). Given the option, owner–builders will invariably opt for a process of phased construction, using cheap *ad hoc* materials at first and replacing them with more substantial materials as funds become available (Lobo, 1982, pp. 6–10).

The phased construction or progressive upgrading approach can provide more affordable space. Building with formal materials such as concrete, concrete block, and baked brick implies sharp reductions in the amount of living area that can be afforded. In Sri Lanka, for instance, researchers determined that 80 percent of households had incomes in 1971 that could finance houses of permanent construction of between only 150 and 250 square feet (Sri Lanka Housing Authority, 1976, p. 227). Similar sizes are reported in Bombay and New Delhi (United Nations, 1962, p. 206).[2] Using the upgrading approach, these same people could afford substantially larger dwellings.

Self-Help Materials and Methods

Self-help technology encompasses an enormous range of materials and methods, from natural regional elements to highly sophisticated industrial by-products. Techniques of construction extend from hastily erected cardboard shacks to elaborately built, earthquake-resistant concrete frames. Since many urban owner-builders find employment as construction workers and laborers in the center city, they bring their field experience to bear in building their own homes. Such borrowed advanced technology, while of interest, is not central to this chapter. Instead, the examination that follows includes a description of the principal materials and methods that might be included under the rubric of appropriate technology, that is traditional local building methodologies, which hold out the promise of affordable and secure housing for the urban poor.

Mud as a Material

Mud is a universally available building material that has been used in all cultures, throughout history, from the village of New Gourna in Egypt (Fathy, 1973, pp. 37–38) to the circular units of Togo and the octagonal *hogans* of the Navajo in the American West (*Cobijo,* 1981, pp. 6, 17). Mud is used in a wide variety of applications in various regions of the world. Principal among them are these:

- Sun-dried brick: adobe
- Mud plaster: mortar
- Tapial
- Burnt brick
- Wattle and daub
- Stabilized soil block units
- Geltaftan

Sun-Dried Brick: Adobe. For best results, adobe must consist of a mix of clay and sand. Mixtures of 50 to 80 percent sand, a maximum of

30 percent clay (restricted because of its expansive qualities), and 15 percent silt are recommended, the latter acting as binder and thermal expansion additive in the mixture (Gallant, 1982, pp. 67–68). Bricks made locally, usually on the land where the house is to be built using reusable wood forms, are structurally adequate for most small houses.[3]

Adobe is best used in hot, arid climates, since rainfall and frost can quickly deteriorate the units (Photo 4.2). In environments with more than 25 centimeters of rainfall annually, special measures can be taken, such as using stone foundations carried above grade to prevent a washout of the base course or the use of plaster coatings.[4] Mud bricks are sometimes reinforced with fibrous material, such as horse or cow dung, animal hair, straw, or vegetable fibers. Units are typically left in the sun to dry for two to three weeks prior to use. Adobe is the cheapest and most readily available material for low-cost home construction, but it is looked on with disfavor by building officials because of its lack of durability and by many owner–builders because of its low prestige. Experiments have been made with a number of binding agents, including plastics, cement asphalt, and industrial wastes, to determine if the disadvantages of mud brick can be offset. In seismic areas and regions where high winds are prevalent, reinforcing internal walls with bamboo, wire, or wood poles is recommended (Gallant, 1982. p. 68).

Photo 4.2 Village of Sart, Turkey. New mud-brick houses under construction. Note the substantial wall thickness, irregular unit dimensions, and use of mud mortar. (Photo by J. C. Waldbaum)

Mud Plaster: Mortar. Mud mortar is used to set adobe, and when reinforced with straw, horsehair, or dung, it produces a serviceable exterior coating on mud-brick walls. This coating is usually whitewashed as an additional protection and is replaced frequently. Sometimes stone or other aggregate is added to the mud plaster to increase its wearing qualities or enhance its appearance. In East African traditional construction, for instance, coral chips are added to plaster for this purpose (Stren, 1978, p. 33).

Tapial. When reinforced with straw or animal dung, placed between parallel rows of form boards, and carefully tamped, mud or *tapial* walls are excellent structural and enclosure elements (Figure 4.1). Because of the skill required and the relatively slow rate of construction, this is not the method selected by the majority of self-help builders, particularly squatters, for whom speed is of the essence. When reinforced with steel rods or wire or bamboo tendons, *tapial* construction has proven to be extremely strong and durable. Andean buildings made of

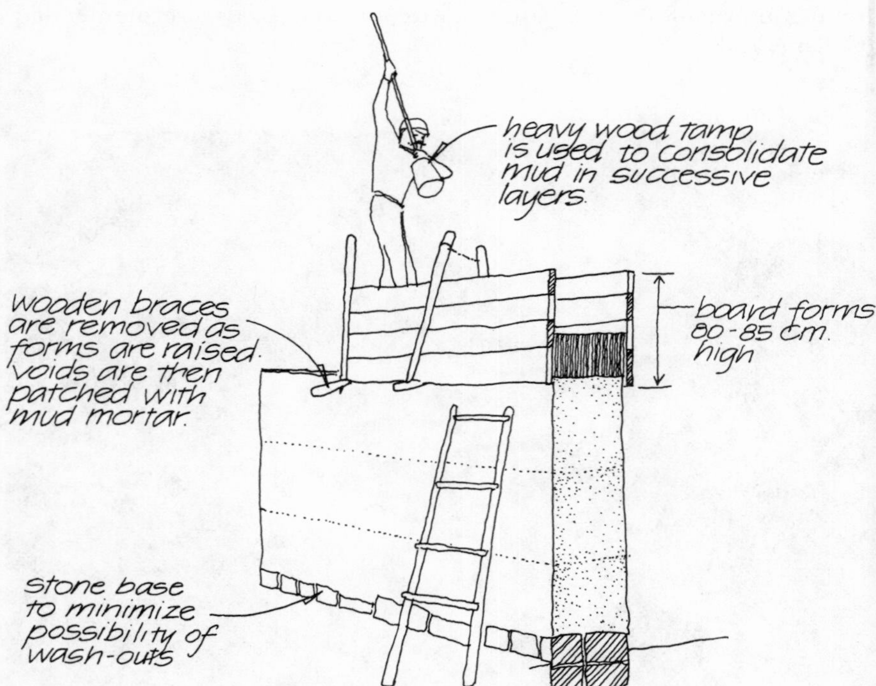

Figure 4.1 *Tapial* construction. Workers tamp mud within braced wooden slip forms, which are raised as each layer is consolidated. Although strong and versatile, this type of construction is not widely used because of the considerable time and skill it requires.

tapial and dating from the sixteenth century are still standing; many have survived several major earthquakes.

Burnt Brick. Hard-burned bricks are in all instances superior to sun-baked adobe units but are necessarily more expensive. Typical strengths of ordinary burnt brick may be in the range of 35 to 105 kg/cm^2 (500–1500 psi), which is to say 2.5 to 7.5 times stronger than adobe units. Field kilns are typically set up where clay is plentiful and where fuel (e.g., wood or coal) is readily available. Units are mold formed, similar to adobe, but are of a smaller size because of the greater density of burnt brick, and are formed into a beehive configuration to create the walls of the kiln. Additional piles of brick are placed inside the kiln, and the outside is then given a coat of mud or sand-lime plaster, which is removed after firing. Although by no means as uniform in quality as modern, machine-operated tunnel kilns, field kilns of this description can produce a highly serviceable product (Photo 4.3).

Wattle and Daub. The wattle-and-daub system consists of a mixture of framing members and mud mortar infill in various combinations. The Masai in East Africa, for instance, use a framework of cut branches to create circular enclosures and apply a mud–dung plaster coating over the armature, which serves as a type of lath (*Cobijo,* 1981, p. 8). Where bamboo is plentiful, the culms may be split to form an excellent lath arrangement and then lashed over a framework of bamboo poles. Mud mortar, reinforced with straw or dung, is then applied.[5] Cement or gypsum plaster is sometimes used as well (Gallant, 1982, p. 186).

Stabilized Soil Block. The low strength and durability of sun-dried mud brick inhibits its use in urban development. Many experiments have attempted to stabilize soil block and the products of several such experiments are now in general use. Soil-cement blocks were the first developed. These consist of a mixture of soil and cement, whose proportions can vary depending on desired strengths, and fine aggregate. For some regions, fly ash is employed as a substitute for up to 20 percent of cement content[6] in order to reduce costs (Government of India, 1970, p. 39).

In the late 1950s and early 1960s the Center for Housing in Central America developed the Cinva-Ram machine,[7] which has been widely used by the International Basic Economy Corporation (IBEC) in Puerto Rico and elsewhere (U.S. Senate, 1963, p. 151). The machine consists of a small, easily moved, compacting press in which soil, cement, water, and other binders are placed and are subjected to manual pressure.[8]

Another form of stabilized block is asfadobe, consisting of a mixture of soil, bitumen, and sand. The unit is not as strong as the soil–cement block but has superior moisture-resisting qualities. In Sudan,

Photo 4.3 Local brick kiln in the sierra, northeast of Quito, Ecuador. Clay is extracted at the site, formed in wooden molds, and burned in the rectangular kiln structure at the hilltop, using locally collected firewood. In the foreground are sun-dried mud bricks, which are also made at this small plant.

asfadobe blocks costing half the price of burnt bricks have been used successfully (Hardoy and Satterthwaite, 1981, pp. 46–47). Other binders that have been tried are lime, molasses, and silicates, including crushed glass, sodium, and calcium (SLHA, 1976, p. 234). Industrial by-products, particularly from the petrochemical sector, have also been experimented with; however, only the soil-cement and asfadobe units are in widespread global use.

Geltaftan. Throughout the Middle East, many traditional village houses have been made of plastered mud brick; the houses usually have vaulted roofs because spanning materials are scarce. The Iranian architect Nader Khalili discovered the ancient use of *kavals,* huge kilns used to make large-diameter clay pipe for the systems of *ganats,* the underground irrigation networks on which Iranian agriculture depends. The *kavals,* having a domed configuration and made of mud brick, had been fired into a single unit during their operation and had managed to withstand centuries of storm and seismic activity. Using these as a precedent, a technique was developed called *Geltaftan,* from the farsi *gel* (clay) and *taftan* (firing or baking) to designate the firing of a complete mud-brick structure. Prior to the accession of the Ayatollah Khomeini, several hundred successful units were erected in Iran (Khalili, 1983, pp. 103, 121, 179, 230–31).

Timber as a Material

Because of enormous demographic growth, many areas once plentifully supplied with timber are now deforested. Therefore, uses of timber are limited generally to squatter settlements, tent structures, wattle-and-daub assemblies, and pole structures. The use of sawn timber for principal structural members is very limited in most parts of the world because of its high cost and unavailability (Parry, 1984, p. 250). Furthermore, because of decay, dry rot, and termites in moist environments, without pressure treatment, timber is often not a suitable material (Gallant, 1982, p. 69).

Squatter Structures. The spontaneous settler will employ virtually any found object in house construction, including scrap lumber and plywood of all kinds. Lumber is highly prized because it is easily connected and has a high strength-to-weight ratio. In the *favelas* of Rio de Janeiro and São Paulo and the *alagados* and *invasões* of Salvador, wood is widely used, although "status-conscious" Brazilians tend to look down on wood (Epstein, 1973, p. 109). The shed-roofed *barracos* of the *favelas* can be built in one or two days, one of the great virtues of light wood framing; and they can be easily moved, a virtue for squatters or precarious settlements.

Tent Structures. The Tuaregs of the central and western Sahara use a combination of straight and curved saplings to serve as a tensed framework to support a covering of either skins (for cold and rainy weather) or screens (for hot and dry seasons). The *Jyyam* of the North African Berbers is an interesting variant on this. The system consists of a modular framework, which produces a 7 m × 13 m tent covered with camel or goatskins, a size determined by the maximum carrying load of a camel, about 700 kilograms (*Cobijo,* 1981, pp. 12, 14). In tropical locations, houses are sometimes built of a framework of light poles, lashed together, which support walls and roofs of thatch. An example of this construction is the domed houses of the Zulus in South Africa (*Cobijo*, 1981, p. 63).

Wattle and Daub. Where saplings are available, the framework for mud mortar construction is often made of lashed poles. In some instances, framing of solid logs with an infill of rock, debris, and wattle and daub, similar to English half-timber construction, is employed. This is exceptional, however, since the joinery and care involved in the assembly involve skills beyond those of the average owner–builder. In Saudi Arabia, scarce timber is minimized in traditional construction by the use of bundled reeds as infill between primary framing members. The entire assembly is then covered with approximately 30 centimeters of dried mud. Roof installations are given a mud and lime plaster coating as well (Galea and Boon, 1981, p. 125).

Bamboo. In 1981 an estimated 2 million tons of bamboo were used for house construction in the Orient alone (*Cobijo*, 1981, p. 61). Applications included beams, frames, columns, and, when cut and flattened, lath and screens (Photo 4.4). When cut into small sections and split into halves, the pieces make excellent roof tile. Where timber is scarce, bamboo serves as structural framing and even as a framework for wattle-and-daub construction. Sections of bamboo have been successfully used as a substitute for steel reinforcing rods. The strength of con-

Photo 4.4 Bamboo dwelling on the west coast of Ecuador. Giant bamboo, *guadua*, is used for all posts, beams, and bracing. It is also employed for lath, screens, railings, and as roof sheathing. In this installation, asphalt-saturated burlap roofing is used instead of cut bamboo tile. (Photo by S. Jacome)

crete improves two to three times with the addition of well-seasoned bamboo rods (Gallant, 1982, pp. 186, 188). Giant bamboo, or *guadua,* as it is called in Latin American countries, is available in many parts of Africa and in South and Latin America. When chemically treated, posts of *guadua* can be set into marshy land or water.

Stone as a Material

Stone is not thought of as a typical material in self-help construction because in many areas, such as Bangladesh and Sri Lanka, it is scarce. Also, the skill needed for stone masonry and the required erection time militate against its widespread use.

Wherever there is moist or marshy ground, self-help builders with access to fieldstone will lay down a layer of stone as a foundation plinth, as discussed in relation to wattle-and-daub construction. Stone is also employed as reinforcing in *tapial* construction at corners, around openings, and below beams (*Cobijo,* 1981, p. 55). Where loose stone is plentiful—for example, along the Adriatic coast in southern Italy—entire villages are made of dry stone construction, for example, the *trulli* of Alborobello (*Cobijo,* 1981, p. 51).

Dry stonework is also used in the Middle East. In Saudi Arabia, traditional houses are built of "garreted" masonry, consisting of large stones with trimmed exterior faces. The interstices are filled with small, fitted stones and pebbles. The entire wall, which is slightly battered inward for increased strength, is then given several coats of mud–lime plaster. Lintels over small window openings are made with logs rather than corbelled stonework (Galea and Boon, 1981, p. 123). By contrast, in Malta, where timber is unavailable, traditional circular homes, *giren,* use stone walls that are gradually battered inward up to the roof to reach a dimension that can be spanned by single stones (Galea, 1981, pp. 211–12).

Probably the most prevalent use of stone is for concrete aggregate. Suitable stone is not equally distributed throughout the world, however, compelling many Third World nations to explore substitutes for stone aggregate. In Bangladesh, for instance, concrete for all but major multistoried buildings uses broken burnt brick for both fine and course aggregate, since both sand and stone are unavailable. Lightweight stone substitutes are also used in many developing nations.

Methods of Construction

In owner-built housing, the roof represents the most difficult and costly item to construct, accounting for as much as 30 to 40 percent of the total cost of the building (KDA, 1966, p. 149; SLHA, 1976, pp. 235–

36). One reason for the enormous popularity of corrugated steel roofing and, to a lesser extent, cement–asbestos roofing, is that their structural spanning capacities minimize requirements for intermediate framing members. In addition, the use of industrialized products carries a special cachet for owner–builders, who often prefer newer materials to traditional ones, even if the latter are cheaper and more serviceable. Corrugated steel roofing is generally installed over a light framing of logs, poles, bamboo, or even light steel members. In moist climates, where the thin (1.5 millimeter) galvanizing layer will not endure, owners may use rust-inhibiting paint or bituminous coatings.

The use of cement–asbestos corrugated roofing is, unfortunately, also widespread. Virtually outlawed in the United States for many years because of its demonstrated carcinogenic properties, which affect both fabricators and end users, cement–asbestos continues to be permitted, even encouraged, in many Third World nations. In the Caribbean, where ground water is scarce, many homeowners use their roofs to catch and store water, with potentially deleterious consequences for the homeowner when the roof is made of asbestos.

Thatch roofs, which are moisture resistant and thermally efficient, are seldom employed in urban development. Reeds and grasses required for thatch are located at increasing distances from urban building sites. Furthermore, considerable time and skill are required to build a good thatch roof, and neither may be available to the self-help builder. Building regulations also restrict use of thatch because of fire hazard and insect and vermin infestation.

Reinforced concrete or concrete-and-hollow-tile construction is used in urban sites where owner–builders develop multistory housing units. In Mexico, the Middle East, and many South American countries, the roof is designed as an *azotea,* or rooftop terrace, and must be strong enough to carry the weight of occupants and furniture. The difficulty of manufacturing and the high cost of deformed steel bars, however, inhibit widespread use of concrete. Few developing nations have their own steel mills or rerolling plants. As a consequence, steel reinforcing bars are one of the principal imports in the Third World and a major contributor to the growing external debt in many countries.

In an effort to reduce the use of steel bars, some countries are experimenting with locally made cored concrete slabs, using welded wire mesh. In the People's Republic of China, local communities are encouraged to make such concrete slabs by developing small-scale manufacturing operations in order to minimize transportation and fabrication costs (Hausmann, 1984, pp. 10–11). Some countries are also experimenting with lightweight substitutes for costly cement. In the Orient, for instance, both burned and raw rice husks are used to produce a light, flexible concrete from which can be made concrete block, mortar, and low-strength concrete. Rice husk ash (RHA) concrete has also been successfully employed in locally made corrugated roofing as a superior alternative to cement–asbestos (Mathur, 1981, p. 1008). Another example is provided by a community in India that successfully developed a nonreinforced fiber–cement corrugated roofing system using coconut fibers (Schaffner, 1984, pp. 17–18).[9]

Asphalt and pitch are abundant in many developing nations and are used in various roofing assemblies. Cardboard, plywood, and steel sheets are often coated with bitumens. Layers of asphalt-impregnated felt are sometimes installed in combination with sod roofs or below clay tile. I have also seen, in Latin America and Asia, a sand–asphaltic cement mixture applied over a framework of light poles and infill that produces a reasonably watertight surface.

Many owner–builders, quite logically, postpone building a floor until basic shelter is provided. Tamped mud or stabilized soil is therefore a common first floor in many owner-built homes for many years, even in multistory buildings. When funds become available, concrete slabs on grade are typical, since basements are rare. The absence of infrastructure also accounts for postponement of floor construction in spontaneous settlements. In Quito, for instance, homeowners in 1985 were experiencing delays of seven to ten years in obtaining water and sewer connections after they had taken occupancy (Hidalgo, 1985).

Occasionally tile or brick units set in sand are used in place of concrete, but this constitutes an exception. In very hot and moist environments, a raised floor is sometimes constructed, made of spaced timbers or bamboo to allow essential ventilation. Even this sensible, ecologically responsive technology is rapidly being replaced, however, by the ubiquitous concrete block and corrugated steel that has become synonymous with Third World development.

Ad Hoc and No-Tech Construction

The previous discussion attempted to outline the principal "official" materials and methods employed in the informal building sector. In addition, ad hoc construction and no-tech construction techniques are used by owner–builders. Typical of these are the Pakistani *jhuggis,* consisting of collections of found objects including tires, cardboard cartons, burlap, automobile parts, and other industrial by-products (KDA, 1966, p. 51).

Sometimes, these ad hoc additions are built in stark juxtaposition with formal construction. In Latin American countries some of the most interesting development takes place on rooftops and adjacent to sterile, multistoried government housing projects. Although forbidden to alter these buildings, enterprising residents find ways to develop creative extensions, often overnight. Ad hoc development usually follows the incremental pattern, discussed above, starting with no-tech enclosures and gradually building refinements over time.

Strategies for Self-Help

Developing nations can provide housing for low-income families primarily in two ways: either build the units and subsidize the construction or provide financial and/or technical assistance to self-help constructors. Strategies for providing assistance to owner–builders fall essentially under three principal headings: upgrading, sites and services, and core–shell programs. It is worth stressing that, sooner or later, most self-help housing, regardless of its precarious character, will likely receive some sort of agency assistance, prompted either by political or humanitarian pressures.

Upgrading

Until fairly recently, most Third World governments tended to perceive existing spontaneous settlements negatively. Programs for new housing have often meant wholesale "slum clearance and replacement, or the provision of incentives for demolition" (KDA, 1966, p. 86). Now, either because of enlightened self-interest or resigned acceptance of an inexorable reality, governments are increasingly inclined to allocate grants, loans, and technical assistance to community upgrading projects. Assistance may take several forms:

- Small construction loans, such as the "roof loans" used in Ghana (Taper, 1980, p. 51)
- Government distribution of formal building materials (e.g., brick, concrete block) at subsidized prices, as outright grants, or as part of long-term financing arrangements
- Planning and design services
- Technical assistance to existing owner–builders, such as that provided by the Peace Corps

Small Construction Loans. The "Swahili house" in eastern Africa provides an example in which traditional construction of *boriti* (mangrove poles), *undongo* (clay–mud wattle and daub), and *makuti* (palm leaf thatch) is incrementally replaced by permanent masonry walls and corrugated steel roofing through a government loan program (Stren, 1978, p. 33). In this example, one of the successful strategies employed was the use of traditional house plans that included provision for lodgers' rooms—a vital source of income for the owner–builder. Unfortunately, many governmental assistance agencies do not recognize this critically important aspect of low-cost housing.

Governmental Distribution of Materials. Distribution is usually limited to stockpiling and supplying key materials such as brick, cement, and block, often as a means of offsetting monopolistic prices at times of unusually high demand. In addition, government agencies can use assistance programs to promulgate new technologies.

Planning and Design Services. Squatters are concerned with obtaining legal land tenure as a first priority. To this end, municipal offices such as the Unidad Ejecutora de Barrios Periféricos in Quito, Ecuador, have been established to provide site planning and design services to existing communities. In addition to preparing metes and bounds documents for the purpose of legal title, the office lays out roads and infrastructure routes. Municipal agencies also may provide technical advice with respect to construction, but usually this has a low priority in relation to other activities (Hidalgo, 1985).

Technical Assistance to Owner–Builders. This assistance can take place in a number of ways. International agencies such as CARE, the Peace Corps, AID, and the World Bank provide professional help, but with the exception of the first two, assistance seldom takes the form of hands-on direct help. Some architects and planners in developing nations attempt to provide technical advice to the informal sector, but this is usually of a design nature and less involved with practical problems relating to building materials and construction. Some of this aloofness arises from class distinctions regarding manual versus intellectual labor. One source of technical assistance for marginal communities is that provided by architectural students, who are increasingly active in providing direct intervention in the planning, design, and construction of informal housing.[10]

Upgrading presupposes that owners have already made an initial investment in land, materials, and labor resources. In situations where the development of open land is anticipated, the use of sites and services schemes is prevalent.

Sites and Services Programs

One conceptual approach to sites and services provides secure land title and basic utility services and leaves construction either to individual families or to mutual construction cooperatives. Another strategy, one employed in Ahmedabad, India, by the Gujurat Housing Board for the Bhadreshwar Housing Colony, in which serviced sites were provided, included a filled foundation enclosure carried to 45 centimeters above grade and toilet and sink enclosures (Mellin, 1984, pp. 5–6). Depending on the degree of physical planning control seen as desirable, there are a number of advantages to the latter scheme. Owner–builders are con-

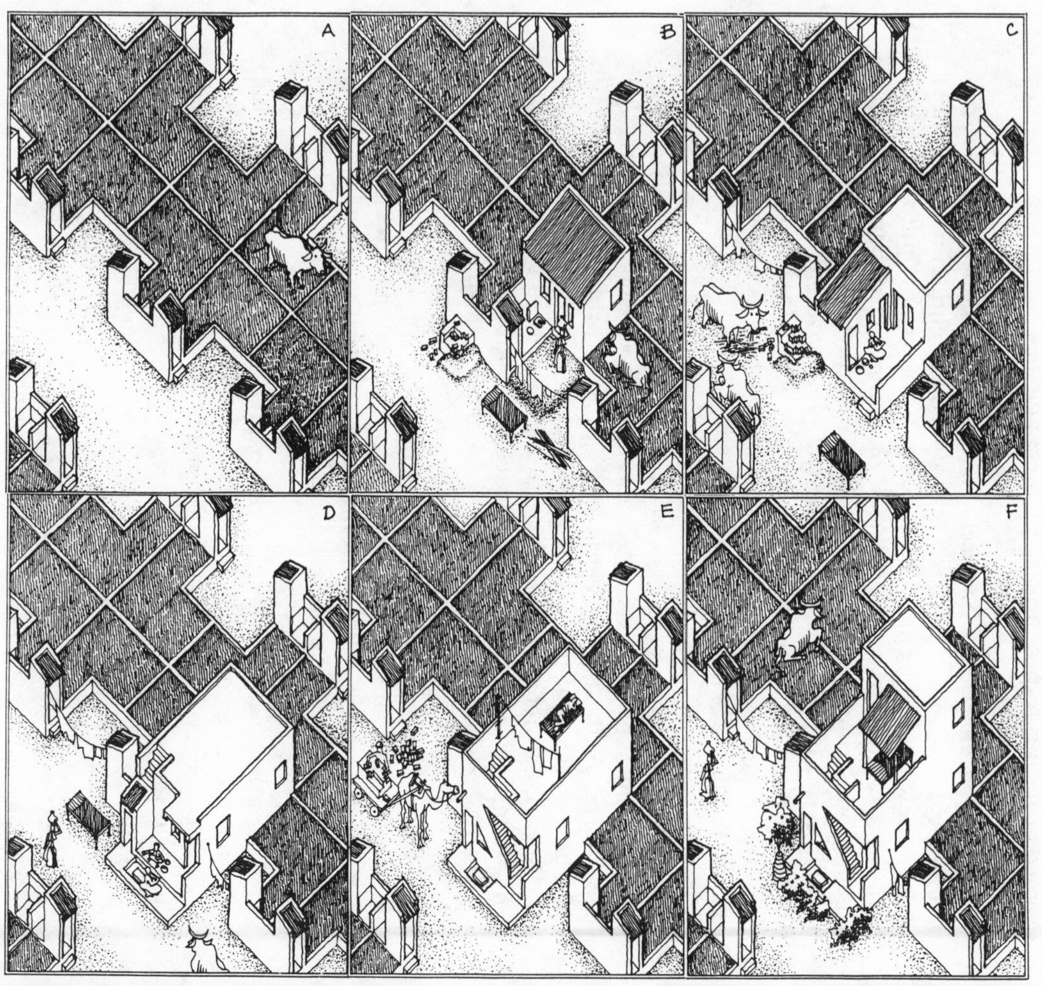
A
B
C
D
E
F

strained to erect houses on a predetermined foundation layout, which sharply limits their size and configuration (Figure 4.2). But the physical character of the total community is predictable to a much greater extent and results in a physical environment with some degree of visual control.[11]

Core–Shell Programs

Core–shell programs carry sites and services schemes a bit further. The government provides an incomplete, serviced unit that owner–builders are expected to finish, often within specified time limits. Core units are provided with a slab on grade, a roof, and a kitchen–bath core that may be complete or may be provided merely with rough plumbing connections. Typically, owners are obliged to build enclosing walls and roofs to meet certain guidelines. In shell units, walls and roofs are provided together with rough plumbing; owners must install interior partitions, finishes, and all fixtures. The remainder of the construction is carried out in one of several ways. In some instances, owner–builders undertake to complete the work without any additional financial or technical assistance. In other cases, the government provides subsidized building materials to low-income residents. In still others, long-term credit is extended to homeowners for the purchase of building materials. Most often, these owner–builders operate in a laissez-faire environment, within the constraints of standards and controls established by government.

Standards and Government Controls

The nature and extent of government regulation of low-cost housing are highly controversial issues. For example, Marxist critics characterize state intervention in the housing process as an imposition of capitalist values and a means of protecting the interests of the governing class (Burgess, 1982, p. 77). According to this perception, standards and codes are enforced to ensure that owner–builders use expensive, profit-generating construction materials whose prices are controlled by state or private monopolies.[12] A more charitable view of regulation is one in which societal concerns for community health, safety, and welfare are expressed in legal terms. In my view, the question of state control over construction is inseparable from its sociopolitical environment.

Figure 4.2 Bhadreshwar housing colony, Gujurat Housing Board project, Ahmedabad, India. Government-provided foundations and utility services established a framework within which incremental self-help construction proceeds as funds become available. (Illustration by R. E. Mellin)

Third World regulations essentially deal with two aspects of construction: size and technical character. Size limitations on dwelling units, which is to say those built or partially built by the state, are normally established to define upper, rather than lower, floor area limits. By contrast, in the United States, minimum sizes are determined, as for example in Federal Housing Administration (FHA) standards, based on an evaluation of spatial requirements relating to family size. In developing nations, floor area allocations are directed toward the equitable distribution of scarce building resources and are unrelated to what might constitute adequate or even humane housing standards. Much of the technical discussion surrounding apartment and house size has to do with culturally determined space perceptions and how extraordinarily small living areas might be made habitable through the interpretative skills of building officials. Thus, the United Nations Habitat report of 1981 states that several Filipino families have no problem sharing one small bath–toilet room and that spatial standards for Bombay (13 m^2) or New Delhi (23 m^2) might constitute adequate living areas for Indian families (United Nations, 1962, p. 206).

The question of quality standards has a direct bearing on unit size as well. Insistence on permanent formal construction forces low-income families to reduce floor area in order to conserve building materials. In the earlier discussion on upgrading, I pointed out that relaxation of rigid controls on materials can permit faster and more commodious construction in the initial phases of development and allow for gradual replacement with more substantial elements when money becomes available (Lobo, 1982, pp. 10, 11; U.S. Senate, 1963, p. 26).[13] While building construction regulations are not always directed toward the application of increasingly rigorous standards,[14] one of the unfortunate aspects of the growth of governmental regulation of urban housing construction has been a tendency toward uniformity and the establishment of constraints on individual initiative and creativity—the mainsprings of the owner–builder in the Third World (Herbert, 1979, pp. 130–31).

Prognosis for the Future

An inherent contradiction in many Third World countries derives from the relative economic success of metropolitan areas. Noncommunist countries, without enforced internal migration policies, are victims of uncontrolled population growth around their major cities (Vining, 1985, p. 41). A critical first step, therefore, in addressing the question of urban housing would be the establishment of policies for decentralization through equitable distribution of services and resources. This has happened peaceably, for example, in Sri Lanka through the use of economic incentives, and in Vietnam and Kampuchea through armed intervention (Vining, 1985, pp. 48–49).

Resource scarcity and reliance on expensive imported Western technologies must also be addressed. Organic cement substitutes, like RHA or brick–concrete slabs (Ahmad et al., 1981, p. 461), are viable alternatives. Furthermore, these imaginative methods are based on conserving local materials and skills and can help maintain existing cultural distinctions, which are becoming increasingly blurred through imports of global technology. Aside from the practical benefits to be had from an appropriate technology posture, there are ethical factors to be considered.

The overwhelming housing problem in developing nations offers an opportunity to examine critically certain basic assumptions concerning the myth of progress we have come to accept as fact. Implicit belief in the perfectibility of technology leading to enduring happiness is a dangerous dream. Technological alternatives are driven by economic exigency, not by human values. A successful strategy for creating both housing and commerce in developing countries would involve decisive efforts to disengage from the global economy and decrease economic dependence on oligopolistic building industries (Bossio, 1984, pp. 356–57).

Architects and planners may be of great help in this regard, if traditional notions of client–professional relationships are redefined. Self-help builders can profit from technical assistance, if it is provided within existing social and cultural frameworks. Helping to impose governmental standards on the one hand and uncritical acceptance of advocacy positions on the other are unsatisfactory roles for architects and planners. An opportunity exists for socially committed architects and planners to serve as mediators between owner–builders and the state in a number of important ways. Beyond providing basic services, such as site and building layouts, professionals with an understanding and appreciation of the entire building process can be of enormous assistance in housing emerging communities. The limited resources of the owner–builder require prudent judgment at every phase of construction, since funds to correct errors are unlikely to materialize. Timely intervention by professionals in this process can therefore be invaluable.

Another fruitful area of involvement relates to development of appropriate building standards. A balance between public safety and welfare and individual economic realities must be struck. To the extent that governments insist on rigorous building regulations, they will have to provide funds to subsidize the millions of families unable to afford to meet them. In the absence of subsidies, however, standards permitting phased construction with respect to quality are unavoidable.

A number of architects with a genuine desire to build quality dwellings for the poor have made significant contributions growing out of basic construction research. Interestingly, the research focus has been on time-honored, traditional methods rather than technological innovations. The works of Hassan Fathy in Egypt and Nader Khalili in Iran provide significant models for successful architectural enterprise in developing countries. This is not to deprecate potential benefits to be derived from a study of emerging technology. Nevertheless, it does underscore the point that technological solutions arising from a nation's cultural and historic traditions provide a promising basis for success.

Conclusion

Self-help builders in developing nations have proven to be a major, if not the most important, resource many countries can rely on in dealing with massive deficits in low-income housing units. Until political means are found to develop more equitable income and land distribution, it is unlikely that governments will find ways to deliver, more effectively, greater numbers of housing units to their poor citizens.

The energy, enthusiasm, and creativity of the self-help construction sector has been overwhelmingly demonstrated in all parts of the world. It would seem that the best course government policy could take would be to expand and improve this indispensable natural resource. In my view, additional building technology experiments, unless they build on traditional methodologies, are doomed to failure. In any event, technical approaches that diminish manual labor are self-defeating in that they serve to expand the population base of the underemployed and unemployed. Instead, assistance programs are needed to join training programs with the production of badly needed low-cost housing, in turn unleashing the substantial construction talents of Third World citizens.

Acknowledgments

The assistance of several colleagues is acknowledged with pleasure. Roberto Carrión, of the Quito office of the U.S. Agency for International Development (AID), was unstinting with his time and advice. Arq. Guido Díaz N., president of Ecuador's society of architects, made available both his excellent judgment and the resources of the association library. Arq. Rolando Moya and Arqa. Evelia Peralta, directors of *TRAMA*, Ecuador's major architectural journal, offered their friendship and considerable reference library. Continued support from the Center for Latin America at the University of Wisconsin–Milwaukee and the Fulbright Commission are also gratefully noted.

Notes

1. Product development in high-income nations tends to be inappropriate for developing countries, with products having excessive and unnecessary characteristics (James and Stewart, 1981, p. 104).
2. Space standards are often related to cultural determinants. I noted, for example, during a visit to the People's Republic of China in 1982, that three- and even four-generation families had no difficulty accommodating themselves to the standard two-room apartment that the central government is building throughout the nation.
3. Although mud brick has a tested strength only one-fourth that of hard-burned brick—that is 500 psi (3.4MN/m^2) compared to 2,000+ psi (13.6 + MN/m^2) for fired brick, it is quite stable in practice and incorporates a technology based on millennia of experience (Tall and Cheong Siat-Moy, 1981, pp. 34–35).
4. Successful experiments were conducted using diluted adhesive as a surface binder over mud brick to create a suitable substrate for cement plaster (Parry, 1984, p. 254).
5. If regionally available, asphalt or pitch emulsion is sometimes added to mud mortar to enhance its waterproofing qualities. The bituminous material is usually cut with kerosene oil and paraffin wax to achieve the desired viscosity (Mathur, 1981, p. 1006).
6. Some experiments have been conducted using organic substitutes for mineral ash to replace expensive portland cement—for instance, rice husk ash (RHA) mixed with lime and sand (Smith, 1984, pp. 8–9).
7. In addition to Cinva-Ram, well-known types include Tek block, Terstaram, and Brepak units. Blocks typically contain cement, lime, ash, or other cement-reducing agents and, occasionally, gypsum (Parry, 1984, pp. 263–64; Stulz, 1984, p. 13).
8. Acceptance of even modest technological innovations, like Cinva-Ram soil blocks, is not always forthcoming and may require local demonstrations (Skinner, 1983, pp. 136–37).
9. Fiber-reinforced cement roofs have been employed, with increasing success, in at least fifteen developing nations. FRC cement sheets lend themselves to permanent formwork and masonry centering (Parry, 1984, pp. 260–62).
10. Many of these are modeled on the Community Design Centers (CDCs) developed in the United States during the 1960s to offer assistance to minority communities.
11. Expansion invariably takes place vertically, however, and often has a deleterious effect on scarce open courtyard space and overstrained municipal infrastructure (Bisharat and Tewfik, 1985, pp. 20–21).
12. Regulation is one of the major reasons developing nations continue to be heavily dependent on imported techniques and to underutilize regional resources (Miles and Parkes, 1984, p. 3).

13. Some countries, such as Tanzania, have required expensive permanent construction within six months at a risk of loss of land tenure. This has been exacerbated by problems with acquisition of key building materials such as cement, which has forced owner–builders either to stop construction or to find other means to complete their homes (Rodell, 1982, pp. 23–29).
14. Imbedded in these building laws is a double standard, which suggests that housing for the poor may have a lower factor of safety than buildings for the wealthy.

References

Abrams, Charles. 1966. *Squatter Settlements—The Problem and the Opportunity.* Ideas and Methods Exchange no. 63. Washington, D.C.: Division of Urban Affairs, U.S. Department of Housing and Urban Developement.

Ahmad, S., V. P. Mittal, and S. A. Salam. 1981. "Tests on Simply Supported Reinforced Brick Slabs." In *Housing—The Impact of Economy and Technology,* ed. O. Ural and R. Krapfenbauer, pp. 415–31. Elmsford, N.Y.: Pergamon Press.

Bisharat, Leila, and Magdy Tewfik. 1985. "Housing the Urban Poor in Amman." *Third World Planning Review* 7(1) (February), 5–22.

Bossio, Juan Carlos. 1984. "Advanced Technologies and Their Implications for the Developing Countries." *Labour and Society* 9(4) (October/December), 345–62.

Burgess, Rod. 1982. "Self-Help Housing Advocacy: A Curious Form of Radicalism. A Critique of the Work of John F. C. Turner." In *Self-Help Housing: A Critique,* ed. Peter M. Ward, pp. 56–98. London: Mansell.

Cobijo. 2d rev. 1981. Madrid: H. Blume Ediciones.

Connolly, Priscilla. 1982. "Uncontrolled Settlements and Self-Build: What Kind of Solution? The Mexico City Case." In *Self-Help Housing,: A Critique,* ed. Peter M. Ward, pp. 141–74. London: Mansell.

Epstein, D. G. 1973. *Brasília, Plan and Reality: A Study of Planned and Spontaneous Urban Development.* Berkeley: University of California Press.

Fathy, Hassan. 1973. *Architecture for the Poor.* Chicago: University of Chicago Press.

Galea, J. M. 1981. "The Development of the Domestic Architecture of Malta in Response to Technological and Economic Force." In *Housing—The Impact of Economy and Technology,* ed. O. Ural and R. Krapfenbauer, pp. 210–27. Elmsford, N.Y.: Pergamon Press.

Galea, J. M., and J. J. Boon. 1981. "The Traditional Architecture of the Asir Province, Saudi Arabia." In *Housing—The Impact of Economy and Technology,* ed. O. Ural and R. Krapfenbauer, pp. 118–34. Elmsford, N.Y.: Pergamon Press.

Gallant, Peter. 1982. *Self-Help Construction of One-Story Buildings.* 2d ed. Information Collection and Exchange Manual M6. Washington, D.C.: Peace Corps.

Government of India. 1970. *Report of the Expert Committee on Methods for Achieving Low Cost Large-Scale Housing Construction in the Major Cities.* New Delhi: National Buildings Organization, Ministry of Health, Family Planning, Works, Housing and Urban Development.

Hardoy, Jorge E., and David Satterthwaite. 1981. *Shelter, Need and Response: Housing, Land and Settlement Policies in Seventeen Third World Nations.* New York: Wiley.

Hausmann, Ulrich. 1984. "The Small Scale Production of Reinforced Concrete Floor Slabs." *Appropriate Technology* 11(1) (June), 10–11.

Herbert, John D. 1979. *Urban Development in the Third World.* New York: Praeger.

Hidalgo, Jenny. 1985. Conversations with the director of the *Unidad Ejecutora de Barrios Periféricos* of the Municipality of Quito, May–July.

James, J., and F. Stewart. 1981. "New Products: A Discussion of the Welfare Effects of the Introduction of New Products in Developing Countries." *Oxford Economic Papers* 33(1) (March), 81–107.

Karachi Development Authority (KDA). 1966. *Proceedings of a Seminar on the Problem of Shelterless People and Squatters in Pakistani Cities.* Karachi, Pakistan: Karachi Development Authority, in collaboration with the Planning Commission and the National Institute of Public Administration, Karachi, March 25–29.

Khalili, Nader. 1983. *Racing Alone—A Visionary Architect's Quest for Houses Made with Earth and Fire.* San Francisco: Harper & Row.

Lobo, Susan. 1982. *A House of My Own—Social Organization in the Squatter Settlements of Lima, Peru.* Tucson: University of Arizona Press.

Mathur, G. C. 1981. "Housing for the Poor in Developing Countries—Impact of Economy and Technology." In *Housing—The Impact of Economy and Technology,* ed. O. Ural and R. Krapfenbauer, pp. 1004–21. Elmsford, N.Y.: Pergamon Press.

Mellin, Robert. 1984. "Sites and Services Case Study: Ahmedabad, India." *Open House International* 9(1), 4–13.

Miles, Derek, and Michael Parkes. 1984. "Housing for the Poor." *Appropriate Technology* 11(3) (December), 1–4.

Parry, John P. M. 1984. "Building Materials and Construction Systems." In *Low-Income Housing in the Developing World,* ed. Geoffrey K. Payne, pp. 249–64. Chichester, England: Wiley.

Rodell, Michael J. 1983. "Sites and Services and Low-Income Housing." In *People, Poverty and Shelter: Problems of Self-Help Housing in the Third World,* ed. R. J. Skinner and M. J. Rodell, pp. 21–52. London: Methuen.

Schaffner, Beat. 1984. "Fibre-Cement Roofing—Helping the Disabled to Help Themselves." *Appropriate Technology* 11(3) (December), 17–18.

Skinner, Reinhard J. 1983. "Community Participation: Its Scope and Organization." In *People, Poverty and Shelter: Problems of Self-Help Housing in the Third World,* ed. R. J. Skinner and M. J. Rodell, pp. 125–50. London: Methuen.

Smith, R. G. 1984. "Rice Husk Ash Cement and Other Cementitious Materials." *Appropriate Technology* 11(3) (December), 8–9.

Sri Lanka Housing Authority (SLHA). 1976. *Housing in Sri Lanka.* Colombo, Sri Lanka: Marga Institute.

Stren, Richard E. 1978. *Housing the Urban Poor in Africa: Policy, Politics and Bureaucracy in Mombasa.* Research Series no. 34, Institute of International Studies. Berkeley: University of California Press.

Stulz, Roland. 1984. "Earth for Construction." *Appropriate Technology* 11(3) (December), 12–13.

Tall, L., and Francois Cheong Siat-Moy. 1981. "Test Results and Strength Prediction of 'Self-Help' Masonry Walls." In *Housing—The Impact of Economy and Technology,* ed. O. Ural and R. Krapfenbauer, pp. 31–49. Elmsford, N.Y.: Pergamon Press.

Taper, Bernard. 1980. "Charles Abrams in Ghana." In *The Work of Charles Abrams,* ed. O. H. Koenigsberger, S. Groak, and B. Bernstein, pp. 49–54. Oxford, England: Pergamon Press.

Terner, Ian D. 1978. "Los Obstáculos al Propietario–Constructor: Un Interrogante a las Tecnologías con Capacidad de Respuesta en la Construcción de Viviendas." In *La Casa Otra,* ed. Edward Allen, pp. 105–24. Cambridge: MIT Press.

United Nations Department of Economic and Social Affairs. 1962. *Report of the Ad Hoc Group of Experts on Housing and Urban Development.* New York: United Nations.

U.S. Senate. 1963. *Hearings before a Subcommittee of the Committee on Banking and Currency, Study of International Housing,* 88th Cong., 1st sess., April 22–25.

Vining, Daniel R., Jr. 1985. "The Growth of Core Regions in the Third World." *Scientific American* 252(4) (April), 42–69.

Ward, Peter M. 1982. "Self-Help, Community Organization and Politics: Villa El Salvador, Lima." In *Self-Help Housing: A Critique,* ed. Peter M. Ward, pp. 175–208. London: Mansell.

Chapter 5

Environmental Issues in Spontaneous Settlements

G. WILLIAM PAGE

Rapid urbanization stresses the natural environment under the best of circumstances, and in Third World cities with large areas of spontaneous shelter, environmental problems threaten both the health of people and economic productivity. Third World countries have not been responsive to environmental problems, in large part because of the many serious national problems considered more important or more politically expedient. The legal implications of uncertain land ownership in squatter settlements has also prevented or delayed governments in many Third World cities from providing a safe water supply and other essential services to spontaneous settlements.

The effects of poverty are of paramount importance in understanding spontaneous settlements and their environmental problems. More than a billion people live in countries that had an average annual income in 1981 of $200 or less. The real per capita income of these people is expected to grow by an average of no more than 1 percent annually (Eckholm, 1982). In contrast, real per capita income growth in developed countries averages 2 to 4 percent per year (World Bank, 1985). Rapid urbanization also negatively affects the standard of living in developing countries. The proportion of the world's population living in urban settlements rose from approximately 14 percent in 1920 to 41 percent in 1980. About 30 percent of the Third World population now lives in cities, with about one-third of these city dwellers living in units they built themselves (Eckholm, 1982). In addition to extensive substandard housing, this rapid urbanization produces chaotic land-use relationships and inhibits the ability of municipalities to provide adequate infrastructure such as transportation systems, water and sewerage facilities, and health services.

Poverty often causes the urban poor in Third World countries to build housing in the most polluted or the least environmentally suitable locations. Land that is unacceptable for formal development is often a target for squatter appropriation. Squatters build on dangerously steep and unstable hillsides, in flood plains, or in other areas prone to natural hazards. They build adjacent to industrial facilities emitting air, water, and noise pollution, and next to sewage outfalls, landfills, or other sources of municipal pollution. Land far from parks, recreational facilities, and public open space is also used. Not only do the poor live in the most polluted environments, they also work in the most health-threatening occupational settings.

Poor environmental conditions in self-help settlements create a serious problem both for the residents and for their countries. Exposure to pollutants, bacteria, viruses, and other infectious agents place these residents at a health risk greater than that experienced by the general population. The poverty and the unhealthy living and working conditions often produce among squatter residents lower resistance and tolerance to environmental insults than exist in the more affluent and healthy portion of the population. The high concentrations of humans and infectious agents in many spontaneous settlements cause residents to be especially vulnerable to epidemics. More generally, the ill health associated with the poor environmental conditions found in spontaneous settlements reduces the labor productivity of Third World countries. Improved sanitary conditions, including improved water supplies and sewage treatment systems, would contribute substantially to ameliorating human suffering and improving the economies of the less affluent countries of the world. In response, the United Nations designated the 1980s as the International Drinking Water Supply and Sanitation Decade in the hope that Third World governments and international aid donors would invest substantially more funds in water supplies and sanitation. This investment is desperately needed in the spontaneous settlements of the Third World's urban centers.

Urbanization, Poverty, and the Environment

Environmental factors in Third World countries link the complex issues of economic development, food production, malnourishment, poverty, urbanization, and spontaneous housing development. These interconnected issues are sometimes referred to as the "poverty resource trap" (World Resources Institute, 1984). In many Third World countries, extreme poverty and pressure from rapidly growing populations combine in a vicious cycle that progressively deteriorates the natural environment and the resource base and is followed by further social and economic impoverishment. The need for food by the large and growing population overtaxes the already fragile natural resource base as the cultivation of marginal and fragile soils leads to soil exhaustion and erosion. In addition, the shortening of the fallow period in slash-and-burn agriculture deprives soil of essential nutrients and causes desertification. The high cost of conventional fuels leads to widespread use of wood as fuel in most Third World countries, and the resulting deforestation causes the use of dung as fuel rather than as fertilizer and soil conditioner. Overgrazing on semiarid lands and overfishing are other examples of environmental problems that cause an increase in poverty. These problems of nutrient exhaustion and soil erosion also produce siltation of rivers, lakes, and reservoirs. The combination of these factors, especially the increase in poverty and the destruction of the natural environment in rural areas, reduces these countries' abilities to support the existing human population. People forced to leave their rural homes because of deteriorating environmental and economic conditions often become residents of spontaneous settlements. Many of these desperately poor migrants lack the resources necessary for even the most modest conventional urban housing.

Health Effects of Spontaneous Shelter Environments

Spontaneous shelter in the cities of developing countries often exists in areas with harsh environmental conditions. Outside experts, public officials, and the residents of such areas recognize these conditions as substantial health threats. A study of the health of residents of a squatter settlement in Lusaka, Zambia, concluded that a hygienic environment would do more for the health of the squatters than all the teaching hospitals of Europe (Schlyter and Schlyter, 1980). The residents of spontaneous housing have responded to many surveys with demands for better sanitation, better water supplies, and better urban services (Leonard and Morell, 1981).

The supply of safe water and the disposal of human excreta are two of the more important health concerns in all spontaneous settlements. Indoor running water is rare. Poor families carry water from distant standpipes or, where standpipes are not accessible, pay cash for water from mobile vendors (Photo 5.1). Under these conditions, water has such a high labor or currency value that it is too precious for use in any but the most essential purposes. Health suffers because water is not used for routine washing and cleanliness. These conditions affect large numbers of people. In Mexico City alone, at least 2 million inhabitants have no running water in their homes (Friedrich, 1984a).

The disposal of human wastes is another serious problem in spontaneous settlement (Photo 5.2). In Cairo, a densely settled city of about 12 million people, one-third of the residents live in buildings that are not

Photo 5.1 Community well under construction in Yogyakarta, Indonesia. (Photo by Carl V. Patton)

connected to any sewerage system (Friedrich, 1984b). In Mexico City, 3 million of the 14 million residents are not connected to the sewerage system (Friedrich, 1984a). Dust from dried human feces contaminates people, houses, and the food eaten every day. In many spontaneous settle-

Photo 5.2 Latrine built over a canal in a spontaneous settlement in Yogyakarta, Indonesia. Water from the canal is also used to clean cooking equipment and eating utensils for a restaurant. (Photo by Douglas C. Ryhn)

ments, nearly 100 percent of the residents are infested with parasites (Friedrich, 1984a). Many squatter settlements use pit latrines, which have a short life of two to three years, for excreta disposal. Land on which to dig new latrines continually is a problem in densely built areas, and family houses are sometimes torn down or relocated to find a suitable location for the new latrines (Schlyter and Schlyter, 1979). In these densely built environments, the quantities of waste introduced to the ground usually result in groundwater pollution that contaminates drinking-water wells.

Many of the more numerous and dangerous diseases in spontaneous settlements are water related. Parasitic diseases caused by protozoa are common in squatter settlements located in tropical climates. These diseases are not common in industrially developed nations located in temperate climates because freezing weather destroys either some stage of the disease vector or the host of the disease vector. The following figures on people suffering from water-related diseases in Third World countries give some rough conception of the dimensions of these problems: trachoma, 500 million; elephantiasis, 250 million; schistosomiasis, 200 million; filariasis, 200 million; malaria, 160 million; gastroenteritis, 100 million; onchocerciasis, 30 million (Eckholm, 1982; Pearson, 1985).

The diseases that afflict residents of spontaneous settlements are part of the cycle of poverty and environmental degradation. Schistosomiasis, a disease of the poor, exists only under unsanitary conditions. Schistosomiasis is a generic name for a series of illnesses caused by liver flukes that are human parasites. Infected humans excrete in their feces the eggs of the liver flukes. Where unsanitary conditions allow the feces of infected humans to enter bodies of water, the eggs hatch and enter water snails as a stage in their life cycle. In their final larval stage, the flukes are free swimming in water, and the larvae can burrow into the exposed skin of humans who come in contact with the infected water. Adult liver flukes cause schistosomiasis, a debilitating and difficult disease to treat (Page, 1987a). A form of filariasis is spread by mosquitoes that breed in polluted puddles in cities (Eckholm, 1982). The combined effects of undernutrition, infections spread by human excrement, airborne infections, and parasites account for nearly all childhood deaths in developing countries (Eckholm, 1982). Some evidence suggests that we have failed in our efforts to eradicate or control these diseases. The progress in extending the life expectancy of citizens of Third World countries slowed in the 1970s and in some areas may be declining (Gwalkin, 1981).

Third World countries also experience many of the same environmental and public health problems experienced by the more economically developed countries, but to a more severe extent. Spontaneous housing often exists immediately adjacent to industrial facilities where industrial residues, by-products, wastes, and spills commonly pollute the environment. Squatter housing may exist next to industries that have located their plants in a Third World country because that country is a "pollution haven" from the more stringent environmental regulations of the economically developed nations. Some health evidence supports the hypothesis of "pollution havens." For example, there is evidence of highly elevated lead levels in the bodies of selected populations in Manila (Bassow, 1979). The median levels of the pesticide DDT in the fat of human breast milk in China, India, and Mexico are from three to seven times higher than the highest median levels of any industrialized country (Pearson, 1985). Birth abnormalities are so high in the industrial city of Cubatão, Brazil, that one-third of Cubatão's children fail to live through their first year (*New York Times,* 1984).

The density of development and lack of planning in spontaneous shelter areas cause the residents to experience acutely many of the environmental problems of urban living. Traffic is chaotic, with cars, trucks, and buses competing with pedestrians, bicyclists, and animals for space. Roads receive much less care in design, traffic signage, and safety engineering than those in the economically more developed countries. In addition to inconvenience, this causes public health problems. In Brazil, traffic deaths per automobile mile traveled are ten times greater than the rate in the United States (Eckholm, 1979). Noise from traffic, industry, and other urban sources produces hearing impairment, sleeplessness, communication disturbances, a decrease in the ability to concentrate, and a reduction in the learning ability of children. Of the 7.6 million people in Bombay, at least 30 percent are affected adversely by noise. Studies in Bombay and Delhi report daytime noise levels as high as 90 decibels and seldom below 60 decibels (Mayur, 1979). The presence of parks, playgrounds, open space, and natural environments are important factors in the quality of life and the level of human welfare. Residents of spontaneous settlements rarely have easy access to these amenities. A common argument is that these environmental amenities are luxuries desired more as individuals gain increased income. But residents of spontaneous settlements who have recently arrived from rural areas place a high value on environmental amenities (Pearson and Pryor, 1978).

Balancing Environmental Concerns with Economic Development

Balancing environmental concerns with the need for economic development is a formidable challenge for Third World countries. Economic development often has been considered to be in direct opposition to achieving environmental protection. This position was enunciated eloquently by the late Indira Gandhi when she said, "How can we speak to those who live in the villages and in the slums about keeping the oceans, the rivers, and the air clean, when their own lives are contaminated? Are not poverty and need the greatest polluters?" (Leonard and Morell, 1981). Leaders of Third World nations are concerned that increased attention to environmental problems by the international community will negatively affect their economic well-being. They have five major concerns:

1. Strict environmental standards, for instance on lead and sulfur in fuel and on herbicide and pesticide residues on agricultural commodities, may adversely affect trade.
2. The high cost of environmental cleanup and protection programs in the developed countries may seriously reduce the amount of aid available for international development assistance.
3. The capital costs of development will increase as developed countries and international aid agencies establish new standards applicable to Third World development projects. (This may also tend to reduce the competitive advantages of Third World countries.)

4. The infusion of sophisticated pollution-control technologies into Third World countries will worsen the problem of developing appropriate technologies.
5. The costs of environmental controls in the developed countries will be passed along, thus increasing the prices of imports (Dahlberg et al., 1985; Leonard and Morell, 1981).

These concerns led many leaders of Third World countries in the 1970s to conclude that any international environmental policy based on the realities of the developed countries would perpetuate the existing international order of affluent economically developed nations and poor Third World nations.

Analysis of the concerns of Third World countries about the effects of environmental controls on their prospects for economic development suggests that these fears may be ill founded. One guiding principle of environmental management is that the marginal or incremental costs of environmental protection should correspond to the marginal benefits achieved or the marginal damages avoided. Difficulties in measuring benefits gained or damages avoided make this simple principle hard to use. The benefits of environmental quality generally do not pass through markets and are often ignored or underpriced as a result. Environmental protection policies that lead to some decrease in conventionally measured gross national product (GNP) may still increase the welfare of the nation if the value of the environmental benefits exceeds the decrease in GNP. The environmental benefits can include the improved health and productivity of workers, as well as improved environmental amenities. Although the allocation of funds to environmental controls in new development may appear to divert scarce resources away from productive use, the long-term costs and benefits should be considered. Damage from pollution may be cumulative, and there may be long delays before it is perceived. Preventive action is almost invariably less costly than remedial pollution control. Moreover, some pollution may result in irreversible changes including the loss of animal species and wilderness areas.

On balance, environmental regulation appears to be worth the expense. A study of the costs of environmental regulation in the United States revealed that pollution control costs have not been a significant source of productivity losses. Those economic losses attributable to environmental regulation, in terms of both measured output and productivity, have declined since the early 1970s when environmental regulations were first enacted (Congressional Budget Office, 1985). Economic losses attributable to environmental damage are estimated at 4 percent of GNP in developed countries, and these countries spend less than 2 percent of GNP on environmental protection (*Environmental Science and Technology,* 1985).

Environmental assessment and planning are important requirements of development projects financed by aid-giving nations and international agencies. In the 1980s, Third World countries and the international community recognized environmental degradation in Third World countries as a significant impediment to economic development. Some Third World nations have adopted comprehensive environmental protection legislation and are strong supporters of the United Nations Environment Program. Many of these countries accept the principle that the most efficient method of production for new development projects is to use modern and environmentally benign industrial processes. Economic development projects that conform to this principle minimize polluting emissions and conserve energy, water, and materials. In some instances, material recovery for reuse within the facility or for resale can recover the cost of the environmentally motivated production process modifications. This principle is also applicable to nonindustrial economic development projects. Investment in renewable resource development can increase productivity by reducing environmental stress such as erosion and nutrient leaching of agricultural soils.

Environmental regulations less stringent than those in most economically developed countries are used by Third World countries to foster industrial development. One Brazilian state, Goiás, went so far as to advertise for investment under the slogan "We want your pollution." Nevertheless, studies have found little evidence that "pollution havens" seriously distort the international pattern of investment (World Resources Institute, 1984). Differences in environmental-control costs are small relative to other production costs, and the traditional determinants of industrial location far outweigh environmental considerations. Multinational corporations have also been accused of taking advantage of the willingness of Third World countries to accept polluting industries because of their great need for economic development. On this point there also appears to be some evidence to the contrary. Studies in the Philippines and elsewhere found that multinational corporations have a better record of pollution control than indigenous corporations (Royston, 1985). Investment in pollution-control equipment may not be as high in Third World countries, and the amount of pollutants released to the environment may be greater than in the more economically developed countries, but despite this, the evidence suggests that multinational corporations play a positive role in introducing and demonstrating pollution-control technology in the Third World.

The effects of the world debt crisis of the 1980s have yet to be fully understood, but may well include a sharp reduction in the effort to improve the environmental quality of Third World countries. Developing countries are under strong pressure to extract resources and raise export production as quickly as possible. They need hard currency to pay their debts. In the short term, environmental measures such as infrastructure development, pollution control, and preservation of ecosystems may be cut back or eliminated because of the urgency of meeting overseas loan payments.

Technological Responses to the Environment

Developing countries face difficult problems in adapting indigenous technology to modern conditions, in importing technological innovations from the developed countries, and in selecting appropriate technologies. Fuel for cooking illustrates this point. In the rural regions of the less economically developed countries, wood is the traditional fuel for cooking. As an indicator of this use, consider that in the developed nations, 8 percent of wood production is used as fuel, while in the developing nations 81 percent is so used (Pearson and Pryor, 1978). With urbanization, many of the rural poor migrate to the cities and continue to use wood as a fuel. Its widespread use results in deforestation that in turn causes erosion, siltation of water bodies, flooding, the damage or destruction of agricultural land, and possible climate modification. Furthermore, burning wood introduces many pollutants into the atmosphere. Emissions of carbon monoxide (CO), nitrogen oxides (NOx), sulfur oxides (SOx), formaldehyde, acetaldehyde, phenols, suspended particulate matter, and benzo-a-pyrene from burning wood produce adverse health effects in humans (Wadden and Scheff, 1983). In densely developed settlements, these pollutants are added to already polluted air.

Indoor air pollution is also an extremely serious problem in spontaneous settlements (Smith, 1984). Cooking stoves are typically vented inadequately and allow dangerous pollutants to concentrate in even the most open of houses. The traditional *ondol* heating and cooking system of Korea illustrates some of these health-related problems. The *ondol* system consists of an excavated kitchen and furnace room with flues running under other rooms to provide heat. The concentration of carbon monoxide in 62 percent of the *ondol*-heated living rooms sampled was greater than 100 parts per million (ppm) (Freeman, 1974). In the United States the standard to protect human health from carbon monoxide in outdoor air is 10 ppm. Furthermore, the manufacture, transport, and use of the anthracite briquets used in the *ondol* system in Seoul was estimated to add 30,000 metric tons of dust to the urban atmosphere and 4,200 tons of ash per day (Freeman, 1974). This alone creates a large proportion of Seoul's solid-waste management problem.

Solving environmental problems in Third World cities is related to the use of appropriate technology. The collection and disposal of solid waste is a good example. In many spontaneous settlements the roads are unimproved and are often impassable by trucks. Thus, solid waste is not collected but is disposed of in shallow holes or large open pits (Schlyter and Schlyter, 1979). An appropriate disposal system would involve choices about the extent of mechanization in collecting and treating solid waste. In collection, compactor trucks and other higher-technology options are often less appropriate than flatbed trucks and handcarts which are more labor intensive (Diaz and Golueke, 1985). In disposal, sanitary landfills are always less expensive than capital-intensive composting facilities or incinerators (Cointreau, 1982; Linn, 1983). Nevertheless, such approaches have to be designed with potential side effects in mind. Improperly designed landfills can contribute to groundwater pollution, and large-scale water treatment and distribution systems may cause serious long-term problems because of groundwater overdraft conditions (Curi, 1986; Page, 1987b). A number of writers have discussed technologies that are appropriate for dealing with environmental problems in developing countries. Monk and colleagues (1984) describe a water treatment plant for a large city that incorporates local materials and labor and has a reduced energy requirement. Hofkes (1984) and Schulz and Okun (1984) present information about small water systems for the urban fringe or rural areas that integrate technology with community involvement. Donaldson (1984) discusses regional water treatment systems in Latin America as a model for developing countries. The Ford Foundation (1971) presents an overview of problems and technologies in the areas of water supply, the removal and treatment of solid and liquid wastes, domestic power supply, and urban transportation.

Spontaneous Shelter and Major Disasters

Because of their location in disaster-prone areas and the lower quality of their structures, spontaneous settlements face numerous major threats. Disaster-prone areas include flood plains, steep hillsides, and land adjacent to hazardous industrial processes. Structures in spontaneous settlements are seldom built according to carefully conceived building codes designed to mitigate the risks of specific locations. For instance, in seismically active regions in developed countries, buildings usually must conform to standards designed to minimize damages from earthquakes. In spontaneous settlements, housing typically is not constructed to provide this protection (Photo 5.3).

Disasters are becoming an even greater threat to life and property. The poor are the most vulnerable to disasters, and among the poor it is the children, the aged, the handicapped, and the malnourished who are most at risk. Both the number of disasters and the number of people affected by them have increased steadily since the 1960s. Most of these disasters have occurred in the Third World (Wijkman and Timberlake,

Photo 5.3 Earthquake damage to a user-built shelter in western Greece. (Photo by Carl V. Patton)

1984). The growing number of people living in the earth's hazard zones have caused this increase, as more people have become at risk. Moreover, spontaneous settlements are often located in hazard zones because the land was left vacant by people with the financial resources to settle in less dangerous areas (Photo 5.4). As previously noted, vacant land in flood plains, on steep hillsides, or adjacent to potentially hazardous industrial plants is often the location of self-help housing. The density of squatter housing in high-risk locations is obviously a concern, for a disaster can affect large numbers of people and has both large-scale immediate and secondary consequences, such as temporary and replacement housing.

Several recent disasters illustrate the effects in hazard-prone areas. The first example is the industrial accident that occurred in Bhopal, India. Bhopal is the capital of Madhya Pradesh state and is a city of 672,000 persons located 750 kilometers (466 miles) south of New Delhi. In 1969 Union Carbide built a small pesticide plant outside the city limits of Bhopal, in an unpopulated area. By 1975, when the plant expanded, squatter settlements had been constructed adjacent to the plant property (Iyer, 1984). By 1984, the large shantytowns of Jaiprakash and Chhola housed many thousands. In the early hours one morning in December 1984, 45 tons of methyl isocyanate gas escaped into the air from a faulty valve. The cloud of deadly gas quickly spread over the adjacent settle-

Photo 5.4 Flooded huts by the Buriganga River, Dacca, Bangladesh. Although rich and poor live side by side, the poor are more vulnerable to disaster. (Photo by Tom Learmonth, Earthscan)

ments and into the city as the residents slept. Over 2,000 people died and 50,000 were injured (Speth, 1984). Most of the victims died of respiratory failure as the gas filled and damaged their lungs. Children and older people whose lungs were either too small or too weak were the most likely to be killed or injured. Many survivors were permanently blinded or suffered other serious damage. Indian officials acknowledge spontaneous abortions, stillbirths, and the births of deformed babies resulting from inhalation of methyl isocyanate gas (Iyer, 1984).

Cubatão, Brazil, is an industrial city of about 100,000 persons located 48 kilometers (30 miles) southeast of São Paulo, between São Paulo and its port city of Santos. Within Cubatão, the spontaneous settlement of Vila Parisi has 15,000 residents and occupies the land between a steel plant, a fertilizer plant, a cement plant, and a steep mountainside. The shantytown is composed of huts, built mostly of wood and cardboard, on stilts over a swamp. The swamp contains a grid of ducts and pipes that carry flammable, corrosive, and explosive materials (*New York Times*, 1984). Pollution has choked off life in rivers and fields and is killing trees on the Serra do Mar Mountains behind the city. Without vegetation to hold the soil, landslides scraped large strips of soil from the 2,000-foot-high slopes (Simons, 1985). The slum is 18 inches below sea level, and high tides regularly overflow the open sewers into the muddy streets. One river boils with chemical effluents, another is blanketed with detergents, and a third occasionally emits toxic clouds. On February 25, 1984, a pipeline rupture and explosion occurred shortly after midnight. When oil burst out of the pipeline and caught fire, it spread quickly across the swampy water beneath Vila Parisi, killing at least 100 men, women, and children and destroying 300 huts, which the police said housed 2,400 people (*New York Times,* 1984).

Bangladesh has roughly 100 million people living in an area the size of Wisconsin, which has a population of only 5 million (Schanberg, 1985). Virtually no unoccupied or uncultivated land is left in the northern parts of Bangladesh. As soil erosion has destroyed farmland, it has contributed to the silt that forms one of the world's largest deltas, where the Ganges and Brahmaputra river systems empty into the Bay of Bengal. The poorest people are pushed southward onto the islands in the delta where they build houses and squatter settlements. Some of these settlements are in the low-lying sections of towns and cities; others are on agricultural land or newly formed islands. On May 24, 1985, a cyclone and resulting tidal wave devastated the lowlands of southeastern Bangladesh, killing an estimated 50,000 people (Schanberg, 1985). A cyclone that struck the same area in 1970 is believed to have killed at least 300,000 people (Weisman, 1985).

Mexico City, with a population of 14 million, has many spontaneous settlements. The city has thirty natural gas storage plants mostly surrounded by shacks and shantytowns (Friedrich and Simpson, 1984). San Juan Ixhautepec is such a settlement adjacent to a gas storage plant in Mexico City. One early morning in November 1984, a series of explosions first destroyed four spherical tanks, each holding about 420,000 gallons of liquefied gas, and then forty-eight smaller containers. The explosion and resulting fire left 365 people dead and 2,000 injured, and it destroyed 30 acres of housing with an additional 30 acres damaged (Friedrich and Simpson, 1984). There were 100,000 evacuees. Mexico has been unable to control squatter settlement of the land adjacent to potentially hazardous industrial facilities in its cities; alternatively, the cost of moving a liquefied gas storage plant is estimated at $30 million (Friedrich and Simpson, 1984).

Mamayes is the name given to a shantytown located in a short, bowlike valley in the green foothills above the city of Ponce, Puerto Rico. Ponce is the third-largest city in Puerto Rico with a population of about 250,000. It is located on the south shore of the island. City officials in Ponce estimate that more than 25,000 squatters live in shantytowns on the edge of Ponce (Nordheimer, 1985). The first half of the 1980s was a time of rapid growth for these shantytowns. The population of Mamayes is estimated to have doubled in that time to about 2,400 people living in makeshift housing up to the 700-foot level on the steep slopes of the mountains surrounding the small valley. In early October 1985, a tropical storm brought three days of rain to Puerto Rico. On Monday, October 7, a wall of earth and rock peeled away from the mountain and destroyed Mamayes in an avalanche of collapsing dwellings, uprooted trees, and suffocating mud. The avalanche destroyed 263 homes and is presumed to have buried 500 people (Treaster, 1985).

Policy Issues

Third World countries experience varied environmental problems, many of which are caused or exacerbated by urgent attempts to become more economically developed. In the past, traditional societies in rural areas produced solutions to environmental problems through slow adaptations. Sometimes it was a process of trial and error, but eventually these societies achieved ingenious and successful adaptations to unusual environmental conditions. As the pace of change has increased dramatically during the past few decades, environmental problems have far outstripped environmental solutions in many countries. This dilemma has been particularly acute for the residents of spontaneous settlements.

Predictions of future environmental conditions in spontaneous settlements include a few positive trends, but many negative trends are expected to continue. In the short term, the world debt crisis poses severe obstacles to achieving solutions to the environmental problems discussed in this chapter. The financial requirements for debt repayment will both preclude using resources to improve environmental conditions and intensify the negative effects of several continuing environmental trends. Urgently needed improvements in water supply and sewage treatment will be delayed. Increased migration to the cities because of deforestation and desertification will remain serious short- and long-term trends. Changes in agricultural practices and the extent of mechanization will also force increasing numbers of poor rural inhabitants to migrate to the cities. Increased construction of spontaneous housing on environmentally unsuitable land will result in an increased number of disasters. The poor health of squatter settlement residents will continue and even become worse.

Positive environmental trends may include the benefits of transferring information and appropriate technology from the more economically developed countries. Industrially developed nations have had to contend with similar problems and are able to provide some advice to less developed countries. Developed nations have had to contend with housing built near sources of constant toxic emissions and have developed technologies and new source performance standards to control the release of pollutants. Problems with abandoned landfills and hazardous waste sites have generated sophisticated environmental monitoring strategies and equipment and techniques to handle toxic materials. Development in environmentally unsuitable locations such as flood plains, steep slopes, and barrier islands has produced land-use planning techniques to limit or control growth. Many transferable lessons are being learned in the economically developed countries from the experience with different policy approaches to avoid and control environmental problems. For example, industries building facilities in developing countries are including modern processes and pollution-control equipment designed to avoid environmental problems. The transfer of such knowledge and appropriate technologies can help Third World countries expand and improve their economies without incurring the more serious environmental damages.

Conclusion

Direct action by governments is required to improve environmental conditions in spontaneous settlements. Continued spontaneous development contributes to significant environmental degradation of the larger urban area and is a substantial threat to the human and economic health of Third World countries. Environmental quality is a "public good," something that benefits everyone but that neither squatter residents nor large corporations can effectively provide alone. Thus government action is needed. The first priority must be controlling future squatter housing. The two basic approaches are providing knowledge to citizens (especially the poor) about the environmentally related risks of residential structures and providing sites and services for future housing.

A policy of increasing knowledge of environmental risks among urban and rural citizens recognizes the critical role of individuals in providing their own safe shelter. Many current environmental risks are not part of traditional cultures, and so there is a clear need for governments to educate citizens about these new dangers. An understanding of the risks from natural and man-made hazards in certain urban locations can help individuals decide where to live. Knowledge about the role of basic sewage disposal and sanitation in densely populated urban areas can help individuals manage these critical functions in their neighborhoods. An awareness of the risks of modern industrial pollutants and sources of exposure to these pollutants in the workplace and inside residential structures can help individuals make decisions about where to live and work, and the tradeoffs associated with these decisions. Providing better information about environmental risks will improve environmental conditions in spontaneous settlements, but it will not solve some of the most critical environmental problems.

Government provision of sites and services for the accommodation of future self-help housing entails immediate costs but has many environmental advantages. Such a policy recognizes the inability of the government to stop spontaneous development and attempts to encourage a more healthy environment in the settlements that inevitably result. Beyond this, the ability to plan for the future development of urban areas has many obvious benefits, such as minimizing the cost of providing government services and locating future residential development in areas that are relatively free from environmental dangers. Installing infrastructure before the development of an area is much less expensive and more easily accomplished than doing so after the residents arrive. Sewer lines, water lines, and limited road systems will contribute greatly to promoting the health and safety of the residents who will eventually occupy the site. These predevelopment investments will be repaid many times over in the long term by the improved health and productivity of future residents.

Providing knowledge to owner–builders, or even providing site-specific infrastructure in urban areas, cannot solve many of the most serious environmental problems. Governments at local, regional, and national levels must take action that treats both symptoms and causes. The symptoms include air and water pollution, noise, and waste products. The causes include uncontrolled population growth, deforestation, soil erosion, desertification, and in its broadest sense, natural resources mismanagement.

Environmental policy needs more attention in all countries. Instead of being an afterthought to the environmental damage caused by other policies, its function should be to anticipate damage, to reduce the negative external effects of human activities, and to promote economic and social policies that expand the basis for sustainable development. Urban centers of Third World countries are places where such a change in environmental policy can produce dramatic improvements. Investments in improved physical and social service infrastructure, in spontaneous settlements in particular and in cities in general, have the potential to release great quantities of untapped creative energies that can be used to raise the standard of living in many less developed nations.

References

Bassow, Whitman. 1979. "The Third World: Changing Attitudes Toward Environmental Protection." *Annals of the American Academy of Political and Social Science* 444, 112–20.

Cointreau, Sandra J. 1982. *Environmental Management of Urban Solid Wastes in Developing Countries.* Urban Development Technical Paper no. 5. Washington, D.C.: World Bank.

Congressional Budget Office. 1985. *Environmental Regulation and Economic Efficiency.* Washington, D.C.: Government Printing Office.

Curi, Kriton, ed. 1986. *Appropriate Waste Management for Developing Countries.* New York: Plenum Press.

Dahlberg, K., M. Soroos, A. Feraru, J. Hart, and B. T. Trout. 1985. *Environment and the Global Arena.* Durham: Duke University Press.

Diaz, Luis, and Clarence Golueke. 1985. "Solid Waste Management in Developing Countries." *BioCycle,* September, 46–52.

Donaldson, David. 1984. "Regional Authorities Support Small Water Systems in the Americas." *American Water Works Association Journal* 78(5), 62–68.

Eckholm, Erik P. 1979. *The Dispossessed of the Earth: Land Reform and Sustainable Development.* Washington, D.C.: Worldwatch Institute.

———. 1982. *Down to Earth.* New York: Norton.

Environmental Science and Technology. 1985. "Environmental Damage Costs Western Industrialized Nations About 4 Percent of Their Gross National Product." 19(12), 1143.

Ford Foundation. 1971. *Infrastructure Problems of the Cities of Developing Countries.* An International Urbanization Survey Report to the Ford Foundation. New York: Ford Foundation.

Freeman, Peter, ed. 1974. *The Urban Environment of Seoul, Korea.* Washington, D.C.: Smithsonian Institution.

Friedrich, Otto. 1984a. "A Proud Capital's Distress." *Time* 124(6), 26–35.

———. 1984b. "And If Mexico City Seems Bad. . . ." *Time* 124(6), 36–39.

Friedrich, Otto, and Janice C. Simpson. 1984. "Fire in the Dawn Sky." *Time* 124(23), 28–29.

Gwalkin, Davidson R. 1981. *Signs of Change in Developing-Country Mortality Trends: The End of an Era?* Development Paper no. 30. Washington, D.C.: Overseas Development Council.

Hofkes, E. H., ed. 1984. *Small Community Water Supplies: Technology of Small Water Supply Systems in Developing Countries.* New York: Wiley.

Iyer, Pico. 1984. "India's Night of Death." *Time* 124(25) (December 17), 18.

Leonard, H. Jeffrey, and David Morell. 1981. "Emergence of Environmental Concern in Developing Countries: A Political Perspective." *Stanford Journal of International Law* 17(2), 281–313.

Linn, Johannes F. 1983. *Cities in the Developing World.* New York: Oxford University Press.

Mayur, Rashmi. 1979. "Environmental Problems of Developing Countries." *Annals of the American Academy of Political and Social Science* 444, 89–101.

Monk, Robert, Terry Hall, and Mohammed Hussain. 1984. "Real World Design: Appropriate Technology for Developing Nations." *American Water Works Association Journal* 78(5), 62–75.

New York Times. 1984. "Oil Blast in Brazil Shantytown Kills 100." February 26, p. 3.

Nordheimer, Jan. 1985. "Hundreds Feared Dead in Puerto Rican Mud Slide." *New York Times,* October 9, p. 1.

Page, G. William. 1987a. "Water and Health." In *Protecting Public Health and the Environment,* ed. Michael Greenberg, pp. 105–33. New York: Guilford Press.

———, ed. 1987b. *Planning for Groundwater Protection.* New York: Academic Press.

Pearson, Charles. 1985. *Down to Business: Multinational Corporations, the Environment, and Development.* Washington, D.C.: World Resources Institute.

Pearson, Charles, and Anthony Pryor. 1978. *Environment: North and South.* New York: Wiley.

Royston, Michael G. 1985. "Local and Multinational Corporations: Reappraising Environmental Management." *Environment* 27(1), 13–42.

Schanberg, Sydney A. 1985. "In Impoverished Nations Such as Bangladesh, Life ls a Tidal Wave." *Milwaukee Journal,* May 29, p. 9.

Schlyter, Ann, and Thomas Schlyter. 1979. *George: The Development of a Squatter Settlement in Lusaka, Zambia.* Stockholm: Swedish Council for Building Research.

Schulz, C. R., and D. A. Okun. 1984. *Surface Water Treatment for Communities in Developing Countries.* New York: Wiley.

Smith, Kirk R. 1984. "Indoor Air: A View from Developing Countries." *Environmental Science and Technology* 18(9), 271a.

Simons, Marlise. 1985. "Pollution Most Foul." *Milwaukee Journal,* May 29, p. 6.

Speth, James Gustave. 1984. "What We Can Learn from Bhopal." *Environment* 27(1), 15.

Treaster, Joseph B. 1985. "Shantytowns Termed Widespread in Puerto Rico." *New York Times,* October 11, pp. 1, 12.

Wadden, Richard, and Peter Scheff. 1984. *Indoor Air Pollution.* New York: Wiley.

Weisman, Steven R. 1985. "Bangladesh Is Struggling to Recover." *New York Times,* May 29, p. 4.

Wijkman, Anders, and Lloyd Timberlake. 1984. *Natural Disasters: Acts of God or Acts of Man.* Washington, D.C.: Earthscan.

World Bank. 1985. *The World Bank Atlas 1985.* Washington, D.C.: World Bank.

World Resources Institute. 1984. *Improving Environmental Cooperation.* Washington, D.C.: World Resources Institute.

III

Contemporary Examples and Lessons

Chapter 6

Informal Settlement in Latin America and Its Policy Implications

ERNEST R. ALEXANDER

The informal settlement process in Latin America is informal only in the sense that it is outside the formal market and institutional system. It is also far from spontaneous. On a continuum from the classic spontaneous invasion *barrios* (Turner, 1967, 1968) to communities that are virtually indistinguishable from planned and approved bourgeois neighborhoods, we can recognize several different kinds of informal settlements.[1] They differ in the motivations that stimulated their growth and in the cast and interplay of actors involved.

Informal settlements are all similar, however, in terms of their basic populations. They are families, generally homeowners, and single individuals, often renting rooms. Some are migrants from the countryside, but most are city dwellers—either natives or earlier immigrants. This primary group of invaders aspires to homeownership and better living conditions than those found in their miserable and overcrowded central-city *inquilinato* (slum) dwellings. Too poor to realize their aspirations in the formal housing market, sometimes without the regular work or predictable money income to become eligible for credit,[2] these families and individuals nevertheless have resources that are mobilized in the process of progressive development to produce informal invasion settlements (Bernal, n.d., pp. 63–70; Cardona et al., n.d., pp. 165–70; Drakakis-Smith, 1981, pp. 59–66; Moser, 1982, pp. 166–67, 171–72).

Informal settlements share two other traits by definition. They are invasions of someone else's land, and they are not formally planned. The settlers may invade land belonging to a government agency, perhaps an open-land conservancy or a park district; an institution, such as a hospital, a university, or often the church; the local government, common, or *ejido,* land, and land reserved for public rights-of-way; or a private landowner (Leeds, 1981, pp. 22–24). Genuine invasions of private property without the owner's complicity are extremely rare because of the associated risks and sanctions; these can be avoided by taking public or institutional land, which is plentiful (Gilbert and Ward, 1982, pp. 105–6). However similar it may be to a legal neighborhood, the invasion community also has not been formally planned or approved by local authorities. It is therefore unprovided, at least in its early stages, with municipal infrastructure and services.

The Informal Settlement Process

Three different kinds of informal settlements can be distinguished by their different motivations and forms of organization: the communal invasion, the organized invasion, and clandestine developments.

The Communal Invasion. This is the classic spontaneous community-based invasion, usually initiated by a group of activists among a larger number of poor households linked by ties of kinship or origin. The invasion is organized in the sense that the timing of the original seizure of the land has to be coordinated, and an understanding about subdivision into lots has to be arrived at. Sometimes this subdivision is informal; sometimes it is formal to the point of obtaining a subdivision layout from a professional or quasi professional (Turner, 1967, p. 171). The Lima *barriadas* described by Turner are of this type, as are some of Bogotá's older *invasiones*. But this kind of informal settlement is becoming increasingly rare. In Cali, for example, during the 1950s these invasions occupied 13 percent of the city's area (compared to 15 percent of informal settlements of other kinds). In the next decade they accounted for only 5 percent, dropping to 4 percent in the 1970s (Centro Interamericano de Vivienda y Planeamiento, 1958; Departmento Administrativo de Planeación, n.d., p. 43).[3]

Gradual infiltration invasion by individual households or small groups of families is another form of communal invasion, for example, the secondary invasion of the Bogotá *barrio* of Las Colinas (Peattie, 1982a, p. 28) (Photo 6.1). More recently, communal invasions have been stimulated by professional invaders. After selling the equity in their lots or renting their houses in an invasion neighborhood where they were among the activist founders, they proceed to organize another invasion (Moser, 1982, p. 70).

The Organized Invasion. The stimulus for the organized invasion comes from outside the community of actual invaders. Often it is political: the informal disposition of public land becomes a source of patronage for establishment politicians (Moser, 1982, p. 70). Parts of the large invasion of Aguablanca in Cali began this way, initiated by both establish-

Photo 6.1 Las Colinas. General view. Note the informal, but not random, placement of structures and dwellings in various stages of development from shacks to three-story houses.

ment political parties, the Conservatives and the Liberals. In Cali this form of invasion, described as *urbanización clandestino control* (DAP, n.d., p. 43), accounted for 11 percent of the city's additional area through the 1960s.

In Bogotá, the original invasion of Las Colinas and the Polycarpa Salavarrieta *barrio,* both occupying unused hospital land, represent another kind of politically organized informal settlement (Peattie, 1982a, pp. 27–28, 34). They were not stimulated by establishment politicians, but were organized by Provivienda, a radical housing consumer organization, linked to the communists, whose program for providing low-income housing spans the formal and informal sectors (Cardona, n.d., pp. 315–19).

Politically organized invasions are not limited to large cities. In the small town of Pitalito in the southern Department of Huila, for example, the *barrio* of Cálamo, making up nearly 15 percent of the town's area, was an invasion of *ejido* land. The invasion was organized by politicians who wanted to bring in voters from the outside to strengthen their support.[4]

The church is another source of political activism that has stimulated organized invasions. Activist clergy, usually parish priests influenced by liberation theology and acting against the orders of their superiors, organize and provide moral support to groups of their slum parishioners for the takeover and occupation of land owned by the church or religious institutions. For example, the *barrio* of El Paraiso in Bogotá is a result of this process.

Clandestine Developments. The third kind of informal settlement cannot be called an invasion, for it is organized by the landowner. Accordingly, I am using the Bogotá Planning Department's designation for these communities: "clandestine developments." There are differences between these developments and formal market urbanization, but the resulting neighborhoods are often indistinguishable after a few years.

Clandestine developments are usually located on the periphery of the city (Gilbert and Ward, 1982, pp. 92–93) on land that has not been zoned or approved for urban development. Consequently, these developments lack urban infrastructure or services and have no assurance of receiving any in the future. The other difference distinguishing clandestine from formal developments is their residents' lack of legal title to their lots.

Several factors mitigate these apparent distinctions between clandestine and formal developments. In their early stages, clandestine developments and invasions alike provide themselves with the services that local governments and utilities withhold (Carroll, 1980, pp. 2, 16, 35). Common standpipes for water are soon put up, or, in areas lacking water pressure, water is trucked in and sold by entrepreneurs. Residents supply themselves with electricity by illegally tapping power lines, and they apply their common efforts to construct rudimentary sidewalks in areas where poor drainage makes this amenity critical. They organize their own solid-waste removal to the nearest municipal collection point, and use private trucks and taxis or jeeps to provide transportation until the bus lines are extended. Paved roads and sewerage are the main infrastructure needs that remain unmet until provided by public agencies.

Infrastructure and services are not withheld indefinitely: in Bogotá clandestine developments and invasions have traditionally been legalized by the authorities (Carroll, 1980, pp. 1–2), and previous to legalization have even received services from public utilities (Gilbert and Ward, 1982, pp. 110–11). In Bogotá (Gilbert and Ward, 1982, p. 106) and other Colombian cities, political patronage has provided, with some delay, informal settlement communities with the same services that legal developments are theoretically assured of in advance. Clandestine developments initiated by landowners with good political connections are virtually assured of regularization after a few years.[5]

The distinction between full legal title and the property rights enjoyed by residents of clandestine developments is also less than critical. Residents are usually assured that they will not be molested or displaced by the authorities (Gilbert and Ward, 1982, p. 105), and their purchase arrangements give them some equity that is negotiable in the informal market (Carroll, 1980, p. 48; Ingram, Pachon, and Pineda, 1982, p. 11). The final regularization that follows completes the transformation of their title to one that is identical to the titles held by originally legal property owners.

Clandestine developments have become the dominant form of informal settlement in Colombia and other Latin American countries. In Bogotá, their share of the total number of additional housing units constructed increased from 30 percent between 1928 and 1938 to nearly 65 percent between 1964 and 1973 (Jaramillo, 1981, pp. 86–87). They accounted for 28.7 percent of the city's total expansion between 1972 and 1982 (Departmento Administrativo de Planeación Distrital, 1984a, p. 2.7). Today, they make up about one-third of Bogotá's residential areas and constitute an important part of the city's land market (Carroll, 1980, pp. 3–4). Cali's *urbanizaciones piratas* made up 10 percent of its expansion in the 1950s, increasing to 26 percent in the 1960s (DAP, 1982, p. 43).[6] At 31 percent, clandestine developments made up the largest single segment of El Salvador's informal housing stock in 1975 (Harth-Deneke, 1981, p. 86).

While the process of land development for clandestine developments is simplified and speeded up by the absence of planning permission, it is by no means simple, and the transfer from developer to resident takes more than a handshake. The developer may be the landowner or a quasi-legal corporation may be set up for this purpose—*empresas communales* (community enterprises), as they are called in Colombia. The process of sale consists of the would-be homeowner purchasing a share in an *empresa communal* that has obtained a lease with option to buy (*arrendamiento con promesa de venta*) the land from the owner (Harth-Deneke, 1981, pp. 91–92). This share represents the purchased lot, which the buyer pays off over several years. With the last payment, the buyer becomes the owner of the lot, with a clear title if the option to buy has been legally exercised, and with a clouded one if it has not. The latter is usually the case until regularization takes place and the original restrictions on sale and development of the land are waived.

The motives of pirate developers in this process are clear: they can sell and realize a profit on land from which they could not otherwise profit. Evidence is mixed on whether profits are inflated (Harth-Deneke, 1981, pp. 95–96) or whether the developer's savings in "soft" costs (e.g., design and legal fees) are passed on to the buyer. According to the best recent study of clandestine developments, their residents have paid about two-thirds of the cost of a legal minimum-norms parcel for a lot that is usually about 25 percent smaller and that lacks municipal infrastructure and services (Carroll, 1980, p. 10).

Although clandestine subdivisions impose significant costs both on their residents and on society (Harth-Deneke, 1981, pp. 82–83), they have to be viewed positively on balance. As Carroll (1980) has stated:

> Pirate subdivisions fulfill a useful function by providing tens of thousands of families with plots of land that they could not otherwise obtain without resorting to invasion. Buyers rarely lose their lots, despite their illegal tenure. Families build homes on the lots, often upgrading them substantially over the years. Missing services gradually arrive, and over time some *barrios* begin to take on a middle-class appearance. (p. 4)

Policy Implications and Responses

It has become generally recognized that conventional in-kind supply programs of low-cost public housing are simply not an adequate response to the enormous and growing housing deficit in developing countries (Hardoy and Satterthwaite, 1981, pp. 254–55). What is needed is the mobilization of communal and nonformal resources represented by the process of informal settlement of invasion communities and clandestine developments.[7] There are basically two different, but not mutually exclusive, ways of accomplishing this: government simulation of the informal settlement process and enlistment of the informal process itself.

The first approach, simulation and supplementation of the informal settlement process, is what sites and services programs try to accomplish. With all their advantages, I suggest that these programs still have too much in common with conventional housing programs to be able to make more than another dent in the growing demand for urban shelter.

The second strategy enlists the informal settlement process itself. This means more than an attitude of benign neglect and occasional delayed acceptance that has characterized Latin American urban settlement policy and government response to invasions and clandestine development to date. Instead, it means recognizing that the informal settlement, consolidation, and progressive improvement of neighborhoods is a process that accomplishes what it does in spite of severe constraints and handicaps. Public policy and programs can intervene to reduce constraints or eliminate handicaps and thus facilitate a process that is a societal asset. Even if this recognition is based on a pragmatic rather than an ideological consensus,[8] this conclusion is compelling. After all, "few governments in the LDCs have any real alternatives to the use and promotion of self-help strategies if real progress is to be made to overcome present housing deficits" (Lea, 1979, p. 53).

In the context of the second policy approach, two forms of intervention have been advocated and tried. The regulation of the land market and the regularization and improvement of informal settlements are reviewed here, together with the sites and services response, to evaluate their potential for mobilizing informal resources and consequently making a significant addition to the provision of shelter.

Sites and Services

Many analysts and observers have advocated sites and services programs as a more appropriate investment of limited resources for low-cost public housing than conventional housing programs (Abu-Lughod, 1981, p. 132; Gómez 1983, pp. 195–96; Harth-Deneke, 1981, p. 105; Oram, 1979, pp. 46–47; Saini, 1979, p. 88). This they undoubtedly are.[9] But they have their limitations.

First, as Hardoy and Satterthwaite have observed, sites and services programs are still substantially more expensive than true informal housing and are thus out of the reach of the very poor (1981, pp. 254–55). Second, they risk "creaming" the population that the formal housing market does not serve, leaving the most marginal to fend for themselves. They also frequently involve more organized suppliers and workshops than the more marginal ones that benefit from genuinely informal construction (Peattie, 1982b, pp. 133–35). Finally, they share with conventional in-kind housing programs an important trait that is both an asset and a limitation: planning.

Planning and design contribute critical elements to the quality of both conventional housing and sites and services projects: norms that ensure the health, safety, and comfort of the ultimate residents; subdivision layouts that are functional, provide for necessary access and services, and are supposed to offer a pleasing and aesthetic environment; and architectural design or technical assistance that ensures the functional and structural adequacy of the dwelling unit. But these attributes also have costs: their actual direct costs and indirect costs in time and effort of the related planning and administrative procedures that are part of formal housing delivery systems all over the world.

The case of Ciudad Bolívar, a large development project in the southeastern part of Bogotá, graphically illustrates the impact of these indirect costs. Planned by the Caja de Vivienda Popular of the Federal District of Bogotá with the participation of other infrastructure agencies and utilities, three-quarters of Ciudad Bolívar's residential area will be in sites and services development, totaling over 10,000 dwelling units. Before any lots can be offered to the people who have already begun to enroll on the waiting lists, the infrastructure planning and design has to be completed, and construction has to be sufficiently advanced so that roads and services will be available on occupation of the lots. The project includes community facilities, such as schools and clinics, that also have to be planned and designed. Neighborhood retail centers, although largely for informally constructed kiosks and market carts, must also be located and designed, as must the construction centers that will enable the *autoconstructores* to purchase their building materials from small businesses at controlled prices. Finally, the plan envisages several core developments of conventional public housing, which also require planning and design (Caja de Vivienda Popular, 1984, pp. 12–17).

At the same time that this formally administered planning and design process was in progress, the informal settlement process was providing its own responses to pressures for an urban land market and the shelter needs of the poor. A large invasion sprang up on land envisaged for ultimate inclusion in Ciudad Bolívar that had not yet been acquired by the Caja (Photos 6.2 and 6.3). This informal settlement, called Jerusalem, is partly made up of incremental spontaneous invasions by individual households, but is, in effect, largely a clandestine development. This

Photo 6.2 Jerusalem. Construction in progress. In the foreground, the site is staked out for construction to begin; to the right is first-stage-invasion construction of tarpaper and corrugated iron.

Photo 6.3 Jerusalem. Invasion housing. More advanced concrete block construction; note the decorative wrought-iron grilles on windows, combining aesthetics, tradition, and functionality. Note also the pirated electrical connection to the front house.

process is now so institutionalized that the sale of some lots in the invasion area is openly advertised, and has been approved, in spite of the absence of development permits or any planning approval, by the Superintendencia Bancearia (*El Tiempo,* 1984).[10] While the planners, architects, and engineers are at work, the informal settlement process is planning and producing housing in a fraction of the time, and at a considerably lower cost, than even the cheapest lot and dwelling in Ciudad Bolívar.[11]

Land Regulation

Land is a fundamental element in the urbanization process, and there are constant calls for effective land regulation (DAPD, 1984a, p.

2.8; Hardoy and Satterthwaite 1981, pp. 226–27; Molina, 1984, pp. 63–64). But often the same analysts who advocate the "public control of land and the acceptance of public responsibility of the supply of land for all uses in accordance with a plan adopted" recognize that the control of land speculation has totally failed (Mabogunje et al., 1978, pp. 39–40). Controls on land speculation and limits on the supply of land approved for development have been ineffective (Hardoy and Satterthwaite, 1981, p. 234) and have not prevented the manipulation of the market by real estate interests (Moser, 1982, pp. 169–70).

In Colombia, for example, the control of land speculation has been ineffective (Gilbert and Ward, 1982, pp. 103, 110). Before 1978, illegal speculators could be fined 10 percent of the value of the prohibited transaction. This was later raised to 100 percent of the value, with the addition of a prison penalty for the developer. Some observers claim that enforcement of these sanctions has resulted in a noticeable reduction of clandestine developments (Planeación Municipal de Cali, 1979, pp. 57–60). Others do not see any significant change (Gilbert and Ward, 1982, pp. 106, 114–15). Observable reduction in the rate of formation of clandestine developments can certainly be attributed to the slowdown in urbanization, which peaked during and after the *Violencia* (the civil unrest of the 1950s and 1960s). Thus the deterrent effects of the above sanctions, which have rarely been applied, are difficult to estimate. Clandestine developments in Bogotá and Cali continue to grow, and the Superintendencia Bancearia, charged with controlling land transactions, does not rigorously enforce the law (Gilbert and Ward, 1982, pp. 112–13) and approves the sale of land that has not been designated for urban development.

Legalization and Upgrading

The legalization and upgrading of informal settlements has been advocated for high priority in low-income housing policy (Perlman, 1981, p. 185; Soto, 1981, pp. 50–51). The need and the potential are there. In Colombia alone, an inventory taken between 1972 and 1975 revealed that informal neighborhoods in sixty-nine settlements contained 617,000 dwelling units and housed a population of 4.5 million (Soto, 1981, p. 51). Legalization and upgrading of existing informal settlements must therefore claim a significant share of the public resources allocated for low-cost housing. But this policy is limited in two ways.

First, legalization and upgrading, or *regularización,* of existing housing is difficult and expensive, although it is still much cheaper than constructing elaborately planned, high-tech public housing. The legalization process itself requires a considerable investment of public resources, since the difficulty and complexity of the procedure preclude the homeowners from accomplishing the transfer of legal title without a good deal of assistance (PMC, 1979, p. 61). Regularization also involves subdivision adjustments, the provision of infrastructure and services, and access to public credit and technical assistance for improving houses and bringing them up to minimal standards. The Las Colinas project in Bogotá, carried out by the Caja de Vivienda Popular between 1967 and 1975 (Peattie, 1982a, pp. 28–33), is a successful example of such regularization and was intended as the prototype for many others (Photo 6.4). This has not happened, and the reasons are obvious: the resources are not available when regularization has to compete with other housing

Photo 6.4 Las Colinas. Regularization (note path and drainage) and construction in progress. Expansion of a house with a new front wall, while the original house (with corrugated iron roof, on left) is still occupied.

programs for limited public funds, and widespread publicly funded regularization would be an incentive for more invasions and clandestine developments.

The second intrinsic limitation of a legalization and upgrading policy is that, by itself, it would make no contribution toward meeting prospective housing needs, since it only addresses the existing deficit. Low-cost housing policy, therefore, must include a mechanism that can address both of these defects. This mechanism must be able to intervene retrospectively in the clandestine development process in order to minimize the rewards and incentives for such development. It must also generate at least some of the money needed to fund the public services involved in regularization. The same mechanism must also be capable of prospective deployment, offering a framework of incentives and sanctions that will encompass all informal construction and assure the eventual funding and provision of infrastructure and services.[12] Such a mechanism is outlined below.

Planning and Administration

Planning and administration of land-use regulations seem to be more a part of the problem than they are a solution. It has become recognized that planning norms in developing countries reflect the values of Western middle-class society (Mabogunje et al., 1978, pp. 8–15; Rodriguez-Espada, n.d., p. 210). Reduced norms are therefore proposed as a way to make housing more accessible to low-income families (Hardoy and Satterthwaite, 1981, p. 268; Mabogunje et al., 1978, pp. 81–83). Several cities in Colombia, including Bogotá, have introduced reduced-norms (*normas mínimas*) policies, but they have had little impact on the supply of low-cost urban housing. The cost of minimum-norm housing has remained significantly higher than that of housing in clandestine developments (Gilbert and Ward, 1982, pp. 109–10).

The problem is that the cost, complexity, and delays of planning administration far outweigh the benefits promised by the planning process. Plans are made, often at a high level of technical competence, but they are not implemented, or when they are, it is after several years' delay.[13] Planning has proven powerless to direct or regulate the process of urbanization and development in cities like Bogotá and Cali. At the same time, the regulatory bureaucracies, such as the Office of Survey and Records (Aparicio, 1983, pp. 50–51), create delays that increase the costs of housing, which the ultimate user pays. Gómez cites the fact that, on the average, three years pass between the transmission of a proposal for housing construction and the availability of developed sites for occupancy. He also points to the 500 administrative steps necessary to urbanize a lot and transfer it to its ultimate resident (1983, pp. 165–67).

The recognition of these flaws in planning does not seem to preclude the advocacy of more planning, better planning, or more coordination. In a planning agency's own reports and recommendations (DAPD, 1984a, pp. 3.5–3.6, 3.7–3.11) such inconsistency is not surprising, given its own vested interest. It *is* surprising to find the same contradiction among many objective observers, beginning with John Turner's conclusion, after his incisive analysis of the informal settlement phenomenon, that "rapidly urbanizing countries desperately need urban planning" (1968, p. 354), and ending with statements by the Colombian observers cited above (Gómez, 1983, pp. 170–71; Rosas, 1984, p. 105).

If planning is unable to provide a framework for urban development and incurs direct and indirect social costs and delays, the inescapable conclusion is that an abdication or significant relaxation of planning powers is called for. More planning or a utopian degree of coordination is not the solution. It is planning that creates the distinction between the legal and the informal housing markets. Therefore, a modification of the planning role in land-use regulation must be an integral component of any policy that aims to mobilize the informal resources of Third World societies.

A Possible Policy for Low-Cost Housing

The preceding discussion presented policy inferences that can be drawn from a clear understanding of the informal settlement process. It also sketched some dimensions of a feasible policy to enlist this process as a major—perhaps *the* major—element of a national housing effort that would seriously address the shelter needs of the very poor, who are the majority of the Third World population. These policy elements include a reorientation of resource allocation priorities, legalization and upgrading of informal settlements, and a revision of the urban planning role in land-use regulation.

A Reorientation of Resource Allocation Priorities from Conventional In-Kind Housing Supply Programs Toward Programs That Facilitate Informal Settlement and Construction. These programs would have first claim on funds allocated for low-income housing. Such funds would be invested in construction credits for *autoconstructores,* assistance to craftworkers and small materials suppliers (*microempresas*), technical advice for self-construction and self-managment (*autogestión*) projects, and the planning, design, and construction of infrastructure for upgrading the informal settlements which are constantly in the process of development.

The Legalization and Upgrading of Informal Settlements. Comprehensive regularization projects must become more frequent. In the priority scale of public attention and investments, they should outweigh conventional housing and sites and services projects. The few such projects that have been implemented, such as Las Colinas, demonstrate their feasibility and prove the fact that each peso spent on legalizing and upgrading informal settlements has many times more leverage in providing housing than money spent in any other way.

A Revision of the Urban Planning Role in Land-Use Regulation. Planning must abdicate its futile attempt to anticipate, direct, and control the informal urbanization process. Conventional land-use planning and regulation should be restricted to the formal market, which should be defined according to a realistic estimate of the relationship between municipal planning and implementation capabilities. The result of such a modification would be to limit the formal market in land zoned for urbanization to the area already serviced and provided with urban infrastructure and to that relatively small increment for which streets, sewerage, water, and electricity supply networks are in an advanced design stage. At the same time, the development of unplanned land on the urban periphery should be deregulated and decriminalized (Ingram, Pachon, and Pineda, 1982, p. 12).

How can this be accomplished? In particular, what kind of institutional mechanism can be set up to channel the informal land market so as to facilitate informal settlement while enabling subsequent upgrading and provision of infrastructure and services? This cannot take place unless the mechanism includes a way of appropriating part of the value of the land improvement for public investment to benefit residents. To be effective and to avoid some of the pitfalls of past efforts in this direction,[14] such a strategy must incorporate appropriate incentives for participation by all relevant interests: landowners and developers, poor households who are the informal settler–purchasers, and public agencies providing infrastructure and services.

I propose the adoption of a modified version of the model used in Mexico for the regularization of the informal settlements of Netzualcoyotl and Ecatepec in the 1970s (Gilbert and Ward 1982, pp. 95–96). A *fideicomiso* (trust) would implement and administer all sales of unzoned and unserviced land on the urban periphery. This *fideicomiso* could be a new organization or it could be an existing regulatory or public implementation agency, such as the Superintendencia Bancearia or the Instituto de Credito Territorial (ICT). A highly appropriate vehicle for the *fideicomiso* could be the Caja de Vivienda Popular in Bogotá and its local equivalent in other cities.[15]

The *fideicomiso* would administer all land sales, both prospective and retrospective, in the informal market. Retrospectively, it would operate much like the present process of regularization, and any future informal settlements that avoided its intervention would automatically come under its jurisdiction. As in Mexico, the *fideicomiso* would be the mechanism for sharing the proceeds of the land sale among the interested parties, providing residents with legal title to their land and financing the provision of infrastructure and services. Payments for retrospective land sales would be adjusted to give purchasing households a substantial discount, perhaps 20 percent, on their payments. This, together with the prospect of obtaining legal title, should be a powerful incentive for residents to cooperate and to divert their payments through the *fideicomiso*. The developer would receive a portion of the payment representing the undeveloped value of the land plus a reasonable profit. This could amount to perhaps 50 percent of the purchase price. The remaining portion—in this partition, 30 percent of the purchase price—would be held in trust for the *barrio* to finance the provision of its infrastructure and utilities and would be credited against the residents' future-betterment tax assessments (*valorización*).

Prospective land transactions would be made only through the *fideicomiso*. A price would be assessed at a proportion of the value of urbanized land, say, 70 to 80 percent, and the proceeds of the sale would be allocated as suggested above. Any sales not concluded in this fashion that result in clandestine developments would again come under the *fideicomiso*'s retroactive umbrella and would be handled through its regularization process.

An illegal land market with side payments to owners and developers might be expected to emerge, but this is unlikely for two reasons. First, there will be a very large supply of land that is potentially developable in this fashion, thus lowering the price in the informal market to the levels that would be assessed for transactions through the *fideicomiso*. Second, buyers would lack the incentive, and sellers the enforcement mechanism, for the fulfillment of purchase agreements at higher prices.

The *fideicomiso*'s intervention should not raise the cost of land for informal settlement. Just as a more generous allowance of *normas mínimas* construction might lower the cost of land (Carroll, 1980, pp. 96–98), the proposed intervention should have the same effect. Ultimately, the land prices set by the *fideicomiso* should reflect a fair market equilibrium for land that includes only the present value of future services provision.

Conclusion

The informal settlement process is complex, but it is clear that it responds to basic shelter needs for those too poor to participate in the formal market for planned and serviced housing. In Latin America, it is also a reaction to defects in local planning, administrative, and regulatory processes and institutions. To mobilize people's own resources in the solution of their housing deficit, governments need to facilitate the development of informal settlements, including clandestine developments.

Such facilitation must consist of several elements including a much higher priority on legalization and upgrading of existing informal settlements and the abandonment of the futile attempt to plan and control the informal urbanization of peripheral land in the major cities. Instead, a *fideicomiso* (trust) is proposed as an institutional mechanism to internalize the improvement values of this land and allocate the value increment among landowners, informal settlers, and funding for infrastructure and services. Such a *fideicomiso,* it must be emphasized, should not be a formal planning body: it will set no standards, design no facilities, enforce no regulations. Its sole function is simply to allocate and distribute the proceeds of land development that takes place anyway.

A more detailed policy analysis of this proposal should be the subject of further research. This would review possible impacts on—and acceptability by—relevant interests and institutions, and would include the development of detailed organizational designs and allocation approaches for various contexts and contingencies. In the final analysis, of course, the feasibility of this proposal depends on the political will of Latin American societies to transcend the limitations of their current societal and institutional structures in a serious effort to help the poor help themselves.

Acknowledgments

This study was undertaken in Colombia under a Fulbright grant; the support and the help of the Colombia Commission for Educational Exchange, its staff and its Director Eng. Francisco Gnecco Calvo, are gratefully acknowledged. Many people shared their experience and insights with me. All of them cannot be recognized here, but special thanks are due to Arch. Jose Ignacio Sanclemente Villalón, director of the Caja de Vivienda Popular, Bogotá D.E., Arch. Oscar Gómez Villa, director of CENAC, and Professor Luis Roberto Martinez M., director of the Department of Urban Planning, Universidad Nacional de Colombia.

Notes

1. I am using this term for housing and neighborhoods that have been developed clandestinely and outside the formal housing market. These include *invasiones* and *urbanizaciones piratas,* which have been called "squatter settlements" (Dwyer, 1975, p. 3).

2. For example, a survey of the original invaders of the Las Colinas *barrio* in Bogotá, Colombia, shows only 14.59 percent of them with any permanent employment (Centro Colombiano de Construcción, n.d.).
3. Colombia's housing deficit has risen from under 200,000 in 1968 to over 560,000 in 1980 (Departmento Nacional de Planeación, 1981, p. 86); its current deficit is over 750,000 dwelling units (Santana and Casabuenas, 1981, p. 199) and will reach more than 1 million units by the end of 1987 (Aparicio, 1983, p. 48). Bogotá (population 4.2 million) and Cali (population 1.7 million) are Colombia's largest and third-largest cities.
4. This is described as "originating under irregular conditions of tenure" (Universidad Nacional de Colombia, 1983, p. 38; personal communication by one of its authors).
5. Numerous examples of this process in Bogotá and Cali were cited in personal communications.
6. This source gives 1 percent as the proportion of clandestine developments and 7 percent as the total of illegal settlement in Cali's expansion of 3,400 hectares between 1970 and 1979. This is an error; it is contradicted by other data published by the same agency, which suggests that nearly 50 percent of Cali's expansion through the 1970s was illegal (DAP, n.d., pp. 10–11).
7. Colombia has significantly increased its investment in low-income housing in general and self-construction and sites and services programs in particular (Isaza and Molina, 1983, pp. 272–73). Cities such as Bogotá and Cali have introduced special programs for subminimal planning norms and construction standards (DAPD, 1984b, p. 31).
8. The ideological dispute is well reviewed in Gilbert and Ward (1982). Proponents of the thesis that encouragement of informal housing is simply another form of capitalist appropriation of labor offer no policy alternative to the status quo short of a radical restructuring of society.
9. The *barrio* of Poblado in the invasion area of Aguablanca in Cali is an excellent example of a successful sites and services program; it is briefly described in Calderón (1983, p. 99).
10. This agency is charged with regulation of commercial transactions in Colombia and, among these, the sale of land. As such, it is an integral part of the land market control system and is referred to again below.
11. This account should not be understood to be derogatory to sites and services projects in general, or in particular to Ciudad Bolívar. The time lapse is endemic to all conventional public projects. Sites and services projects and targeted low-cost housing assistance are still preferable to massive conventional public housing, as shown by comparing Colombia's and Venezuela's programs (Handelman, 1979).
12. In the land-regulation context, the Superintendencia Bancearia's subdivision control and its threat to confiscate illegal developments and hand them over to the Instituto de Credito Territorial for administra-

tion, or, later, to administrate them itself, were supposed to be such a mechanism (Gilbert and Ward, 1982, pp. 112–13). Its relative failure may be due to several flaws: (*a*) inconsistent and sometimes ineffective administration; (*b*) lack of resources and a consistently low level of enforcement; (*c*) lack of incentive for the residents to cooperate in transferring their payments from the illegal developer to the agency.

13. For example, in the 1972 structural plan for Bogotá, the stages for infrastructure construction and the retention of a greenbelt (Llewelyn-Davies et al., n.d., pp. 14–15, 94–99, 108–10) have not been implemented. The implementation of infrastructure in major cities follows the adoption of master plans by four to five years (Gómez, 1984, p. 168).

14. For example, the failure of the ICT and the Superintendencia Bancearia in their confiscation of illegal developments (Gilbert and Ward, 1982, pp. 112–13); part of the reason for this may have been that developers, who were losing their entire profit, and settlers, who were expected to continue to pay the entire purchase price of their land, had a mutual interest in sidestepping the confiscation requirements, over which legal sanctions were powerless to prevail.

15. This proposal resembles suggestions advanced by Gómez (1984, pp. 195–96) and Robledo (1980, pp. 28–30) and similar ideas (e.g. Harth-Deneke, 1981, p. 103; Mabogunje et al., 1978, pp. 85–86) for an effective redefinition of the public role in assuring adequate land supplies to meet low-income housing needs.

References

Abu-Lughod, Janet. 1981. "Strategies for the Improvement of Different Types of Lower Income Urban Settlements in the Arab Region." In United Nations Centre for Human Settlements (HABITAT), *The Residential Circumstances of the Urban Poor in Developing Countries,* pp. 116–34. New York: Praeger.

Aparicio, Rafael Martínez. 1983. "La Vivienda Popular: Factor de Reactivación Económica y Nuevas Fuentes de Desarrollo Nacional." In *Controversia Sobre el Plan de Vivienda Sin Cuota Inicial,* ed. Fabio Giraldo Isaza. Bogotá: CAMACO, pp. 47–56.

Bernal, Segundo. n.d. "Algunos Aspectos Sociólogicos de la Migración en Colombia." In *Las Migraciones Internes,* ed. Ramiro Cardona Gutiérrez, pp. 55–101. Bogotá: ASCOFAME Division de Estudios de Población.

Caja de Vivienda Popular. 1984. "Informe de Labores: Primer Semestre 1984." Bogotá, June 20. Mimeo.

Calderón, Rivera Mario. 1983. "El Primer Año en una Política de Vivienda." In *Controversia Sobre el Plan de Vivienda Sin Cuota Inicial,* ed. Fabio Giraldo Isaza. Bogotá: CAMACO, pp. 93–100.

Cardona Gutiérrez, Ramiro. n.d. "Asentamientos Espontaneos de Vivienda: Aspectos Sociales de los Programas de Mejoramiento." In *Las Migraciones Internes,* ed. Ramiro Cardona Gutiérrez, pp. 311–27. Bogotá: ASCOFAME Division de Estudios de Población.

Cardona Gutiérrez, Ramiro, Alan B. Simmons, and Ethel Rodríguez-Espada. n.d. "Migración a Bogotá," In *Las Migraciones Internes,* ed. Ramiro Cardona Gutiérrez, pp. 119–77. Bogotá: ASCOFAME Division de Estudios de Población.

Carroll, Alan. 1980. *Pirate Subdivisions and the Market for Residential Lots in Bogotá.* World Bank Staff Working Paper no. 435. Washington, D.C.: World Bank.

Centro Colombiano de Construcción. n.d. "Las Colinas: Estudio de Habilitación Urbana de un Barrio de Invasion en Bogotá, Colombia." Bogotá. Mimeo.

Centro Interamericano de Vivienda y Planeamiento (CIVP). 1958. *Siloe: El Processo de Desarrollo Communal Aplicado a un Proyecto de Rehabilitación Urbana.* Bogotá: CIVP.

Departamento Administrativo de Planeación (DAP). 1982. *Annuario Estadistico de Cali 1981.* Cali: Municipio de Cali.

———. n.d. *Distrito de Aguablanca: Diagnóstico y Plan de Inversión 1984–1989.* Cali: DAP, Municipio de Cali.

Departamento Administrativo de Planeación Distrital (DAPD). 1984a. *Bogotá año 2000: Plan de Desarrollo Económico y Social.* Bogotá: Alcaldía Mayor de Bogota, DAPD.

———. 1984b. "Crecimiento de Bogotá D.E. Colombia 1890–1980." Bogotá: Alcaldía Mayor de Bogotá D.E., DAPD Unidad de Mejoramiento y Coordinación de Barrios Division de Coordinación y Programación. Mimeo.

Departamento Nacional de Planeación (DNP). 1981. "La Edificacion de Vivienda en Colombia," *Revista de Planeación y Desarrollo* 13(3) (July–December), 11–90. DNP: Unidad de Programación Global y Unidad de Desarrollo Regional y Urbano.

Drakakis-Smith, David. 1981. *Urbanisation in the Development Process.* London: Croom-Helm.

Dwyer, Denis John. 1975. *People and Housing in Third World Cities: Perspectives on the Problem of Spontaneous Settlements.* London: Longman.

Gilbert, Alan, and Peter Ward. 1982. "Low Income Housing and the State." In *Urbanization in Contemporary Latin America: Critical Approaches to the Analysis of Urban Issues,* ed. Alan Gilbert with Jorge Hardoy and Ronaldo Ramirez, pp. 79–127. New York: Wiley.

Gómez Villa, Oscar. 1983. "La Politica de Vivienda y la Reactivacion Economica." In *Controversia Sobre el Plan de Vivienda Sin Cuota Inicial,* ed. Fabio Giraldo Isaza, pp. 165–78. Bogotá: CAMACO.

Handelman, Howard. 1979. *High Rises and Shantytowns: Housing the Poor in Bogotá and Caracas.* American Universities Field Staff Report. Hanover N.H.: American Universities Field Staff.

Hardoy, Jorge E., and David Satterthwaite. 1981. *Shelter, Need and Response: Housing, Land and Settlement Policies in Seventeen Third World Nations.* New York: Wiley.

Harth-Deneke, Alberto. 1981. "Quasi-Legal Urban Land Subdivisions in Latin-America: A Solution or a Problem for Low-Income Families." In United Nations Centre for Human Settlements (HABITAT), *The Residential Circumstances of the Urban Poor in Developing Countries,* pp. 82–115. New York: Praeger.

Ingram, Gregory K., Alvaro Pachon, and Jose Fernando Pineda. 1982. *The City Study: Summary of Results and Policy Implications.* World Bank Research Project RPO 671–41. Washington, D.C.: World Bank.

Isaza, Fabio Giraldo, and Ismael Molina. 1983. "Instituciones Financieras de la Vivienda en Colombia." In *Controversia Sobre el Plan de Vivienda Sin Cuota Inicial,* ed. Fabio Giraldo Isaza, pp. 247–86. Bogotá: CAMACO.

Jaramillo, Samuel. 1981. *Producción de Vivienda y Capitalismo Dependiente: El Caso de Bogotá.* Bogotá: CEDE, Faculdad de Economía, Universidad de los Andes.

Lea, John P. 1979. "Self-help and Autonomy in Housing: Theoretical Critics and Empirical Investigators." In *Housing in Third World Countries: Perspectives on Policy and Practice,* ed. Hamish S. Murison and John P. Lea, pp. 49–53. London: Macmillan.

Leeds, Anthony. 1981. "Lower Income Urban Settlement Types: Process, Structures, Policies." In United Nations Centre for Human Settlements (HABITAT), *The Residential Circumstances of the Urban Poor in Developing Countries,* pp. 21–61. New York: Praeger.

Llewelyn-Davies, Weeks, Forestier-Walker & Bor, in association with Kates, Peat, Marwick & Co., Coopers & Lybrand, n.d. *Plan de Estructura para Bogotá: Informe Tecnico Sobre el Estudio de Desarrollo Urbano de Bogotá Fase 2.* Bogotá: Republica de Colombia, Banco Internacional de Reconstruccion y Fomento, Programa de las Naciones Unidas para el Desarrollo.

Mabogunje, A. L., J. E. Hardoy, and R. P. Misra. 1978. *Shelter Provision in Developing Countries: The Influence of Standards and Criteria.* New York: Wiley.

Molina, Humberto. 1984. "Vivienda, Reactivación y Crecimiento Económico," In *Controversia Sobre el Plan de Vivienda Sin Cuota Inicial,* ed. Fabio Giraldo Isaza, pp. 153–64. Bogotá: CAMACO.

Moser, Caroline O.N. 1982. "A Home of One's Own: Squatter Housing Strategies in Guayaquil, Ecuador." In *Urbanization in Contemporary Latin America: Critical Approaches to the Analysis of Urban Issues,* ed.

Alan Gilbert with Jorge Hardoy and Ronaldo Ramirez, pp. 159–90. New York: Wiley.

Oram, Nigel. 1979. "Housing, Planning and Urban Administration." In *Housing in Third World Countries: Perspectives on Policy and Practice,* ed. Hamish S. Murison and John P. Lea, pp. 42–48. London: Macmillan.

Peattie, Lisa R. 1982a. "Settlement Upgrading: Planning and Squatter Settlements in Bogotá, Colombia." *Journal of Planning Education and Research* 2(1) (Summer), 27–36.

———. 1982b. "Some Second Thoughts on Sites-and-Services." *Habitat International* 6(1/2) (Winter), 131–39.

Perlman, Janice E. 1981. "Strategies for Squatter Settlements: The State of the Art as of 1977." In United Nations Centre for Human Settlements (HABITAT), *The Residential Circumstances of the Urban Poor in Developing Countries,* pp. 168–90. New York: Praeger.

Planeación Municipal de Cali (PMC). 1979. "Problemas Legales y Institucionales de la Vivienda Popular en Cali." Cali: PMC, October. Mimeo.

Robledo Uribe, Fabio. 1980. "La Vivienda Popular en Colombia." *Revista Arco* 234 (July), 23–25.

Rodriguez-Espada, Ethel. n.d. "La Incorporación de los Migrantes en la Estructura Económica y Social de la Ciudad de Bogotá," In *Las Migraciones Internes,* ed. Ramiro Cardona Gutiérrez, pp. 179–217. Bogotá: ASCOFAME Division de Estudios de Población.

Rosas, Luis Eduardo. 1984. "Desarrollo Urbana, Planificación y Bienestar." In *Controversia Sobre el Plan de Vivienda Sin Cuota Inicial,* ed. Fabio Giraldo Isaza, pp. 101–5. Bogotá: CAMACO.

Saini, Balwant. 1979. "Site Development and Sanitary Services." In *Housing in Third World Countries: Perspectives on Policy and Practice,* ed. Hamish S. Murison and John P. Lea, pp. 88–99. London: Macmillan.

Santana Rodríguez, Pedro, and Constantino Casabuenas Morales. 1981. "Hacia una Política de Vivienda Popular en Colombia." In *La Vivienda Popular Hoy en Colombia,* ed. Pedro Santana Rodríguez, pp. 191–282. Bogotá: CINEP.

Soto Sierra, Pedro Javier. 1981. "Un Nuevo Enfoque en las Soluciones Habitacionales para Sectores de Muy Basos Ingresos." In *La Vivienda Popular Hoy en Colombia,* ed. Pedro Santana Rodríguez, pp. 45–55. Bogotá: CINEP.

El Tiempo. 1984. "Ciudad Bolívar Últimos Lotes 50,000," classified advertisement, no. 31. June 4.

Turner, John F. C. 1967. "Barriers and Channels for Housing Development in Modernizing Countries." *Journal of the American Institute of Planners* 33(3) (May), 167–80.

———. 1968. "Housing Priorities, Settlement Patterns and Urban Development in Modernizing Countries." *Journal of the American Institute of Planners* 34(6) (November), 354–63.

Universidad Nacional de Colombia (UNC). 1983. *Pitalito: Plan de Ordenamiento Territorial y Urbano 1983–1998*. Bogotá: UNC, Facultad de Artes, Departamento de Planificación Urbana.

Chapter 7

The Growing Housing Crisis in Ecuador

DAVID EVAN GLASSER

An examination of the present housing situation in Ecuador reveals a similarity to the uncontrolled urban growth experienced by most developing nations and represents a microcosm of the housing crisis at present overwhelming Ecuador's South and Latin American neighbors. A study of Ecuadorian housing is particularly useful because the country's small population of 8.6 million (1982 census) and relatively recent squatter settlements, which followed the oil boom of 1972, provide a case study of a nation not yet overwhelmed by urban realities. Furthermore, Ecuador has provided a range of governmental initiatives in assistance to low-income dwellers that furnishes valuable data on self-help housing in developing nations.

In Ecuador housing patterns are largely determined by uncontrolled speculation in urban land, a consequence of historic racial and class domination of land ownership and monopolistic control of primary building construction materials. The most insidious and lasting influence, however, has been the land-ownership profile produced by the peculiar institutions established by the Spanish conquest and its aftermath.

Ecuador's Land-Ownership Profile

Between 1517 and 1533, Spanish adventurers, never numbering more than 2,000, led by Sebastian de Benalcazar, managed to defeat an indigenous army of over 500,000. In Quito and other Ecuadorian cities, plans were laid out in accordance with Spanish custom and included public squares, marketplaces, cathedrals, street grids, and other peninsular planning elements. This policy was soon followed by the infamous *encomienda* and *repartimiento,* which were expected perquisites to *conquistadores* from a grateful crown (Hurtado, 1983, pp. 13–21). The *encomienda* involved forced expropriation of Indian-held cultivated lands. The *repartimiento* had to do with the assignment of a specified number of Indians to carry out agricultural, mining, and construction work.

Although land ownership theoretically remained in Indian hands, it became increasingly clear that the settlers had no intention of returning these lands, which had been carefully cleared and cultivated by the natives through the institution of the *minga* (*Ñucanchic Minga,* 1984, pp. 5–11). This practice, employed throughout the Incan empire, involved broad participation by Indian worker squadrons in the construction of roads, canals, monuments, and other community projects. The *minga* also defined acceptable moral and ethical standards for the Incan society, wherein all land was owned by the community or, rather, held in trust for the entire society by the Inca, the hereditary Sun-king. The Spanish conquerors shrewdly subverted these traditions for their benefit, both with respect to land appropriation and exploitation of labor, the continuing effects of which are still very much evident in the low-cost housing sector.

The Catholic Church, as an institution, as well as individual priests, purchased substantial tracts of land from the crown, so that in 1539, only six years after the establishment of Spanish Quito, royal decree had to be issued curtailing religious acquisition of lands and rents.

From 1537 to 1539, religious establishments acquired more than half of the recorded *haciendas* (estates) (Hurtado, 1983, pp. 13–21). By the eighteenth century the major portion of land was in the hands of the church, principally the Companía de Jesús, which still maintains huge holdings.

The persistence of patterns of exploitation of indigenous lands and labor was such that in 1680 the *Codigo Indiano* (Indian Laws) explicitly forbade slavery, the so-called *huasicama* (forced personal service), and forced communal work based on the model of the *minga.* From the initial establishment of the Spanish colonies in general and in Ecuador in particular, a pattern of extraction rather than investment was set in place with reliance on agricultural rather than industrial wealth. Land ownership in Latin America, instead of industrial or mercantile establishments, became the principal source of wealth for both Spanish and native-born settlers.

Only members of the propertied class could be members of the ruling town councils, the paternalistic character of which is still reflected in the present political structure of Ecuador. As recently as 1962, twenty-eight of the thirty-four *diputados* in the unicameral Senate were *hacendados* (landowners) (Hurtado, 1983, p. 66).

The Ecuadorian war for independence from Spain between 1809 and 1820 was initiated by colonial settlers determined to maintain the status quo in the face of liberalizing tendencies abroad. The French and American revolutions, with their ideas about the inalienable rights of man, were not widely known in South America and had little or no influence on the wars of independence (Hurtado, 1983, pp. 47, 49). There was, in consequence, no appreciable improvement in the working conditions and legal status of the Indians after independence. The taciturn acceptance by the indigenes of the political shifts in Ecuador over the years is movingly captured in this traditional saying:

> *El amo viene, el amo se va*
> *La tierra queda, el indio queda*
> (The landowner comes, the landowner goes
> The land stays, the Indian stays)
> Moncayo (1981, p. 176)

Stimulated by national efforts to increase foreign exchange, the coastal areas began to produce major export crops of cacao and fine straw for panama hats, creating an unprecedented demand for salaried workers and generating the impetus for the first of several internal migrations. This in turn contributed to the growth of Guayaquil and its establishment as the major port city of Ecuador.

Housing Demand and Land Speculation

Until 1950, the year in which Ecuador became a major banana-exporting nation, migration within Ecuador from rural to urban areas and from sierra to coastal regions was related to the search for wage-based employment and a desire to escape from the oppressive conditions of the *haciendas*, primarily those in the sierra. After 1950, the character of internal migration altered substantially in both dimension and objective. With an increased income derived first from banana exports and subsequently from the state-owned petroleum industry, successive military governments (1972 to 1979) invested heavily in manufacturing capacity, producing an increased demand for industrial workers in the larger cities. This refocusing of economic activity, together with the search for amenities and opportunities supposedly available in the urban centers, accounts for the increase in the urban population from 27.3 percent of the nation in 1950 to 51 percent in 1985, half of which is in Quito and Guayaquil (Achig, 1983, p. 23).

An additional factor that contributed to urban migration was the passage of agrarian reform laws in 1964 and 1973, directed to transferring land to Indian *huasipungeros* (sharecroppers), with the intention of maintaining a productive rural agricultural population. How these laws were contravened and served instead to accelerate the rise of spontaneous uncontrolled urban settlements is described below.

The preceding summary describes a nation in which a small number of wealthy landed families were provided with the means to construct substantial estates and villas, first in the cities and then in outlying areas as urban expansion occurred. In effect, lack of concern for urban housing for workers and the poor and the absence of long-range planning were embedded in the earliest policies of the Spanish settlers. A pattern of laissez-faire development became established that now threatens to overwhelm the major urban areas of Ecuador. Housing for workers and the lower classes was built on marginal land from the outset of the colony, using available resources such as tamped earth and adobe (Moncayo, 1981, p. 175). The original settlers, concerned with the productive organization of their agricultural estates and with building their cities in accordance with peninsular models, did not make adequate planning provision for housing workers and Indians. As a consequence, the historic center of Quito, originally well articulated and organized, became increasingly less so as the city expanded, first concentrically and then linearly, when practical considerations of building made it imperative to follow the north–south interandine corridor axis.

In 1940 there was evidence of some peripheral development near coastal cities, at Guayaquil in particular, owing in part to the growing role of Ecuador in banana exports (*Ecuador—20 Años,* 1984, p. 10). At the same time, although to a lesser extent, *urbanizaciones* (ad hoc developments) began to appear in the previously preserved downtown historic districts of Quito as the landed class began to move northward. Eventually, the historic *quintas* (urban villas) were subdivided by the departing landlords, or their intermediaries, to accommodate large numbers of needy families. Typical is the case of one antiquated *quinta* in downtown Quito. In a building that originally housed a single family and dependents, 25 families with 128 persons are now sheltered, unprovided with any municipal services. Current estimates describe 88.6 percent of *barrio* housing as substandard with respect to deficiencies in all infrastructure systems. In Ecuador, as in many Latin American cities, new rural migrants find that moving to unsatisfactory inner-city dwelling units is a necessary intermediate step in the process of establishing themselves in one of the burgeoning peripheral neighborhoods.

From 1948 to 1960, during an era of domestic tranquility and rising prosperity fueled by the banana boom, capital formation occurred similar to that which took place at the turn of the century as a result of cacao exports. Stimulated by international concern for the growing housing problem in developing nations and, in Ecuador, with the encouragement of President Kennedy's Alliance for Progress, the Banco Ecuatoriano de Vivienda (BEV, the Ecuadorian housing bank) was formed in 1961–62 in an effort to provide a mechanism for the construction of low-cost housing (*Ecuador—20 Años,* 1984, p. 13).

In the mid-1960s oil was discovered in eastern Ecuador and by 1972 was generating substantial national income, initiating a short-lived spurt in construction. The inflow of capital into the country, however, had a concomitant impact on real estate prices that soon reduced construction activity and generated an enormous influx of immigrants into urban centers in search of employment and improved living conditions. The resulting land speculation is cited as one of the principal reasons for the rapid diminution in building construction between 1973 and 1977 (Achig, 1983, pp. 54–57).

Then as now, development of land without infrastructure was ostensibly prohibited by the municipality. Nevertheless, through the use of intermediaries, forerunners of today's *lotizadores* or *urbanizadores piratas* (illegal or pirate land developers), wealthy owners sold off parcels of land on an installment basis to property-hungry peasants, leaving the city to provide roads, utilities, street lighting, transport, and other services at public expense (Photo 7.1). The example of Quito is noteworthy insofar as total disregard for the public welfare is concerned. In 1922, in order to expedite land sales, an amenable municipal government, members of which were substantial landholders who would benefit from flexible legislation, established a range of residential neighborhoods with designated rankings (e.g. *primera, segunda, tercera*) that determined minimum lot size, number and type of public amenities, infrastructure, and so on (Achig, 1983, p. 71). This extraordinary measure had the desired effect sought by its framers; the socioeconomic segregationist character of neighborhood subdivision was consolidated to the economic benefit of a handful of private property owners at the cost of the community. The resultant tenfold increase in speculative land values is not an isolated instance, as the modern examples cited below demonstrate. Between 1922 and 1975 the city limits of Quito expanded from 249 hectares to 6,166 hectares, an increase of 2,093 percent (Achig, 1983, p. 68). Between 1963 and 1975, land prices increased throughout Quito, ranging from 33.3 percent to 194 percent in the central historic district, to 798.5 percent in the fashionable northern suburbs. The most extraordinary rise was recorded in the modern central district just north of the colonial center, at a rate of 14,900 percent (Carrión et al., 1978, pp. 60–61).

A consequence of the land speculation has been the creation of an artificial scarcity of land in Ecuador's cities, most notably in Quito. While well-serviced available land in the center city, adjacent to employment, schools, hospitals, parks, and other municipal services remains vacant, Quito is struggling to provide minimal services to its rapidly expanding peripheral communities.

In addition, a number of serious technical problems are arising from unplanned growth in the sierra. Quito, Bogotá, La Paz, and other Andean cities have similar morphologies. Initial settlements are typically

Photo 7.1 *Urbanizaciones.* A hastily assembled illegal land sales operation in downtown Quito.

established in sheltered valleys between the mountain ranges, following a north–south axis. Subsequent expansion takes place in the immediate area of the center and then to the north and south along the valley floor where fertile soils and accessible building sites facilitate development. When the linear character of the city becomes too extended to accommodate efficient transportation and utility networks, expansion occurs in the east–west direction onto the foothills and steep mountainsides. Work opportunities and social amenities at the center provide additional incentives for the establishment of precarious settlements in a concentric relationship to the core. In Quito, the city limit, or *Cota,* has been set for some time at 2,850 meters above sea level, the topographic contour serving as a convenient municipal boundary, determined in large measure by the upper limits of the pumping capacity of the city water system. Planning officials, concerned with proliferation of unplanned peripheral growth, point out that Quito's economic and technical capacity to provide services above the 2,850-meter level will be severely strained. Moreover, they predict that continued unplanned growth will have long-term negative ecological consequences for both the irregular communities and the city as a whole (*Comercio,* 1985c).

The difficult slopes of the Andes typically motivate builders to fill in the *quebradas* (ravines), often with disastrous results. One notorious example is provided by the Mena II community, one of the settlements that came about as a result of the Comité del Pueblo movement, a Quito-based group of squatters demanding land and financial assistance for housing development (*Ecuador—20 Años,* 1984, p. 14). The land on which Mena II was founded in 1922 was purchased, of necessity, at the lowest possible cost and is inhospitable in every respect: poor soil for gardening, stunted vegetation, severe erosion problems, and, worst of all, its location directly over the site of a number of abandoned salt-mine tunnels. Municipal engineers made a perfunctory investigation at the time and assured the city and dwellers that potential problems could be accommodated. In time, the community became established to the point where city services of all kinds were provided. In 1982 huge cavities began to appear beneath houses and streets, which caused several virtually to disappear as a result of subsidence owing to inadequate subsurface drainage. In its quest to obtain land for housing sites, the community of 6,000 had covered over three *quebradas,* carried out apparently with technical assistance from the municipality (Gomez, 1984, pp. 75, 81).

Housing Deficit Projections

The *Glosario de Términos de Asentamientos Humanos* (1978) describes housing deficit as derived from a combination of factors:

- An absolute lack of housing, comparing the difference between numbers of households and number of available units
- A relative deficit in relation to conditions of overcrowding and requirements for replacement of deteriorated units
- Unemployment and/or underemployment resulting in income levels too low to pay for housing and its constituents: land, materials of construction, labor, and financing (p. 39)

This general definition was further refined by the Junta Nacional de Vivienda (JNV), the national housing board, in its 1974 classifications for various types of available dwelling units in relation to its long-range plan for housing development in Ecuador (*Ecuador—20 Años,* 1984, pp. 113–14). The JNV established three basic categories of dwelling units. The first included houses, country homes, and apartments classified as adequate with respect to both size and services. The second included units determined to be currently inadequate, but improvable either in regard to their construction, size, or services. These would include rented rooms, cabins, and shacks. The third category included all additional structures considered inadequate for human habitation and unsuitable for rehabilitation or improvement.

According to the census of 1982, in accordance with these criteria 566,491 dwelling units out of a total of 1,572,358 were characterized as inadequate. To this number, government housing officials add an additional 300,000 or more units to cover population growth since 1982, currently estimated at 200,000 to 250,000 persons per year (at a national average of 5 members per family this translates to between 40,000 and 50,000 new households annually), and the provision for eliminating all multiple occupancy of single family units. The resulting figure of approximately 900,000 units is the generally used current figure employed in establishing housing goals and programs (*Comercio,* 1985e; *Ecuador—20 Anõs,* 1984, p. 114).

Projecting forward to the end of the century, assuming a uniform rate of population increase, the Census Bureau calculates a total requirement for 1,055,755 new dwelling units from 1983 to 2000, which, added to the present deficit, produces a target of approximately 1,600,000 new dwelling units if decent housing is to be provided for all Ecuadorian families by the end of the twentieth century. Thus, somewhere between 100,000 and 150,000 housing units per year will be needed to accommodate both the demographic increase and systematic replacement of deficient dwellings.

The government of President León Fébres Cordero, elected in 1984, ran a successful campaign using the effective slogan *Pan, Techo, Empleo* (Bread, Shelter, Work). As part of his comprehensive housing development strategy, the JNV and BEV were instructed to set in motion the so-called Plan-Techo program, whose main focus was to be the provision of basic shelter for families at the lowest-income levels. This initiative replaced efforts begun in prior administrations to provide core units, such as the Piso-Techo projects in which simple floor slabs on grade and roofs were provided to poor families for completion through self-help construction efforts. It is not my intention at this point to enter the debate over the effectiveness and ethical posture of self-help housing (see Burgess, 1982, pp. 79–85; Turner, 1982, pp. 99–113), although I concede several points raised by Burgess with respect to the commodity status of housing in developing nations. More to the point is the government's purposeful move away from user-developed housing to a program directed toward the building industry, material suppliers, banking interests, and finally the residents. Ecuador has clearly opted to employ the trickle-down theories at present operative in the United States private housing sector in relation to its low-cost housing programs. Critics of Plan-Techo see many parallels between the United States and Ecuadorian housing efforts and predict similar results.

Plan-Techo

The government intends to produce 100,000 housing units annually, primarily directed to low-income population sectors. In order to accomplish this objective, an upper sales limit of fifty times the minimum wage, currently established as S/.8,500 a month (about $80 a month), or about 425,000 sucres, was set as the maximum price of a medium-size unit. An average low-income Ecuadorian family was estimated to have about S/.5,000 a month available for amortizing a fifteen-year loan at 21 percent, which would imply a home not exceeding S/.500,000 (about $4,800). To meet the stringent goals of the Plan-Techo program, prototypical units with an average floor area of 36 square meters (about 400 square feet) were projected using the most basic construction techniques, estimated at S/.6,000 a square meter (about $5.50 a square foot). Also included in the calculation was the assumption that land would be available at unit costs of S/.2,000 a square meter (less than $2 a square foot). An essential component of the plan was the financial structure, which called for long-term loans at rates of 21 percent, well below the then current market of 28 to 29 percent. A key factor in Plan-Techo, this loan rate represents a subsidy that will eventually depend on the nation's solvency with respect to both its internal and external obligations.

The program calls for units to be built by building contractors and sold to residents at stipulated prices. The BEV, Instituto Ecuatoriano de Seguridad Social (IESS), JNV, and savings and loan organizations, together with contractors and landowners, if serving as project sponsors, would receive from the Central Ecuadorian Bank up to 75 percent of total project costs for a two-year period at annual interest rates of 21 percent and would be obliged to repay loans as units were sold. A stipulation of Plan-Techo is the limit of S/.30,000,000 available to individual developers, which is intended to spread work to a large number of sponsors and discourage the employment of multinational contractors whose systems depend on economies of scale.

That there would be criticism of Plan-Techo for social, political, and economic reasons was a foregone conclusion. Certainly, architects and planners were outspoken about the program's deficiencies, attributing to its operation land speculation, monopolization of building materials, and unfair municipal legislation (*Hoy*, July 30, 1985, p. 10A). Most interesting, however, from the standpoint of critical analysis, are the editorial comments prepared by the *Cámara de Construcción de Quito,* which represents the building industry, to whom the major benefits of the program were directed (Cámara, 1984). The following summary of the key points provides a useful description of the principal factors affecting contemporary Ecuadorian housing.

Land Acquisition. Municipal-held land in Ecuador is inadequate to meet the demand for low-cost housing, and as a consequence, land speculation has increased to the point where building sites within the government's guidelines are unavailable (*Hoy*, July 30, p. 2A).

Construction Cost Control. The impact of monopolization within the Ecuadorian construction industry was alluded to earlier. At present there are only four companies importing cement, two importing steel, and correspondingly low numbers in other key sectors such as glass, aluminum products, and electrical and plumbing supplies. There is unquestioned evidence of stockpiling and price fixing of construction materials, stimulated in large part by government programs such as Plan-Techo. The establishment of government policies to force acceleration of production and imports in anticipation of demand and the establishment of national warehouses with stockpiles of necessary materials at controlled price levels are recommended (Carrión et al., 1978, p. 15).

Land Tenure/Legal Restrictions. Increased flexibility on the part of provincial and municipal governments with respect to legal constraints on housing development is recommended. The question of land tenure is the primary concern for most low-income families, and obtaining the *escritura* (land deed) is of overriding importance in spontaneous settlements around Quito.

Project Finances. The government of Ecuador, through the Plan-Techo program, is promulgating the construction of four types of dwelling units of differing size and sales price, directed to buyers at the bottom of the income ladder on the basis of projected family income and ability to pay. The largest unit proposed, for families of six and more members, at 45 square meters is less than half of the minimum floor area required for federally financed housing in the United States. The Cámara estimated a cost of S/.679,300, including realistic land costs, overhead, and a profit margin of 10 to 12 percent, compared with the government's target sales price of S/.425,000.

A projected 37 percent increase in sales price is a consequence of the revised calculations. These new price levels would virtually foreclose the possibility of home ownership for families at the lowest-income levels, whose capacity to pay even the rates established by Plan-Techo is seriously in question. While the government has based its plans on assumptions related to minimum salary levels, the fact is that many Ecuadorians earn wages well below this level, and many operate within the informal income sector relying principally on a barter economy. According to a summary estimate, all of the low-income and lower-middle-income classes, constituting 67.2 percent of the population, fall below the S/.400,000 credit qualification level; thus, two-thirds of the population could not qualify for the minimal housing proposed in the Plan-Techo program.

Foreign Companies and Loans. At present, building companies from Mexico, Spain, France, Sweden, and the United States are in Ecuador and are interested in low-cost housing production, a fact that deeply troubles the Ecuadorian construction industry. The government, in an effort to fulfill its campaign promises, has shown itself willing to entertain various alternatives if it means increased production of badly needed units. Nevertheless, arrangements with foreign construction firms have invariably meant obtaining external credits, thereby adding to the already unmanageable foreign debt. Virtually everyone involved with the development of housing in Latin America deplores the impact of external indebtedness on developing nations in general and low-cost housing policies in particular (*Milwaukee Journal,* 1983). The $48 billion debt endangers the fragile emergent democracies on the continent and serves to exacerbate income disparity among class levels, since austerity programs directed toward debt service invariably curtail social housing programs (Burgess, 1982, p. 82).

San Enrique de Velasco

San Enrique de Velasco, located in northwest Quito, is only one of more than 200 marginal communities formed in the past twenty-five years. It represents a paradigm for such neighborhoods throughout Ecuador with respect to its formation and its relationship to government policies.[1] The community, settled from 1964 to 1967 in the Parroquia Cotocollao district of the city, is located in the foothills of the sierra, immediately adjoining the exclusive club Tenis Quito. The site consists of 25 hectares and was originally owned by the Freire family. Under the terms of the 1964 Agrarian Reform Act, the Freires were obliged to sell their property to the *huasipungeros* (sharecroppers), who then had limited cultivation rights on the property in return for labor provided to the landowner. The 1964 Act had as its principal objective the return to agricultural production of certain lands held by absentee landowners and their distribution to sharecroppers who had lived on and farmed these parcels. Ostensibly directed toward increased social equity and utility, the act was subverted by the landholding aristocracy from its outset and, in consequence, had marginal impact on land tenure for the underclass.

The limited number of small farms resulting from the agrarian reform in large part reflects actions by the large landholders, who, in anticipation of the 1964 act, forcibly removed *huasipungeros* from the most fertile lands to arid, unprofitable sites. This was coupled with a move to increased mechanization on large farming tracts (Achig, 1983, p. 23), which explains to a great extent the increased immigration of rural workers to Quito, Guayaquil, and sixteen or so medium-size cities between 1964 and 1971. In San Enrique de Velasco, the owners readily transferred the steeply sloped, clayey land to the sharecroppers. In fact, governmental intervention often serves to create and enhance the exchange value of urban land to the benefit of landholders, even when the land is of marginal value (Carrión et al., 1978, pp. 14–16; Yunovsky, 1976).

The *Patrimonio Familiar Agrícola* (Agricultural Family Landholding Act) was passed in 1967 to protect Indian land rights and in response to efforts to subvert land reform. Indian families without machinery, equipment, or the means to obtain them found themselves with land but without the technical or financial resources to produce at more than subsistence levels. Consequently, many *huasipungeros* found that they had no alternative but to sell to third parties through intermediaries in contravention of the 1967 law. This, together with the subdivision that occurred through inheritance, transformed the community from an original 8 lots to 273 lots, ranging in size from 176 square meters to 6,405 square meters, 90 percent of which are without current legal title. The community has a population of 881 persons in 189 housing units, roughly evenly divided between single and two-family units.

The process of moving San Enrique de Velasco from its precarious formation to legal status within the municipality represents a formidable undertaking for the planning authorities. The intitial step involves the neighborhood's being registered as such in accordance with the 1966 *Ley de Cooperativa y su Reglamento* (Law for the Formation and Regulation of Housing Cooperatives) which provides for the formation of *cooperativas* and *precooperativas* and grants legal status to new communities. The next critical step is the extension of municipal boundaries to encompass the new community. San Enrique de Velasco is situated at 3,000 meters above sea level and, until recently, above and beyond the city limits, established at topographic contour 2,850. In June 1985, legislation legalized eighteen settlements, including San Enrique de Velasco (*Comercio*, 1985f). An estimated 200,000 persons in over 200 settlements, representing one-fifth of Quito's present population, will eventually receive legal status as property owners as a result of the program. Unless and until major structural changes with respect to distribution of land and resources are brought about, this process of ex post facto legalization will remain the norm in Ecuador.

Once assigned cooperative status and included within the city limits, San Enrique de Velasco was entitled to receive the services of the office of Barrios Periféricos (an administrative agency for marginal neighborhoods), which undertook a complete topographic and boundary survey; an inventory of the location, type, and construction character of all existing structures; and a socioeconomic survey in order to prepare a comprehensive site plan (Figure 7.1). The present law calls for the municipality to (*a*) accept the built environment as found; and (*b*) discuss with the *cooperativa* any proposed changes to land distribution, circulation, open land, and so on. Through the active participation of the board of three elected community representatives, a majority of families was consulted and eventually approved site modifications.

With respect to the economic viability of the San Enrique de Velasco community, surveys carried out by the Barrios Periféricos provide compelling evidence that the government's ambitious Plan-Techo program cannot reach the most needy at the bottom of the income ladder. For instance, only 9 percent of the community could be described as being above the subsistence level of S/.10,000 ($95) a month and only 54.3 percent of the population was defined as employable. Of the employable, only 48.6 percent are gainfully employed. Thus, only one-quarter of the community can be described as wage earners.

Educational levels of residents of San Enrique de Velasco are characteristic of most squatter settlements. The overwhelming majority, 66 percent, has completed only primary school. An additional 14 percent has completed some secondary schooling. Of the total, 18.9 percent of residents eighteen years old and older have some degree of literacy. In spite of the relatively limited educational experience of the community, most families express a great desire for increased educational opportunities for their children. This points up a recurrent planning problem faced by settlements such as San Enrique de Velasco. In their initial stages, site layout is either done ad hoc or with the help of *urbanizadores* more interested in quick sales than in thoughtful planning. Land for communal amenities such as parks, health services, schools, and the like is either forgotten or reduced to a minimum in order to maximize profits. Consequently, when government intervenes, as in this instance, land redistribution is needed, which invariably causes technical and emotional problems for the residents.

The community lacks all basic services, and its dwelling units are generally of inadequate size and construction. Currently under consideration are plans for installation of septic tanks and communal water taps, which represent the extent of government authorization. Also being studied are legal and economic mechanisms to permit homeowners to improve and expand their houses. This is particularly problematic because the absence of land deeds and the lack of affiliation with

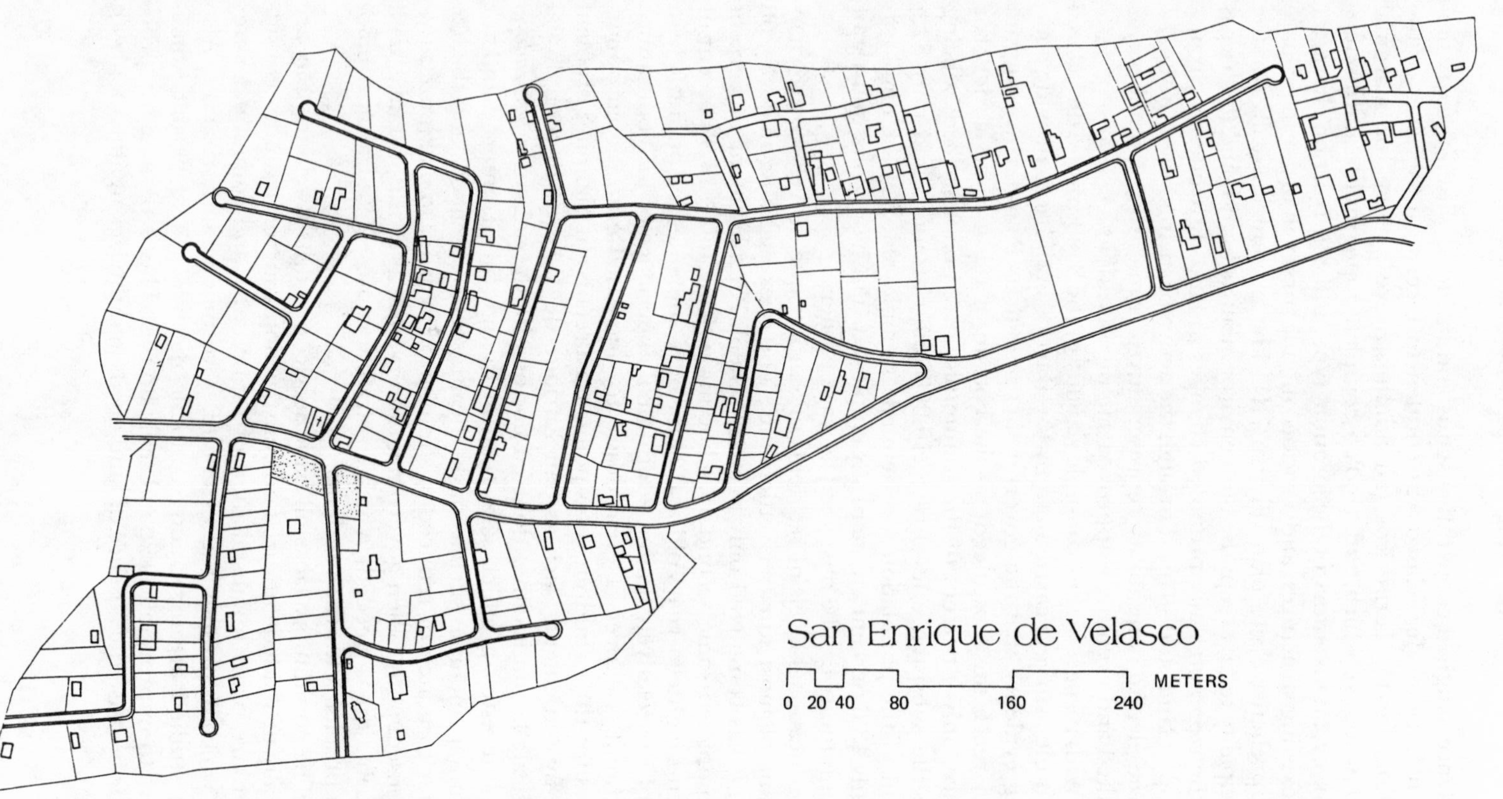

Figure 7.1 San Enrique de Velasco. The site plan shows existing homes and the consolidation of existing road patterns in accordance with municipal standards and lot boundaries. This kind of drawing provides the basis for legalization of land tenure and future civic improvements within the community. (Illustration by Lesley Bain)

IESS, to which only regularly employed workers can belong, make obtaining financial credit almost impossible.

Policy and Funding Issues

The IESS does not provide coverage for all Ecuadorians, particularly not for those most in need of assistance. Nevertheless, together with the BEV it represents the main source of housing mortgage money for middle- and lower-middle-class families. The present government, in undertaking the Plan Techo program, has discovered that acquisition of sufficient funds at rates within the ability to pay of low-income residents is a major obstacle to its implementation. Recently, the president of Ecuador attempted executive action to force the autonomous IESS to make available long-term mortgages at 10 percent annual interest rates to low-income families (prevailing rates are 28 percent to 29 percent). Many critics viewed this attempt on the part of the national government to tamper with a self-sustaining agency as an action that would reduce IESS to bankruptcy (*Comercio,* 1985a).

Pressures within Ecuador to distribute costs of social housing across the financial spectrum have resolved themselves in highly contrasting ways. On June 11, 1985, the National Congress passed legislation exempting holders of mortgage obligations from any income tax, as a measure intended to stimulate housing construction through increased credit fluidity (*Comercio,* 1985b).

Recognizing the crisis proportions of the housing deficit in Ecuador and the potential danger of autocratic intervention from the executive branch, the governing council of IESS reluctantly determined to allocate 20 percent of its mortgage funds for those affiliates with incomes below the S/.8,500 limit (*Comercio,* 1985d).

Some organizations, such as the Asociación Latino Americano para Habitación, Urbanismo y Arquitectura (ALAHUA), a privately funded architectural and planning organization that promotes low-cost housing in Latin America, envision densification strategy as a potential key to financial and physical success. This approach makes possible land sales to newcomers and generates income that the community and individuals can use for improvements. In the view of many Ecuadorian planners, the resulting increased density has the additional benefit of serving to reestablish the urban street, which random settlement has all but obliterated. Experience has shown, however, that *barrio* settlers tend to resist efforts at increased densification, even to their economic disadvantage. As has been pointed out, secure land tenure is the uppermost consideration in all irregular settlements, and attempts to modify property boundaries often meet with strenuous resistance (Castells, 1983, pp. 88–93; Turner, 1967, p. 11). Thus, Ecuadorian planners are faced with the compound problem of attempting to resolve the growing housing deficit while undertaking to maintain the urban character of the cities. In most Latin American countries these goals have proven to be mutually exclusive.

Conclusion

Present governmental efforts to provide low-cost housing in meaningful quantities are inadequate to meet current demands of 40,000 to 50,000 new households per year in addition to replacement of substandard units. Land acquisition and legalization are central factors in providing low-cost housing. Programs that encourage limited-cost, low-profit housing construction without concomitant efforts to acquire land through eminent domain or other means are unlikely to be successful, in view of the present uncontrolled speculation in land prices fueled by government efforts to solve the housing problem.

Subsidies for social housing are a necessity but are politically difficult to obtain. Redirection of nationally derived tax revenues makes more economic sense than does reliance on international programs such as the Agency for International Development (AID), which exacerbates an already compromising external debt. The banking community in Ecuador will have to develop a more flexible system of credit allocation with respect to low-income sectors. The ability of housing *cooperativas* to obtain long-term loans is a sine qua non for their continued development and maintenance. A precedent in this regard was established in 1982 by the Cooperativa Santa Faz in Rio Bamba where a small number of families obtained a privately financed mortgage to develop a self-help-constructed housing project. The abilities and desire of low-income settlers to build houses and meet debt obligations is not fully understood or appreciated by either private or public credit-granting agencies. The evidence shows that when continued homeownership is at stake, bank repayments are scrupulously made by most settlers (Photo 7.2).

Government intervention in purchasing, storing, and distributing building construction materials is necessary if cost containment is a serious objective. Monopolization of supplies in a growth economy is a fact of life in Ecuador and Latin America in general. Additional measures to reduce reliance on imported materials and methods are needed as well. This is a complex issue, since local building codes often establish standards of construction that, in the view of many, are unreasonable and unrealistic where low-cost housing is concerned (Achig, 1983, p. 11; Connolly, 1982, p. 156). Even more difficult to resolve is the resistance many settlers evince with respect to available and appropriate technologies.[2] The desire for modernity and contemporaneity seems to outweigh common-sense financial considerations for many marginal residents.

Photo 7.2 Self-help house in Rio Bamba. The upper-level rental unit was added by the owners after ownership of land was consolidated and the basic house completed.

Thus, many unfinished concrete frame and brick houses may be seen where adobe dwellings might have long since been completed (Photos 7.3 and 7.4).

Until major shifts in the mechanisms of economic distribution occur in Ecuador, incremental development of existing communities represents the most effective means of achieving progress in social housing. Government efforts to legalize land in existing neighborhoods, and to provide planning services, basic infrastructure, and eventually funding for improvements to existing units, while imperfect in many respects, seem to be realistically directed and offer some hope for the consolidation of viable neighborhoods for low-income residents.

Further efforts with respect to financial and technical assistance for upgrading projects are needed. The ability of Ecuadorians to undertake their own housing construction has been amply demonstrated. As in most developing nations, through their own resources, the people have been able to provide housing that the government could not offer. The most productive investment available to the nation is in this form of activity. Unfortunately, policies necessary to provide meaningful assistance to low-income self-help builders are unlikely to materialize in the present political climate, which favors continued support to the formal sectors of the economy.

Photo 7.3 San Enrique de Velasco. Rapidly erected *mediaguas* (leantos), which will be improved and expanded over time.

Photo 7.4 San Enrique de Velasco. Concrete frame and block construction with plastered facade, which is preferred by most residents over houses built with indigenous materials.

Acknowledgments

I gratefully acknowledge the contributions of a number of Ecuadorian colleagues without whose assistance I could not have completed this work. Arq. Guido Díaz Navarrete, president of the Colegio de Arquitectos Ecuatorianos, Nucleo de Pichincha, explained the intricate workings of Ecuadorian housing politics. Dra. Jenny Hidalgo, director of the Unidad Ejecutora de Barrios Periféricos of Quito, provided many hours of instruction regarding the planning and social realities of Quito's squatter settlements. Arq. Fernando Chavez, of the Asociación Latino Americano para Habitación, Urbanismo y Arquitectura (ALAHUA), provided a model of enthusiasm for the rights of the homeless. Dra. Susana Jacome introduced me to the best and the worst of Ecuador. I also express my appreciation for support provided by the Center for Latin America at the University of Wisconsin–Milwaukee for several summers of research and finally for the assistance provided by the Fulbright Commission, both in Washington, D.C., and Quito.

Notes

1. Much of the following information derives from a series of discussions with the principal municipal planning officer in charge of the Unidad Ejecutora de Barrios Periféricos in Quito (Hidalgo, 1985).
2. See Chapter 4 for a more complete discussion of self-help construction.

References

Achig, Lucas. 1983. *El Proceso Urbano de Quito.* Published under the auspices of the Centro de Investigaciones (CIUDAD) and the Colegio de Arquitectos (CAE) (Nucleo de Pichincha) Tercer Mundo.

Burgess, Rod. 1982. "Self-Help Housing Advocacy: A Curious Form of Radicalism, A Critique of the Work of John F. C. Turner." In *Self-Help Housing: A Critique,* ed. Peter M. Ward, pp. 55–97. London: Mansell.

Cámara de la Construcción de Quito. 1984. *Boletin/Tecnico Informativo* no. 19 (November). Entire issue devoted to a detailed critique of Fébres Cordero government's housing program entitled *Plan-Techo.*

Carrión, Diego, et al. 1978. *Quito, Renta del Suelo y Segregación Urbana.* Quito: Coleccion Premio, Ediciones Quito.

Castells, Manuel. 1983. *Movimientos Sociales Urbanos.* 7th ed. Mexico City: Siglo Veintiuno Editores.

El Comercio (Quito). 1985a. "IESS Se Afectaría si Se Aplica Formula para Plan-Techo." June 12, p. A1.

———. 1985b. "Congreso Aprobo Reforma a Ley de Impuesto a al Renta." June 12, p. A2.

———. 1985c. "Es Indispensable Planificar Crecimiento de Quito." June 14, p. C8.

———. 1985d. "IESS: 20% de Prestamos Hipotecarios Asignarán para Vivienda Social." June 24, p. D1.

———. 1985e. "Estudian Política de Vivienda en Ecuador." June 27, p. A6.

———. 1985f. "Legalizan 18 Asentimientos en Barrios Periféricos." June 29, p. A2.

Connolly, Priscilla. 1982. "Uncontrolled Settlements and Self-Build: What Kind of Solution? The Mexico City Case." In *Self-Help Housing: A Critique,* ed. Peter M. Ward, pp. 141– 74. London: Mansell.

Ecuador—20 Años de Vivienda (Ensayo). 1984. JNV–BEV Gobierno Constitutional 1979–1984. Quito: Impresion Editorial Fraga, July. Limited edition publication describing housing policies in Ecuador over the past twenty years.

Glosario de Términos de Asentamientos Humanos. 1978. Mexico City: Secretaria de Asentamientos Humanos y Obras Publicas (SAHOP).

Gomez, Nelson. 1984. "La Mena II, un Barrio de Quito con una Lesión Congeita." In *Quito, Aspectos Geográficos de su Dinamismo. Documentos de Investigación* no. 5, pp. 75–81. Quito: CEDIG.

Hidalgo, Jenny. 1985. Conversations with the director of the Unidad Ejecutora de Barrios Periféricos, a separate agency of the Quito Planning Department charged with dealing with the recent influx of peripheral neighborhoods in the city, May 25 to July 29, 1985.

Hoy (Quito). 1985. "Plan-Techo Es una Farsa." July 30, pp. 2A, 10A.

Hurtado, Oswaldo. 1983. *El Poder Político en el Ecuador.* 5th ed. Quito: Editorial Planeta del Ecuador.

Ley de Cooperativa y Su Reglamento. 1966. Municipal law no. 1031, promulgated September 20, 1966. Published by the Municipio de Quito.

Ley de Reforma Agraria. 1964. Registro Nacional de Derechos de Autoridad no. 0644. Quito: CEPSI.

Milwaukee Journal. 1983. "The Latin Debt Bomb." Series reprinted from issues of *Milwaukee Journal,* December 4–9.

Moncayo Andrade, Abelardo. 1981. "Pensamiento Económico de Abelardo Moncayo Andrade." In *Colección de Historia Económica,* no. 1. Guayaquil: Banco Central del Ecuador y la Universidad de Guayaquil, Facultad de Ciencias Económicas.

Ñucanchic Minga. 1984. Publication in Quechua and Spanish explaining the Incan practice of the Minga. Quito: CEDEP, Centro de Educación Popular.

Turner, John F. C. 1967. "Barriers and Channels for Housing Development in Modernizing Countries." *Journal of the American Institute of Planners* 33(3) (May), 167–81.

———. 1982. "Issues in Self-Help and Self-Managed Housing." In *Self-Help Housing: A Critique,* ed. Peter M. Ward, pp. 99–113. London: Mansell.

Yunovsky, Oscar. 1976. "La Renta del Suelo a la Configuración del Espacio y Medio Ambiente Urbanos." Paper presented at the Eleventh Congreso de Planificación, Guayaquil, Ecuador.

Chapter 8

Meeting Shelter Needs in Indonesia

CARL V. PATTON AND LEKSONO PROBO SUBANU

Meeting shelter needs takes on a special significance in Indonesia, which has one of the lowest per capita annual incomes of all countries in Southeast Asia ($580), a rapidly growing population with half of its members under twenty years of age, and little in the way of public infrastructure. Less than 9 percent of Indonesia's population is served by public piped water systems, and an even smaller percentage has access to public sewerage systems (Department of Public Works, 1984).[1] Even with these limitations, the people of Indonesia have managed to house themselves, albeit a major portion of the need is filled by user-built and temporary housing in the nation's *desa* (rural villages) and *kampung* (urban settlements).[2] A substantial portion of Indonesia's housing stock—perhaps half of its 28.4 million units—was built by the people who occupy it.

Most of Indonesia's population growth is taking place in its urban centers, which grew at a rate of 5.3 percent a year between 1971 and 1980. Yet only one-quarter of the country's population of 162 million now lives in urban areas. The majority of these urban residents lives in the larger centers, with more than 8 million living in Jakarta, the nation's capital and largest city, and half of the total urban population living in the ten largest cities. Although there is a transmigration effort to spread the population more evenly across the country through voluntary or induced migration of families from the crowded areas of Java to agricultural areas on the outer islands, best guesses are that the rural-urban shift will continue and will result in continued rapid growth in the urban areas (Hamer et al., 1986, pp. 12–16).

Demographers place Indonesia's year 2000 population near 200 million, with well over one-third of these people living in urban areas. This urban population growth has many implications. Important among them are the increasing demand for urban housing and for employment to provide a means for consumers to purchase housing and related services. One estimate is that 200,000 new urban housing units will have to be constructed annually to meet the country's housing need by the year 2000 (World Bank, 1980, p. 2).

In this chapter we discuss the current housing dilemma in Indonesia, describe the nature and character of *kampung,* report on the Indonesian government's Kampung Improvement Program, and analyze the positive and negative aspects of the *kampung* as a means of providing needed low-cost housing.

The Extent of User-Built Housing

It is not possible to determine precisely the number of temporary or user-built housing units in Indonesia. The 1980 census shows 30,263,273 households (6,167,198 urban households) living in 28.4 million housing units of all types, 22.8 million of these units being in rural areas and 5.6 million in urban areas. Most self-help housing is located in rural areas, and as much as 80 percent of the rural units are, in whole or part, user built. In urban areas, this figure is somewhat lower, with estimates of up to 50 percent for some places. As an example, for the Special Province of Yogyakarta, which includes the city of Yogyakarta and four *kabupaten* (counties), housing is grouped into four quality categories, based on the materials used for roofs, walls, and floors. The lowest class (category IV) is likely to be the most temporary. About 45 percent of the housing in the city and the surrounding urbanized area is in this class, as compared to 90 percent of the rural housing (Statistical Office, 1980). If we can assume that the temporary housing units are user built, a rough estimate can be made of the amount of such housing in Yogyakarta. It seems reasonable to assume that a substantial proportion of housing in Indonesia, perhaps 50 percent or more, is user built.[3]

We assume that a house does not have to be built by the owner from the ground up to qualify as user or owner built. But a house designed by the owner and completely built by workers under the supervision of the owner would not qualify as user built. The boundary in Indonesian urban areas may well be moving toward the latter extreme, as most housing in the urban *kampung* is being built in varying degrees with the help of skilled labor. Even in the rural *desa* the more difficult tasks, such as carpentry, are being carried out by skilled workers, while the owner handles the less-skillful components, such as foundations and walls. Labor-intensive tasks, such as the erection of bays and installation of roofs, may be done with mutual help of the neighbors (the *gotong royong* tradition). Some of the more purely owner-built housing in the urban *kampung* is constructed this way, employing the mutual help of old neighbors from the original villages who come expressly for the occasion.

The *Kampung* as a Type of Settlement

The *kampung* is a very important part of the Indonesian city, as approximately two-thirds of the urban population lives in such areas. The Indonesian word *kampung* is typically used to refer to a certain type of residential area in the city, as opposed to the word *desa,* which means a village or rural residential area. The word *kampung* also carries the idyllic connotation of homeland or place of birth. We are examining the *kampung* as an urban residential area with certain characteristics.[4]

Historically, *kampung* were autonomous settlements or villages located on pockets of rural land or on the fringes of Indonesian cities. As these areas became more crowded, their standards of sanitation remained low, with the resulting prevalence of disease and poverty. City administrations became concerned about the effect the settlements might have on the living conditions of the city as a whole—referring actually to the European parts of the city. Although it took much effort to overcome associated legal and financial problems, such autonomous villages were finally abolished and incorporated into the municipal administrative hierarchy (Cobban, 1970, pp. 138–61). One consequence was that city governments then became responsible for improving the living conditions within *kampung*.

Today's cities are also incorporating surrounding settlements into their administrative domains, but for a different reason. They wish to control the extension of urban activities. This explains why cities like Semarang, which has expanded to several times its original size, contain large percentages of rural areas (80 percent) and rural agricultural populations (20 percent). Other cities, like Yogyakarta, have been unable to expand their administrative boundaries, even though the surrounding villages are quickly turning into residential areas with definite urban characteristics.

The original *kampung* residents were typically rural, generally less educated than the average urban dweller, poor, and considered to be lower class. This is how the word *kampungan* came to mean uncivil or ill-mannered behavior. Nevertheless, *kampung* residents have retained many of the positive aspects of rural life, such as social traditions, neighborliness, community cohesiveness, and the *gotong royong* tradition, by which many services that otherwise would have to be paid for can be rendered on an exchange basis among neighbors. This system has been deliberately maintained, even though some *kampung* residents are becoming less interested in participating in such community activities and would prefer to pay for services.

There are basically two kinds of urban *kampung*. One is the consistently poor and overcrowded centrally located *kampung*; the other is the less crowded, peripheral, and typically higher-income *kampung*.[5] The poorer, overcrowded *kampung* are filled with houses packed so closely together that to reach a house one may have to squeeze through between the walls of other houses. These *kampung* are usually located on appropriated or marginal land close to the activity centers of the city, in many instances behind a row of middle- to high-income houses or stores. We shall refer to these as *central kampung*. The proximity of central *kampung* to activity centers makes them attractive to the poorer segment of the population and to unskilled migrants. Activity centers are their primary source of income as low-level public servants, food peddlers, garbage collectors, scavengers, or other informal-sector workers. With these low-paying occupations (approximately a dollar a day), the residents of central *kampung* cannot afford conventional housing and have to revert to self-help housing, often building houses out of scrap materials on appropriated private or government land. These people live closely together and lose most of their privacy in order to live cheaply and near their workplaces.

The overcrowding of the central *kampung* is a relatively recent phenomenon. The larger cities on Java have been receiving increasing flows of rural migrants since the end of World War II, and these migrants typically settled in the central *kampung*. As the original central *kampung* became overcrowded, the incoming migrants began to settle on marginal lands such as river banks, in abandoned Chinese cemeteries, along railways, and on private or government-owned vacant land close to the centers. As time went by and no public action was taken against the squatters, these new central *kampung* became established residential areas, although with primarily temporary housing and no definite status of land ownership. This process of *kampung* formation is still occurring and is a massive headache for urban governments wishing to keep an orderly city. The size of central *kampung* varies from 15 hectares to 120 hectares with densities ranging from 350 to 1,250 persons per hectare (Silas, 1984a, p. 72).

The second kind of urban *kampung*, the peripheral *kampung*, is less crowded and has better-constructed houses with higher-income residents. These *kampung* are generally located farther from urban activity centers, but still within easy reach of most urban services. They may be in peripheral areas either within or outside the municipal boundary line. Not being the primary target of rural migrants, and having larger tracts of land, the peripheral *kampung* retained most of their spaciousness well into the 1960s. As the national economy improved, and more people could afford better housing, people began to consider these peripheral *kampung* as land resources, and middle-class families started to move into them. This movement caused increased building densities, but it introduced better-constructed houses into the *kampung*, increasing the value of *kampung* land.[6] With the movement of higher-income families into *kampung,* there appears to be a beneficial relationship between lower- and higher-income families, with the lower-income people providing services, for pay, to the higher-income people.

Problems of Land Ownership

Kampung are often located on government-owned land or, as are many central *kampung,* on appropriated private land. Although squatting is prohibited on government land, and the law provides for criminal sanctions, little has been done to remove squatters except from areas near waterways, along railways, and in greenbelt zones. When the law against squatting was passed, it contained a provision for legalization of squatter occupations prior to 1954. Furthermore, regulations prohibit evictions by public organizations or individuals without the consent of the mayor.

Kampung housing on appropriated land generates land-ownership problems. On the one hand, the squatter risks making a capital investment that may be taken away when the ownership of the land comes into question. On the other hand, the owner of the land may not be able to regain control of the land after it has been used for some time by squatters.

Many existing *kampung* are slated for removal over the next ten to fifteen years, but moving the squatters to another area presents a problem. On Java, the problem is especially troublesome because of the *ngindung* system, a feudal mechanism of exchange, where a landowner allowed a person or family to build a house on the land in exchange for services rendered to the owner. This problem exists in Yogyakarta where many large landowners lived close to the urban center (the *Kraton*). These landowners, members of the sultan's court, allowed people to live on their lands under the *ngindung* system. The servants and domestics felt honored to be allowed to live there and could hardly be called squatters! With this system, however, after some decades, more buildings must be put up to house later generations, and the persons occupying the land take root. It becomes difficult to make them vacate their homes, and it requires substantial effort and funds for the original landowner to clear or sell the land. Court settlements have resulted in users having to buy the land if they wish to remain. *Kampung* relocations are negotiated on a case-by-case basis, with a settlement price established for the dwelling owner.

Part of the difficulty over land tenure can be traced to the lack of land registration. The process is time-consuming, and the informal fees are so high that there is little incentive to register and obtain a title for land. The government recently launched a national program to register land ownership, but this does not eliminate the problem for the landless residents of the urban *kampung*.

Credit for home improvements is also difficult to obtain in Indonesia. Banks and individuals are not likely to lend funds because of the lack of security of title. Even when loans are secured by a registered title, it is difficult to remove a mortgagee from the property if there is a default on the loan. Fortunately, the credit situation has improved significantly, especially for the lower-middle-income group and those above that level. The national development corporation, PERUMNAS, has been producing low-cost houses that can be acquired with long-term loans (up to twenty-five years) at low interest rates. Housing developers have been given incentives and credit facilities to subdivide land and build houses that can be bought on credit from the bank. However, these facilities can be used only by people who can show evidence of ability to repay the loans. This can hardly be done by new migrants from the villages or street vendors who cannot guarantee a steady income. To them, self-help *kampung* housing is still the best answer to their shelter needs.

The Indonesian government has recognized that *kampung* provide a major source of shelter for poor households. A nationwide Kampung Improvement Program (KIP) has been established in the hope of improving shelter conditions. Before analyzing that program, however, we describe several *kampung* and present the pros and cons of the *kampung* as a source of low-cost housing.

Kampung 1

Located on the urban edge of Jakarta, this peripheral *kampung* houses several hundred people on nine to fifteen hectares. The residents of this *kampung* tend to be poor, unlike the residents of some peripheral *kampung*, who may have moderate incomes. This *kampung* developed on privately owned land over the past twenty years, and now nearby land is being developed with expensive homes in the $100,000 to $150,000 range. A stark contrast exists between the small, self-help homes of the *kampung* and the so-called estates across the road (Photo 8.1). Until recently, this *kampung* existed as a somewhat isolated community with its own small shops, grocery, community well, and mosque. Being sparsely settled, the area provides large amounts of lush green space for its inhabitants, in contrast to the dense development of Jakarta. Residents either own their homes, which they most likely built themselves over time, or rent from another resident of the *kampung* for approximately $7.50 a month.

Photo 8.1 *Kampung 1.* The stark contrast between housing for the poor and the rich is vividly demonstrated here. The houses of the poor are soon to be replaced by more of the same luxurious housing.

Residents of this *kampung* face an increasingly common problem. The owner of the property, which is now ripe for urban development, wishes to sell the land to a developer. The squatters will have to leave. Although the *kampung* residents will receive some compensation because the government requires developers to purchase the houses they have built, the residents will most likely relocate in another *kampung* for economic reasons.

Kampung 2

Located on government-owned land on the bank of a river in Yogyakarta, this central *kampung* contains approximately 300 houses and 1,500 people. In addition to private residences, this *kampung* includes a mosque and an architect-designed library with a student dormitory on its second floor, both of which were built by residents as cooperative ventures (Photo 8.2). As is true in many central *kampung,* these people helped build one another's homes. Those who do not own their homes rent from others for approximately $15 a month. As in all *kampung* and villages, a night watch has been organized, with residents assigned specific nights for guard duty.

While this *kampung* provides affordable housing and ample open space, it also experiences many of the problems inherent in *kampung* developments, most notably the lack of water and sewerage systems and paved streets and footpaths. Furthermore, its location on a river bank, with the inevitable pollution of the river, signals forthcoming government action to remove the *kampung* and resettle the residents. Local planners and architects report that the issue is still under debate, with one side favoring resettlement and the other side favoring improvement of environmental conditions to make the place healthier and more livable. Although the government would pay to resettle the residents, including their extended families, the *kampung* residents may come out on the short side of the arrangement. The resettlement area is expected to be too far from the residents' current jobs with the result that they will not be able to commute to their old places of employment. Although the government is supposed to find relocatees jobs in the new area, this is not always accomplished satisfactorily.

Photo 8.2 *Kampung 2*. Architect-designed library and dormitory. Note the similarity to one of the buildings illustrated in *Kampung 3*, which was designed by the same priest–architect.

Kampung 3 and 4

Also located in Yogyakarta, these *kampung* are tucked into the hillside along a small river, a short distance from one another. *Kampung 3* backs onto a commercial area of many small tire-repair shops and extends under a highway viaduct. The location of the shops is against the law, but the government chooses to let them remain. Most of the workers live in their shops, and some have families living on the river bank below.

Kampung 3 is a rare case of an architect-designed *kampung*. It is actually part of a scheme created by a priest–architect to provide transition housing for the poorest of the poor. Most of these people live as scavengers or *becak* (trishaw) drivers or engage in other marginal employment. The idea is to utilize and maintain land on the steep river bank while providing housing for poorer people. Arguing that the steep banks will otherwise deteriorate, the architect designed a system of embankments and a complex of buildings made of inexpensive materials (Photo 8.3).

With thirty to forty homes and up to 200 people in the *kampung*, the site is still under development. The density of this *kampung* is much greater than that of *Kampung 1* or *2*, but open space is available along the

Photo 8.3 *Kampung 3*. The system of embankments strengthens the steep slope. In the background are the tire-repair shops facing the street above. The architect's touch is apparent in the two-story buildings in the center.

flood plain at the river's edge. The *kampung* also contains a multipurpose building for community activities plus several well-crafted houses. One structure is especially noteworthy—a two-story bamboo unit designed by the priest-architect that uses a concrete drainage way as its foundation.[7] Storm water simply flows under the house into the river.

Kampung 4 is a newer settlement downriver from *Kampung 3*. It used to be a squatter settlement where thieves and pickpockets disappeared when pursued, and where prostitution existed. Unlike *Kampung 3*, it was built without the benefit of an architect's services. A few years ago, a social worker from a local church began to work with these people, helping them to improve their way of life and defending them against the harshness of law enforcement (Photo 8.4). Threatened with eviction because the site was slated to become a sanitary landfill, the social worker succeeded in getting the local *camat* (district chief) and *lurah* (village head) to recognize the rights of these people to live there and to have resident status. Nevertheless, their long-term future on the site is uncertain. These people live in entirely self-help houses that are constructed primarily from scrap.

Photo 8.4 *Kampung 4*. The social worker is coming to conduct reading classes in the meeting room (*Balai Pertemuan*) built by the residents. The houses are situated around and oriented toward this meeting room.

Kampung 3 and *4* are both relatively new settlements located on environmentally sensitive lands—the deep and steep banks of the river. Unlike the older *kampung,* built also on environmentally sensitive lands along the same river, whose residents have been living there since before World War II and are more firmly established in the urban socioeconomic structure, *Kampung 3* and *4* are not apt to be the recipients of government improvement programs. In fact, their very existence is starkly illegal, and because of their small size and transitory nature, it is not likely that they will survive for a long time.

Some of the houses in these riverside *kampung* are built in the flood plain so that during the rainy season, when the river rises quickly, residents may have to evacuate their homes. They simply move out when the river is up and move back when it recedes. This occurs once every few years, and most residents accept it as a fact of life, perhaps a necessary cost of living in a convenient, centrally located area where transportation costs are minimized and employment opportunities are maximized. Beyond these factors, most residents of these *kampung* could not afford comparable housing in an authorized housing area.

Kampung 5

Located near *Kampung 2,* this new *kampung* is springing up on a Chinese cemetery (Photo 8.5). One important feature of the *kampung* is that the squatters organized and distributed the land among themselves and even allocated land for the necessary pathways. Since the land straddles the municipal boundary line and is somewhat isolated, the squatters can have a freer hand. They are willing to invest in a house because the Chinese cemetery legally belongs to the sultan, and he is known to be very sympathetic to squatters. They also know that some of the nearby *kampung* built on Chinese cemeteries were eventually recognized.

The people of *Kampung 5* are building their houses among the tombs; a few are even building their houses *around* the tombs. While some of the tombs have been abandoned by relatives, many are still visited every year. The relatives say they do not really mind the squatters; they are even glad that someone is living close by because they can be sure that the tombs will always be clean. The houses here are mostly user built and are of a better quality than those at *Kampung 4* because most of the residents of *Kampung 5* are better-off financially.

Kampung Governance

Kampung governance has several levels, beginning at the smallest unit with an area called the *rukun tetangga* (RT), made up of approx-

Photo 8.5 *Kampung 5.* Owner-built house being built in the so-called *kampung* style using wooden columns, bamboo roof structure, and clay tile roofing. Note the Chinese tombs on the far side and the volleyball "court" beyond.

imately thirty families. The next larger unit is the *rukun kampung* (RK), called the *rukun warga* in Jakarta, which contains perhaps a hundred families. The *Ketua* RT is a volunteer coordinator for the RT, and the *Ketua* RK is the volunteer coordinator for the RK program and services. Next, there is the *lurah*, the local government employee who is responsible for several *kampung*. The RT serves as a link between local residents and the *lurah*. For example, *kampung* residents who need to obtain an ID card or driver's license first go to the RT, who clears the necessary papers for contact with the *lurah*, the government administrator of the *kampung*. In the villages and rural areas, the *lurah* is elected. In the urban areas, the *lurah* is appointed by a higher official of government and is paid for providing services as a formal, local government employee (see Figure 8.1).

Community services are supported in part through taxes. In addition to the new, nationally enforced income tax and the value-added tax incorporated into the price of goods, there are two land- or housing-related taxes. One is a formal tax on land and homeownership and is based on the size of one's dwelling and land. There are also local neighborhood "taxes" that are paid as development contributions and are used to maintain streets and drainage channels, for the hiring of a *kampung* guard, and for other community services.

Positive Aspects of *Kampung*

The benefits of *kampung* living have been suggested in the preceding pages, but it would be useful to enumerate the positive aspects and then balance them with a review of the disadvantages of the *kampung*. Perhaps above all, *kampung,* especially the central *kampung,* are a source of affordable housing for people who would not be sheltered as well or at all if they did not exist. These urban *kampung,* both the central and peripheral ones, are typically conveniently located in relation to shopping, work, and transportation, providing a real economic benefit to their residents.

Kampung also serve as a source of capital investment. Over the years, by building incrementally, the *kampung* resident can amass, in the form of house and land, a sizable investment. While the primary intent is not to trade up, capital accumulation does occur, and if not sold or traded for a profit, the *kampung* house provides security for family and future generations. Even if eventually evicted, there is a good chance that the squatter will be compensated or otherwise gain from the *kampung* holding through economic and social contacts.

The activities of the *kampung,* from shared construction with traditional methods to the mutual provision of common services, create a sense of community and group pride. A value carried over from the traditional village, this community cohesiveness is a positive aspect of *kampung* life. The fact that the *kampung* enables the extended family to live together or nearby contributes to this cohesiveness.

Negative Aspects of *Kampung*

In order not to romanticize *kampung,* it is important to recognize that they do contain poverty, and some residents express feelings of hopelessness and despair. *Kampung* are also beset by inadequate and often nonexistent water and sewerage systems, and they lack other public facilities such as schools, fire protection, and post offices. The absence of these services is no small price to pay for the advantages cited above.

Because public services are not always provided, *kampung* residents must join together to purchase those they need. While this may at first seem to be a disadvantage, *kampung* residents have pointed out that it allows them to pay only for those services they really want. Furthermore, jointly providing *kampung* services such as nightly guard duty is a reflection of the traditional cohesiveness that makes *kampung* life more positive.

Residents living in *kampung* located on government or private lands must live with the fact of uncertain land tenure and the related, often constant, threat of eviction. To the extent that *kampung* are located in environmentally sensitive areas, there is a negative impact on the land and nearby residents.

On balance, the positive aspects of *kampung* appear to outweigh the negative ones. This is certainly true from the standpoint of *kampung* dwellers seeking low-cost shelter. The government also recognizes the *kampung* as providing the basis on which to build a stable, healthful living environment. The Indonesian Kampung Improvement Program (KIP) is intended to capitalize on these advantages.

The Kampung Improvement Program

The Indonesian government has set forth a three-part program for the country's housing sector.[8] Aimed mainly at the shelter problems of low- and middle-income households, the program includes a low-cost standard house-building program, a sites and services program, and a *kampung* improvement program. Although work is going on in all three areas, the KIP holds the promise of affecting the greatest number of Indonesians. In addition to the central government's modified KIP, which is discussed here, there is a smaller-scale, community-based KIP that can be initiated by local communities.[9]

KIPs are relatively easy to undertake, for they do not require much in the way of feasibility studies or engineering plans. The KIP also has the potential to improve the lives of more Indonesians at a lower cost and greater economic return than other options. As a comparison, during the last five-year national plan, 500,000 low-income residents were to benefit from the KIP, while 84,000 persons were to benefit from the sites and services program (World Bank, 1980, p. 7). Figures for Jakarta show that the sites and services approach costs about $225 per capita, while the KIP approach costs about $40 per capita (Department of Public Works, n.d., p. 12). The major part of the difference appears to be attributable to the variation in the cost of building new versus improving existing services. In general, the KIP approach affects more structures at a lower cost in less time. The economic rate of return for the KIP is estimated at 21 percent, whereas the rate of return for sites and services is estimated at 15 percent (World Bank, 1980, pp. 48–49). Up to 75 percent of the households in *kampung* slated for improvement fall below the poverty line.

Overall, the KIP also promises to be the better approach to widespread shelter improvement in Indonesia. For example, during the 1979–84 *Repelita* (*Re*ncana *Pe*mbangunan *Li*ma *Ta*hun: Five Year Development Plan), 230 cities and towns had implemented a KIP, with more than 400 additional cities and towns planning to begin KIPs during the fourth *Repelita* (1984–89). The national development corporation, PERUMNAS, on the other hand, increased housing by only 150,000 units during the last *Repelita* and plans to build 300,000 units during the fourth *Repelita* (Silas, 1984b, pp. 36–37).

The KIP is intended to be a systematic and unified physical, social, and economic development project that operates at the national, provincial, and city levels of government. Five objectives for the KIP have been stated (Department of Public Works, n.d., p. 3):

- Reduce deficits in household consumption of essential goods and services.
- Increase human capacity, incomes, and productivity.
- Increase households' and enterprises' control of capital assets and access to credit.
- Promote social and economic stability and reduce vulnerability within *kampung*.
- Promote self-help and self-reliance among *kampung* people.

The government hopes to achieve these objectives by coordinating existing agency programs at the three levels of government, making use of existing financing supplemented by new budget allocations, spreading the KIP to all designated urban growth centers, and integrating existing *kampung* into the city structure.

The KIP involves not only the provision of physical improvements such as sewers, water, and roads but also health, social, and economic improvements, although physical improvements have dominated the KIP approach. The basic idea is to provide a foundation on which *kampung* residents can build a viable existence without fear of losing their investment and being dislocated. From this base, people would be helped to move to a level where they could obtain municipal services and afford to pay the taxes to finance these services.

KIPs are intended to have four components (Department of Public Works, n.d., p. 64):

- Physical infrastructure (roads, footpaths, sewerage systems)
- Social services (health, education, recreation)
- Economic programs (technical assistance, credit to small businesses, job training)
- Home-improvement programs (credit, materials, technical assistance)

In order to avoid an excessive emphasis on the physical component in KIPs, minimum *and* maximum standards have been adopted. Minimum standards are intended to define a base or floor and to focus attention on less costly incremental improvements. Maximum standards have been established in order to restrict high-cost/low-return improvements and avoid the conversion of *kampung* into middle- or upper-income areas that cause the original *kampung* residents to be bought out of the area (Photo 8.6). In practice, an attempt is made to provide a relatively full

Photo 8.6 Kampung Improvement Program. Modest improvements, such as the paving of pathways and construction of drainage systems, raise the sanitary conditions and visual appearance of *kampung*.

range of improvements within a *kampung* in order to make a substantial improvement in the hope that it will generate other improvements.

KIP standards are defined in terms of cost per hectare of upgrading, and this determines the level of service to be provided. Three cost standards have been established: a *threshold* level at $4,480 per hectare, a *minimum* level at $9,600 per hectare, and a *desirable* level at $16,000 per hectare. Under the last national development plan, the goal was to serve 50 percent of the *kampung* areas needing improvement in the target cities (World Bank, 1980, p. 4). In order to generate more upgrading, the central government provides grants of up to half the program costs of improving to the minimum standard 50 percent of the *kampung* area, if the city will provide the other half. A similar incentive program exists for water-supply modernization.

Criteria used to select and rank *kampung* for upgrading include worst environmental conditions, highest density, oldest age, proximity to existing infrastructure networks, and willingness and interest of the community in a KIP (World Bank, 1980, p. 32). Other policy concerns for physical improvements include minimal disturbance of existing houses by fitting new infrastructure within the existing layout of the *kampung,* compensation and relocation assistance for families whose houses are eliminated by the project, and long-term land rights to households occupying public land prior to the implementation of the KIP.

In order to provide garbage collection and health and education services efficiently, KIP efforts are aimed at *kampung* of at least 10,000 persons, or several *kampung* are served as a group in order to reach this size. It has also proven more cost effective to use a general contractor to coordinate work among several *kampung*.

Efforts are made to coordinate the KIP with other national programs, such as those in health (vaccination, hygiene, mobile medicine), education (nonformal education, literacy education, vocational skills), development (roads, bridges, drainage, village centers, small markets, and public bathing, clothes washing and sanitary facilities), technical assistance to small industries, and home-improvement loans (Department of Public Works, n.d., pp. 40–42).

At the local level, three groups are involved in the planning and implementation of the KIP: the citywide KIP Steering Committee, the Kecamatan Project Committee, and the Kampung Committee (Figure 8.1). The KIP Steering Committee is appointed by the city mayor and is comprised of the heads of the various city departments responsible for aspects of the KIP. This group coordinates the planning, implementation, maintenance, and evaluation of the activities of the units involved in the KIP. The Kecamatan Project Committee is chaired by the *camat* (the district chief) and is made up of representatives of city departments, elected *kampung* residents, and *lurah* from the involved *kampung*. The committee reviews the *kampung* proposals from its jurisdiction, and the *camat* serves as project officer. The Kampung Committee, made up of the *lurah,* heads of neighborhood and block groups, and other *kampung* residents, identifies projects to be carried out in its *kampung* and recommends improvement priorities.

Although the planning process varies from one *kampung* to another, generally the process begins when a Kampung Committee submits an improvement proposal through the *lurah* (who chairs the Kampung Committee) to the *camat.* The *camat* evaluates the *kampung* proposals and presents a recommendation to the mayor, who submits it to the KIP Steering Committee. The steering committee evaluates the proposals against the needs of the *kampung* and selects target *kampung.* The city planning department prepares a preliminary design and budget with the executive secretary of the steering committee. The projects then go to the project committees of the *kampung* areas (comprised of the *camat, lurah,* RK, and RT). The *camat* prepares a list of KIP projects for the steering committee, which forwards the list to the mayor and city council for final approval. Meanwhile, city technical departments develop detailed plans and cost estimates. This process takes about eight or nine months.

Learning from the KIP experience, the Indonesian government has launched other programs directed toward *kampung* improvement through various departments using national as well as local funds. One

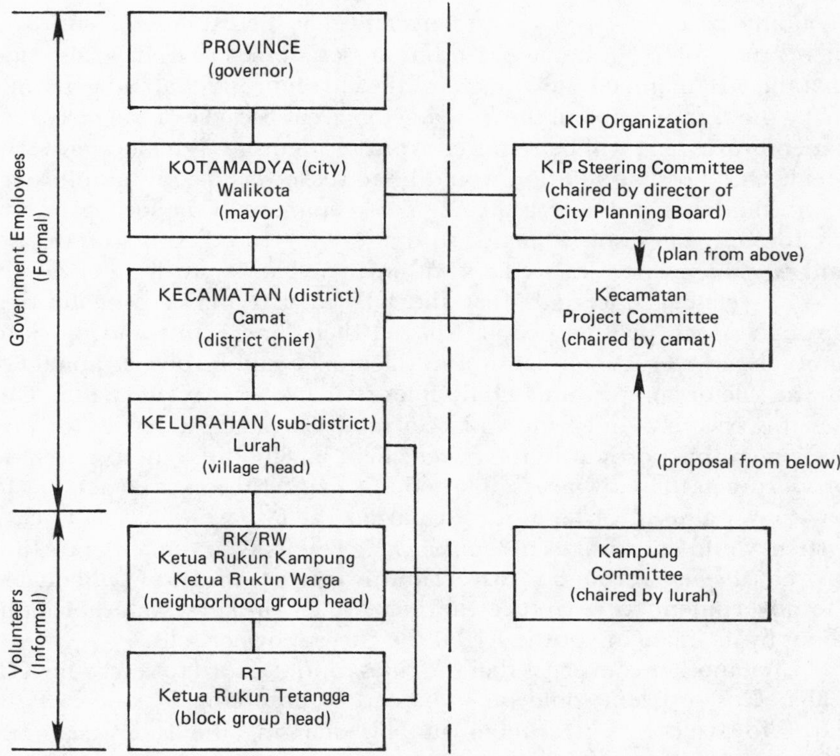

Figure 8.1 Indonesian local government organization.

of these programs, the Urban Residential Area Improvement Program, is reported to be successful in three respects (Silas, 1986). First, the criteria for selection of recipient *kampung* have resulted in the selection of *kampung* that truly need the program. Second, the participation by residents has been effective; in fact, their contribution, in terms of labor as well as funds, has considerably expanded the coverage of the program beyond planned targets. Third, the cost of these internally funded programs is substantially lower than that of the KIP programs supported by international funds, resulting in comparable physical and socioeconomic improvements. These findings emphasize again the importance of self-help in the improvement of *kampung.*

Selected KIP Problems and Solutions

Local observers have identified a number of problems associated with the Kampung Improvement Program. But for each problem, there are potential remedies. It has been argued that the KIP may destroy the economic base for *kampung* residents and that the expense of improvements may force out home-based businesses. Some critics have also said that the KIP might cost too much for the current residents and generally make the cost of living in the *kampung* too great because of the increased expenditures that will be required from residents and the local government. One possible solution would be to set lower maximum improvement standards and permit the *lurah* to keep more of the local property tax for *kampung* improvements, so that the increased costs to residents and *kampung* businesses are kept within an ability to pay.[10]

A related concern is that the KIP may result in gentrification through which process people will sell their land rights and move to another *kampung*. A solution to this dilemma could involve a capital tax on the sale of land within a Philippines-style tax-assessment system. Under this system, homeowners place a value on their properties for tax-assessment purposes, with the government having the right to purchase properties at these owner-established fair market prices if owners try to set a low value in order to avoid paying their share of taxes. Such a system would encourage current *kampung* residents to remain in the improved *kampung* through relatively low property taxes and would enable the government to recapture the increase in property value brought about by its financing of the KIP if the current owner sells.

Yet another concern is that the cities cannot afford to repay the KIP loans. This problem could be addressed by enforcing maximum standards to avoid overinvestment and by changing the Indonesian tax structure to keep a greater percentage of tax revenues at the local level. Of course, without raising taxes overall, this implies a shifting of revenues from the state to municipalities. But such a shift might be in the national interest as a relatively low-cost way of improving urban living conditions.

Shortage of funds for the KIP has always been a problem. The promotion of more self-help and user-building activities would reduce the labor component of KIP funding. Building materials could be provided, and the *kampung* residents could be organized to contribute manual labor. This would require some form of training or apprenticeship program to be included in KIP packages. Another benefit would be enhancement and preservation of the building skills of the people. As Silas (1986) has described, *kampung* residents are willing to contribute money in order to improve their environment. Also, funds from other (sectoral) sources are often available at the local level. Organizing and coordinating funds from the various sources would result in more efficient utilization and, consequently, larger coverage of improvement projects.

Maintenance has been lacking in some improved *kampung*, and the fear is that the KIP funds may, in the long run, be wasted. The response to this problem would seem to be the development of programs to induce *kampung* residents to maintain communally the *kampung* infrastructure. These efforts would be built on the tradition of *kampung* community cohesiveness and mutual help (*gotong royong*), which is carried over from rural life, and would recognize that a KIP must be a continuing process to be successful.

Finally, some squatters fear losing funds spent on improvements to housing on land they do not own. A solution to this problem might be a land registry as part of the KIP. Such a registry could legitimize the title of squatters and encourage home improvements, even in *kampung* where a KIP is not scheduled for some time.

Policy Issues and Prospects

The Indonesian urban population is increasing rapidly, and thus it will face extraordinary housing demands as a large, young population forms more households. The Indonesian government is well aware that it will not be able to provide publicly all the necessary low-cost housing, and that the KIP efforts will help shelter many people. Yet it is hard to believe that this effort alone can provide all the shelter needed. It also seems inefficient to relocate *kampung* once they have rooted on sensitive lands. One of the more severe problems for *kampung* dwellers in urban areas is finding suitable land close to their places of work.

The planner's instinct is to suggest ways in which land could be demarcated for *kampung* before the fact, to avoid problems of development on sensitive lands. (This approach might or might not include a sites and services component.) But planners and policymakers must remember that market forces cause people, including squatters, to settle in certain parts of the city, for example, near workplaces, transportation, and water supplies. These services or facilities are typically located near the center of the city, where the only land available to squatters is the sensitive land along river banks and railways. Furthermore, not only squatters choose these areas; high-income people seek the same locational advantages. Consequently there is typically a mixture of high- and low-income people in these sensitive areas, with the houses of the higher-income people next to the street and those of the lower-income people behind them. The high-income people need (physical) help from the low-income people, and by providing these services, the latter are able to secure money needed for survival in the urban area.[11] A demarcation policy should respond to this symbiotic relationship and be supportive rather than repressive, especially for new immigrants. A supportive environment can help migrants cope with the more stressful urban situation. A repressive or inhibiting environment can cause maladaptive behavior and eventually lead to government "muscle" policies, such as eviction, clearance, and even closing the city to immigrants—policies that seem to fail.

Were a demarcation policy to be established, however, the Indonesian planning system and bureaucratic support structure might not be able to cope with such an approach—it requires a system of land registry, a means of financing the purchase of sites, and widespread planning and administrative skills. With rapid growth and urbanization, the difficulty lies, in part, with setting up these procedures quickly, before *kampung* spring up on sensitive lands. Since *kampung* will continue to be the dominant source of low-income housing in Indonesia for decades to come, jumping ahead of the invasion–improvement–relocation cycle is the challenge before the Indonesian government.[12] This challenge might be met by reserving land for *kampung* development as part of formal village and urban plans. This would be a clear policy statement that the Indonesian government has recognized the value of the *kampung* and the KIP in housing its population. Such a policy statement would call the potential value of the Indonesian KIP to the attention of other governments, aid agencies, and practitioners.

On a national scale, policies for developing smaller, secondary cities could also be pursued to divert the flow of rural migrants from the large urban centers and thus relieve them of some of the pressure of spontaneous housing development.[13] The smaller cities can function as buffers or stopping-off points for migrants on their way to the larger cities, and some of these migrants might stay permanently in the smaller cities. These secondary cities could become the primary recipients for rural migrants from the immediate surroundings by providing jobs in the informal or service sector. Toward this end, Rondinelli (1983) proposes three essential actions to be taken in developing secondary cities: (1) strengthen the economies of existing secondary cities; (2) stimulate growth and diversification of smaller towns and market centers; and (3) strengthen the physical, economic, social, and political linkages among secondary cities, and between them and larger and smaller settlements. This distributive policy is very much in accord with the national development goals of Indonesia and might well be pursued along with KIP activities.

Acknowledgments

Some of the research for this chapter was conducted by the authors as part of a cooperative agreement between the School of Architecture and Urban Planning (SARUP) at the University of Wisconsin–Milwaukee, and the Jurusan Teknik Arsitektur (JUTA) at the Universitas Gadjah Mada, Yogyakarta, Indonesia, sponsored by the Midwest Universities Consortium for International Activities with funding from the World Bank. Useful comments on the chapter were provided by Haryadi, Harry Miarsono, and Douglas Ryhn.

Notes

1. In urban areas, less than 40 percent of the population has access to a safe public water system and one-quarter of the population disposes of its untreated human waste in streams and rivers (Department of Public Works, 1984).
2. It should be noted that in the Indonesian language no letters are added to nouns to indicate a plural form.
3. Silas (1984b) has estimated that *kampung* housing constitutes between 60 and 75 percent of Indonesia's urban housing stock.
4. For further discussion of the meaning of the word *kampung,* see Atman (1975) and Williams (1975).
5. More than a decade ago, Atman classified *kampung* as rural (*desa*), semirural, semiurban, and urban (1975, pp. 217–18). We prefer to use *desa* to refer to rural settlements and *kampung* to refer to urban settlements. We believe *central* and *peripheral* are better descriptors of urban *kampung* because the classification captures the location–density–income characteristics of today's *kampung.*
6. Apparently such gentrification has been occurring for some time (Williams, 1975, p. 340).
7. This housing was described in the design periodical *ASRI* (Suhanda, 1985).
8. Indonesia did not have a formal national housing policy until 1975, although local policies and programs existed earlier. Local housing cooperatives funded by central government credits existed between the mid-1950s and mid-1960s but produced only 1,250 units. Other local cooperatives have built similar small numbers of units, but without assistance from the government.
9. For a concise history of the KIP, see Silas (1984a). The first KIP efforts began as early as 1924. There are now five or more KIP approaches. Early KIPs focused on provision of basic infrastructure. Later KIPs increased in scale. The two better-known approaches are the modified KIP (a top–down government public works program) and the W. R. Supratman KIP (a bottom–up, smaller scale, community-based approach). Essentially all KIPs are public works programs.
10. A number of taxes commonly assumed to be local taxes, including property taxes, are collected by the provincial government. Revising the method for collection and distribution of these taxes would be no small task.
11. See Williams (1975) for additional discussion of the value of this mixing of classes.
12. A continuing research project on approaches to improving the environmental quality of *kampung* has been initiated by the SARUP–JUTA research team.
13. This is not to suggest direct intervention to force migrants into

certain areas but to encourage the shift indirectly through economic and management efforts. Researchers have suggested that this be done by improving national sectoral and urban management policies (Hammer et al., 1986).

References

Atman, Rudolf. 1975. "Kampong Improvements in Indonesia." *Ekistics* 40(238) (September), 216–20.

Cobban, James L. 1970. "The City of Java: An Essay in Historical Geography." Doctoral dissertation, Department of Geography, University of California, Berkeley.

Department of Public Works. 1984. *Selected Problems in the Provision of Infrastructure in Urban Areas.* Jakarta: Republic of Indonesia, Department of Public Works, National Urban Development Strategy Project.

———. n.d. *Kampung Improvement Program: Toward a National Policy.* Jakarta: Republic of Indonesia, Department of Public Works.

Hammer, Andrew M., Andrew D. Steer, and David G. Williams. 1986. *Indonesia: The Challenge of Urbanization.* Working paper no. 787. Washington, D.C.: World Bank.

Rondinelli, Dennis A. 1983. *Secondary Cities in Developing Countries: Policies for Diffusing Urbanization,* vol. 145. London: Sage Library of Social Research.

Silas, Johan. 1984a. "The Kampung Improvement Programme of Indonesia: A Comparative Case Study of Jakarta and Surabaya." In *Low-Income Housing in the Developing World,* ed. Geoffrey K. Payne, pp. 69–87. New York: Wiley.

———. 1984b. "Resource and Process of Low Income Urban Housing in Surabaya, Indonesia." *REGOL,* December, 36–44.

———. 1986. "Social, Economic and Health Impacts on Residents of Kampungs Receiving the Urban Residential Area Improvement Program in the Province of East Java." Unpublished research paper.

Statistical Office of the Special Province of Yogyakarta. 1980. *Survey on Housing Conditions in the Special Province of Yogyakarta.*

Suhanda, Anda. 1985. "Profil: Romo Mangunwijaya; Membangun Lingkungan yang Sehat bagi Masyarakat Kecil." *ASRI* 30 (July), 88–91.

Williams, David. 1975. "Jakarta's Kampungs." *AD,* June, 339–43.

World Bank. 1980. *Indonesia Staff Appraisal Report, Fourth Urban Development Project.* Washington, D.C.: World Bank.

Chapter 9

Hong Kong's Floating Settlements

BRUCE TAYLOR

Visitors approaching Hong Kong by air can see evidence of its most serious housing problems even before their plane lands at Kai Tak airport. The rooftops of urban Kowloon give an indication of the density of settlement in the main urban section of Hong Kong, an area comprised of the northern shore of Hong Kong Island and the Kowloon Peninsula (Figure 9.1). According to the 1981 Hong Kong census, average population density in the urban area was 28,479 persons per square kilometer, and densities reached a peak of 165,445 persons per square kilometer in the lower-income district of Sham Shui Po in Kowloon (Hong Kong Government, 1985a, p. 284).

Overcrowding is a dominant characteristic of many of Hong Kong's residential districts. It manifests itself in a number of ways—traffic-clogged streets, overloaded public transport, and high noise levels—in addition to the obviously low quality of housing provided by the packed tenement buildings. This overcrowding is traceable to a number of interrelated and complementary causes. Among them are rapid population growth and a shortage of developable land. Over the years, these problems have led the government to mount massive efforts to provide housing, reclaim land from the sea, and cut down mountainsides for suitable building sites.[1]

Population and Housing Pressures

Despite the government's best efforts, population pressures in Hong Kong have proven so great that demand for housing often has rapidly exceeded supply. This situation, familiar in many Asian cities, particularly affected Hong Kong when waves of immigrants arrived in

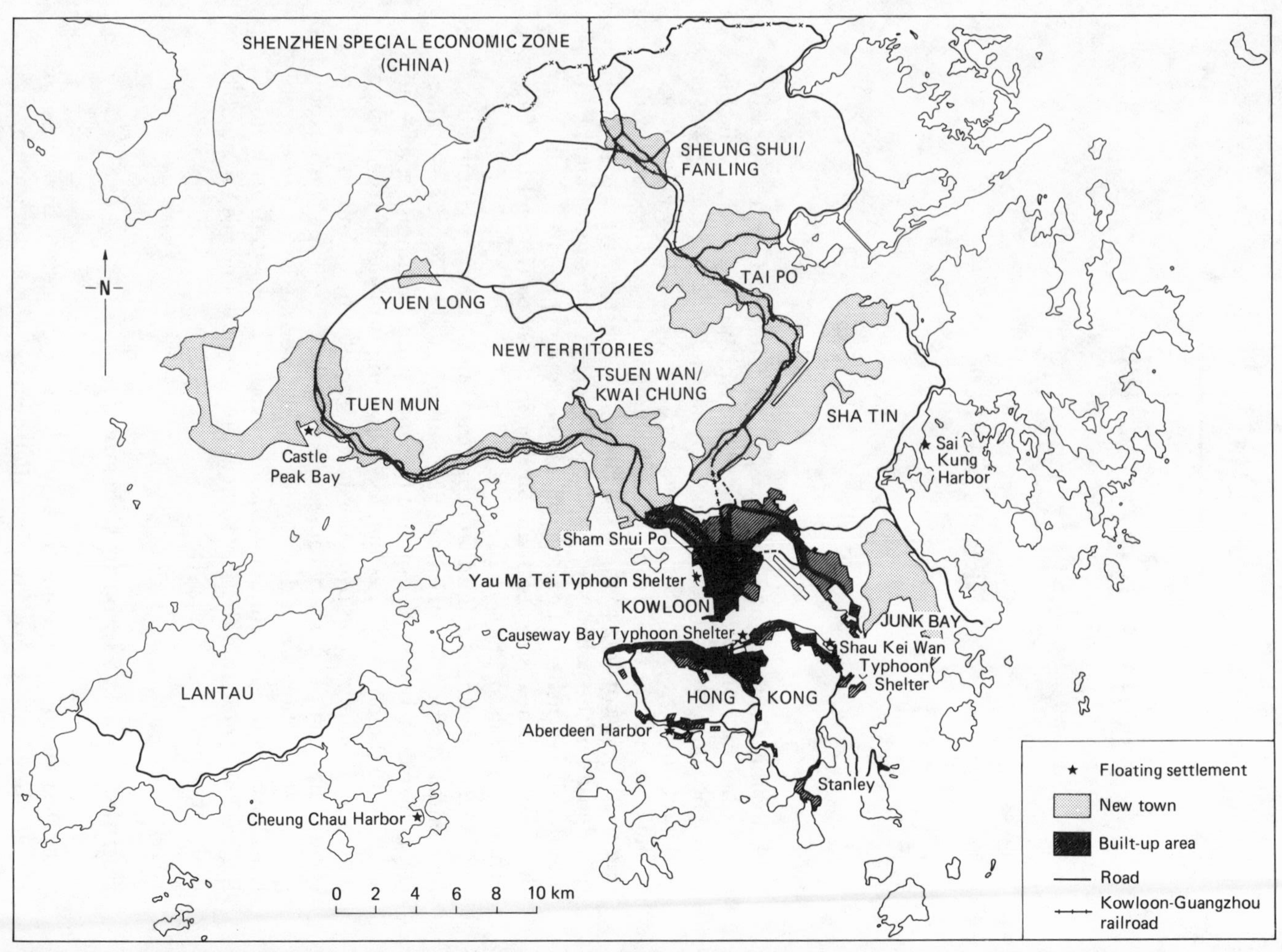
SHENZHEN SPECIAL ECONOMIC ZONE
(CHINA)
SHEUNG SHUI/
FANLING
TAI PO
YUEN LONG
NEW TERRITORIES
TSUEN WAN/
KWAI CHUNG
TUEN MUN
SHA TIN
Sai
Kung
Harbor
Castle
Peak Bay
Sham Shui Po
Yau Ma Tei Typhoon Shelter
KOWLOON
JUNK BAY
Causeway Bay Typhoon Shelter
Shau Kei Wan
Typhoon
Shelter
LANTAU
HONG
KONG
Aberdeen Harbor
Stanley
Cheung Chau Harbor
N
0 2 4 6 8 10 km
Floating settlement
New town
Built-up area
Road
Kowloon-Guangzhou
railroad

the territory from China in the early 1950s and the late 1970s. The consequence in Hong Kong has been much the same as elsewhere: the appearance of squatter colonies on the steep slopes fringing the urban area or on neglected agricultural land in the more rural New Territories. More insidious, perhaps, because it is less observable, is the partitioning and repartitioning of tenement buildings into small cubicles and cocklofts providing virtually no privacy and having only limited access to communal washing, bathing, and toilet facilities.[2] These tenement slum dwellings, some no more than twenty years old, remain remarkably persistent even as the squatter communities are gradually resettled (Bristow, 1984, pp. 218–30; Keung, 1985).

The Hong Kong government's responses to these housing problems are well documented, both by the government (Hong Kong Housing Authority, 1981) and by other commentators (e.g., Keung, 1985; Pryor, 1983; Yeung and Drakakis-Smith, 1982) and hence need little comment here. Since the 1950s, the government has constructed low-cost public housing on a scale probably equaled nowhere else in the world.[3]

These public housing estates are made up of high-rise tower blocks, usually thirty or more stories tall, housing 15,000 to 25,000 people in an integrated residential community that includes landscaped playgrounds, commercial centers, schools, community halls, and other neighborhood-oriented facilities. Since 1973, the bulk of public housing has been built outside the urban area in Hong Kong's decentralized new towns, of which there were seven in 1985 (Figure 9.1).

Less well known outside Hong Kong are the government's parallel efforts to complement the public housing construction program. To house victims of natural disasters, displacees from buildings condemned as unsafe, and former squatters whose areas are cleared for redevelopment, the Housing Authority administers temporary housing areas (THAs) and transit centers.[4]

The government also engages in upgrading selected squatter areas where the land is not likely to be needed for development. Facilities such as fire breaks for safety purposes, street lighting, public toilets, and paved sidewalks are introduced into squatter communities through this program. With nearly 480,000 people still living in land-based squatter areas in Hong Kong (Hong Kong Housing Department, 1985), the need for this program will exist for the foreseeable future.

Figure 9.1 Urbanized areas and major floating settlements in Hong Kong. (Illustration by S. L. Too)

Floating Settlements as an Alternative Housing Form

Some of the visitors who fly over Kowloon on their approach to Hong Kong's airport may later eat at a "floating restaurant" during their stay in the territory, most likely at Aberdeen on Hong Kong Island's southern coast (Figure 9.1). Others will enjoy boat trips that pass through the small harbor at Aberdeen. Both restaurant goers and pleasure cruisers catch glimpses in Aberdeen Harbor of one of the globe's more unusual forms of spontaneous settlement. On hundreds of boats ranging from small sampans to massive seagoing junks, families live out their daily lives—sleeping, eating, washing, even working on board—and they remain largely oblivious to the tourists' inquisitive scrutiny. The scene is repeated in some of the territory's other sheltered harbors, less frequented by tourists, with the floating communities representing the vestiges of one of Hong Kong's traditional ways of life (Photo 9.1).

Floating settlements have a long history in Hong Kong, as indeed they do elsewhere in China (Anderson, 1972). The British colonizers of Hong Kong in 1841 found fishing villages well established at the locations of today's Aberdeen and Stanley; the majority of these indigenous residents probably spent much of their lives on their boats (Hong Kong Government, 1985a, p. 292). Living on board their vessels made considerable sense to people who had to put to sea each day to maintain their livelihood.

But the floating settlements of that day also had a strong ethnic identity. The boat dwellers were mostly of two culturally and perhaps ethnically distinct groups, the Tanka and Hoklo people (Anderson, 1972, pp. 1–4), considered to be "different" and indeed socially inferior by most Han Chinese. Historically they were treated as virtual outcasts; on occasion, they were forcibly prevented from settling on land. One consequence of such treatment was the creation of a unique cultural inheritance that, while recognizably Chinese, has distinctive traits of its own (Anderson, 1972; Kani, 1972). Many customs traceable to the "boat people" are now part of Hong Kong's general folklore.

In modern times these floating settlements have persisted despite the rapid increase in the construction of low-cost housing on land. At least three reasons explain why some boat people choose to remain in their seaborne communities. First, there is the undoubted economic appeal of boats as housing units. Though a new seagoing junk can cost the equivalent of several years' earnings for a fishing family, many of the boats moored in the floating settlements are older vessels—some are very decrepit and unlikely to stand up to ocean use. With rents for small private housing units (not cubicles or cocklofts) in central urban locations often topping HK$2,000 per month even for units of indifferent quality, and with newer public housing flats renting for HK$400 to $600 a month when available, boat dwelling is an attractive option for some

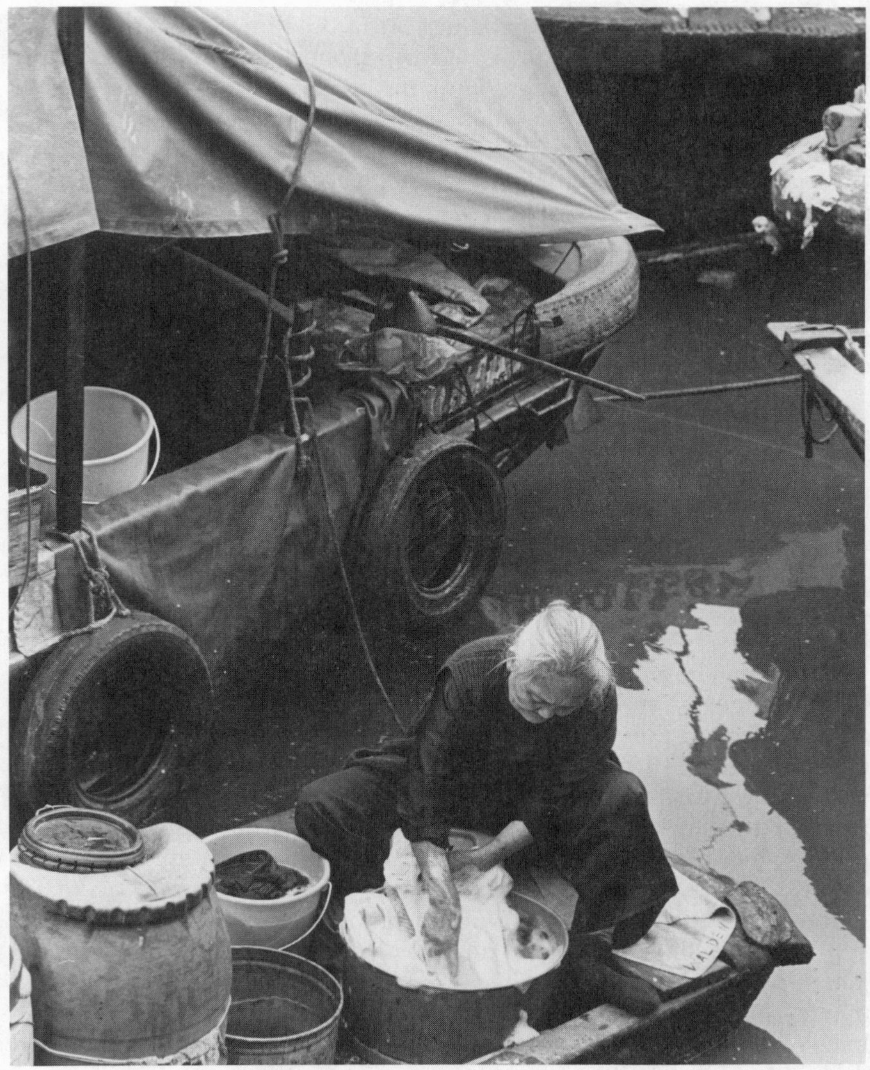

Photo 9.1 At work in the Causeway Bay Typhoon Shelter. (Photo courtesy of Information Services Department, Hong Kong Government)

families raised in the tradition. Many floating colonies also have the advantage of a location near some of Hong Kong's larger employment centers, which public housing in the more remote new towns does not possess.

A second reason for the persistence of floating settlements is the life style sustained by fishing families, particularly those whose vessels do not have deep-sea fishing capabilities. As in the nineteenth century, it is still necessary for these boats to put forth from sheltered ports each day. Although the traditional sailing junk has died out in Hong Kong, some households continue to maintain a livelihood through shallow-water fishing with diesel-powered vessels. From their standpoint it is practical to remain on board and make the fishing vessel their domestic quarters as well.

Still another reason that floating settlements have persisted is the desire among some residents, mainly the older ones, to maintain their traditional culture. This perceived need to maintain an identifiable life style has decreased, however, as opportunities on land have expanded, and many fisherfolk have taken jobs in factories.

Anatomy of the Floating Settlements

In line with their historical status as fishing communities, floating settlements appear in a number of the sheltered harbors along Hong Kong's coastline (Kani, 1967; Lo, 1983, p. 158; see also Figure 9.1). Some of these are artificial harbors created by breakwaters, while others are natural embayments along the coast. Particularly in the artificial shelters, the floating communities must share the harbor waters with other forms of shipping. In Yau Ma Tei Typhoon Shelter, probably the busiest sheltered harbor in the territory, the dwelling boats of the floating population mingle with flat-bottomed container lighters ferrying shipping cargo back and forth between shore and the oceangoing container vessels moored farther out in the harbor (Photo 9.2). In Causeway Bay Typhoon Shelter an even more incongruous combination appears, with a colony of sampans located cheek-by-jowl with the pleasure boats of the wealthy tied up at the Royal Hong Kong Yacht Club marina (Photo 9.3).

The dwelling boats give an initial impression of visual disorder. They vary considerably in type, size, and condition. The larger junks may be 35 to 50 feet in length; sampans are considerably shorter, perhaps only 15 to 20 feet, and shallower. The traditional junk is a roomy design that historically saw usage as a freighter. When used for dwelling purposes, cabins for the family and the crew, if any, are found below deck, and storage holds are provided for food, household items, and, on working fishing boats, the daily catch (Kani, 1967, pp. 24–27). Sampans used as living quarters normally have a wooden shelter built above deck, which houses the family, with the shallow hold used for storage. On both types of boats canvas awnings, drab green or brightly colored, may be fitted for added protection from the elements.

Meals are cooked on board with simple cookstoves. With refrigeration normally impossible, most boat-dwelling families purchase fresh

Photo 9.2 Aerial view of Yau Ma Tei Typhoon Shelter. (Photo courtesy of Information Services Department, Hong Kong Government)

Photo 9.3 Dwelling boats and pleasure craft share the Causeway Bay Typhoon Shelter. (Photo courtesy of Information Services Department, Hong Kong Government)

foodstuffs each day, the typical shopping pattern for most Hong Kong residents until only recently. Water is obtained from taps onshore or may be purchased from floating vendors at about HK$.50 per bucket. Sanitation on the boats is primitive. Modern chemical toilets are almost unknown, and most sewage from the junks and sampans is simply discharged into the surrounding waters. Laundry is festooned everywhere, adding to the sense of visual anarchy found in the floating settlements.

The condition of the dwelling boats ranges from well maintained, albeit cramped by the standards of land dwellers, to totally decrepit. Some of the permanently moored junks are a weather-beaten gray, obviously not painted for many years. Others, most likely the working vessels, are worn but evidently seaworthy and serviceable. Occasionally a new boat can be spotted, distinguishable by the lighter brown color of unweathered wood. The gaily painted fishing junks of former days are less common now, and on many dwelling boats the brightest splashes of color are provided by paper handbills and leaflets, adorned with Chinese characters symbolizing happiness, prosperity, and fortune, plastered on the walls above deck.

Many boat residents have no connection with the shore except by access over other boats. A continuous flow of feeder sampans and rowboats ferries people back and forth to the shore, and carries foodstuffs and drinking water out to the boats (Photo 9.4). The larger permanently moored boats often have a smaller boat tethered alongside that serves as the family's private transport.

The water surrounding many dwelling boats is littered with assorted flotsam carried in from the outer harbor or thrown overboard from the boats. An unpleasant smell of raw sewage permeates the air in some of the larger communities, indicative of seriously polluted waters. This pollution is not entirely the product of the floating communities, as discharging untreated sewage from homes on land into the harbor is still common in Hong Kong. Noise pollution may also be a problem when harbor traffic is busiest, although the floating settlements are on the whole quieter than most neighborhoods on land.

The floating settlements are poorly supplied with community facilities and social services, despite the efforts of private clan associations, cooperative marketing societies (e.g., the Fish Marketing Organization), and charitable groups. Education, health care, and social services aimed at the young or the elderly almost inevitably are provided by facilities on land. Formal religious activities center on temples built on land, the best known of which are dedicated to Tin Hau, the Queen of Heaven and Protector of Seafarers. Most religious observances, however, are less formal and may be conducted on board the boats. The need to go ashore for medical treatment, for education, or for any dealings with government officials, including social welfare organizations, means that relative to their counterparts on land, the boat dwellers find it much more difficult to take advantage of Hong Kong's modern infrastructure of community facilities. Some may opt out altogether, choosing instead to rely on the clan or extended family as a source of support—as is still traditional among more rural or less Westernized Chinese.

Photo 9.4 Feeder sampan in Shau Kei Wan Typhoon Shelter. (Photo courtesy of Information Services Department, Hong Kong Government)

Explaining the Decline of Floating Settlements

Despite the reasons given above for the persistence of the seemingly anachronistic floating communities down to modern times, the most striking characteristic of these settlements is that they are continuously shrinking. Table 9.1 shows the decline in "marine population" (the census term) between 1911 and 1981. It is evident from the table that the

Table 9.1. Change in Hong Kong's Marine Population, 1911–81

Year	*Marine Population*	*Percentage of Total Population*
1911	61,798	13.5
1921	71,154	11.3
1931	70,093	8.3
1941	154,000[a]	10.6
1961	136,802	4.4
1966	102,520	2.7
1971	79,894	2.0
1976	59,050	1.3
1981	49,747	1.0

Sources: Kani (1967, p. 17), and census data of the Hong Kong Government, Census and Statistics Division (1983).
[a]Estimated number.

floating communities are less and less attractive to Hong Kong residents; at current rates of decline, they may disappear by 1996 (Lo, 1983, p. 157).

Several explanations are possible for this phenomenon, which distinguishes Hong Kong's floating communities from most other spontaneous settlements found in less developed countries, including those covered in other chapters of this book. Perhaps the most compelling is the gradual lessening of population pressures on Hong Kong's land-based housing stock, with the continued high construction rate of public housing and the curbing, since 1980, of immigration to Hong Kong. As most boat dwellers are longer-term residents of Hong Kong, they are eligible for a permanent public housing unit immediately on reaching the head of the waiting list for public housing; that is, if they have bothered to apply—many have not. They thus are in an advantageous position to benefit directly from the government's intensive efforts to build more public housing. Many land-based squatters, in contrast, do not have the requisite ten years' continuous residence in Hong Kong and are eligible only for less desirable housing in a THA.

On some occasions the government has provided special allocations of public housing units to boat dwellers. For instance, in 1984–85 the Housing Authority relocated 105 families from Yau Ma Tei's floating community to Fanling new town in a special voluntary resettlement exercise (Hong Kong Housing Authority, 1985, p. 78), an offer rejected by about 400 other families because Fanling was thought to be too far away. This special program is in line with the general government policy of encouraging resettlement of people in the floating communities without actually compelling it (see *South China Morning Post,* 1985a, p. 1; *South China Morning Post,* 1986, p. 13).

In general, as housing availability on land gradually increases, the economic motivation for continuing to live on boats lessens. This especially is true for boat dwellers who are employed on land, sometimes at a considerable distance from the harbors where their boats are moored. Despite continuing high land prices, the availability of more secure and more spacious housing on land undoubtedly will attract a still larger number of boat dwellers.

Aside from the overall state of Hong Kong's housing market, social and economic motivations among boat dwellers encourage them to leave the floating communities. With nine years of education now compulsory in Hong Kong, the children of boat dwellers are receiving their education in schools based on land—an opportunity that many of their parents never had. These children are no longer useful for operating a fishing vessel, and inevitably it is only a short step for many from being educated on land to being employed there and forsaking their families' traditional livelihood. At school the children also are culturally assimilated into the mainstream of land-dwelling children, eliminating or lessening any perceived importance children might attach to maintaining the floating life style of their parents. The same process has been noted among younger generations of New Territories villagers with respect to their agricultural heritage (Lee, 1981).

Economically, the fishing industry, along with farming, has slowly declined in importance with the expansion of a land-based manufacturing economy in Hong Kong. The shallow seas off Guangdong Province are being overfished by coastal fishing vessels from China and Macau, as well as Hong Kong (Chu, n.d.). Fishing families who remain in the trade are turning to steel-hulled diesel vessels with the capability of venturing much farther into the South China Sea. The capital investment required for these modern ships is beyond the means of many boat dwellers; some enter cooperative arrangements with other operators, but many give up fishing for land-based pursuits. The more modern vessels that remain in operation also require smaller crews. Thus, even among families who remain in fishing, some family members are likely to be displaced to land. Equally important, modern diesel trawlers are much less adaptable as dwelling vessels than are traditional junks. They do not normally anchor in the midst of typhoon shelters, and when fishing in the deep seas, they may be away from port for days at a time. Neither factor is conducive to establishing family living quarters on board.

A final explanation for the dwindling population of Hong Kong's floating settlements is the gradual increase in incomes and the resultant enhancement of social aspirations that characterizes much of Hong Kong society. For many families with increased means, what may once have been adequate residential environments are now unacceptable. Westernization of Hong Kong's culture may play a role in this, but more significant is the overall level of prosperity evident in the community. A change in community attitudes toward housing standards does not, of course, affect floating settlements alone. Older public housing estates, developed to low standards in the 1950s basically as emergency shelter, are being demolished or renovated into more modern units as their inadequacies become increasingly evident (see Drakakis-Smith, 1979; Myers, 1981).

Government Policy and the Floating Settlements

From the standpoint of Hong Kong's administrators, there are important legal differences between boat dwellers and land-based squatters. By virtue of their illegal occupation of government land ("Crown Land") or, occasionally, land leased to a private landholder, the latter are technically in violation of Hong Kong law—even if, as in some squatter communities, the law is so weakly enforced that unofficial markets develop for squatter "property" (Smart, 1985). Consequently, they must face the prospect that their homes will be cleared at one time or another. In contrast, Hong Kong's boat dwellers are not violating any law by congregating in the territory's typhoon shelters. Their legal position is similar to that of today's New Territories villagers whose ancestors lived in the same village at the time of the British lease in 1898. The right to occupy their property or boat is respected by the law, and if their property is required for a public works project, or if their sheltered harbor is reclaimed for urban redevelopment, they are entitled to rehousing, and in many cases to compensation for their losses.

Although Hong Kong's floating communities have the stature of legitimate settlements, as opposed to the nonlegitimate squatter communities found on land, this does not mean that boat dwelling receives encouragement from the government. The fundamental policy adopted toward boat dwellers by the authorities in Hong Kong is to encourage their resettlement on land in public housing accommodations that are also used to resettle the land-based squatter population. To this end the government urges boat dwellers to register on the waiting list for public housing, and from time to time it makes alternative housing accommodations available even for boat-dwelling families not on the waiting list (as in 1984 and again in early 1986). At the same time, the government encourages boat dwellers to make use of the array of social services provided on land. In terms of living conditions facing the boat dwellers, the government has acted to eliminate some of the worst hazards to the health and safety of the floating population; otherwise, though, its position is best characterized as "benign neglect."[5]

The safety of boat dwellers has been vastly enhanced by the availability of sheltered anchorages known as *typhoon shelters*. These are constructed and maintained by the marine authorities in Hong Kong to serve all shipping at times when tropical cyclones threaten Hong Kong, but they provide special benefits for the floating communities that nestle in their relatively protected waters. Most of Hong Kong's permanently moored dwelling boats are located in sheltered anchorages. The stresses on older hulls are very much lessened when boats are anchored in a shelter, and, of course, the chance of an entire community being blown out to sea in a serious storm is eliminated.

Although they provide safety advantages, typhoon shelters may become seriously polluted because of the difficulty in achieving adequate tidal flushing of their waters. In the past, untreated sewage from land has been channeled to the sea through underwater sewage outfalls or along land conduits (*nullahs*), and some of these have discharged into typhoon shelters, adding to the pollution problem created by waste discharges from dwelling boats. The government's planning guidelines now require sewage outfalls to discharge their loads outside the typhoon shelters, and some existing outfalls are planned to be relocated.

Within these areas of safe harborage, the government has made little direct effort to improve living conditions. There are no programs, for instance, that would encourage the continued upkeep of dwelling boats in habitable condition. Nor are there programs to upgrade the infrastructure accessible to the floating communities, as there are in some land-based squatter settlements—although admittedly some of the improvements made on land have no relevance to a floating community. It might be feasible, though, to consider mooring floating chemical lavatories within the settlements or providing piped water through undersea connections.

In terms of social services, the government has not put a great deal of effort into developing mobile or floating facilities that could serve boat dwellers at their homes, perhaps with one eye on the diminishing clientele that such facilities might serve. Instead, the expansion of social service availability on land, through the government's Social Welfare Department and through private agencies, is felt to be sufficient to meet the floating population's needs. Outreach efforts directly aimed at the floating population are mostly the province of church-related organizations. Several Catholic priests in particular are known in the community as spokesmen for the boat people and articulators of their needs.

The indirect policies that may have long-term implications for the welfare of Hong Kong's floating population begin with the territory's longer-term plans for physical development. In 1984 the government completed studies aimed at developing a plan for Hong Kong's physical growth through the 1990s, recognizing that after completion of the current new towns by 1991, a new strategy for land development would be required (Pryor, 1985). This Territorial Development Strategy (TDS) was drawn up through the use of sophisticated methodology, including the use of computer optimization models designed to compare alternative land development strategies in terms of minimizing their cost to the government or to the broader community (Choi, 1985). For the boat dwellers, the direct effect of the TDS will be the loss through reclamation of some of their present anchorages. Particularly hard hit will be the community at Yau Ma Tei, since the typhoon shelter there is slated for reclamation at an early stage in the development program (Hong Kong Government, 1985b).

To date, no government publication commenting on the Territorial Development Strategy has made reference to any plans for relocating the floating settlements affected by reclamation. Locations for possible new typhoon shelters have been noted, suggesting the possibility that a community of boat dwellers might be relocated en bloc to a different shelter. It is more likely that the government will renew its efforts to relocate the floating communities on land.

A more immediately controversial policy affecting boat dwellers concerns immigration control. Since late 1980, illegal immigrants to Hong Kong from China have been repatriated whenever found. Only persons with exit papers ("one-way permits") issued by the Chinese government are allowed permanent entry into the territory. In 1984 more than 26,000 people emigrated to Hong Kong in this way. Somewhere between 180,000 and 200,000 others are waiting for their chance to emigrate (*South China Morning Post,* 1985b, p. 8).

The floating population falls into a gray area in Hong Kong's immigration legislation. A boat-dwelling man from Hong Kong who marries a woman from China is allowed to bring her on board his boat, and into Hong Kong waters, as long as he remains engaged in fishing. The woman is not allowed to leave the boat, however, unless she needs urgent treatment on land in, say, a medical emergency. In effect, she becomes one of the boat's crew in the eyes of immigration officials, and unlike other cases where families are separated, she does not require a one-way permit from the Chinese authorities to enter Hong Kong. Estimates of the number of "boat brides" range from 800 to 1,000, with the largest numbers in Yau Ma Tei and Aberdeen typhoon shelters.

Difficulties with this arrangement can arise in two ways. First, if a family becomes eligible for resettlement, those who are Hong Kong residents (almost always the husband and any children born in Hong Kong) can move to accommodations on land, whereas legally the others cannot. Not wishing to split up families, the government has responded by not including any households in this situation in its resettlement offers. Second, and more crucially, if the husband takes up employment on land, the wife and any China-born children become illegal immigrants, liable to be repatriated at any time. The situation becomes critical when a family cannot sustain its livelihood from fishing and turns to other employment, as many boat dwellers have done.

Matters came to a head in late 1984 when fourteen boat-dwelling women whose husbands had taken up factory employment petitioned the authorities to be allowed to stay in Hong Kong. The government's eventual response was to order them to return to China and apply for one-way permits through the established channels. The plight of the boat brides received considerable media attention during the summer of 1985, but despite this and despite appeals from social service organizations and political pressure groups, the government stood firm in its decision. The case highlighted the uncertain legal status of other boat-dwelling families and brought the floating settlements—for a time, at least—sharply into the public consciousness (*South China Morning Post,* 1985b, p. 8, 1985c, p. 8, 1985d, p. 1).

Implications for Other Spontaneous Settlements

The floating communities in Hong Kong are distinctive in a number of ways from most other forms of spontaneous settlement, including the land-based squatter settlements found elsewhere in Hong Kong. They are not of recent origin, but instead represent a uniquely evolved adaptation by a distinctive cultural group to the needs created by their mode of life. The floating settlements tend not to be dominated by an informal economy. Instead, most of the floating workforce hold jobs, although not lucrative ones, in the formal manufacturing sector or in fishing. In addition, the floating communities enjoy a status as tolerated, if not completely welcomed, elements in Hong Kong's highly diversified physical and social fabric. They are a well-accepted part of Hong Kong's extraordinarily heterogeneous culture.

This distinctive character does not mean that Hong Kong's floating settlements are only an interesting curiosity with no possible relevance for policymakers outside the territory. From the standpoint of planning and housing officials in other less developed countries, the continuous shrinkage of Hong Kong's floating settlements merits an especially close examination—both the ways by which shrinkage is brought about and the consequences it imposes on those who remain afloat and those who resettle ashore. Three questions suggest themselves immediately: (1) the representativeness of the conditions that combine to produce a decline in the size of floating settlements; (2) the possible problems posed by the adjustment of spontaneous settlers into regularized conditions; and (3) the problems created for settlers who remain when spontaneous settlements are reduced in size.

Representativeness. Earlier in this chapter several explanations were suggested for the shrinkage of Hong Kong's floating settlements. Included were elements relating to economic trends in Hong Kong, to government housing policies, and to social and cultural characteristics of the floating population. Many of these factors are closely linked to Hong

Kong's distinctive political status as a quasi-independent city–state, and to its past success in establishing a thriving economy based on export-oriented manufacturing, which provides alternative employment for residents engaged in agriculture and fishing. These conditions differ from those found in most other cities of the Third World, and they must be accounted for when considering whether any of Hong Kong's experiences relative to the shrinkage of its floating population are transferable to other localities.

For instance, Hong Kong's status as a separate political unit gives the authorities a great deal more control over the flow of rural–urban migrants than exists for the administrators of the typical Asian, African, or Latin American city. Whereas migration from the countryside to the cities in most nations is unhindered by political boundaries, prospective migrants from rural China to Hong Kong must obtain permission from both governments—the granting of which is tightly controlled. The boat brides controversy illustrates the direct effect that Hong Kong's rigid immigration controls have on the growth of spontaneous settlements. The shrinkage of Hong Kong's floating communities, and the expected stabilization and eventual decline in land-based squatter settlements, owes a great deal to the removal of any source of continued population growth other than natural increase, which itself is on the decline in Hong Kong (Hong Kong Government, 1983).

The public housing program in Hong Kong also differs radically from the norm in most developing countries. Hong Kong's program, with its emphasis on a large volume of construction and a high level of capital expenditure, may not be the appropriate model for other Third World cities, where resources that can be allocated to housing programs are more scarce (Mabogunje et al., 1978; Yeung and Drakakis-Smith, 1982). The resettlement of boat dwellers into new housing on land is occurring in tandem with the rapid increase in the number of low-cost flats available in Hong Kong. If the public housing program were not progressing at such a rapid pace, the economic incentives for remaining in the floating communities would be much stronger. For cities and regions where the availability of low-cost subsidized housing is limited, Hong Kong's experience in resettling at least part of this group of spontaneous settlers (not to mention the much larger group of land-based squatters) is unlikely to be directly applicable.

Officials in these other cities and regions are encouraged by many housing analysts to think in terms of in situ modernization of squatter settlements, directed self-help provision of basic housing, or sites and services development, rather than in terms of high-rise, high-technology capital construction. It is interesting to consider what sort of programs might appear in Hong Kong if officials were thinking in equivalent terms when responding to the needs of the floating population. They might introduce initiatives such as the following:

- Financially supporting the systematic maintenance of dwelling boats, through periodic capital grants or by engaging the expertise of specialists in boat building.
- Encouraging the expansion of communally supplied social services within the floating settlements, making use of the organizational capacities of government social workers. (Day care for children, in particular, is a pressing need.)
- Supplying additional infrastructure to serve the floating communities, such as permanent moorings (resembling those, perhaps, in a traditional marina).

There is little prospect of such programs appearing in Hong Kong. This is directly traceable to the government commitment to conventional public housing, which the authorities consider to be highly successful. Although the need may not exist in Hong Kong, it certainly cannot be assumed that equivalent needs do not exist in places where different conditions prevail (see the essays in Yeung, 1983).

In general, explanations for the decline of Hong Kong's floating population center on economic and cultural forces operating within the territory, which fortuitously create conditions that favor the movement of the floating population out of the spontaneous settlements and into more traditional communities based on land. Perhaps the most significant implication policymakers in other localities can draw from Hong Kong's experiences with its floating communities involves the importance of such elements of the "social and economic climate" prevailing within a city in determining the future of spontaneous settlements. Even in the absence of an active resettlement program for the floating population, Hong Kong has seen some success in reducing their numbers.

Adjustment to "Regularized" Conditions. When boat dwellers are resettled into land-based housing, some adjustment problems inevitably arise, above and beyond the normal ones associated with any household move. For breadwinners leaving the fishing industry, there is the need to adapt to the routinized setting of the factory floor. For spouses and children, often pressed into service on fishing vessels for minor maintenance to the equipment, drying nets, or other repetitive tasks, determining the best use of free hours necessitates some adjustment. For all, there is a change in the social environment from the more insular, tightly knit community found within the floating settlement to the larger, more heterogeneous, and more anonymous setting prevalent in housing estates.

As has happened in other resettled squatter communities, the notion of maintaining and properly using community property may take some getting used to; in a floating community most amenities are individually owned. Hence getting the new settlers to make good use of parks, playgrounds, community halls, and the other amenities provided in a housing estate may be difficult at first. If resettlement of the floating population is scattered and piecemeal, the effects resulting from fragmentation of the boat dwellers' established social networks may be quite pronounced. It is notable and welcome that the Housing Authority in Hong Kong offers to resettle a number of boat-dwelling families together in the same area.

Problems Created by Planned Shrinkage. As Hong Kong's floating communities diminish in size, the remnants become less and less economical to service either by government agencies or by private commercial or charitable organizations. Social welfare facilities directed principally at the floating population, for instance, serve a smaller and smaller market under present conditions. The problem of maintaining an adequate level of urban services in a setting where the clientele is declining in size has been touched on with respect to slum areas in American cities (Heilbrun, 1979), and it is possible that with active progress in the drive to eliminate or regularize spontaneous settlements in developing countries, the issue will come up more often in the future. An entire squatter community cannot always be resettled or upgraded at one time, perhaps because of limited resources or spending constraints imposed by the government, and the problem then arises of providing services economically to those that remain.

Several questions concerning policy toward shrinking spontaneous settlements immediately suggest themselves. At what point is it permissible to withdraw public services, such as a primary school or a community health care center, that function in a shrinking spontaneous settlement? Should the entire community pay a higher average cost for these services as a consequence of maintaining less-well-used facilities in such areas? Is it ever justified to clear or relocate the remnant of a shrinking settlement purely on the grounds that it is expensive to service? In the 1950s an argument similar to this last one was made by government officials in Hong Kong in relation to land-based squatters; they believed that the cost of constructing resettlement housing was less, in the long run, than the cost of providing either humanitarian relief after squatter-area fires or preventative health care (Drakakis-Smith, 1979; Keung, 1985). These questions have not yet been faced with respect to the floating population, partly because the per capita expenditure question does not arise in the floating communities (most social services are located on land and serve land dwellers as well as the floating population) and partly because of the small size of the boat-dwelling community. There is also, of course, no immediate alternative use for the waters occupied by the floating communities—unlike the case with land-based squatter settlements. If an entire floating settlement is ever relocated in the future, it will most likely result from the reclamation of its sheltered anchorage to provide more land for urban development.

Indeed, questions like these have no ready answers, and perhaps this is one reason they are seldom raised in the context of the housing problem in developing countries. Yet if a nation is successful in stemming the growth of spontaneous settlements, or in relocating a majority of its squatters into higher quality or more permanent housing, questions of this nature eventually will arise. Housing officials and planners then may find themselves interchanging one set of difficult policy issues for another.

Conclusion

The longer-term prospects for the survival of Hong Kong's floating settlements are rather dim. Certainly the government is exerting its best efforts to encourage boat dwellers to relocate on land, and its efforts are aided by a growing perception within the floating communities that land-based life styles offer more economic and social opportunities. It is premature, though, to suggest that floating settlements will suddenly disappear, and certainly this cannot be expected in the immediate future. At the earliest it will be 1995 before all land-based squatters in Hong Kong can be resettled into subsidized units, and this government-set target date is thought to be overly optimistic by many observers. It appears that no special priority will be given to compel the resettlement of the floating population, and no doubt at least a tenacious remnant will persist in retaining their traditional life style despite periodic inducements to leave. An apt comparison here is with rural New Territories villages, which have lost much of their younger population but retain, for the time being, their elderly residents, who subsist as marginal farmers, supplementing their meager earnings by remittances from relatives who have emigrated (see McGee and Drakakis-Smith, 1981).

It is in the short- to medium-term, during which floating settlements will shrink without completely disappearing, that Hong Kong policymakers will face their most daunting task. Is it possible for a spontaneous settlement to be reduced in size, stripped of the majority of its younger population, gradually weaned away from its traditional means of livelihood (fishing), and perhaps eventually relocated to an altogether new site, without creating intolerable strains on the remaining residents or totally disintegrating the community? Hong Kong's treatment of its floating population in the years to come represents an interesting prototypical example. Although the circumstances surrounding the case may be idiosyncratic and not fully representative of conditions elsewhere, it bears watching by policymakers in other places who look forward to a time when the growth of spontaneous settlements might be reversed.

Notes

1. Concern over land shortages has inspired the formation of a high-level government committee that focuses on questions of providing land for new development. Several planning studies aimed at determining the longer-term development potential of Hong Kong were also commissioned (Pryor, 1985). Surprisingly, these latter studies concluded that Hong Kong has more than enough developable land to meet needs related to future population growth.
2. One other factor that contributes to overcrowding is the high prices paid by private developers for building parcels, partly reflecting the government's practice of selling land at competitive auction (Kwok, 1983). Private developers concentrate their energies on housing for the middle and upper classes, which normally commands higher rentals for an equivalent-size site than does lower-income housing.
3. In 1973 the authorities set a goal of rehousing 1.8 million residents in standard-quality housing over a ten-year period, with the aim of eliminating substandard housing in squatter areas and private tenements. Although this ambitious goal was not realized, the past decade has seen an expansion of the public housing construction program, with over 36,000 new rental and ownership flats completed in 1984–85 alone (Hong Kong Housing Authority, 1985, p. 8).
4. In 1985 there were forty-eight THAs housing some 132,000 people (Hong Kong Housing Authority, 1985, pp. 104–5).
5. Of potentially greater impact are the implications of government policies in tangentially related areas—notably land-use planning and immigration control—which are not directly aimed at the floating communities, but which have an indirect effect on living conditions there.

References

Anderson, Eugene N. 1972. *Essays on South China's Boat People.* Taipei: Orient Cultural Service.

Bristow, Roger. 1984. *Land Use Planning in Hong Kong.* Hong Kong: Oxford University Press.

Choi, Y. L. 1985. "The LUTO Model and Its Applications in Hong Kong." *Planning and Development* 1(1), 21–31.

Chu, David K. Y. n.d. "Government Policies, Economic Development and Ecological Feedbacks at the Land–Water Interfaces of China, with Special Reference to Guangdong Province." Unpublished discussion paper, Department of Geography, Chinese University of Hong Kong.

Drakakis-Smith, David. 1979. *High Society: Housing Provision in Metropolitan Hong Kong—A Jubilee Critique*. Hong Kong: Centre for Asian Studies, University of Hong Kong.

Heilbrun, James. 1979. "On the Theory and Policy of Neighborhood Consolidation." *Journal of the American Planning Association* 45(4) (October), 417–27.

Hong Kong Government. 1985a. *Hong Kong 1985*. Hong Kong: Government Printer.

———. 1985b. *Planning for Growth*. Hong Kong: Government Printer.

Hong Kong Government, Census and Statistics Division. 1983. *Demographic Trends in Hong Kong 1971–82*. Hong Kong: Government Printer.

Hong Kong Housing Authority. 1981. *The First Two Million*. Hong Kong: Hong Kong Housing Authority.

———. 1985. *Hong Kong Housing Authority Annual Report 1984/85*. Hong Kong: Hong Kong Housing Authority.

Hong Kong Housing Department. 1985. Unpublished report on 1984–85 Squatter Survey. Quoted in press release, Hong Kong Housing Authority, October 24.

Kani, Hiroaki. 1967. *A General Survey of the Boat People in Hong Kong*. Hong Kong: Southeast Asia Studies Section, New Asia Research Institute, Chinese University of Hong Kong.

———. 1972. "The Boat People in Shatin, N.T., Hong Kong: The Settlement Patterns in 1967 and 1968," *Chung Chi Journal* 11(2) (October), 57–65.

Keung, John K. 1985. "Government Intervention and Housing Policy in Hong Kong." *Third World Planning Review* 7(1), 23–44.

Kwok, Reginald Y. W. 1983. "Land Price Escalation and Public Housing in Hong Kong." In *Land for Housing the Poor*, ed. Shlomo Angel et al., pp. 328–47. Singapore: Select Books.

Lee, Rance P. L. 1981. "The Fading of Earthbound Compulsion in a Chinese Village: Population Mobility and Its Economic Implication." In *Social Life and Development in Hong Kong*, ed. Ambrose Y. C. King and Rance P. L. Lee, pp. 125–60. Hong Kong: Chinese University Press.

Lo, C. P. 1983. "The Population: A Spatial Analysis." In *A Geography of Hong Kong*, ed. T. N. Chiu and C. L. So, pp. 105–23. Hong Kong: Oxford University Press.

Mabogunje, A. L., J. E. Hardoy, and R. P. Misra. 1978. *Shelter Provision in Developing Countries*. Chichester: Wiley.

McGee, T. G., and David Drakakis-Smith. 1981. "Sap Say Heung—Emigrant Villages in Hong Kong." In *Urban Hong Kong*, ed. Victor F. S. Sit, pp. 160–66. Hong Kong: Summerson Eastern.

Myers, John T. 1981. "Residents' Images of a Hong Kong Resettlement Estate: A View from the 'Chicken Coop.'" In *Social Life and Develop-*

ment in Hong Kong, ed. Ambrose Y. C. King and Rance P. L. Lee, pp. 21–36. Hong Kong: Chinese University Press.

Pryor, E. G. 1983. *Housing in Hong Kong.* Hong Kong: Oxford University Press.

———. 1985. "An Overview of Territorial Development Strategy Studies in Hong Kong." *Planning and Development* 1(1), 8–20.

Smart, Alan. 1985. "The Squatter Property Market in Hong Kong: Informal Regulation and the State." Unpublished discussion paper, Centre of Urban Studies and Urban Planning, University of Hong Kong.

South China Morning Post. 1985a. "Brides in Limbo Are a Political Time-Bomb." February 24, p. 1.

———. 1985b. "Boat Brides' Saga Sparks Talks Call." July 6, p. 8.

———. 1985c. "The 14 Boat Brides Must Leave—and That's Final." July 10, p. 8.

———. 1985d. "Brides Take Last Option." July 24, p. 1.

———. 1986. "Typhoon Shelter Boat People Offered Homes." January 31, p. 13.

Yeung, Yue Man, ed. 1983. *A Place to Live: More Effective Low-Cost Housing in Asia.* Ottawa: International Development Research Center.

Yeung, Yue Man, and David Drakakis-Smith. 1982. "Public Housing in the City-States of Hong Kong and Singapore." In *Urban Planning Practice in Developing Countries,* ed. John L. Taylor and David G. Williams, pp. 217–38. Oxford: Pergamon Press.

Chapter 10

Low-Income Settlements in Monrovia, Liberia

LINDA LACEY AND STEPHEN EMANUEL OWUSU

In African cities, government officials concerned with shelter provision are faced with numerous constraints, including rapid population growth, increasing urbanization, stagnant economies, and shortages of materials. Finding ways to house the rapidly growing populations in Africa is an immediate need. The situation is critical in Monrovia, Liberia's federal capital and largest city, where earlier efforts at producing low-income housing estates are being replaced by concurrent strategies including sites and services, core housing, and community upgrading.

In this chapter we examine the evolution and the growth of communities within Monrovia, Liberia, and discuss how residents have produced shelter for themselves. We also examine the role of the government in providing shelter to the urban poor and indicate alternative strategies that officials can pursue.

Population and Economic Pressures

Most sub-Saharan African countries are doubling in population every twenty to twenty-five years. Projections made by the United Nations (1985) indicate that from 1980 to 2000 Africa will increase in population by 401 million, or 81 percent. Accelerated growth has resulted in high proportions of the population being under fifteen years of age; in future years, this will keep birthrates high in spite of declines in fertility.

While populations are growing rapidly, economic development is stagnant in some countries and is even declining in others. World Bank statistics indicate that per capita income fell between 1973 and 1983 in sub-Saharan Africa (World Bank, 1984a). Long-range projections by the World Bank also indicate declines in gross domestic product (GDP) in most sub-Saharan countries. For Zambia and Liberia, where the GDP grew an average of 5 percent per year between 1960 and 1970, estimates indicate that from 1970 to 1982 the average annual growth rate was only .9 percent. Countries such as Uganda and Ghana experienced declines in GDP between 1970 and 1982 (World Bank, 1984a). Because of these trends, promoting income-generating activities and feeding, educating, and providing health care services to growing populations will take higher priority than the physical development of cities.

Although government resources are expected to decline for urban development, most urban centers will experience high levels of population growth. In 1950, 14.8 percent, or 32.6 million Africans, resided in urban centers. By 1980, 28.7 percent, or 136.7 million, lived in urban locales. By the year 2000, 42.2 percent, or 370 million, will be urban dwellers (United Nations, 1985). Urban growth has not been evenly distributed. In absolute numbers, select centers, such as capital cities, have been the prime receivers of new urban dwellers. Although many residents are migrants to these locales, a sizable number are urban-born as a result of high levels of urban natural increase.

Whether migrants or urban-born, most residents in sub-Saharan African cities are poor and without adequate resources, and large percentages of city dwellers reside in inadequate housing (Table 10.1). In the Republic of Cameroon, over 87 percent of the population lives in substandard areas in the cities of Douala and Yaounde. The proportion exceeds 70 percent in Ibadan, Lome, and Rabat. Most of the data presented in Table 10.1 were collected in the early 1970s, and urban growth has doubled the size of many of these cities since then. This suggests

Table 10.1. Populations Living in Slums and Spontaneous Settlements, Selected African Cities

Country	*City*	*Year*	*Percentage*
Cameroon	Douala	1970	87
Cameroon	Yaounde	1970	90
Kenya	Nairobi	1970	33
Kenya	Mombasa	1970	67
Malawi	Blantyre	1970	56
Morocco	Casablanca	1971	60
Morocco	Rabat	1971	70
Nigeria	Ibadan	1971	75
Senegal	Dakar	1971	60
Sudan	Port Sudan	1971	55
Togo	Lome	1970	75
Tanzania	Dar-es-Salaam	1970	50
Upper Volta	Ougadougou	1972	52
Zaire	Kinshasha	1970	60
Zambia	Lusaka	1969	48

Sources: Drakakis-Smith (1980); United Nations (1976).

that, in absolute numbers, even more residents are now crowded into old settlements or have created new communities in these cities.

Faced with limited resources for urban improvements but growing numbers of low-income families, planners, housing providers, and other urban administrators are forced to search for low-cost strategies to meet the needs of residents in African cities. In the 1960s and early 1970s, a number of governments developed low-income housing estates, complete with dwelling units and public facilities. Blitzer, Hardoy, and Satterthwaite (1981) indicate that few of the urban poor benefited from these projects in Nigeria, Egypt, and Kenya. In recent years, efforts to meet the needs of low-income families have focused on low-cost, self-help programs through which residents assist in providing their own shelter and community services. The shift in strategy is helping African governments improve living conditions for a larger number of urban residents.

In Monrovia, an estimated 70 percent of the city's residents are poor. Yet most families have obtained shelter and related services by their own means or through family or tribal ties. Although resources for urban development are limited, strategies have been pursued by the government to improve living conditions in the city. Efforts began in 1970 when the Liberian government established the National Housing Authority (NHA) to provide shelter for the poor. In the first phase of activities, five low-income housing estates were built. Because of the large numbers of low-income households, these units met only 1.83 percent of the housing need. To reach a larger number of residents, the NHA shifted its priority away from housing estates to self-help measures—sites and services schemes and community upgrading activities. In order to understand the evolution of these policies, we begin by tracing the development of Monrovia and the growth of low-income communities.

The Growth of Monrovia

In 1816 the American Colonization Society was founded to resettle free Negroes and freed slaves in the country of their forebears. The land bought by the Colonization Society in 1821 later became part of the Republic of Liberia. Settlers from America arrived in 1822. The first settlement was named Christopolis, but in 1824 it was renamed Monrovia in honor of President James Monroe of the United States (Gnielinski, 1972). In the early nineteenth century the new city consisted of the Kru, Bassa, Vai, and Grebor tribal communities, Americo-Liberians (freed slaves and free Negroes), and Africans from neighboring countries (Johnston, 1904).

Monrovia grew slowly during the early 1900s; rapid growth did not occur until after World War II. Under the administration of President Tubman, Liberia established an open-door policy to attract foreign capital and investments to the country. Tubman's economic policies led to the development of Monrovia's Free Port and the establishment of a number of industries.

Increased economic activities within the city attracted migrants from rural areas within the country and Africans from surrounding nations. Between 1947 and 1962 the city increased by 62,700 inhabitants. Census reports for 1962 and 1974 indicate that the city received another 120,000 inhabitants during this period. Srivastava estimated that 80,000 of these persons were migrants—14,000 international and 66,000 internal migrants (1980, p. 44). International migrants came from neighboring West African countries such as Guinea, Sierra Leone, Ghana, and the Ivory Coast and from developed countries such as the United States and Lebanon. Most internal migrants were short-distance movers from the three bordering counties of Lofa, Grand Bassa, and Bong. While 37 percent were interurban movers, the majority were from rural environments (Srivastava, 1980).

Between 1974 and 1982 Monrovia received another 125,800 new residents through natural increase and migration. From 1982 to the year 2000, 630,000 residents are expected to be added to the city. Monrovia dominates the economies of both rural and urban centers and is the prime receiver of migrants. The next largest urban center is Buchanan, with a population about one-tenth that of Monrovia.

Communities within Monrovia: Fraenkel's Observation in 1958–60

Fraenkel (1964) provided a comprehensive analysis of communities in Monrovia during the initial phase of rapid urban growth. She described the city as a conglomeration of about ten settlements and communities. Many of these areas evolved along tribal or religious lines. In 1958 Fraenkel observed that most communities consisted of members from the same tribal group. Only a few, such as Old Kru Town (now West Point), Bishop's Brook, and the Kwi Street community had diverse populations. Within most tribal and multiethnic communities, however, a wide range of socioeconomic levels was represented. Many of the established settlements surrounded the core of the city—Bishop's Brook, Bassa, Loma Quarters, Old Kru Town, Vai Town, and Snapper Hill—and some had origins dating back to the nineteenth century. Kru villages existed at the northern base of present Monrovia at the time when the first free Negroes arrived in 1821 (Johnston, 1904). Figure 10.1 shows the location of these communities in 1960.

When individuals and families arrived in Monrovia, extended family members and community-based traditional leaders assisted newcomers in obtaining shelter, jobs, and welfare services. Most established settlements within the city had governors or urban tribal chiefs who were

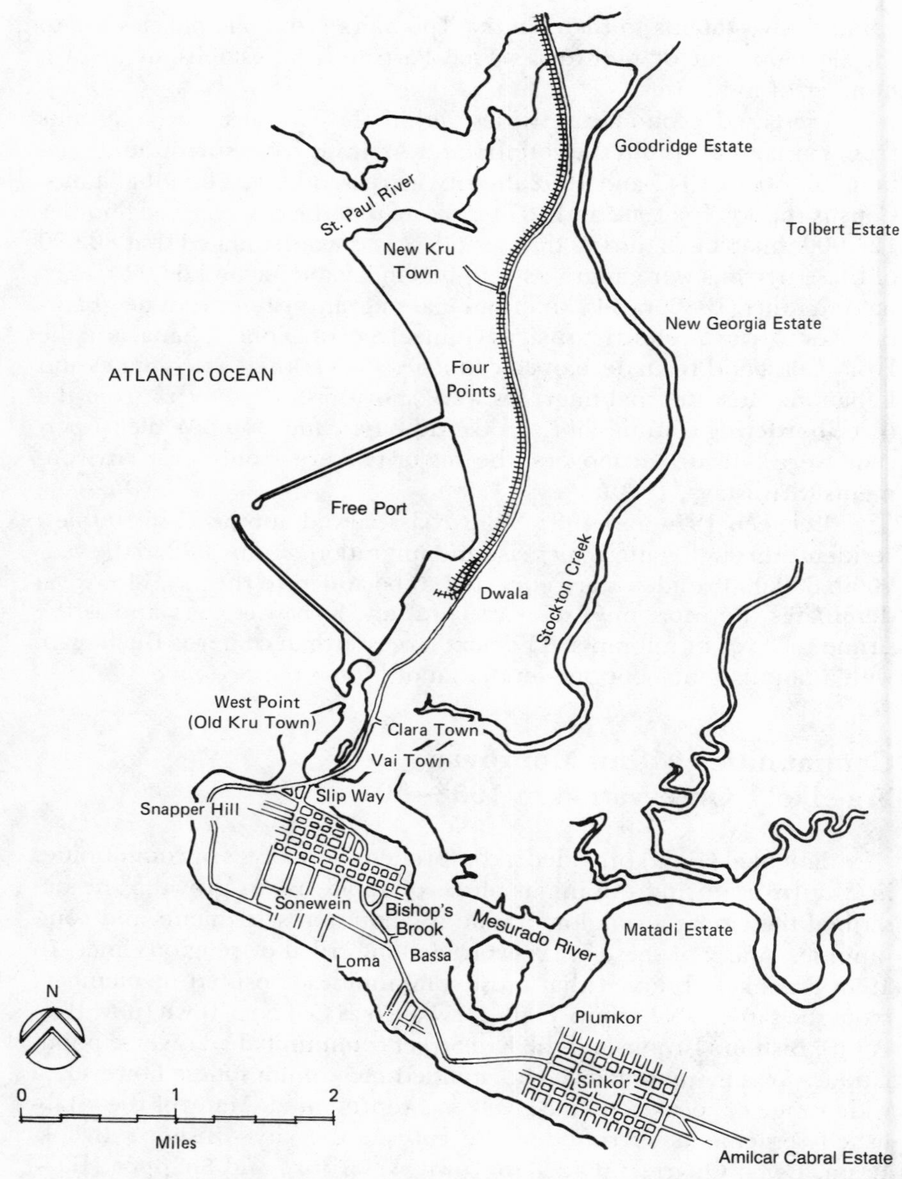

Figure 10.1 Communities within Monrovia, based on Fraenkel's observation in 1960, and the housing estates. *Source:* Fraenkel (1964, p. 46). (Illustration adapted by Harry Miarsono)

allocated varying levels of legal and administrative power over their communities by city officials. In three communities—New Kru Town, Vai Town, and the Bassa Community—traditional organizations developed land corporations to assist residents in obtaining shelter. The Kru, then the largest ethnic group in the city, had established the most complex system of administration and developed the largest land corporation in the city. In Kru settlements, the head of the community has the title of governor. Before 1916, the governor was chosen by Kru Town residents. At present, the governor is appointed by the president of Liberia and is assisted by a vice-governor and seven councillors, who represent the various subtribal groups of the Kru. The councillors act as assessors at the court of the Kru governor, assisting the governor in the role of urban tribal head.

Appointed in 1916, Governor Davies formed one administrative unit for all Monrovia Kru and developed the Kru Corporation. Monies for the corporation came directly from dues received from tribal members. While the corporation assisted needy families and provided legal services to community members, its largest venture was the provision of land for households evacuated in 1945 when the government decided to build a breakwater for the Free Port. The Kru Corporation, with some financial assistance from the government, purchased 52 acres of land about five miles north of the town center. Any individual of Kru origin could purchase one-eighth of an acre of land for $100 (Fraenkel, 1964). (The U.S. dollar is used as local currency in Liberia.) By 1958 Fraenkel observed about 250 houses, well spaced and built on a street plan.

A smaller land corporation was established in the 1920s by an American Negro Baptist pastor who wished to provide a place of residence for his congregation, which consisted mostly of members of the Bassa tribe. Nearly 27 acres of land were obtained. Anyone of Bassa descent who joined the church could purchase a plot of land for $12. Within the community, an elementary school was built along with a courtroom for the Bassa governor. In 1930, the deed for land in Vai Town was granted by the Liberian government. Anyone of Vai descent could claim land without payment. Fraenkel noted that many Vai residents leased their land to others or rented rooms. A paramount chief and a Council of Advisers had administrative charge of Vai Town and its land. These and other tribal associations enabled communities to assist families and new migrants in finding work and shelter in Monrovia.

Present-Day Communities in Monrovia

Fraenkel's observations were made over twenty years ago when Monrovia's population was about 80,000; at present it is over 330,000. Older communities have expanded to house new migrants who have joined relatives and friends, entirely new settlements have emerged at the periphery of the city, and within middle-class and elite neighborhoods small pockets of makeshift settlements have emerged. An estimated twenty-two low-income communities exist in greater Monrovia. The communities range in size from 5,000 to 36,000, and most continue to experience high levels of population growth, with the largest settlements experiencing the most growth. It is estimated that Sonewein grew from 21,079 in 1975 to 28,610 in 1980; West Point from 19,667 in 1975 to 25,367 in 1980; and Sinkor from 21,859 in 1975 to 29,663 in 1980 (World Bank, 1984b). Within most of these communities, household sizes range from 4.0 to 5.8 persons.

The World Bank (1984b) estimates the absolute poverty income level for Monrovia at $281 per capita per year; in 1980, 60 to 70 percent of the population of greater Monrovia fell below this level. The Liberian government has made even higher estimates of poverty. Based on household-level data collected from 1979 through 1985, the National Housing Authority has estimated that Monrovia's urban poor constitute close to 80 percent of the city's total population (Republic of Liberia, 1985a). Unemployment is high in Monrovia, ranging from 45 to 52 percent (Futures Group, 1983, p. 26; Republic of Liberia, 1985a, p. 4). Staff within the National Housing Authority predict that unemployment will grow worse, which implies that the number of urban poor will also increase.

In most low-income communities one sees a variety of housing, such as makeshift shelters built from wood siding or corrugated tin and cardboard, concrete block units, and wooden frame houses. The variety of structures reflects land ownership, land availability, migration intentions, and the different socioeconomic levels of households found within the communities. Some families achieve economic mobility and attempt to improve their shelters within their existing communities. Within West Point, the largest and most congested settlement where land is owned by the government, one occasionally sees concrete blocks slowly replacing makeshift materials as households improve their socioeconomic status (Photo 10.1). Once the new home is completed, the old shelter is taken down carefully and the materials are sold to community members.

Land is scarce in West Point, and newly arriving families build structures in unsafe areas, often in close proximity to rivers, community garbage dumps, and makeshift human-waste-disposal facilities. Families have built shelters on the bank of the estuary of the Mesurado River, which floods during the rainy season.

In New Kru Town, where the Kru were able to buy small plots of land through their corporation as early as 1945, a variety of new and older modern residential structures exist. Although makeshift housing is built increasingly as the community continues to expand, concrete structures are still in the majority.

Photo 10.1 Makeshift housing in West Point, Monrovia. Such housing is slowly being replaced by concrete block structures as families achieve socioeconomic mobility.

The availability of facilities such as water, electricity, and sewerage systems has not kept pace with the rapid growth of Monrovia. Many residents in low-income communities lack these services or pay a substantial proportion of their small incomes for them. The water supply system in Monrovia consists of public standpipes, metered connections, wells, self-contained roof collection systems, and water from the sea or river. While 40 percent have access to public standpipes, many must rely on a variety of other sources (World Bank, 1984b).

Of critical concern is inadequate sewage disposal. The sewerage system in Monrovia covers only 30 percent of the city. The lack of means to collect human waste leads to health problems, including outbreaks of cholera, which have been estimated at 400 to 500 cases a year since 1974 (World Bank, 1984b). Few public toilets exist. Residents in West Point, in particular, rely on makeshift toilets built over the river or sea. Many residents are charged fees to use such facilities.

The poor spend a large proportion of their income on energy, in part because of its cost, but also because of the inefficient way in which services are obtained. While the middle and upper classes rely on electricity as a primary source of energy, nonelectric sources meet most of the needs of the poor. Charcoal, kerosene, firewood, gasoline, and batteries are used for cooking, heating, lighting, ironing, and small-scale businesses. Access to electricity is limited, and most users obtain it through illegal wiretaps. Only 8 percent of West Point households have electric connections, and of these 400 connections, only 50 are legal (World Bank, 1984b). Illegal connections are very easy to make, provided the family can afford the $75 to $150 for the hookup, but they are dangerous and can lead to fires.

As the city continues to grow rapidly, increasing demands will be placed on its limited resources and infrastructure. Numerous health hazards, especially for children, exist in these communities, but funds for improvements remain limited.

Low-Income Housing Estates

In the initial stages of rapid urban growth, the Liberian government ignored housing problems in urban centers and put financial resources into other development sectors. The provision of housing for the urban poor was viewed as the responsibility of extended family members and the tribe, who acquired housing for new urban dwellers through the private sector or through illegal squatting.

Supportive efforts to meet the needs of the urban poor did not emerge until 1970 when the government established the NHA. The administrative duties of the housing authority were established in part by advisers from the United Nations in 1969. In the early years of the NHA, most of its activities focused on the establishment of housing estates in Monrovia. Five major estates were developed between 1970 and 1980, providing 1,479 housing units intended for low-, middle- and high-income families (Republic of Liberia, 1980). Land costs within the core of Monrovia were extremely high, so the housing authority obtained land on the periphery of the city. All five projects are located about two to five miles outside the center of the city. By 1980, Amilcar Cabral Estate had 72 units serving 350 Liberians, the Stephen A. Tolbert Estate had 414 units with a population of 2,000, the E. J. Goodridge Estate had 576 units housing 3,000 persons, and New Georgia contained about 226 units housing 1,000 persons. The Matadi Estate was specifically designed for middle- and upper-income families, with the intent of charging higher rents to subsidize the rents for the other four units. Planned to accommodate 905 households, about 191 units have been completed.

The Liberian government financed most of the cost of the housing estates for a total expenditure of about $15.8 million. The individual estate costs were Amilcar Cabral, $667,200; S. A. Tolbert, $5,588,640; E. J. Goodridge, $7,741,440; and New Georgia $1,802,000. An additional $14.6 million was borrowed from Citibank, an American commercial bank, to finance the Matadi Estate (Republic of Liberia, 1980). The high costs of the units reflect the building standards used. Units were built of brick or concrete in a modern style. An example of a unit in one of the older estates, Stephen A. Tolbert, is provided in Photo 10.2. The units were designed to accommodate small families. The grounds are well maintained, and most families have planted flowers and small shrubs around their units.

Most units in the estates are provided on a rental basis and are managed and maintained by the NHA. The housing authority employs staff for a full range of services including road repairs, building maintenance, groundskeeping, and garbage collection. The rental system was designed to generate revenues to construct additional units. In order for the government to recover costs from the units and develop a surplus of revenue for new units, it had to attract tenants with reliable incomes and charge rents that would generate sufficient revenues to pay for the units. The monthly income for the target population in Amilcar Cabral, S. A. Tolbert, and E. J. Goodridge was $200 to $400; in New Georgia, it was $75 to $150; and in Matadi, $500 to $1,300.

Few low-income families benefited from these housing estates; most units went to the middle class. Rents were far beyond the means of most residents of the low-income communities in Monrovia. As indicated in Table 10.2, most residents in low-income communities pay far less rent for their units than the fees charged in the estates. In West Point, the median rent is approximately $20, and 11.4 percent pay between $1 and $9 a month (Republic of Liberia, 1985a). Surveys conducted by the NHA also indicate that many residents do not pay cash rents. A variety of services are rendered in place of money.

The NHA estimates that 11,720 new households enter Monrovia's housing market each year (Republic of Liberia, 1985b). About 80 per-

Photo 10.2 A two-bedroom duplex unit constructed in the Stephen A. Tolbert Estate in 1976.

Table 10.2. Household Characteristics of Selected Low-Income Communities in Monrovia

Communities	*1980 Population*	*Household Size*	*Median Monthly Income*	*Percentage Homeowners*	*Median Monthly Rents*
New Kru Town	19,727	4.85	$110.72	30.00	$15.30
West Point	25,367	5.20	87.00	30.50	19.95
Plumkor	6,768	3.10	118.82	26.40	12.83
Dwala	3,560	4.43	153.87	30.63	18.33
Four Points	4,309	4.48	108.67	31.10	15.40

Sources: Republic of Liberia (1985); World Bank (1984b).
Notes: Some households also pay rent by providing services such as labor. These figures do not represent these households.
The Liberian government uses the U.S. dollar as its local currency.

cent of these households are poor and are unable to produce adequate shelter for themselves. While millions of dollars were invested in the NHA conventional housing units between 1970 and 1980, little was done to meet the shelter requirements of the growing number of urban poor during this first phase of activity. The housing units provided by the NHA are estimated to have met less than 2 percent of Monrovia's present requirement of 85,257 units.

Meeting the Needs of the Urban Poor

By the late 1970s and early 1980s there was growing concern about the needs of the urban poor among high-level government officials and staff within the NHA. It became apparent that the poor represented the majority of residents in Monrovia and required far more than housing to improve their living environment. This realization led to a shift in housing strategies. Concurrent strategies such as sites and services, core housing, and community upgrading activities are now being pursued to benefit a larger segment of the urban poor. Although a few additional housing units have been built since 1980 in the existing housing estates, new units are now being built within existing low-income communities such as New Kru Town and West Point.

A pilot sites and services project has recently been completed in the New Georgia Estate with grant money from The U.S. Agency for International Development. The NHA decided to experiment with this strategy before undertaking a large-scale project. Approximately 43 acres of land have been allocated to provide 550 plots, 100 core units with kitchens and bathrooms, and a few complete demonstration units. An example of a core unit is provided in Photo 10.3. The kitchen and bathroom

Photo 10.3 A core housing unit, kitchen and bathroom, in the New Georgia Estate, 1986. About 100 core units are under construction.

are provided, and families are given a floor plan to guide the construction of additional rooms.

At present, the 100 core units have been sold and 418 plots of land are for sale. Serviced plot sizes range from 1,750 to 2,555 square feet, and costs range from $1,450 for the smaller plots to $2,124 for the larger plots. Households are expected to make a downpayment of 3 percent and pay monthly mortgages of $14.50 to $21.50 for a twenty-year period. An extra $2.50 is charged for community services. Families purchase the core units that range from $4,539 to $5,983, with monthly mortgage payments ranging from $45 to $58.50. These families also pay the extra $2.50 for community services. The monthly income range of the primary wage earner is $100 to $226 for those purchasing plots and $150 to $300 per month for those purchasing core units. Other requirements for the plots and core units include the following:

1. Liberian citizenship, and residency in Montserrado County for the past five years.
2. The purchaser must be at least eighteen years old.
3. Construction of the unit must begin within ninety days.
4. The plot or core must be occupied for a minimum of three years.
5. Residents must agree not to sell the plot or house for three years, and to offer it first to the NHA.
6. Residents may not own any other residential property in Montserrado County.
7. Purchasers are limited to one plot or core unit in New Georgia.

In the initial plans for the project, loans for home development were part of the package. Unfortunately, banking institutions in Liberia are facing critical financial problems and are unable to provide small-scale home construction loans to low-income households. Because of this, there is no limit on the amount of time that it takes for families to complete their units.

To assist households in building safe, reliable shelter and maintaining healthy living environments, guidelines, regulations, and technical assistance are provided. The NHA provides each household with four alternative floor plans. Those households that wish to use their own design must obtain permission from the housing authority. Buyers are required to build flush toilets and bathrooms that are connected to the sewer line, use fireproof materials, limit construction to two floors, finish and paint the outside walls, and have ceiling heights in living areas of at least seven feet. Households are also allowed to operate businesses within their homes provided that they do not create noise or air pollution. In addition to shelter, other services provided as part of the New Georgia Estate include three licensed schools, three health care clinics, several churches, two markets, a few shops, and two large playing fields. These services were built as part of the housing estate rather than as part of the sites and services project.

It is too early to evaluate the success of this demonstration project. The core units are being built by families and hired labor, and the application process for the serviced plots has just begun. In June 1986 we observed lines of applicants for the serviced plots. Most had heard of the project through radio and television advertisements sponsored by the NHA. In the site office, applicants were provided with simple but detailed information booklets and were given oral presentations on the concept of sites and services, as well as tours of the demonstration units.

The New Georgia Estate became the location for the project in part because of the availability of land and existing services and facilities. Since New Georgia is located on the periphery of the city, families with higher incomes (who can afford transportation costs to jobs) are more likely to apply for the serviced plots and core units. Poorer residents in older communities such as West Point, where people are within walking distance of informal-sector employment and business opportunities, are not likely to apply for fear of being moved away from employment opportunities.

To provide services for the poorest households, the government is pursuing community upgrading projects in several settlements. In order to target upgrading activities to low-income communities, the NHA investigated the needs and priorities of residents in seven communities in Monrovia and fifteen urban and rural locales throughout the country. The comprehensive study took the six years between 1979 and 1985 to complete and represents a major step in involving the poor in program design.

In Table 10.3 we provide information on the rank order of priorities of residents in selected communities of Monrovia. In New Kru

Table 10.3. Needs and Priorities of Residents in Selected Communities in Monrovia

	Communities					
	New Kru Town		*Dwala*		*Four Points*	
Population	19,727		3,560		4,309	
Percentage homeowners	30.0		30.6		31.1	
Percentage ranking of priorities (multiple responses)	Public toilet	88.30	Public toilet	63.14	Public toilet	83.66
	Clinic	63.95	Street lighting	46.58	Water supply	54.11
	Street lighting	63.15	Clinic	43.46	Clinic	47.87
	Water supply	62.72	Water supply	42.84	Street lighting	39.75
	Schools	57.73	Garbage	38.36	Schools	39.65
	Street paving	56.41	Transport	34.87	Electricity	30.80
	Garbage	48.21	Street paving	31.87	Employment	30.70

Sources: Republic of Liberia (1985); World Bank (1984b).
Notes: Some households also pay rent by providing services such as labor. These figures do not represent these households.
The Liberian government uses the U.S. dollar as its local currency.

Town, one of the larger communities, resident priorities included public toilets, a health care clinic, street lighting, water, schools, street paving, and garbage collection. Similar priorities were observed in other communities. Few households indicated housing as a top priority. Instead, they stated needs that are beyond their ability to provide for themselves.

The information from the surveys is being used to allocate resources for community upgrading. A full range of activities has just been completed in West Point by the NHA with assistance from AID. Projects include the construction of four sanitation units, a market center with forty-nine stalls to provide jobs and incomes for community residents, a primary school, thirty-six new rental units, and two miles of roads.

The Cost-Recovery Issue

The total cost of the West Point project was $950,000. Recovering project costs has been a major problem in most African countries. User fees and property taxes are the major sources used to recover costs. In West Point an alternative cost-recovery system is being implemented. The school and road will be managed by the government, but the income-generating facilities, such as the shopping center, public baths, and rental units, were handed over to a community-based cooperative founded in 1983. Any resident can join the cooperative for $1 and become a voting member for $5. The cooperative will own, manage, and maintain the community facilities and explore alternative ways that it can provide additional facilities and services. Members receive a share in the profits, and voting members can decide on ways to use resources for other upgrading activities.

To assist the cooperative, detailed management and financial guidelines and training have been provided by AID and the NHA. It is estimated that the projects can generate about $50,000 a year: $17,600 from the market stalls, $12,000 from the rental housing, and $5,600 per public bath facility.

It is difficult to project the success of this strategy. Only 30 percent of the residents are homeowners in West Point. Of the 6,833 households in the community, 4,749 rent their accommodations (Republic of Liberia, 1985a). Nevertheless, it is a relatively stable community. A survey by the Society of African Missions (1984) found that the average length of stay is 9.28 years. Given the permanent nature of the community, the West Point Cooperative can be a success. While this alternative method will take years to recover costs, it has created community responsibility for the projects and has established an environment that will facilitate other kinds of self-help projects.

The NHA has also encouraged the involvement of other agencies in community improvement efforts. Through a $10 million loan from the World Bank, the Monrovia City Corporation, which in past years focused on physical planning activities, is engaged in upgrading activities in three low-income communities: Clara Town, Sonewein, and Slip Way. Access roads are being improved; and drainage systems, sewerage systems, communal water points, and security lights are being provided. Community facilities such as primary schools, clinics, community centers, and marketplaces are also being expanded or constructed depending on need. Training in areas such as finance and municipal management is also being promoted so that staff can better coordinate community upgrading activities and devise alternative strategies for funding this level of activity. A summary of services completed is presented in Table 10.4. About 30 percent of the property taxes collected in the city are allocated to the Monrovia City Corporation. A proportion of the tax money will be used to repay the loan.

While the West Point upgrading project is turning into a success story, the Monrovia City Corporation faces a number of problems. Once upgrading activities occurred, the communities became attractive places in which to live and work. In most of the communities, however, residents are renters. Landlords are raising rents, since they can now attract higher-paying residents, and these increases are forcing some of the poorest households out of their communities. This problem raises the issue of land tenure. Without legal title to land, the poor can easily be displaced by upgrading activities. To improve the living conditions of the poor, legal rights to the land must accompany upgrading activities. Once residents feel secure within their communities, then it is possible to organize residents to maintain upgrading services and generate human and financial capital to expand services.

Table 10.4. Upgrading Activities Completed by the Monrovia City Corporation through the Monrovia Urban Development Project

	Communities		
	Slip Way	*Clara Town*	*Sonewein*
Population in 1980	9,988	N.A.	28,610
Upgrading activities			
Toilets with showers	7	11	10
Health clinics	1	1	1
Community centers	1	1	1
Elementary schools	1	1	1
Market	—	1	—
Roads, footpaths and drainage (in meters)	620	2,500	1,100
Sewerage (in meters)	750	1,950	380
Water lines (in meters)	900	1,900	800

Source: Interviews with Monrovia City Corporation Staff, June 1986.

Future Policies in the Light of Severe Financial Constraints

As in most low-income countries in sub-Sarahan Africa, funds for urban development are declining in Liberia. The share of government resources allocated for urban development and housing during the First National Development Plan, 1976 to 1980, amounted to 3.4 percent, or $26 million. In the Second Development Plan, 1980 to 1985, only 2.9 percent, or $18 million, was allocated to this sector. While housing providers and urban planners are implementing a wider variety of strategies to improve the residential environment of the urban poor in Monrovia, only a few communities are being reached with the resources that are available. This raises a number of issues. What financial avenues exist to fund additional urban development projects? Who should pay for urban improvements? What mechanisms exist to involve the poor in providing services for themselves?

To promote urban development in future years, housing officials and urban planners must pursue a number of concurrent strategies in low-income countries that can (1) generate revenues for urban development; (2) reduce the costs of urban improvements; (3) spread services and facilities to larger numbers of households; and (4) control rapid urban growth. Efforts to reduce costs and spread the benefits of urban development can include careful selection of low-cost appropriate technology for infrastructure improvements and housing construction; improved targeting of activities to the poor; coordination of activities and strengthening of linkages among government agencies, the formal and informal economic sectors, and community groups; and involvement of the poor in the provision of housing and related services. The development of an urban taxation system and the establishment of user fees for services such as water and electricity are strategies that can be pursued to generate revenues for urban improvements. To control rapid urban growth, governments must pursue both urbanization strategies and fertility regulation programs, since urban growth is a product of migration and natural increase.

The financial future of Liberia is bleak, and all the strategies above must be investigated. But their success will depend on the ability of the government both to create a partnership with low-income households to enable them to help themselves and to promote income-generating activities.

In established communities where urban governors and urban tribal chiefs continue to provide administrative and community services, the NHA and others involved in urban development must collectively work with these leaders to mobilize residents for community self-help activities. Joint efforts among planners, housing providers, local community leaders, and residents are needed to identify community problems, set specific goals and targets, develop alternative strategies to reach different segments of the community, and identify human and financial resources to aid in program implementation. Members of the community can also be called on to help resolve problems that arise during implementation and maintenance. Within many of the low-income communities in Monrovia, signs of participatory efforts exist. Citizens have collectively built churches and cleared play areas for children. The West Point Cooperative also provides evidence that participatory self-help efforts can be promoted. Household-level studies and community-group information-exchange sessions are needed to explore the kinds of self-help projects that communities can support.

Government officials must also play a stronger role in promoting income-generating activities in low-income settlements. More attention must be devoted to the informal economic sector, since it provides a large proportion of the urban poor with jobs. In most communities, a full range of skilled and unskilled economic opportunities exists. There are carpentry shops, tailor shops, and family-run fishing industries, in addition to numerous small retail stalls.

Photo 10.4 shows some of the small boats that dock on the edge of West Point, bringing in fish that will be smoked and sold by women in the community, throughout Liberia, and in surrounding countries. Providing loans to such small-scale businesses, expanding existing marketplaces, and building new market areas will assist larger numbers of families in improving their incomes and, consequently, their living environments.

Two significant changes must occur for a government–user partnership to work. First, government officials must create stable environments for low-income residents. Families must be given legal rights to

Photo 10.4 West Point is well known for its family fishing industries. Small fishing boats can be found at the far end of the sandbar. The fish are caught by husbands, brothers, uncles, and cousins and are smoked by the women and sold throughout Liberia and surrounding countries.

the land where they reside if officials wish to utilize fully the financial and human resources of residents. Second, urban officials must expand their role in the provision of shelter and related services. They must become both providers and facilitators of urban development. Dennis Rondinelli and Shabbir Cheema (1985) provide an excellent summary of the role of government as a facilitator. To their model, which includes needs assessment, determination of standards, financing and planning assistance, quality control, and cost-reduction efforts, we add another element: training. Substantial amounts of time must be spent training community members in community organizing, management of community-based upgrading projects and small family businesses, building construction, and maintenance. As facilitators of urban development, urban professionals must promote the involvement of low-income residents in all aspects of service delivery—identifying community needs and priorities, project and program planning, implementation, evaluation, and maintenance.

While self-help strategies will spread services to larger numbers of families, they are nonetheless short-term solutions. The major problem facing Monrovia is rapid urban growth. Government officials must explore ways to control this growth. Strategies that should be pursued include fertility-regulation programs, regional growth efforts such as the development of secondary cities or agroindustrial centers, and integrated rural development programs.

Conclusion

African towns and cities are experiencing rapid urban growth, and the majority of the new urban dwellers are poor and unable to provide shelter and basic services for themselves. With assistance from donor agencies, strategies have been pursued to improve the residential environment of the urban poor. The first efforts focused on low-income housing estates, but proved to be extremely costly while yielding limited shelter to the urban poor. In response, the 1970s focused on low-cost self-help strategies that could meet the needs of large numbers of low-income households. Sites and services schemes, progressive housing, and community upgrading activities were pursued in African countries such as Kenya (Muwonge, 1982), Malawi (Pennant, 1983), Tanzania (Mghweno, 1984), and Zambia (Jere, 1984).

The few studies of the experiences of African countries indicate that problems existed in reaching large numbers of the poor and in recovering costs, particularly for community upgrading activities (World Bank, 1983). Financial resources for additional urban development projects are limited. Consequently, African governments are exploring alternative ways to share the responsibility of meeting the shelter and related needs of the urban poor. Since most of these countries lack a strong formal private sector with which to share costs, expenses must be shared with low-income households.

The success of this government–user partnership will depend on the ability of the NHA and other agencies involved in urban development to implement changes. The first, and probably the most difficult issue they must address, is land tenure. Legal rights to the land where households reside must be given to residents to motivate them to improve their living environment. Also, the roles of urban officials must be expanded. Government officials must become both providers and facilitators of urban development and self-help processes. As the Liberian government relies increasingly on community residents to provide for themselves, community education programs and training must be expanded. Educational programs on environmental health, as well as information on home improvements, can assist residents in creating healthy environments for themselves and their children. Last of all, new organizational frameworks must be developed to coordinate the activities of agencies, public and private institutions, and community groups involved in the urban development process.

Acknowledgment

A short article, "Self-Help and Related Shelter Programs in Liberia," based on this chapter has appeared in the *Journal of the American Planning Association* 53 (2) (Spring 1987), 206–12.

References

Blitzer, Silvia, Jorge E. Hardoy, and David Satterthwaite. 1981. "Shelter: People's Needs and Government Response." *Ekistics* 48(286), 4–13.

Drakakis-Smith, David. 1980. *Urbanization, Housing and the Development Process.* New York: St. Martin's Press.

Fraenkel, Merran. 1964. *Tribe and Class in Monrovia.* London: Oxford University Press.

Futures Group. 1983. *Liberia: The Effects of Population Factors on Social and Economic Development. RAPID.* Washington, D.C.: Futures Group.

Gnielinski, Stefan. V. 1972. *Liberia in Maps.* New York: African Publishing Corporation.

Jere, Harrington. 1984. "Lusaka: Local Participation in Planning and Decision-making." In *Low-income Housing in the Developing World,* ed. Geoffrey K. Payne, pp. 55–68. New York: Wiley.

Johnston, Harry. 1904. *Liberia.* London: Hutchinson.

Mghweno, Joram. 1984. "Tanzania's Surveyed Plots Programme." In *Low-income Housing in the Developing World,* ed. Geoffrey K. Payne, pp. 109–23. New York: Wiley.

Muwonge, Joe W. 1982. "Intra-Urban Mobility and Low-Income Housing: The Case of Nairobi, Kenya." In *Housing the Urban Poor in Africa,* ed. M. K. C. Morrison and P. C. W. Gutkind, pp. 57–80. Syracuse: Foreign Aid Comparative Studies Series no. 38.

Pennant, Thomas. 1983. "Housing the Urban Labor Force in Malawi: An Historical Overview, 1930–1980." *African Urban Studies* 16, 1–15.

Republic of Liberia. 1974. *1974 Census of Population and Housing.* Monrovia: Ministry of Planning and Economic Affairs.

———. 1979. *Liberia: Geographical Mosaics of the Land and the People.* Monrovia: Ministry of Information.

———. 1980. *National Housing Authority 1980 Annual Report.* Monrovia: National Housing Authority.

———. 1985a. *Report on Survey and Feasibility Studies Conducted by Socioeconomic and Technical Section, 1979–1984.* Monrovia: National Housing Authority.

———. 1985b. *Shelter: Newsletter.* January. Monrovia: National Housing Authority.

Rondinelli, Dennis A., and G. Shabbir Cheema. 1985. "Urban Service Policies in Metropolitan Areas: Meeting the Needs of the Urban Poor in Asia." *Regional Development Dialogue* 6(2) (Autumn), 170–90.

Society of African Missions. 1984. *West Point, Monrovia, Liberia: Development Project Report.* Washington, D.C.: Society of African Missions.

Srivastava, Mohan L. 1980. "Migration to Liberia." In *Demographic Aspects of Migration in West Africa,* ed. Kunniparampil C. Zachavia, pp. 1–80. World Bank Staff Working Paper no. 414. Washington, D.C.: World Bank.

United Nations. 1976. *World Housing Survey, 1974.* New York: United Nations.

———. 1985. *World Population Prospects: Estimates and Projections as Assessed in 1982.* Population Studies no. 86. New York: United Nations.

World Bank. 1983. *Learning by Doing: World Bank Lending for Urban Development, 1972–1982.* Washington, D.C.: World Bank.

———. 1984a. *The World Development Report 1984.* New York: Oxford University Press.

———. 1984b. *Liberia: Monrovia Water, Power and Urban Projects Analysis and Strategies for Improved Access to Services by the Urban Poor.* Working Document on Liberia. Washington, D.C.: World Bank.

Chapter 11

Commercialized Rental Housing in Nairobi, Kenya

PHILIP AMIS

The conventional view of squatting in Third World cities involves the illegal occupation of land and user construction of shelter. The settlements so formed are often politically autonomous, under a permanent threat of demolition, and outside the legal system. Characteristically the urban poor build their own shelters on land they do not own, using anything they can lay their hands on. This user construction is occurring partly because private capital does not find such a sector attractive for investment in view of the insecurity associated with possible demolition (Roberts, 1978, 147–48). Once security is established and financial returns become available, however, capital for the construction of rental housing is attracted to this sector, regardless of the legal position. This process is transforming the nature of low-income urban housing in some Third World countries (Angel, 1983).

Nairobi, for example, is now a city of tenants. Over the last twenty years, squatter housing has been so transformed that by 1985 the city was characterized by the operation of the private rental sector, albeit illegally. In the first section of this chapter I discuss the developments behind this transformation of squatting. I then consider specific Kenyan and Nairobi experiences and analyze this process within Nairobi's four main settlements. I follow this by an examination in one unauthorized settlement of the operation of the commercialized rental sector and its policy implications.

The Transformation of Squatter Housing

Illegality as an aspect of squatting has generally discouraged capital investment in spontaneous settlements. Nevertheless, it is security for capital investment that matters rather than illegality per se. As such, the relationship between security and expected rates of return influences whether capital penetrates this sector. Through such mechanisms the two aspects of squatting—the illegal occupation of land and user construction—are related. Indeed, the notion that illegality and user construction are essential elements of squatting refers to a special case that has been popularized by much work in Latin America. My aim is to show that illegality and the intervention of capital are not always incompatible and that it is perfectly feasible for the private sector to operate in such illegal areas, thus preempting the existence of user construction.

Before continuing, it is relevant to elaborate on what determines security and expected rates of return for capital investment. Four developments seem to have influenced security or the de facto acceptance of unauthorized settlements.

The first and most clearly associated development has been the emergence since the 1960s of pro-squatter literature. The thrust of this new orthodoxy was that squatters could meet their own housing needs. These ideas were reinforced by a general shift in development philosophy toward the informal sector, small-scale production, and basic needs.

The second factor was that the process of rural–urban migration was inevitable. The rationale behind the demolition of squatter housing was partly a belief, especially in Africa, that migration would be temporary. Increasingly it became obvious, whatever policy was pursued, that urban growth would continue unabated. In the end there was little option but to accept unauthorized settlement (Wegelin, 1983). It was on this unlocked door that the humanitarian lobby was pushing.

The third development was World Bank involvement in urban shelter projects after 1972. This involved attempts to harness the ability of squatters to house themselves. The projects took the institutional form of settlement upgrading and sites and service schemes (Skinner and Rodell, 1983). The World Bank also exerted pressure, usually in the form of conditions on loan agreements, on Third World urban administrations to accept and stabilize unauthorized areas. Hence, in the mid-1970s the most marginal of the urban population was to discover that the World Bank had become its patron. This process of leverage in changing urban policy was particularly clear in Kenya and the Ivory Coast.

The final development is related to the preceding one, namely, the forces that explain the World Bank's involvement in supporting unauthorized development. The idealist view is that academic pressure with humanitarian motives and the Robert McNamara ideology account for this policy shift. This is not entirely convincing. Similarly, a crude materialist interpretation in terms of reducing wages by reducing housing costs is also unsatisfactory. First, this logic has always existed and does not explain the timing of a specific historical intervention. It also fails to explain a policy pursued and promoted in a wide variety of economic conditions (from Mexico and Brazil to Senegal and Kenya). It seems therefore that the underlying logic behind an acceptance policy must be sought at the political level. The acceptance of unauthorized settlements is a relatively painless, and potentially profitable, way to appease the urban poor in the Third World. The increasing mobility and ability of international capital to change locations at short notice is likely to make these political considerations more, rather than less, important.

At the macro level, these are the trends that are moving Third World administrations toward a more laissez-faire acceptance policy regarding unauthorized settlements. Therefore, whatever the precise legal position, the security for capital investments is likely to be increasing. We must also consider the expected rates of return in this sector in relation to alternative sources of investment. This expected return is clearly vital in attracting capital investment and will reflect the prevailing economic conditions within a specific country.

The level of competition within this sector is important in determining expected rates of return, and access to land and the extent of monopoly in this access are important in determining competition. Recent research confirms that the main determinant of shelter is the availability of urban land for development. The more land available, the lower the return, and this implies less attraction for capital investment. In contrast, the emergence of a monopoly tends to create land scarcity and higher returns with considerable attraction for capital (Angel, 1983, p. 22).

Within each historical and national context, these variables influence the security and rates of return for capital investment, which in turn determine the commercialization of low-income (unauthorized) housing. Change in these variables is transforming the concept of squatting.

Unauthorized Development in Kenya and Nairobi

The specific backgrounds of Kenya and Nairobi are significant in the emergence of the rental sector in unauthorized settlements. Kenya's colonial experience is that of a settler state. European involvement included establishment of a white agricultural export economy as well as administration. Land was taken from the African population to achieve this. Simultaneously, the African population was prohibited from growing cash crops and was seen as a labor reserve for the agricultural sector. The existence of this white-settler agricultural economy sharply differentiates Kenya, together with Algeria, Zimbabwe, and South Africa, from the rest of Africa.

Nairobi was the service center of this settler economy, and its location was a result of its being a convenient halting place in the construction of the Uganda Railway. It was originally conceived as a European city where Africans were tolerated only for their labor power. To achieve this, a pass-law system was established to restrict African migration. Nairobi was systematically racially zoned in the major plans of 1905, 1927, and 1948 (Van Zwanenburg, 1972). The main aim of the zoning was to achieve a disease-free urban environment with a minimum of public expenditure.

The result of this was extremely unequal land distribution, which means that for the impoverished African majority, the availability of urban land has been and still is severely restricted. Indeed, not until 1954 were Africans allowed to own leasehold property in Nairobi. Thus, until recently the Kenyan government attempted to control rural–urban migration, and by implication, urbanization. A related colonial legacy is that of housing and planning standards that cannot possibly be implemented given the economic conditions facing the majority.

Nairobi has experienced rapid growth. In 1962 its population was 343,500. By 1983 it had risen to 1 million. This represents an annual urban growth rate of approximately 5 percent, although since 1979 the rate seems to be declining to 4 percent. In terms of rapid urbanization, Nairobi has much in common with the general African context. As a result of its settler inheritance, however, few cities have been so inappropriately prepared to accommodate such an increase.

First, Nairobi has the extremely unequal land distribution inherited from racial residential planning so that in 1972 there were 8 inhabitants per acre in the ex-European zone, 32 in the Asian zone, and 400 in the African zone (Kimani, 1972). Second, Nairobi's planning and building bylaws were designed to maintain standards for a settler minority; consequently they are totally inappropriate to the economic position facing the majority. In this situation, where public housing programs have made little serious impact, the majority have increasingly sought shelter in the unauthorized sector.

The growth of the unauthorized sector has been spectacular, increasing from 500 units in 1962 to 22,000 units in 1972 (Chana and Morrison, 1973, p. 216). By 1979 a rough estimate would give 110,000 unauthorized units, housing approximately 40 percent of Nairobi's population. A recent study confirms the 40 percent estimate (Development Planning Unit, 1985). Without a cadastral survey, all such figures are little better than intelligent guesses. Nevertheless, the population estimates for the four main unauthorized settlements within Nairobi are given in Table 11.1.

Political and economic developments since the 1960s have resulted in the stabilization of these four main settlements, while others have been consistently destroyed. The emergence of the private rental sector has been an integral part of the development of these settlements. This process has both been encouraged by and resulted from capital availability and the private sector's intervention. As I mentioned above, for most

Table 11.1. Populations of Major Unauthorized Settlements in Nairobi

Year	*Mathare Valley*	*Kwangware/ Dagoretti*	*Kibera*	*Korokocho/ S. Karobangi*
1960	—	18,000	3,000	—
1965	3,000	30,000	6,000	—
1970	35,000	41,500	11,000	2,000
1975	65,000	65,000	20,000	5,000
1980	120,000	90,000	60,000	40,000

Sources: Estimates from Chege (1981); Hake (1977); HRDU (1971); Temple (1974); Waweru and Associates (1976).

Third World urban administrations there were many pressures toward such a policy. Within Nairobi, the emergence of rental housing in Dagoretti and especially housing companies in Mathare Valley after 1969, a cholera outbreak in 1972, and a major loan from the World Bank in 1978 were all significant in this gradual shift. I consider them in turn, together with the experience of the four main settlements. This provides the background for an analysis of one specific settlement.

The Process of Unauthorized Settlement

Dagoretti, located approximately 7 kilometers from the city center, is one of the main unauthorized settlements in Nairobi. Until 1964 it was outside the municipal boundary, and as such was part of the Kikuyu agricultural reserve. This area, along with much of the central province of Kenya, experienced land consolidation in the 1950s, which was a restructuring from communal to private ownership. Throughout this period, indeed starting from the 1940s, landowners began to construct a few simple mud-and-wattle structures for renting to lodgers (Memon, 1982). This process greatly accelerated in the mid-1960s. Helped by administrative confusion and inaction combined with severe housing pressure in Nairobi, the landowners, now ex-farmers, began to construct blocks of one-room timber units in considerable numbers on their plots. As one put it, "I am finding it more profitable to grow people than maize" (Memon, 1982, p. 153). The most significant fact about this development of low-income unauthorized housing was its profitability. Even at modest rent levels, capital investment could be recouped within one or two years (Memon, 1982). This discovery was not lost on other would-be landlords and speculators.

In 1969 a series of events took place that were to revolutionize housing in Nairobi's main unauthorized settlement, Mathare Valley. The inhabitants of Mathare felt that demolition was imminent and decided to form a cooperative to buy the land on which they were squatting in order to ensure their future security.[1] This movement to form cooperatives included both original squatters and later arrivals who had bought such property. Unfortunately, as these cooperatives sought to buy the land on which they collectively squatted, the price skyrocketed. In a sense their action created a land market that did not exist. Previously this land had a deflated and unrealizable value, partly as a result of the uncertainty associated with the squatters, but also due to the general fall in Nairobi real estate values associated with the political uncertainty at independence (Richard, 1970, p. 7).

As a result of this rapid increase in land prices, it became necessary for these cooperatives to seek additional funds, since with their limited resources they were unable to afford to buy the land on which they squatted. These cooperatives or companies effectively went public and sold shares. They had no difficulty in selling shares and attracting funds, since the expected rate of return was high, perhaps through evidence from Dagoretti on the grapevine, but both urban and rural land has always been perceived as a safe investment in Kenya. The effective control of these companies in terms of share ownership became increasingly dominated by individuals from outside Mathare Valley.

By the end of 1969 new companies composed entirely of outside members were being formed to buy land in Mathare Valley (Richard, 1970, p. 7). Until the spring of 1970, six of the eight companies buying land in the Mathare Valley originated there. For these first companies, the average share price was 500 Kenya shillings (500/-). (At that time one Kenya shilling = $.14; 500/- = $70). After the spring of 1970, however, of the seven companies buying land, only two originated in Mathare. For this group, the average share price was over 3,000/- ($420). This increase illustrates the growing recognition of the profitability of such housing development. The high cost of the shares also illustrates the increasing outside involvement of speculative property developers as opposed to the resident urban poor. These outsiders could see that despite the high cost of shares—land costs only slightly less per acre than in Muthaiga, Nairobi's diplomatic enclave—Mathare Valley represented an excellent site for urban development (Photo 11.1). It was one of the most accessible underdeveloped tracts of urban land from the city center (Richard, 1970, pp. 7–8). The strong suggestion was that these outside funds were from influential sponsors, even from sophisticated real estate developers (Jorgenson, 1977, p. 141). Clearly this fundamentally alters the situation and represents very different interests from those of squatters collectively attempting to buy the land on which they illegally live. The formation of such external companies provides the clearest example of the involvement of private capital in the rental sector in unauthorized settlements.

These outsiders were eager to start house construction, presumably to yield some return on their investment. Initially, they investigated

Photo 11.1 Mathare Valley. Units built by the housing companies. (Photo by Gary Gray)

legal housing development. Given the official minimum requirements, this was too expensive.

> After considerable hesitation the companies elected to ignore the regulations and begin construction. They in effect invaded their own land, building unauthorized housing according to their own plans and [to] suit their own needs. The risk paid off handsomely. No demolition orders were issued, and returns on investment were very high. (Richard, 1970, p. 8)

The lack of demolition was attributable in part to the proximity of the general election in November 1969. It also seems likely that there was some tacit agreement with the Nairobi City Council and the government.[2] Since the original squatters had increasingly lost control of their companies to outsiders, much of this development was not in their interests in terms of shelter but was motivated by profit for the shareholders. The limited objective of owning the land on which their houses rested was swept aside in an orgy of speculative back-to-back wooden tenement building. In some cases the original squatters were subjected to more eviction pressure from the companies than they were from either the state or the former Asian landowners (Housing Research and Development Unit, 1971; Richard, 1970; F. Temple, 1973, p. 272). Partly this pressure reflected the financial control of outsiders, but it would also seem that the more sophisticated were able to confuse the original squatters and take advantage of their limited education. This was clearly put by a spokesman for the, appropriately named, Quick Service Company, who said: "They [squatters] are becoming a bother. They are still sitting on land we purchased and we would like to demolish the shanties and put up new houses" (*Nation,* August 13, 1970, p. 1).

The rationale here is clearly that of an urban real estate developer. The return on capital investment in this tenement housing was spectacular—in the range of 50 to 100 percent (Hake, 1977, p. 159; HRUD, 1971, p. 62). This profitability has transformed the entire provision of low-income housing in Nairobi. During a sixteen-month period between 1969 and 1971, the companies built 7,628 room-units in Mathare Valley, doubling its population (F. Temple, 1973, pp. 268–75) and transforming its character and type of housing.

In Dagoretti and Mathare Valley unauthorized rental structures emerged on private land. The emergence of similar developments on public land was more dependent on the administration's adopting a policy of de facto acceptance and control. This has been the case with the other two major unauthorized areas, Kibera and Korokocho.

In the progression to an acceptance policy, the 1971 cholera outbreak was significant. In 1963 the Nairobi City Council claimed that the provision of water to unauthorized settlements would legitimize the existing illegal situation. Therefore, the council would not connect Mathare

Valley to the water system despite the residents' stated ability to pay for the service. Instead, through community action, money was raised and a pipe laid that was subsequently attached to an adjacent private plot. The water that was legally obtained on this plot was then resold privately to the settlement. This system proved inadequate. The outbreak of cholera in Nairobi in 1971 cut through legal and technical difficulties, and water standpipes were installed within five days in Mathare Valley and Kibera (Hake, 1977, pp. 154–55). The fundamentally self-interested nature of this action by the authorities was obvious (F. Temple, 1973, p. 280).

This installation of infrastructure was the first example of a policy of limited acceptance, resulting in the development of a dual policy. Hence, alongside the stabilization of certain settlements, others, notably small inner-city sites without the benefit of political patronage, were being demolished. In this context, the Nairobi River Valley site was demolished at least five times between 1969 and 1978. The most spectacular demolition occurred in 1977 when the entire site was demolished and approximately 10,000 inhabitants were moved to form the nucleus of the newest large unauthorized settlement, Korokocho. This savage demolition seems to have been a preemptive strike by the Nairobi authorities prior to signing a $50 million loan for urban projects with the World Bank. A key condition of this loan was a policy of freezing existing unauthorized settlements; both demolition and permitting unauthorized development were to be stopped.

This is the legacy behind the Korokocho settlement on public land 15 kilometers beyond the eastern edge of Nairobi. In this situation, the administration seems to have had some role in the layout of plots. Private landlords are developing rental accommodations on these plots similar in structure to those at Dagoretti and Mathare Valley. The sector remains highly profitable; the initial capital outlays were being repaid within two years (Kabagambe and Moughtin, 1983).

The Private Rental Sector in the Unauthorized Settlement of Kibera

To understand better the dynamics of the private rental sector, I examine the phenomenon in Kibera, an unauthorized settlement in West Nairobi. Kibera is one of the four main unauthorized settlements within the city. Historically the site has been associated with the Nubian community in Kenya. The colonial administration allowed the Nubians to settle in the area because they were an important element in the colonial military. In a legal sense the land in Kibera is all government owned; however, the colonial authorities allowed these Nubians to settle as "tenants at will." In the area's subsequent history we can see how claims to settle in the area shift from being based on ethnicity (i.e., Nubians only) to being based on more strictly economic criteria (i.e., ability to pay). This process mirrors the general capitalistic transformation within Kenya from "traditional" communal rights to land to private individual title deeds. Throughout Kibera's history, its urban settlement and development has had no formal legal basis. Yet property relations and ownership do exist in a de facto sense.

During the mid-1950s the Nubians were able to profit from their privileged position within the colonial administration by being allowed to construct additional rooms explicitly for rental purposes. The financial returns were exceptional and have been estimated at an annual capital return of 171 percent (N. Temple, 1973). The administration tacitly accepted this development, perhaps in return for Nubian loyalty to the colonial state. The Nubians were in a particularly advantageous position during the State of Emergency or Mau-Mau uprising from 1952 to 1960 because they were trusted by the state. Second, the official policy of removing the Kikuyu from Nairobi would have left them able to exploit the potential housing openings created by the encouraged migration from Western Kenya. By 1972 the settlement had grown to around 17,000 inhabitants composed of a private rental sector of a limited scale and some user construction on the fringes of the site. At this stage the local administration was passive toward unauthorized urban development.

During 1974, however, the local administration gained effective control over land allocation and was thus able to intervene in the unauthorized housing market. The administration began to allocate permission to build in Kibera. In order to support this allocation process, it threatened to demolish any new housing built without permission. The local administration thus intervened in this unauthorized sector by allocating protection for new construction.

This policy was partially the result of individual changes in local political and administrative positions. Nevertheless, as a result of this informal control, and aided by the continuing high demand, Kibera experienced something approaching a real estate bonanza. Approximately 1,400 new structures were built, tripling the area's population in five years. In 1979 the population reached 62,000. It is this new informal urban development that I now examine to illustrate the recent changes that have occurred within the provision of low-income shelter in Nairobi. The result has been that yesterday's squatter is today's tenant.

Allocation of Informal Building Rights

The allocation of informal building rights gives access to a lucrative source of capital accumulation and is a major resource controlled by the local administration. These rights are informal rather than legal and amount to an assurance of protection from demolition for individual allottees. Since the legality of this allocation process is at best debatable, political patronage is important in providing protection.

The local administration itself has become a client of more powerful political backers. Indeed, the recent history of "stop–go" regarding the availability of land is a function of shifts within these networks of political patronage. These networks are often internal to the Kenyan public administration, and in many cases the landlords are also members of the administration. This was true of 35 percent (ten of twenty-nine) of the large landlords identified in my study. The local administration may be returning favors, consolidating potential clients, or rewarding friends or tribesmen by informally providing free land for urban development. Inevitably information on such matters is difficult to obtain, but it is rumored that bribes change hands as well.

The process by which individuals use their position within the public sector to their own financial advantage has been well documented in Kenya. In fact, this straddling between the two economic sectors is considered to be the hallmark of Kenya's emerging bourgeoisie (Swainson, 1981). Nonacademic commentators might call it corruption. Within Nairobi, the allocation of building rights is generally an important source of political patronage for politicians and the administration.

This interpretation is consistent with some of my data on landlords. The predominance of Kikuyu among the large landlords in Kibera—seventy-one (66 percent) of those I surveyed were Kikuyu, while twenty-four (22 percent) were Nubian—is probably a result of patronage by the predominantly Kikuyu administration and politicians who were attempting to consolidate their power base. It should be noted, however, that these Nubians were all relatively recent recipients of land for building, and such allocations were likely made in order to forestall any potential opposition from them. Individuals involved in the allocation of building rights are often seen as collaborators with outsiders by the remainder of their community.

The Dynamics of the Rental Sector

To prosper in the rental sector, landlords must have access to land and capital and have estate management skills. I have already addressed how landlords secure land; below I discuss the access to capital. The third component, estate management, involves the collection of rents, finding new tenants, and day-to-day maintenance. Clearly this function is only a constraint for absentee landlords, and is discussed later.

The original squatter who starts to rent out several rooms has few problems, providing there is access to both land and capital (i.e., personal savings). This situation represents the emergent unauthorized private rental sector, which has a long historical legacy within the "African locations" in Nairobi (Bujra, 1973). But there is an inherent contradiction in the expansion of a small-scale landlord's operation. As the scale of operation increases, and as access to land becomes politically controlled, the landlord may have difficulty securing land and capital. To resolve this dilemma, the small-scale landlord must look elsewhere, including to patrons, to gain access to land and additional capital funding. The result is that the small-scale operator loses autonomy. Of course, some members of the Nubian community are able to fulfill these two functions through their own resources. This also seems to be true of the Kikuyu landowners in Dagoretti. Given the profitability of the sector, however, there is pressure on small-scale landlords to depend on external capital to increase the scale of their housing operations. From the other point of view, this can be seen as one way in which external capital penetrates this sector. These pressures are clearly at work in the housing companies in the Mathare Valley.

On public land, as in Kibera and Korokocho, the political control of land in unauthorized settlements facilitates the emergence of large-scale operations. Land may be directly allocated to those with sufficient capital, even though they do not live in the area, permitting a scale of operation that otherwise would be restricted by the general poverty of the settlement. This is not to say that a small-scale sector does not also exist, but the above are the mechanisms that encourage the commercialization of low-income housing and its increasing dominance by large-scale landlords.

The most obvious and important point about this rental sector is that it is a commercial operation, albeit illegal. The construction is subcontracted and involves a division of labor (Photo 11.2). Unlike user construction, the production, consumption, and ultimate ownership of the dwelling involves different individuals. Profits are extremely high. For example, the annual capital return on a ten-room structure I investigated in Kibera in 1980 was 131 percent. After only eight months, the landlord's rental income was pure profit, since maintenance and running costs are more or less nonexistent. The fact that the housing stock constructed is explicitly for rental purposes and not for owner occupation is suggested by the high average number of rooms per structure in the settlement: 10.33. Similarly, the average landlord lets over 12 rooms (Photo 11.3).

The distribution of room ownership among the landlord group within Kibera is revealed in Table 11.2.[3] The 32 percent of the landlords owning, as a group, the smallest number of rooms control only 10 percent of the available room-units, while the 6 percent letting the largest number of rooms are able to command fully 25 percent of the housing stock. Here can be seen the scale of ownership and its concentration. For example, four individual landlords control 571 rooms in Kibera, or 5

Photo 11.2 Kibera. Unlike user construction, the private sector involves substantial amounts of subcontracting in the building process.

Photo 11.3 Kibera. Private-landlord-developed housing. Each block will contain more than ten one-room units.

percent of the entire housing stock, giving each landlord an empire in excess of 100 room-units. While such a scale of operation is atypical, it is worth considering the financial rewards it represents.

Within a year at most, landlords will be able to recoup their initial capital outlay, and after this the rental income from 100 units will yield a monthly income of approximately 10,000/- (assuming an average room rent of approximately 100/- a month). This income will also be tax free, being impossible to declare. Even on a more modest scale, a landlord owning 30 units will have a monthly income of 3,000/-, after the initial capital is recouped (Photo 11.4). This is equivalent to the salaries from some middle-ranking white-collar jobs in Nairobi. Nevertheless, it is important to realize that for some individuals, this rental income represents their only source of income. In particular, for those who are landless and without employment in Nairobi, this rental sector provides the

Table 11.2. The Magnitude of Landlord Holdings in Kibera

Number of Rooms Let	*Number of Landlords*	*Total Number of Rooms*
30+	52 (6%)	2,762 (25%)
16–29	106 (12%)	2,177 (20%)
8–15	463 (51%)	5,039 (45%)
0–7	289 (32%)	1,141 (10%)
Total	910 (101%)[a]	11,119 (100%)

[a]Does not add to 100% because of rounding.

Photo 11.4 Kibera. The door numberings (38 and 39) give an indication of the concentration of ownership. This landlord will be letting out at least thirty-nine room-units.

income for their survival. Similarly, this small-scale urban landlordism provides an important source of economic security for many women, for whom income alternatives are closed. Consequently, while some of these landlords are well-off, it would be a mistake to underestimate the number of the urban poor who depend solely on this sector for a livelihood.

It is apparent from the above figures and from direct observation that the capital involved in the large-scale rental operations could not be exclusively generated locally. In fact, a high level of absentee landlordism was found among persons who let out more than twenty units; 64 percent lived elsewhere in Nairobi or Kenya, while 14 percent lived elsewhere within the settlement. This leaves only 22 percent living with their tenants as resident landlords.

Landlord–Tenant Relationships

Table 11.3 presents a social profile of Kibera. I have attempted to relate the social backgrounds of tenants and small and large landlords in terms of the International Labor Organization (ILO) income profile of Kenya. Some landlords are from social backgrounds markedly different than those of their tenants. It would be fair to say that no Kenyan occupational group is uninvolved in some way or another with the Kibera housing market, whether as landlord or tenant. Also worth noting is the variety within both the landlord and the tenant population. At one extreme are doctors, top civil servants, and managers from both the public and private sectors among the landlords. But there is also a significant landlord group from among the urban poor. Similarly, it would be a mistake to assume that all the tenants are on the bread line; some hold down middle-ranking clerical jobs but choose to live in such areas to

Table 11.3. A Profile of Tenants and Landlords in Kibera

ILO Urban Categories, 1976	*Monthly Income*	*Tenants*	*All Landlords*	*Large Landlords (more than 20 units)*
1. *a.* Owners of medium enterprises in commerce, industry, and services *b.* Rentiers *c.* Professionals *d.* Managers and top bureaucrats	2,500/- plus	0	17%	31%
2. *a.* Skilled employees in formal sector	1,667/- to 2,499/-	1%	22%	38%
3. *a.* Clerical employees in formal sector *b.* Semiskilled employees in formal sector *c.* Owners of some informal-sector enterprises	500/- to 1,666/-	48%	55%	31%
4. *a.* Unskilled employees in formal sector	250/- to 499/-	37%	6%	0
5. *a.* Informal-sector employees and smaller entrepreneurs	below 250/-	14%	0	0

Source: ILO (1979), table 2.11, p. 43.

minimize their expenditure on housing. Also in contrast are tenants who are some of the poorest citizens of Nairobi, without a regular income and for whom each day represents a battle for survival. In the middle, as the table shows, there is a degree of similarity between the circumstances of landlords and tenants. Suffice it to say, however, that if all the landlords actually lived in the settlement, the outward appearance of inequality would be greater than it is today, where the differences among the living conditions of many inhabitants are already striking.

Within commercialized settlements, landlord and tenant relations are generally hostile. The average rent (in 1980) was 99/- for an average room of 15 square meters constructed from mud and wattle with a corrugated iron roof. The rent levels are not subject to legal controls; thus by 1983 the rent levels were around 220/- (Janet Seeley, personal communication, 1984). This gives an annual increase between 1980 and 1983 of 30 percent. Since there has not been a corresponding increase in incomes since 1980, it is clear that within the settlement, and in fact throughout Nairobi, rent levels have increased much faster than incomes.

The survey revealed that the average tenant spends 14 percent of household income on housing services. This is less than the international agencies' arbitrary figure of 20 percent for low-income urban dwellers, but it is important to understand its economic context. The average tenant household income in the survey was 756/- a month, but a significant group (38 percent) had incomes below 600/- a month or suffered from insecurity of income. The figure of 20 percent might seem low, but the crucial point is that both World Bonk consultants and the Kenyan Central Organisation of Trade Unions (COTU) estimate that 625/- a month are required for a family in Nairobi to fulfill its basic nutritional requirements alone (COTU, 1980; Republic of Kenya, 1980). The general poverty of the settlement is borne out by the fact that in one section of the settlement the Catholic Relief Service estimates that 50 percent of the children suffer from malnutrition as judged by ratios of weight and height to age. In such a situation it is not surprising that paying rent represents a major financial difficulty for most tenants. Since 1980, this problem has been considerably aggravated. Therefore, to suggest that such individuals are not paying enough on housing is little short of criminal.

As might be expected, landlord–tenant relations center on the monthly rent payment, for which the ultimate sanctions for nonpayment are physical violence and immediate eviction. Examples of both are fairly common, and horror stories of such behavior abound. There is also some variation in landlords' behavior toward their tenants' problems that range from sympathy to total insensitivity. Paradoxically, it seems that the smaller-scale landlords who are socially nearest their tenants are the harshest landlords. But for these landlords, their tenants' rent is often their primary source of livelihood.

For tenants, flexibility in rent payment is important, as they attempt to meet regular rent payments from an irregular income. Unfortunately, 39 percent (thirty) of the tenants in my survey must pay their rent when it is requested, with no negotiating for an extension. Those who are unable to borrow money from kin or employer are sooner or later forced to go to the moneylender. Here the rate, albeit illegal, is 20 percent a *month!* Clearly such a situation further impoverishes the urban poor.

Turning now to landlord–tenant relations from a landlord or estate management perspective, we find that many landlords employ intermediaries to carry out the tasks of rent collection, maintenance, and choice of new tenants. To the interview survey, 28 percent (twenty-four) of the tenants responded that their landlord used such an intermediary.

For landlords who do not live in Kibera, this estate management function may prove difficult; the rent collector may run off with the rent money. Intermediaries may often be used to disguise the identity of the owner, since it is politically embarrassing for affluent Kenyans to be seen to be involved in such cutthroat activities. The ruthlessness and inequality of some aspects of this sector would appear to offend even the highly instrumental and capitalistic moral norms of modern Kenya—"Eat or be eaten," as the Kenyan novelist Ngugi Wa Thiong'o (1977) puts it.

Nothing typifies the social transformation that the commercialization process has wrought in unauthorized settlements as much as this formalization of the landlord–tenant relation combined with a refusal to admit to ownership. Clearly the fact that individual landlords seek to hide their identity says a lot about the nature of this unofficial rental housing market.

Effects of the Capitalist Rental Market

The capitalist rental market operating within unauthorized settlements is growing, and a number of effects can be identified. The first effect is the tendency for the poorest individuals in such settlements to be pushed out. The rent increases since 1980 are likely to have greatly escalated this. Unfortunately there are no data that describe the impact of this process. At one level, tenants may move to cheaper rental accommodations. This process seems to be occurring within Kibera through a "bumping down" phenomenon that has been noted elsewhere in Nairobi. Higher-income inhabitants are increasingly forced to look for accommodation in lower-income areas.

A second effect may involve individuals who cannot afford to stay in the rental market reverting to self-construction elsewhere. This may be possible on the extreme periphery of Nairobi. Hence we might postulate a rent curve nearing zero at some distance from the city center. Nairobi is predominantly surrounded by high-quality agricultural land, however, and the possible conflict in land use makes owner-constructed housing a debatable option. The importance of such an option is a crucial question for the future, since rent levels (in unauthorized settlements) are increasing rapidly, especially in relation to stable or even falling incomes (Amis, 1987). This rent inflation may be an unforeseen outcome of the policy instigated by the World Bank concerning the stabilization of unauthorized settlements. Demolition is to be stopped, but so too is expansion. Thus land supply is restricted in a situation of increasing demand which forces up prices.

The commercialization of squatter housing is also having interesting social implications. The traditional U-shaped nature of Swahili architecture is being replaced by functionally cheaper single blocks. The social advantages of the former in terms of semipublic space are abandoned in favor of the profitability of the latter. Profit-maximizing behavior also seems to be increasing among landlords: room sizes in new structures have shrunk to 3 meters by 3 meters, which is the minimum size that will accommodate two beds.

A fourth effect of the capitalist nature of this sector is the overriding of ethnic loyalties and prejudices by economic motivations. Landlords prefer mixed-tribe tenants to make collective action by tenants more difficult. Such a strategy also reduces the chance of the landlords' tribesmen attempting to seek favors in the payment of rent on the basis of some tribal loyalty. Despite this, I came across two instances where tenants appeared to negotiate collectively with their landlord with some measure of success. A rent strike in a shantytown may not be far off.

Another result of this commercialization process is the increasing importance of mobility *within* such settlements (Muwonge, 1980). This is in strong contrast to owner construction where there is very limited mobility because individuals remain in the houses they have constructed. The data from Kibera reveal substantial residential mobility; 56 percent of the tenants had lived elsewhere in Kibera, which includes 33 percent who have lived in two separate Kibera villages, while 6 percent had lived in three separate villages. The estimated average length of stay in each unit is 2.58 years, which is comparable to the residential mobility of tenants in the United States, which is thought to be the world's most residentially mobile society.

Yet a sixth impact of commercialization is that, for the tenants, the problem has moved from insecurity stemming from mass demolition by the state of an entire settlement to insecurity from individual eviction by landlords for failing to pay the rent. Here we can see capitalism's general tendency toward individualization, with the result that increasingly the strain of Nairobi's housing problem is being borne by the landlord rather than by the state.

The Marketability of Unauthorized Rental Housing

A second stage in the commercialization process has begun to develop. Unauthorized housing itself is becoming marketable. Thus it is starting to become possible for landlords to sell such rental blocks. In one case a prospective buyer was able to raise a 49,000/- loan from a bank for this purpose. This second-stage capitalist transaction does not depend on political connections and gives some indication of the real value of such connections. A hypothetical landlord in a two-year period might do the following, based on conservative estimates from my data: build a ten-room unit for 12,000/-, rent it out for two years (28,000/-), then sell the block for 40,000/-, which would result in a net overall profit of 56,800/-. To achieve such a return within two years on an initial investment of only 12,000/- is staggering. Such are the rewards in modern Kenya for knowing the right people. The existence of this second-stage market suggests that it is still considered to be a safe investment for individual economic security and that there is a general lack of alternative economic investments. It also suggests that some individuals are excluded from patronage networks that would enable them to buy such property at 12,000/- rather than 40,000/-. A similar process has been noted in Latin American squatter settlements where the majority of inhabitants bought their plots from original squatters (Gilbert, 1981). In Latin America the original squatters are getting a cash reward for their nerve in occupying land, whereas in Kenya landlords who sell out are realizing a monetary gain for being connected to the local administration.

It is worth emphasizing that the housing market I have been describing is not supposed to exist, according to the conventional view. It has no legal foundation, and politically and socially it is convenient for the Kenyan elite to ignore it. Capitalism's ability to transcend social barriers and situations and revolutionize the productive forces together with its inherent exploitation are well illustrated in the shantytowns of Nairobi.

Policy Implications

At a policy level, this commercialization of unauthorized rental housing is encouraged. Government policy holds that Nairobi's housing shortage is to be solved by the market. This policy, which is promoted by the international aid agencies, includes the recognition and ultimate legalization of unauthorized settlements that will ease the operation of the private sector therein. Alongside this commercialization process is a parallel trend toward political recognition and legitimization, albeit given reluctantly. For the state, it seems easier and more effective in terms of social control and economics (taxes, ratable values, etc.) to integrate such settlements rather than demolish them. Within Nairobi, the sheer scale of this unauthorized private sector is important in encouraging its integration.

Unfortunately, the extreme poverty of urban areas may make integrationist policies difficult to pursue. One of the advantages to earlier squatters in Nairobi was that they were effectively able to exit from the housing market and thus live in urban areas rent free. In a situation of increased political control, unless one has good access to the administration, that option virtually ceases to exist, with the result that one must search for a room to rent. Consequently it seems that the urban poor are being forced into a capitalist rent relationship they cannot afford and that may affect their health. The danger here is the creation of a relatively well housed but malnourished population. The trends in rents and wages since 1980 have greatly exacerbated this problem. Urban poverty may well become less visible as it is effectively forced off the streets and into the living room. Such a situation has occurred in such diverse places as Singapore and Scotland, which suggests that such an idea is not as absurd as it may sound. Indeed, the evidence of Nairobi's sites and services scheme points toward such a situation.

Shantytown housing is an important source of capital accumulation, but at what expense and to whose benefit? Is housing so important that we should push individuals toward malnutrition as they divert more and more of their meager incomes away from food and toward housing? The devil's advocate might suggest that the urban poor would do better to eat all their money and sleep on the streets rather than enter into a housing market they cannot afford.

Acknowledgment

This chapter is an extension and illustration of an earlier article, "Squatters or Tenants: The Commercialization of Unauthorized Housing in Nairobi," which appeared in *World Development* 12 (1)(1984), 87–96.

Notes

1. These cooperatives are in fact structured as companies. The terms *housing companies* and *housing cooperatives* are used interchangeably.
2. According to informants, this tacit acceptance was from the highest possible source. These housing companies would be allowed to proceed with unauthorized housing development if at some later date they redeveloped the site with legal (i.e., formal) housing. Since 1981, this agreement has come home to roost with disastrous consequences. The

word is now out that the companies must redevelop the site, and plans are being drawn up by consultants, many of whom work in the low-cost field themselves. Unfortunately Mathare Valley contains many people (100,000+) who live in the housing companies' own informal-sector housing development. In order to simplify this urban redevelopment problem, so it is implied, these housing companies have resorted to arson of their own property. Since 1981, there have been four or five major fires in the valley; the largest, in November 1982, left 10,000 individuals homeless (*Financial Times,* November 24, 1982, p. 1). It is important to understand that as a result of the bylaws, the present inhabitants (i.e. tenants of Mathare) will not be able to afford to live in the formally redeveloped Mathare Valley. For them, the process is *not* renewal or redevelopment; it is eviction.

3. The fieldwork data used in this chapter come from three main sources: direct observation, an intensive landlord and tenant survey, and an overall landlord survey for the new sections of Kibera. It is again worth mentioning that because of the sensitive nature of the subject, reliable data were not always available. Consequently I sometimes have to rely more on "impressionistic" sources. The data were collected in 1980–81.

References

Amis, Philip. 1984. "Squatters or Tenants: The Commercialization of Unauthorized Housing in Nairobi." *World Development* 12(1), 87–96.

———. 1987. "Migration, Urban Poverty, and the Housing Market: The Nairobi Case." In *Migration, the Labor Market, and Social Order,* ed. J. S. Eades, pp. 254–75. London: Tavistock.

Angel, S., et al. 1983. *Land for Housing the Poor.* Singapore: Select Books.

Bujra, Janet M. 1973. *Punwani: The Politics of Poverty.* Report submitted to the Economic and Social Research Council, London.

Central Organisation of Trade Unions, Kenya (COTU). 1980. *The Cost of Living in Kenya as Related to Low Income Workers.* Nairobi: COTU.

Chana, Tara, and Herbert Morrison. 1973. "Housing Systems in the Low Income Sector of Nairobi, Kenya." *Ekistics* 36(214), 214–22.

Chege, Michael. 1981. "A Tale of Two Slums." *Review of African Political Economy* 20, 74–88.

Development Planning Unit (DPU). 1985. *Nairobi Project.* London: University College.

Gilbert, Alan. 1981. "Pirates and Invaders: Land Acquisition in Urban Colombia and Venezuela." *World Development* 9(7), 657–78.

Hake, Andrew. 1977. *African Metropolis: Nairobi's Self-Help City.* London: Sussex University Press.

Housing Research and Development Unit (HRDU). 1971. *Mathare Valley, a Case-Study of Uncontrolled Settlement in Nairobi.* Nairobi: University of Nairobi.

International Labor Organization (ILO). 1979. *Planning for Basic Needs in Kenya.* Geneva: ILO.

Jorgensen, Niels. 1977. *Housing Finance for Low-income Groups.* Rotterdam: Bowcentrum.

Kabagambe, Denis, and Cliff Moughtin. 1983. "Housing the Poor: A Case Study in Nairobi." *Third World Planning Review* 5(3), 227–48.

Kimani, S. M. 1972. "Structure of Land Ownership in Nairobi." *Journal of East African Research and Development* 2(2), 101–24.

Memon, P. 1982. "The Growth of Low-income Settlements: Planning Response in the Peri-urban Zone of Nairobi." *Third World Planning Review* 4(2), 145–58.

Muwonge, Joe W. 1980. "Urban Policy and Patterns of Low Income Settlement in Nairobi, Kenya." *Population and Development Review* 6(4), 595–613.

Ngugi Wa Thiong'o. 1977. *Petals of Blood.* London: Heinemann.

Republic of Kenya. 1980. *Kenya Low-Cost Housing By-Law Study.* Nairobi: Ministry of Urban Development and Housing.

Richard, Joan. 1970. "The Land Buying Movement in Mathare Valley." Paper prepared by the Town Planning Department, Nairobi.

Roberts, Bryan. 1978. *Cities of Peasants.* London: Edward Arnold.

Skinner, Reinhard J., and Michael J. Rodell, eds. 1983. *People, Poverty and Shelter: Problems of Self-Help Housing in the Third World.* London: Methuen.

Swainson, Nicola. 1981. *The Development of Corporate Capitalism in Kenya 1918–1977.* London: Heinemann.

Temple, Fred. 1973. "Politics, Planning and Housing Policy in Nairobi." Doctoral dissertation, Department of Political Science, Massachusetts Institute of Technology, Cambridge.

Temple, Nellie. 1973. "Redevelopment of Kibera." Draft manuscript. Nairobi: University of Nairobi.

———. 1974. *Housing Preferences and Policy in Kibera, Nairobi.* Discussion Paper no. 196. Nairobi: Institute of Development Studies, University of Nairobi.

Van Zwanenberg, Roger. 1972. "History and Theory of Urban Poverty in Nairobi: The Problem of Slum Development." *Journal of East African Research and Development* 2(2), 165–203.

Waweru and Associates. 1976. *Planning and Engineering Analysis, Nairobi Sites.* Low Cost Housing and Squatter Upgrading Study Progress Report No. 7. Nairobi.

Wegelin, Emiel. 1983. "From Building to Enabling Housing Strategies in Asia: Institutional Problems." In R. J. Skinner and M. J. Rodell, eds. *People, Poverty and Shelter: Problems of Self-Help Housing in the Third World,* pp. l06–24. New York: Methuen.

Chapter 12

Abusivismo and the *Borgate* of Rome

ALBERT GUTTENBERG

Macche' proletari d'Egitto! (What kind of proletarians are these, anyway?) So runs a recent caption in the special features section of the Roman daily *Il Messaggero* (Testa, 1985, p. 6). This exclamation was provoked by an action of the Italian Senate to extend the *Condono Edilizio,* the pardoning of unauthorized housing, from October 1983 to March 1985.[1] It was an action that threatened to open the door to the legalization of all dwellings illicitly constructed or modified between these two dates—a move later quashed in the Chamber of Deputies. The legitimation of illegal housing by any of a variety of means is no rare event in Italy. Some Italians have come to count on such actions almost with the same certainty that they count on the seasons to change. *Le cose si aggiustano* is the way they express it: Things work out in the end.

The irony of the headline—its feigned surprise—reflects another certainty: Gone are the days of the romantic shantytown, gone the "noble struggle of the classic proletariat to establish the people's right to the city. All that remains is the right to be 'abusive' " (Testa, 1985, p. 6).

The columnist's cynicism is supported by a study his newspaper conducted in collaboration with Censis, an Italian social research institute. Interviews of a sample of 1,145 residents of illegal housing (containing 300 families) constructed after 1981 and located in Rome's extreme eastern edge revealed the following:

"Almost one-half of the sample studied (45.6 percent) had a net annual income estimated at between 20 and 40 million lire," compared with an average for Lazio [Rome's region] of 36.5 percent. As further indicators of their status, 60.3 percent of those sampled own an automobile with a cylindrical capacity greater than 1,600 cc; 5.3 percent have second homes in the mountains or at the seashore and "57.3 percent of the current generation possess at least one color television set." Of the sample, 16.4 percent are considered to be rich. Occupational data confirm the impression of a comparatively well-off component of the Italian population; 46.1 percent are white-collar employees mainly of public agencies such as ATAC [trams and autobuses], ENEL [electric utilities] and Alitalia; 22.0 percent are self-employed workers, merchants, and artisans; and 5.4 percent are entrepreneurs and executives. Clearly, this is no proletariat (Testa, 1985, p. 6).[2]

While they may not be representative of the total universe of illegal housing in Rome's periphery, these findings and the manner in which they are reported are enough to indicate the controversy that surrounds the subject.

The extent of any activity outside the law is hard to define with exactitude; nevertheless, there is evidence enough that illegal building is not a passing phenomenon in Italy, nor is it confined to Rome. This form of lawbreaking is nationwide, but it is most common in the south where 50 percent of construction is said to be illegal (Amorosino, 1985, p. 18). At the beginning of 1977 there were 750,000 illegally constructed rooms in Rome, a number equal to 20 percent of the city's total stock and involving about 9,000 hectares (6 percent) of its 150,000 hectares of land (Comune di Roma, 1981, p. 21). The geographic distribution is indicated in Figure 12.1. Although there is no district in Rome without its share of illegal construction, the principal locales are the settlements at or beyond the city's developed edge, but well within its boundaries—the *borgate.*

What, precisely are these *borgate* and what relation do they bear to illegal housing? Let us begin with a few definitions.

First, it is important to note that illegal construction is not limited to residential building. Although illegal commercial and industrial structures are subjects that merit study in themselves as well as in relation to illegal housing, in this chapter we are concerned solely with illegal *housing* construction.

Illegal construction of whatever type is called *abusivismo* in Italy and those who practice it are *abusivi* (Photo 12.1). According to Fera and Ginatempo (1982) *abusivismo* (henceforth understood to apply to illegally constructed housing) is to be distinguished from autoconstruction, with which it is frequently confused. The latter denotes a dwelling built by a person for self-occupancy using family and friendly labor and is most commonly rendered in English as self-help housing. The same authors make a further distinction between autoconstruction and autopromotion, meaning by the latter those cases in which the future user hires somebody else to do the job. The reason for the mixup between illegal housing and self-help housing is that in Italy a vast amount of autoconstruction takes place outside a municipality's building regulations or its general regulatory plan and in this sense is abusive or illegal.

For historical reasons, which I examine, *abusivismo* is also frequently confused with improvised housing—hovels, shacks (*baracche*), and shantytowns (*borghetti*). Again the correspondence between the two phenomena is only partial, since, in Italy, *abusivismo* is also practiced by the comparatively well-off.

Finally, I would distinguish between *abusivismo* and squatting, which became prominent in the 1970s as part of a general civic protest movement. Squatting is the illegal occupation of land or buildings by nonowners. *Abusivismo,* in contrast, as used here, is the violation of public land use and building regulations.

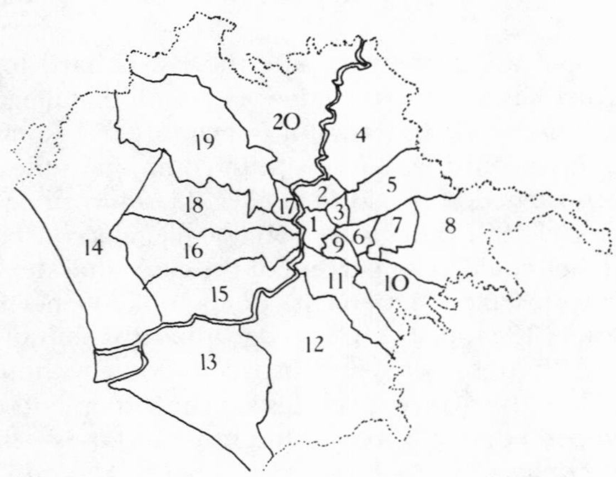

District	*Zone F1 [hectares]*	*Zone O [hectares]*	*Consolidated Subdivisions [hectares]*	*Total [hectares]*
4	124.10	50.00	18.50	192.60
5	150.00	109.00	70.00	329.00
7	333.70	—	—	333.70
8	409.00	978.00	248.20	1,635.20
9	—	32.00	—	32.00
10	373.70	394.00	36.00	803.70
11	—	25.00	—	25.00
12	152.10	264.00	—	416.10
13	229.20	1,134.00	116.60	1,479.80
14	347.20	547.00	46.30	940.50
15	10.00	84.00	203.00	297.00
16	327.10	138.00	7.60	472.70
18	121.60	85.00	—	206.60
19	744.80	317.00	204.80	1,266.60
20	508.20	275.00	97.70	880.90

Figure 12.1 Territory involved in illegal expansion in Rome as of 1978. Zones F1 were settled in the 1950s; Zones O were settled after the 1950s. *Source:* Comune di Roma (1981, p. 21). (Illustration adapted by David Loehr)

Abusivismo comes in two forms: construction, without permission, of an entire edifice; and minor violations in existing structures, including works of repair, maintenance, and restoration, unless required for health or safety (Amorosino, 1985, p. 18). Clearly *abusivismo* is, first, a juridical phenomenon. Were there no laws or plan to regulate the time, place, and manner of construction, it would not exist. In a special sense, therefore, the cause of *abusivismo* is the city plan.

Indeed, from a legal point of view, the history of *abusivismo* in Rome is the story of a wave of regulatory plans chasing a wave of peripheral development.[3] The plans chase the unauthorized construction, but some *abusivi* intend all along to be caught for the benefits it brings—streets, sewers, schools, playgrounds (Photo 12.2). It is this "condoning" of illegal construction that many Italians resent as unfair. "Why should someone get a public break that I have to pay for?" Americans would call it a "ripoff." Marxists turn this explanation upside down. For them, the ripped-off ones are the *abusivi,* who are forced to pay with their own labor for what the state ought to provide. Thereby the state dodges the cost and the social responsibility of housing the poor.

Lately, *abusivismo* is coming to be seen in a different light, not as a swindle or as class exploitation, but as a social and economic insurgency cutting across all classes, occupations, and age groups. According to this view, what unites the disparate elements is dissatisfaction with the legal housing production system to the extent that they have literally taken

Photo 12.1 Luxurious *abusivismo.* An illegal villa in the *borgata* La Romanina. (Photo by Francesco Perego)

matters into their own hands. In addition to constituting a society of "do-it-yourselfers," what the *abusivi* have in common is a place, not a static, fixed location but a moving part of the region—the periphery, meaning the expanding edge of the metropolis and beyond. *Abusivismo* in its consolidated form is essentially a phenomenon of the periphery and is not to be understood apart from the history of the periphery and its past and present uses.[4]

Historical Background

To understand the land uses of the periphery, one must go back to the turn of the century and even earlier, to a time when reformers in all Western countries were grappling with problems of population growth and spatial expansion. Industrialism and participation in the international division of labor were the forces that drove the progressive cities of Europe, including those of northern Italy, and caused them to grow. Rome, however, was different. In Rome the spur to urban growth was political rather than economic. A century ago its rural hinterland was populated by large landholders and their almost feudal dependents. In an economy so elementary "there existed no quarters [within the city] for the rich and the poor, there was not enough rich to form a special quarter." Instead, they divided their residence between a "place in the

Photo 12.2 Waiting for infrastructure at Borgata Finocchio. It may take years for service to reach this location. (Photo by Francesco Perego)

city and a villa in the country side" (Piazzo, 1982, pp. 15–16). As for the indigenous Roman poor, they remained organic to the city and constituted the servants, maintainers, and objects of benevolence and charity of princes and cardinals (Piazzo, 1982, p. 16).

Quite another type of Roman poor were the migratory workers who began to come to Rome in the 1880s and 1890s. In large part they consisted of the rural unemployed, the castoffs of a rationalizing agriculture, who were finding work in the riot of building that followed national unification and the establishment of Rome as the nation's capital (1870). In the beginning, these uprooted people would return to their villages in Lazio or Abruzzi at the end of a summer's work. More and more, however, they were disposed to remain in Rome during the entire year, finding whatever shelter they could on the steps of churches, under the gates and archways, and by the side of railroad tracks. Such "dwelling places" were soon augmented by improvised hovels in the lee of ancient aqueducts or other public structures (Photo 12.3). The outcasts might gain a precarious foothold within the city, but always, especially in periods of slack building, the tendency was to push them beyond the walls and outside the gates of Rome. Thus the periphery early became a place beyond the law for the "emarginated," a place for discarded people and activities.

Photo 12.3 Tor Fiscale. Necessitarian *abusivismo*. Although greatly diminished, such housing persists. A shanty leans on a Roman aqueduct with a medieval tower. (Photo by Francesco Perego)

The hard lot of the Roman poor was not entirely ignored. Certain reform impulses began to manifest themselves. There was, for example, the private initiative to build housing for workers in the industrial quarter of Testaccio.[5] Unions were also forming and beginning to undertake cooperative housing projects. A landmark year for reform was 1903, which saw the advent of the liberal Giolitti government (Procacci, 1984, pp. 461–81). One of its noteworthy accomplishments was the founding of the Istituto Autonomo per le Case Popolare (IACP), headed by the finance minister, Luigi Luzzatti. With the energy imparted to the pioneering enterprise by this able man, there were some notable beginnings, particularly at San Saba where the aim was to produce better popular housing at a lower cost (Insolera, 1976, pp. 82–83). Ernest Nathan, the liberal mayor of Rome (1907–13), introduced further reforms, including an increase in public education, measures to improve public hygiene, the limiting of land speculation in the interest of more and better housing for the people, the encouragement of citizen participation in municipal affairs, and city ownership of such basic services as trams, electricity, and water (Insolera, 1976, p. 82). Unfortunately, the reform energies generated in these years were not sufficient to overcome the inertial forces of abuse and neglect, and they were soon dissipated in the growing turbulence of Italian national politics.

The unification of Italy and the establishment of Rome as its capital set in motion the migratory flows that led to this first episode of *abusivismo.* Future events followed a similar pattern: large-scale immigration and expulsion of the poor to the periphery (Comune di Roma, 1983, p. 17). In the Fascist era resettlement became official policy (i.e., government sponsored). Mussolini's purpose was to restore Rome to its ancient physical and political grandeur, a project that required the clearing of the slums that had grown up in the vicinity of many of the city's most famous piazzas (San Pietro, Barberini, Venezia). To receive their former inhabitants, twelve official *borgate* (villages, hamlets) ringing the city were built between 1924 and 1940, often under the watchful eye of neighboring military installations but with little useful infrastructure to support them. An estimated 40,000 to 50,000 people were deported to these *borgate,* the first of which were exceedingly rude and unhygienic one-story structures. Though government created, even these settlements were "abusive" in the sense that they were outside the perimeter of the 1931 regulatory plan. Their importance is that they provided the nuclei for future rounds of unauthorized peripheral development (Piazzo, 1982, pp. 29–30).

During and immediately after World War II, migration to Rome accelerated, as thousands thronged to the "open city" to escape the conflict. In the 1950s, the legal population of Rome increased by more than 500,000, and in the following decade by more than 600,000. The consequence was a mushrooming of *baracche* constructed on public and private land, of whatever materials came to hand. The same period saw an intensification of illegal subdivision (Clementi and Perego, 1983, pp. 292–97).

Then the tide turned. In the early postwar period, *abusivismo* of the shantytown variety reached its highest point and began to recede. By the mid-1960s it was replaced by a different, and perhaps more intractable, variety. A "metamorphosis" in spatial relations was occurring in the Rome region, attributable in part to the growth of the tertiary sector of the regional economy, occasioned by the rise of a complicated and extensive state bureaucracy, and the emergence of a consumer economy of regional and national dimensions. A second and related cause was the decentralization of people and resources to the hinterland, spurred by the widespread use of the automobile, the new space requirements of modern commerce and industry, and the continuing congestion of central Rome (Comune di Roma, 1983, p. 11).

With decentralization came a change in the character of *abusivismo* and the *abusivi* themselves. Looking back, scholars discern three major phases in the process. The first, roughly the 1950s, is characterized by the movement of impoverished immigrants to the periphery, driven there by earlier official fiat in the Fascist era or later by rising land values in the center as the city became the destination of thousands from other parts of Italy, notably the south and Rome's own region of Lazio. The defining feature of *abusivismo* in this phase is that the spontaneous housing constructed was for personal use with labor supplied by family and friends. A low-grade, rude, relatively unserviced ambiance was a concomitant characteristic of this period (Comune di Roma, 1983, pp. 11–12). A second phase dates from the 1960s with the great distribution of publicly constructed infrastructure that began to fill the Rome region in that decade. Gradually, it became an environment capable of meeting the consumption standards of a burgeoning middle class, thereby losing some of its aura of rudeness and marginality. This, plus the family savings realized through autoconstruction, provided the opportunity for a hitherto family-type, dependent workforce (the major component of the first migration) to convert itself into an independent workforce. Workers grew more skilled. More important, their skills were now for sale. Where previously they had built their own houses, they now built for others and for profit. A new *abusivismo* was coming into existence, and with it was developing a separation, geographic as well as economic and social, between the old and new periphery, the first based on autoconstruction, the second on production for the market (Comune di Roma, 1981, pp. 14–15).

A third phase, beginning in the 1970s, and continuing to the present, represents the expansion and consolidation of the new *abusivismo* (Photo 12.4). In this phase, the earlier settlers have been joined increasingly by middle-class immigrants pushed to the *borgate* by the hous-

Photo 12.4 Two generations of *abusivismo*. On this lot in Borgata Gregna, multilevel construction is proceeding before the demolition of an earlier one-story illegal hut. (Photo by Francesco Perego)

ing shortage in the city and by the shrinking buying power of the lire (Comune di Roma, 1983, p. 72). "In the period 1970–80 the production of official housing reached the level of only 120,000 units, compared with 250,000 in the 1960s, while the same decade (1970–80) saw an illegal output of 100,000 units" (Bartolozzi, 1983, p. 7). By 1975 one out of every four inhabitants of Rome lived in an unauthorized structure (Bartolozzi, 1983, pp. 6, 7).

The forces that maintain the illegal system in its current flourishing state are multiple. One factor is the city's chronic financial plight, the result in part of the national government's parsimony. Revenue-sharing funds from the national government have in the past been slow in coming, and since the late 1970s have been reduced. Only a minor fraction of Rome's resources derive from real estate taxes. Lacking sufficient funds, the city has been unable to provide the infrastructure on which both public and legal private housing depend.

A second factor is the readiness of agricultural landholders to capitalize on their holdings by illegally dividing them into smaller lots for sale. These land oligopolists have not been merely the passive suppliers of land. They have actively manipulated the market, making use of the regulatory plan in the process. A common practice is to buy up lots that have been cheapened by being zoned "unbuildable" and then to secure a change in the plan that renders the same lots developable (Fried, 1973, p. 118).[6]

The chronic inflationary pressures that boost the cost of legal housing in the private sector are a third factor. Among these pressures must be counted the regulatory plan itself with its constraints and requirements on developers that add to the cost of land and housing, resulting in a more expensive product than can be provided by the *abusivi* (Bartolozzi, 1983, p. 7; Fried, 1973, p. 113).

Among the factors that have impeded legal housing production and consequently encouraged *abusivismo* is the poor performance of the public sector. In the 1960s it managed to produce only 4,400 of the 11,000 additional units required to house the shantytown population.

The Geography of *Abusivismo*

As noted, every regulatory plan has run panting after the unauthorized development that eluded the grasp of its predecessor. Consequently, the phenomenon has spread outward from the center, but not in perfect circles. The wave has moved faster in this direction and slower in that, depending on such variables as terrain, accessibility, and prevailing land use.

The major push, in terms of land area covered and rooms constructed, has been easterly along the roads to Prenestina, Casalina, and Tiburtina (Figure 12.1, Districts 8 and 10)—this owing to the strong railway and highway ties to the city. A second thrust is to the southwest (District 13), again because of good transportation, particularly the rapid transit line connecting Rome with Ostia on the coast. The abusive settlement between via Trionfale and via Boccea (Districts 18 and 19) constitute a north–south spoke displaced westward by the hilly terrain to the north of the center (District 20). Not all the expansion has been radial, however. The strip of coast from Fiumicino to the Arrone River has seen the rise of much illegal settlement in the form of vacation houses. Finally, there are certain remote settlements, illegal extensions of some of Rome's neighbors, such as Setteville di Guidonia, Frascati, and Bracciano (Comune di Roma, 1981, p. 21).

In addition to exhibiting directionality, spontaneous development is also concentric in its layout. A number of concentric areas, called Zones F1 and Zones O, have been identified within many districts. The F1 Zones are located closer to the center and comprise the illegal development that sprang up mainly in the 1950s and that was "recuperated," that is to say, rectified and included in the 1962 regulatory plan. The O Zones are located farther from the center and are the sites of more recent waves of illegal settlement. Whereas in the F1 Zones the settlements are substantially homogeneous, the O Zones are characterized by a wider diversity of social types "depending on the sectors of the city in which they arise" (Comune di Roma, 1983, p. 9). It is these two zones whose contrast constitutes the old and new periphery referred to above.

Figure 12.2 indicates the relationship of the illegal settlements to the major features of the region they impact. To those already mentioned (major roads, railways, coastline) must be added parts of the Agro Romano because of their low potential for profitable legal real estate investment, public open spaces such as parks and cemeteries, areas earmarked for public housing, unbuildable zones by reason of watery terrain, archaeological zones, and zones reserved for industry (Comune di Roma, 1981, p. 23).

Demographics

Despite its origins, Roman *abusivismo* is far from a Third World, shantytown operation. Instead, it is a highly complex system for acquiring and developing land for residential (and nonresidential) purposes, both for personal use and for profit, and on a scale large enough to be regarded as complementary to and competitive with the legal production system, public and private. From an economic standpoint, the basic features of the system are acquisition of illicitly subdivided public or private land; lower production costs effected by means of autoconstruction or autopromotion and by the use of cheaper materials; the avoidance of taxes, building permits, and social security contributions; the reduction of heavy carrying costs by the pacing of construction according to the means of the builder; and the willingness on the part of the occupant to forego, for an indefinite period, modern services and environmental amenities in the expectation of eventual legalization and the provision of the usual residential infrastructure (Clementi and Perego, 1983, pp. 33–34). These practices allow housing prices 30 to 40 percent lower than those in the legal sector (Bartolozzi, 1983, p. 8).

With such a price advantage and with these frontier characteristics, it is not surprising that the *borgate* are settlements in which younger families predominate (Comune di Roma, 1983, pp. 38–39). There are more teenagers than in the older parts of the region and far fewer individuals age sixty and over. Men slightly outnumber women, as one might expect in a frontier society. The inhabitants of the *borgate* tend to be less educated than the average Roman, but this difference has been narrowing with the increasing presence of middle-class immigrants (Comune di Roma, 1983, p. 84). According to a recent survey, 54 percent of the Zone O residents moved there so that they could acquire an affordable home (Comune di Roma, 1983, p. 101). But other life-style preferences have figured in their decisions to move, notably the desire for a shorter journey to work (11.5 percent), a more tranquil environment (6.1 percent), and nearness to friends and relatives (7.2 percent) (Comune di Roma,

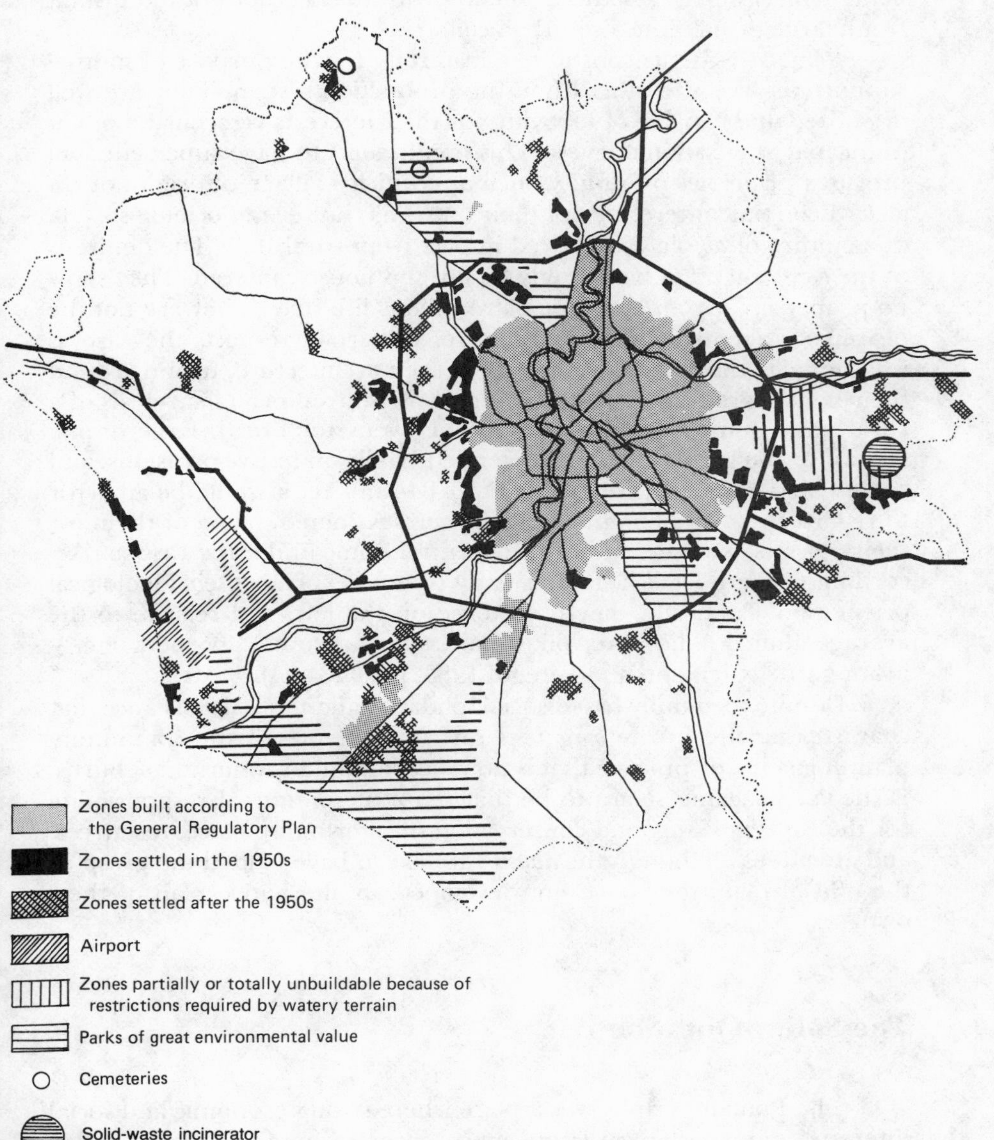

Figure 12.2 Compatibility of abusive settlements with various kinds of restrictions. *Source:* Comune di Roma (1981, p. 24). (Illustration adapted by David Loehr)

1983, p. 102). These are not unlike the motives that have been impelling many Americans to resettle in small towns outside, but not too distant from, large or medium-size urban centers.

Borgate residents constitute a fraternity for the purpose of mutual support vis-à-vis the official housing production system. They are well organized and capable of lobbying for their interests vigorously, both at municipal and national levels. This bond seems to have superseded all previous principles of affinity, such as ethnicity, village of origin, or dialect. Economic interest is not their only link, however. Sociologists talk of a culture of *abusivismo* derived in part from rural Italy. The denizens of the *borgate* tend to be strongly family and house centered. They show no propensity for an eccentric or rebellious life style. They are not the bearers or agents of a counterculture. In certain respects they are as traditional in their habits as they are in their architecture. In and around their houses are frequently to be found the souvenirs and survivals of a rural past: outdoor laundries, outdoor ovens for bread, large dining rooms for the gathering of the extended family on festive occasions, and so on (Clementi and Perego, 1983, pp. 84–85). Yet it would be an error to regard them as so many rural villagers. As noted, many of them (or their parents) were deportees from central Rome under the Fascists. According to Piero Della Seta, this early trauma explains their ideological orientation. Politically, they tend to be on the left, and relative to the average Roman, they are, on social issues—divorce, abortion, etc.—avant garde (Clementi and Perego, 1983, pp. 123–24).

Despite the family-based social solidarity and mutual assistance that characterizes life in the *borgate,* I saw no evidence of the community planning spirit or practice that is now so common in American suburbs. Particularly lacking seems to be that sense of communal responsibility for the care, policing, and conservation of interfamily space, resources, and amenities. Although the *abusivi* appear to have eluded the grasp of the official plan, they have not developed an alternative plan of their own.

The Policy Question

The Roman periphery is a place where strong economic and social interests converge. Large landowners, eager to subdivide, meet developers looking for cheap land and low- and middle-income families intent on acquiring affordable dwellings in a more tranquil environment than the older, denser parts of the city allow. At the base is a pool of experienced masons (*muratori*) who, after meeting their own demands, sell their surplus labor for profit. The question of legality aside, there is nothing wrong with any of these motives. The trouble is in how they are pursued and their effects on the environment. Leonardo Benevolo has described the environmental consequences of *abusivismo:*

> The choice of location corresponds to no general design and passes indifferently over areas zoned as developable, agriculture, open space, archaeological. . . . The hydrological, functional and landscape damage is almost irreparable—the most evident manifestation being the congestion caused in the infrastructure network (streets, sewers, installations) that can be rectified only at colossal expense. The structure of each settlement is almost always reduced to its most elementary form: strings of lots served by stringy streets of the narrowest sort in order to increase the area of saleable land. (Clementi and Perego, 1983, p. 70)

To this dolorous recital one might add the moral cost of *abusivismo:* cynical and widespread law evasion. As recent events prove, the problem is not likely to yield to governmental penalties such as those imposed by the recent *Condono Edilizio.* When it went into effect, there were widespread protests and civil disturbances in southern Italy, particularly in Sicily and Calabria, led largely by communist mayors and assessors. One result has been a progressive weakening of the 1985 law's original precriptions. What, then, is to be done?

A better understanding of the complex nature of *abusivismo* is fundamental to any resolution of the problem. It is therefore heartening that there have been some conceptual advances, so that Italian planners and planning analysts are now in a better position to assess and respond more adeptly to this problem. Whereas before they spoke simply of *abusivismo,* they now distinguish between different types of *abusivismo.* This advance is reflected in the following classification:

> 1. *the abusivismo of necessity* motivated by the search for any kind of affordable shelter;
> 2. *the abusivismo of choice* tied to the desire for a different kind of home whether in cultural or locational terms;
> 3. *the abusivismo of convenience* deriving from a wish to protect savings [in an inflationary environment];
> 4. *the abusivismo of speculation* determined to exploit, without hesitation, every opportunity that offers a return to investment capital. (Comune di Roma, 1983, p. 7)

The first category represents those who have no alternative but to evade the law. They build illegally in order to live. The others do so in order to live better. Borrowing John Seeley's categories, the first group are "necessitarians," the rest are "opportunists" (Seeley, 1959). As noted, necessitarian *abusivismo* is definitely on the wane, even if it has not disappeared entirely (Clementi and Perego, 1983, p. 389). Owing to the decline in immigration and a general rise in living standards during the

1970s, the shacks and shanties have diminished markedly (Clementi and Perego, 1983, pp. 47, 389).

Not so with opportunistic *abusivismo,* which is now the dominant strain and growing wildly (Photo 12.5). Here one must ask the rock-bottom question: Do the Romans really want their *abusivismo?* The official response is an emphatic no. But in Italy, as elsewhere, the correspondence between what people believe and what they will espouse publicly is notoriously low. Who would openly condone breaking the law?

This is not to imply that there are no real interests opposed to illegal housing. The organized builders of Rome, for example, resent the competition they get from the autoconstructors. The planning profession is against unregulated autoconstruction, not only for the damage it does, but also for thumbing its nose at every known planning principle and dictum. Rhetorically, at least, the Union of Borgate (a residents' association) is on record as opposing it as playing into the hands of speculators (Clementi and Perego, 1983, p. 129).

Environmentalists also weigh in against *abusivismo.* Families in regular structures are outraged when they find their dwellings overshadowed or their views blocked by an illegal add-on story across the street or an entire new building (Fried, 1973, p. 106). Nevertheless, if we attend to deeds rather than words, it is hard to avoid the impression that there is considerable weight on the side of the *abusivi.* Certainly the groups who benefit from the current system are numerous and influen-

Photo 12.5 Colle Mentuccia. An example of the latest and most speculative generation of *abusivismo.* (Photo by Francesco Perego)

tial: the landowners, small and large, who insist on their right to do as they please with their land; would-be *borgatari,* who are still in the process of acquiring their own dwellings and have no doubt that they prefer them to whatever the public housing program might provide, if anything; leftists, who still wish to see in the residents of the periphery an "emarginated" outcast population whose illegal autoconstruction is justified by the state's failure to meet its social responsibility to provide decent housing for all; and the church, with its real estate interests and political ties to the large landholders. Some architects and planners also seem to be softening in their attitude to the *abusivismo* problem, which they lay in part to the failure of their professions to satisfy the residential tastes and preferences of the people. To some extent their attitude also reflects the emergence of a sociological and anthropological perspective that views the *borgate* as a cultural phenomenon rather than a design and planning monstrosity perpetrated by speculators.

So, while there is much public hand-wringing over *abusivismo,* there is very little effective action against it. After measuring the phenomenon in all its dimensions with admirable precision, when it comes to proposals, analysts retreat into sonorous generalities, for example, that the problem will have to wait for a legislative initiative that will bring within one framework all the "individual and collective interests that converge in abusivism" (Comune di Roma, 1983, p. 107). Or, considering the alternatives, they dismiss them one by one. Fines and penalties and the like are too weak. Public housing is too bureaucratic. State-assisted autoconstruction is more promising, but here, too, there is hesitation: wouldn't it constitute a license to continue the same wild development under new rules? *Abusivisimo,* some suggest, might be "choked off" at its sources in the labor market, in investment practices, and in access to material and equipment—theoretically interesting, but just how it would be done and where the political power would come from is left unanswered. The same holds true with such draconian measures as the demolishing of the illegal settlements and the resettlement of their residents elsewhere in official communities built in conformity with planning norms. Who, since Mussolini, would dare try? What remains is what the city authorities have been practicing from the beginning—*recupero,* that is, ex post facto regularization, the inclusion of the illegal areas in the next round of public service supply, and the coordination of *abusivismo* with the legal housing market (Comune di Roma, 1983, p. 107). An example of the regularization measures available are those being brought to bear on certain of the newest settlements on the far periphery of Rome: a program for providing water, sewers, and lighting by the municipal water and power company (ACEA); plans for public transport, schools, and cultural centers; a speeding up of the process of correcting illegal buildings; and the protection of the rights of lot owners to a house on that lot or, failing that, the provision of an alternative lot in an area dedicated to low-cost housing (Clementi and Perego, 1983, p. 390).

While land remains the principal form of wealth in Rome and construction the main industry, it is doubtful whether anything more than *recupero,* "action after the fact," is possible with respect to Roman *abusivismo.*[7] "Action before the fact," that is, prevention, will probably have to wait for the creation of alternative sources of public and private wealth. It will probably also have to await the maturation of social attitudes in the Roman population, as was the case in America. The national self-control that we associate with American environmentalism was not there from the beginning. It was a belated response to the devastation wrought by western settlement—cutover forests, dustbowls, flooded plains. And only recently has this early conservationist reaction been reinforced by certain cultural trends—the cult of nature, resource scarcities, escapism—that have been strong enough to generate and sustain an effective environmental movement.

In a sense, the *borgate* are Rome's frontier and the *borgatari* its settlers. A feast of land faces a land-hungry populace. Not until their hunger is assuaged can we expect an effective stand against *abusivismo.* By that time, of course, it may be too late.

Acknowledgments

This chapter was prepared after a research trip to Rome in the summer of 1985. For the invaluable assistance and guidance they provided, I am indebted to the following: Anna Maria and Bruno Ambrosi de Magistris, Gerardo Bartolozzi, Alberto Clementi, Umberto De Martino, Nella Ginatempo, Federico Malusardi, Francesco Perego, Pietrenzo Piazzo, Gianluigi Scanferla. The helpful comments of Nico Calavita and Raffaella Nanetti, who read this chapter in manuscript form, are gratefully acknowledged.

The photographs of the illegal settlements of the Roman periphery are by Francesco Perego, taken in 1983 in the course of a research project, sponsored by the University of Rome, on the growth processes of contemporary urban peripheries of which he was co-director. The photographs are reproduced here with his permission.

Notes

1. The Law of February 28, 1985, n. 47, the *Condono Edilizio,* sets forth rules regarding the control of building and planning activity and provides against future violations by specifying sanctions. Other measures expedite planning and building procedures and pertain to the

squaring or reconciling of illegal settlements with established urban planning norms (see Amorosino, 1985, p. 9).

2. Unauthorized construction by the middle class is occurring in other countries as well, including Yugoslavia, discussed in Chapter 13, and Greece (Patton and Sophoulis, 1983).

3. The 1909 plan overtook and legitimized the residential construction at Porta Pia, which had risen outside the perimeter of the 1893 plan; and the 1931 plan caught up with and incorporated development at Monte Sacro, Garbatella, and Monteverde Nuovo, all beyond the reach of the plan of 1906 (Comune di Roma, 1981, p. 10).

4. In the historic center, *abusivismo* takes the form of the illegal subdividing of apartments or additions or restructuring in violation of preservation norms. Illegal land-use changes, as, for example, from residential to commercial/office, also constitute a form of *abusivismo* common at the center.

5. The results, however, were a far cry from a decent working-class district. From 1883 to 1907, Testaccio stood incomplete, overcrowded, and without clinics, schools, or laundries (Insolera, 1976, pp. 65–69).

6. Speculation and corruption are by no means limited to large landholders (see Fried, 1973, p. 101).

7. "In the capital, the square meter is the unit of measure for wealth; it is the real currency." Gianfranco Piazzesi quoted in Fried (1973, p. 101).

References

Amorosino, Vittorio. 1985. *Guida Al Condono Edilizio* (Law of February 28), n. 47. Rome: Edizioni Cie Rre.

Bartolozzi, Gerardo. 1983. "Sviluppi Dell'Abusivismo Urbanistico–Nella Area Romana–Provvedimenti Locali Per il Recupero Urbanistico e La Sanatoria Amministrativa Dei Nuclei Spontanei-Rapporti Con Il D.D.L. Nazionale e Relativi Aspetti Tecnici." Paper presented at Convegno sul Tema Abusivismo e Condono Edilizio, Rome, November 21.

Clementi, Alberto, and Francesco Perego, eds. 1983. *La Metropoli "Spontanea"—Il Caso di Roma.* Bari: Edizioni Dedalo.

Comune di Roma. Ufficio Speciale del Piano Regolatore. 1981. *II Recupero degli Insediamenti Abusivi,* ed. Anna Maria Leone. USPR Document no. 1. March.

———. 1983. *Le Zone "O" di P.R.G: Roma. Indagine Sulla Struttura Urbana e Sociale dei Nuclei Edilizi Spontanei. Rapporto finale ricerca,* ed. Giacchino Belli, Roberto Pallotini, and Giovanni Ranuzzi. Ufficio Risanamento Borgate. November.

Fera, Giuseppe, and Nella Ginatempo. 1982. *Autocostruzione—Marginalita' O Proposta.* Reggio Calabria: Casa del Libro Editrice.

Fried, Robert C. 1973. *Planning the Eternal City.* New Haven and London: Yale University Press.

Insolera, Italo. 1976. *Roma Moderna—Un Secolo di Storia Urbanistica—1870–1970.* Turin: Piccola Biblioteca Einaudi.

Patton, Carl V., and Costas M. Sophoulis. 1983. "Great Expectations: Illegal Land Development in Modern Greece." *Ekistics* 50(301) (July/August), 259–64.

Piazzo, Pietrenzo. 1982. *Roma-La Crescita Metropolitana Abusiva.* Rome: Officina Edizioni.

Procacci, Giuliano. 1984. *Storia Degli Italiani.* Bari: Editori Laterza.

Seeley, John. 1959. "The Slum: Its Nature, Use and Users," *Journal of the American Institute of Planners* 25(1) (February), 7–14.

Testa, Alfonso. 1985. "Macche' Proletari d'Egitto!" *Il Messaggero,* May 26, p. 6.

Chapter 13

Squatter Housing in Yugoslavia

BORIS PLESKOVIC

Squatting and unauthorized development are rare phenomena throughout the controlled economies of Eastern Europe and the Soviet Union. A notable exception is in socialist, nonaligned Yugoslavia, where squatting has appeared on a relatively large scale and represents a substantial addition to the urban housing stock. Although squatting has never been accepted as an alternative form of housing in Yugoslavia, it has been tolerated to a great extent and has been indirectly responsible for some positive, if limited, changes in urbanization and housing policies.

This chapter presents the evolution of squatter housing in Yugoslavia and the city of Ljubljana; describes current trends, major causes, and consequences; and discusses important characteristics of the population of the squatter areas concerned. The chapter ends with an overall evaluation of government housing policies, discusses lessons learned from the experience, and provides some conclusions directed toward future housing policy. Such issues are better understood against the background of urbanization and housing policy in Yugoslavia.

Urbanization in Yugoslavia

Rapid urban growth in Yugoslavia is a phenomenon only of the past thirty-five to forty years. Between the two world wars, Yugoslavia had a backward economy with an underdeveloped industry and few urban centers. After World War II, the country implemented an economic model that favored rapid industrialization. Although the majority of the population at the time was rural, very limited attention was paid to the development of agriculture. The agricultural system was largely inefficient, overreliant on climatic conditions, and could not support a growth in population. As a result, disguised and seasonal employment and underemployment, especially in the less developed southern regions, characterized agriculture in Yugoslavia (Pleskovic and Dolenc, 1982). After 1965, emigration to Western Europe was encouraged to ease severe unemployment problems, but this policy did not relieve any significant amount of urbanization pressure. On the contrary, returning migrant workers represented a significant proportion of squatters in some Yugoslavian cities. The employment situation worsened with the introduction of tractors and other agricultural mechanization during the 1970s, which rapidly increased the amount of surplus labor in the countryside.

The consequent drift from the rural areas has been reinforced by the socioeconomic attractions of the cities through industrialization. To a large extent, the rapid postwar urban growth has reflected both push factors in the rural areas and pull factors in cities. The result of the rural migration and accelerated industrialization has been a rapid increase in the urban population. In 1947, over 80 percent of the Yugoslav population was rural; by 1985, the proportion living in urban centers exceeded 45 percent. The proportion of the population engaged in agriculture in the less developed southern regions, which accounts for 37 percent of the total population, decreased from 72.9 percent in 1947 to less than 30 percent in 1985. The composition of the gross material product (GMP) of Yugoslavia has changed in favor of industry. The share of industry in GMP[1] increased from 12.8 percent to more than 40 percent between 1947 and 1985.

The primacy that has characterized urban growth in most developing countries has not occurred in Yugoslavia, where the six largest regional capitals have shared in the growth of primary city functions and have thus offered dispersed targets for migration (Table 13.1). There has been, however, net out-migration from the less developed agricultural regions to the more developed northern industrial regions. This

Table 13.1. Population and Household Growth, Major Urban Centers of Yugoslavia, 1953–81 (in thousands)

	Population				*Households*			
City	*1953*	*1961*	*1971*	*1981*	*1953*	*1961*	*1971*	*1981*
Belgrade	593	942	1,209	1,470	135	319	491	484
Zagreb	456	459	733	855	104	164	249	288
Split	98	132	185	235	14	40	214	246
Ljubljana	157	206	257	305	N.A.	69	88	109
Sarajevo	N.A.	213	359	448	N.A.	64	101	136
Skopje	168	270	388	556	27	58	96	123

Source: Federalni Institut za Statistiku (1985).
N.A. = Not available.

migration has put additional pressures on cities and housing demand and has contributed to the formation of some squatter and slum areas in northern cities.

The average growth of urban population in Yugoslavia was 3.1 percent from 1965 to 1973 and 2.8 percent from 1973 to 1983 (World Bank, 1985). This rapid urban growth has brought great pressure on housing availability, to which the government has been unable to respond because of limited financial resources. During the past decade, Yugoslavia has been devoting approximately 4 percent of its gross domestic product (GDP) to housing investment, which represents an increase over earlier decades.

Housing Policy Formation

Housing demand in Yugoslavia has been met through different supply measures, which have changed significantly over time. Immediately after World War II and up until 1950, government policy emphasized repair and reconstruction of existing dwellings rather than new construction, because more than 25 percent of the prewar stock of houses had been destroyed. Also, in order to provide for a more equal distribution of existing housing, all dwellings with more than three apartments were brought under social ownership.[2] Rent control was also introduced nationally during this period for all housing not privately owned. New housing construction was limited, with only about 5,000 new dwelling units built each year. From 1950 to 1956, there was greater emphasis on investment in new dwellings; more than 200,000 new units, mostly one- and two-bedroom apartments, were built. Housing was the responsibility of the federal government, and all financing for construction came from its budget.

In 1957 a new system for financing housing construction was adopted, with the creation of housing funds at the communal and republic levels. Funds came from collecting 10 percent and subsequently 6 percent of the gross personal income of employees. These funds were administered by Communal Housing Authorities, which promoted and bought new housing stock through publicly owned construction companies (Bassin, 1984). With these funds, over 350,000 new units were built between 1956 and 1965 (Table 13.2). In addition, the private sector, which accounted for nearly 60 percent of total housing construction, built 485,000 units. Nevertheless, until 1960, the increase in the number of units lagged behind the number of new households, so the housing deficit increased by 290,000 units (Dubey, 1975). This was the result of both an increase in population and a decline in average household size. From 1960 to 1965, the response of the government to this housing shortage was to lower standards and build smaller apartments.

Table 13.2. Number of Dwellings Built in Yugoslavia, 1956–83 (in thousands)

Year	*Public*	*Percentage*	*Private*	*Percentage*	*Total*
1956–60	126	46	153	54	279
1961–65	226	40	332	60	558
1966–70	225	35	409	65	634
1971–75	238	35	446	65	684
1976–80	267	37	444	63	711
1981–83	169	39	264	61	433
Total	1,251	38	2,048	62	3,299

Source: Federalni Institut za Statistiku (1985).

From 1965 to 1974, several market mechanisms were introduced into the economy. The responsibility for resolving the housing problems of their employees was transferred to the self-managed (worker-owned) production enterprises, and the Communal Housing Authorities were abolished. Enterprises were now responsible for collecting 4 percent of the gross personal income of their employees for housing construction; this was a decline from the 10 percent and 6 percent collected earlier. These funds were used in part by the enterprises, although a portion was transferred to the communal and republican housing funds. The funds left with enterprises were used either to build apartments (for rent or sale) for their employees or to grant housing credits. Commercial banks were also given an important role in the credit system for housing construction. The construction of apartments in the public sector was carried out by independent construction companies. Financing for the construction of apartments came from enterprise credits, commercial bank loans, communal housing funds, or private savings. Most new apartments were sold as condominiums because controlled rents were insufficient to cover even basic maintenance costs, let alone provide financing for new investment in rental housing.

An attempt to raise housing rents to a more economic level failed, and fewer rental apartments were built during this period. The introduction of market mechanisms (e.g., liberalization of credit and prices) increased the role of private housing construction. Average yearly construction during the period was about 130,000 units, of which 35 percent was publicly built and 65 percent privately built (Table 13.2). In spite of the considerable increase in housing construction, a large discrepancy between housing supply and demand remained. According to the 1971 census, there was a housing deficit of 507,000 dwellings in Yugoslavian urban areas.

As a consequence of the housing shortage, squatter housing emerged on a relatively large scale. It became evident that low-income households could not afford adequate housing, even with loans from their enterprises or from commercial banks (Bassin, 1984). Part of the reason for this situation was the inadequate financing schemes and extremely expensive and inefficient public housing construction. As a result of the high prices of apartments and the general economic situation, the buying power of enterprises was reduced to a minimum, which resulted in the purchase of a minimal number of apartments, to be used only by the most essential employees, usually professionals (Jankovic, 1972). Funds left for enterprise housing credits were usually distributed evenly to a large number of applicants but in very small amounts. At the same time, commercial banks required large down payments, up to 50 percent of the purchase price of an apartment, and offered relatively short-term (ten to fifteen years) loans (Dubey, 1975). Some of these policies were corrected during the next planning period.

Following constitutional changes in 1974, each commune and republic was permitted to adopt independent policies and set housing standards. The self-managing Housing Interest Associations were formed. Like the Communal Housing Authorities before them, the associations operated on a communal basis, and the communal assemblies defined the percentage contributions, which varied from 4 to 6 percent of gross personal income, for general housing development. Approximately 10 percent of these funds was used for the creation of a Solidarity Housing Fund in each commune.

The Solidarity Housing Fund was to provide apartments for low-income families and individuals who did not have sufficient financial resources to solve their housing problems, especially young families and individuals who were retired or disabled. The solidarity fund also was a partial response to the growing numbers of squatters and slums in the larger cities. The role of the fund has been very positive; it has helped clear many slum areas and provide their occupants with housing. In fact, the system of housing finance and construction introduced in the early 1970s has been fairly successful in resolving the housing problems of the poorest households. Although small pockets of "shanty" dwellings remain in some urban centers, their growth has been more or less stopped. The housing problems of the lower-middle-income households, who are not eligible for aid from the Solidarity Housing Fund and who cannot afford to buy or build their own dwellings, have not been resolved satisfactorily.

A recent slowdown in the growth rate of new housing construction has resulted from a general economic recession and increased price controls on public housing. Construction companies have often preferred to invest in the more profitable office and factory construction, where prices are not controlled, but private-sector housing construction has continued to account for over 60 percent of the total construction. Table 13.2 shows that from 1956 to 1983, 3.3 million new dwellings were added to Yugoslavia's housing stock. This is a considerable achievement in terms of numbers of dwellings, but there has been less progress in the quality of housing. In urban areas more than 80 percent of the dwellings do not have central heating and more than 30 percent do not have running water. There are also large variations between regions in the quality and quantity of housing. In 1983, for example, only 42 percent of the urban dwellings in the least developed region, Kosovo, had running water, whereas the figure in the most developed region, Slovenia, was 92 percent (Federalni Institut, 1985).

In spite of considerable construction efforts and several changes in housing policies, housing shortages exist in all major urban centers. Rural areas have a housing surplus. Although rural–urban migration has slowed recently, especially in the more developed northern regions of the country, the demand for urban housing has increased with higher incomes and the continuing decline in average household size. Some of the housing shortage has been filled by squatting.

Evolution of Squatter Housing in Yugoslavia

Squatting has been a widespread response to the housing shortage in Yugoslavia. The Yugoslavian name for this phenomenon is *crne gradnje,* or black housing,[3] which means dwellings built illegally. In general, such dwellings are built without building permits by their inhabitants and are located along the city periphery on land not necessarily zoned for residential development. In such areas, land has not been nationalized, and prices are lower. If the authorities discover the houses during the construction process, the houses can be demolished. Once the walls and the roof are built, long, tedious legal proceedings are needed to remove the squatters. Squatting is extensive in urban Yugoslavia, particularly in the larger cities (Table 13.3), but as we see later in the chapter in relation to Ljubljana, many squatters are at least semilegal. Approximately 90 percent of the squatters have built dwellings on private land; the remainder are on public land belonging to communes or regional administrations. There is no organized invasion of land (e.g., Doebele, 1977). Instead, most squatters build individually or in small groups along the peripheries of cities or on land purchased from farmers or other owners.

Squatter housing appeared in Yugoslavia as it moved from a low-income country to middle-income status. A few squatters arrived between 1950 and 1960 (Ravbar, 1978). Intensive construction of squatter houses started after 1960, accelerated after 1966, increased steadily until 1980, and then began slowly to level off, although there are many variations among different cities.

The government did not give any organized attention to the phenomenon of illegal housing until several thousand units were built around most urban centers. In the early 1970s, when squatters reached

Table 13.3. Illegal Housing as a Proportion of Private Housing Construction, Selected Yugoslavian Cities, 1961–67

City	*Illegal Housing as Percentage of Total*
Belgrade	52.1
Zagreb	39.5
Banja Luka	41.9
Osijek	66.8
Split	49.3
Novi Sad	49.3
Pristina	36.3
Smederevo	69.9
Tetovo	39.0
Tuzla	58.9

Source: Finci (1972).

such proportions that in many larger cities every second newly built house, and in smaller cities every third or fifth, was illegal, city and local governments initiated several surveys, seminars, and studies of the problem. One such study estimated that in 1972 more than 1 million of Yugoslavia's 22 million inhabitants lived in illegal houses (Kobe et al., 1973). Another study reported that in more than 20 percent of regional centers in the republic of Bosnia and Herzegovina, more buildings were built without permits than with permits in the early 1970s (Dzankic, 1972).

The most comprehensive attempt at estimating the scope of the squatter problem was organized by the Permanent Conference of Yugoslav Cities. During 1967 this institution carried out a survey of seventy-three Yugoslavian cities that showed that more than 36,000 squatter dwellings had been constructed between 1961 and 1967. The proportion of illegal housing in the analyzed cities represented about one-half of the total private construction (Table 13.3). Most squatters located next to highways in zones planned for recreation, industry, or housing—zones close to the city that could easily be connected to infrastructure facilities (Finci, 1972).

The analysis of seventy-three cities showed that housing construction was more or less chaotic in terms of disorganized and discontinued land-use patterns and infrastructure development (Photo 13.1). It also identified the presence of slums in larger cities including Belgrade, Zagreb, Sarajevo, Skopje, and Nis. The slums are relatively small in terms of number of housing units, however, and are an exception rather than the rule. This contrasts with the situation in some developed countries, including the United States, and in many less developed countries,

Photo 13.1 Ljubljana. A typical slum. These areas usually consist of a small group of barracks on the periphery of the city.

where slums can reach enormous proportions. Another difference between the typical developing country and Yugoslavia is that squatters and slums are rarely found in the centers of Yugoslavian cities.

In general, the construction quality of illegal houses is relatively high. Although variations exist among different cities, the overall quality of squatter construction in many ways resembles organized middle-income housing (Photo 13.2). Squatters in Yugoslavia are not the poorest segment of the population. The majority of them are low-skilled and semiskilled workers (factory workers, carpenters, bricklayers, plumbers, construction workers, electricians, mechanics, etc.). The poorest segment of the local population is taken care of by the state, especially since 1974, and is provided with subsidized rental housing or solidarity housing. Most inhabitants of slums are recent migrant workers who moved to the city from other regions or republics; squatters typically originate from within the city region.

The list of causes for black housing in Yugoslavia is a long one and is dealt with in detail in the next section. The illegal housing problem has been enormous, and the government's basic policy guidelines to redress the problem have had two components: the demolition of illegal buildings and the undertaking of preventive measures. Neither policy has been systematic, long-term, or comprehensive. The results of government attempts to deal with the problem have produced only statistical data and a very small number of demolished houses (Dzankic, 1972). The government at first intended to clear specific areas needed for city growth and relocate the affected populations into public housing. This is an expensive procedure. Little official clearance has taken place, other

Photo 13.2 Ljubljana. Squatter houses on the periphery of the city. Note their high quality and standard of construction.

than for road developments or for the removal of the worst slum areas. When land use and infrastructure plans have been developed for affected squatter areas, however, recognition of the squatters as part of the city proper has resulted. Sooner or later, these locales have been provided with infrastructure improvements.

Concern for the future has been left to the city inspector, to whom this is only a secondary task. Furthermore, because of inadequate staffing and a lack of both technical equipment and support from other institutions, city inspectors cannot prevent continued illegal construction. The result of such policies has been an increased number of illegal buildings and a massive and united opposition by citizens to the clearance of such buildings. The inability of inspection offices to deal with the problem can be seen from the fact that in 1972 a total of 39 percent of the illegally constructed dwellings were indicated for clearance by inspectors, and only 3 percent of the buildings were demolished (Dzankic, 1972).

The most recent statistical data show that between 1976 and 1982, 149,502 new illegal dwellings were constructed in Yugoslavia, while 394,622 housing units were built by the public sector (Table 13.4). The proportion of illegal buildings to total public housing construction was much higher in the less developed regions: the number of squatter units constructed was equivalent to 65 percent of the total number of public housing units constructed. On average, 68 percent of the squatters are workers; in some cities the percentage is even higher, for example, in Belgrade 80 percent, Split 86 percent, and Novi Sad 94 percent (Anojuic, 1986). The largest squatter settlement in Yugoslavia is on the out-

Table 13.4. Public and Squatter Housing Construction in Yugoslavia by Major Republics–Regions and Their Capital Cities, 1976–82

	Number of Units Constructed			Number of Units Constructed	
	Public Housing	Illegal Buildings (squatters)		Public Housing	Illegal Buildings (squatters)
Yugoslavia	394,622	149,502	*Capital Cities*	176,590	57,694
Less developed regions					
Bosnia-Herzegovina	50,348	33,152	Sarajevo	14,444	19,065
Kosovo	4,011	3,191	Pristina	2,322	1,248
Macedonia	32,649	20,555	Skopje	19,892	10,480
Montenegro	5,956	4,897	Titograd	3,537	1,393
Total	92,964	61,795		40,195	32,186
More developed regions					
Croatia	96,080	26,797	Zagreb	46,819	7,748
Serbia	110,182	41,423	Belgrade	57,360	13,523
Slovenia	63,412	6,271	Ljubljana	23,390	3,283
Vojvodina	31,984	13,216	Novi Sad	8,826	954
Total	301,658	87,707		136,395	25,508

Source: Stalna Konferencija Gradova (1985).

skirts of Belgrade. This squatter settlement, Kalucerica, contains about 20,000 inhabitants and was recently legalized. Interesting features of this settlement include a relatively large rental market of rooms and high-quality housing construction.

In spite of the enormous size of the squatter problem in Yugoslavia, very few illegal buildings have been demolished recently, and no comprehensive policies have been implemented to redress the housing shortage (Anojuic, 1986). The large numbers of surveys, studies, conferences, and official meetings that took place in all major cities during the early 1970s have never been repeated. Since then, the problem has been left to city governments, which tend to deal with it in more or less similar ways. One city that has been the subject of recent extensive research on squatter housing is Ljubljana. This city has the highest per capita income in Yugoslavia, and its policies are often followed or studied by other cities. For these reasons, it is a useful case study.

The Growth of Ljubljana and the Provision of Housing

Only five cities in Yugoslavia contain more than 250,000 people. One of them, Ljubljana, is expanding very rapidly. Ljubljana is the capital of the most developed northern republic, Slovenia. Between the world wars it was a small industrial center of about 70,000 persons. In

1953 it reached a population of 157,000, which doubled by 1981 to 305,000 inhabitants (see Table 13.1). This very rapid growth has resulted in many problems for the city planners. At present, however, the greatest single problem facing Ljubljana is its housing shortage, with the resultant construction of substantial numbers of squatter houses.

Squatting in Ljubljana has been a feature of the city since the 1960s (Ravbar, 1978). In the early 1970s, illegal buildings constituted half of all private housing construction. Because of the growing size of the problem, city authorities laid down basic policy guidelines in the 1972 "Black Housing Law" after previous legislation designed to encourage general house building had failed to achieve any notable success (Krietmajer, 1974). The 1972 law had three primary objectives:

1. *Prohibition of infrastructure connections (water, electricity, sewerage) to illegally constructed buildings.* This measure, designed to discourage future illegal construction, failed with the realization that people should not live without water and electricity connections. Squatter buildings were given temporary infrastructure facilities.
2. *Prevention of further widespread growth of black housing.* The law shortened legal procedures for the clearance of buildings in areas not zoned for housing construction and empowered local authorities to demolish any black house built after 1972. In the face of continued widespread squatting, an attempt to clear illegal housing has failed because no feasible alternative housing has been available.
3. *Tolerance of black housing.* The law provided that an illegally constructed building not be demolished immediately, but only be registered as a "building designated for demolition," thus allowing for later legalization. This measure had a dual purpose. On the one hand, it was assumed that it would discourage future squatters because inhabitants of squatter housing would be uncertain about the future of their housing. On the other hand, it gave the authorities time for a detailed survey of "critical" buildings, as well as an excuse to delay the socially and politically infeasible demolition of all squatter housing.

After acceptance of the law and on the recommendations of the republican urban inspectorate, five communes of the city decided to carry out a detailed survey of black housing. The survey categorized black housing into (1) areas for legalization; (2) areas for identification (with possible legalization); and (3) areas for clearance.

The 1974 survey showed that the city contained 2,484 illegal buildings, of which 85 percent were residential dwellings, 4 percent barracks (slums), and the rest either illegal reconstructions and additions or illegally built industrial buildings. Of all identified squatter housing, 56 percent consisted of finished buildings; the remainder were under construction. Infrastructure connections were significant: 56 percent of buildings had electricity, 54 percent water, and 4 percent sewerage connections; 31 percent had no infrastructure. Thus, nearly all the squatters were able to obtain the most essential infrastructure facilities.

Socioeconomic Characteristics

The survey showed, surprisingly, that the squatter population did not belong to the poorest segment of the population, but consisted of average and below-average household categories. Heads of households living in squatter housing were neither socially disadvantaged nor well-to-do. The average family size in the squatter area was 3.5, slightly larger than the 2.9 average of the city. In most (64.4 percent) households there were two full-time workers; 30.6 percent of households had one full-time worker (Table 13.5). In general, unemployment in Ljubljana was negligible and found only in slums.

Most employment was located in and around the city center. Over 70 percent of the squatters were employed in the social sector,[4] which in a socialist country like Yugoslavia means permanent job security (tenure) and a steady income. Only 2 percent of squatters were full-time farmers. Around 12 percent were either self-employed or employed in the small

Table 13.5. Socioeconomic Characteristics of Squatter Households, 1971

Number of family members	1	2	3	4	5	6+
Percentage in squatter households	6.7	9.5	30.3	41.7	7.3	4.5
Average percentage for Ljubljana	25.2	18.3	20.5	18.8	9.8	7.4
Number employed per squatter household	1	2	3	4+		
Percentage	30.6	64.4	3.8	1.2		
Income per capita[a]	0–499	500–999	1,000–1,999	2,000+	N.A.	
Percentage	9.9	43.8	36.0	3.8	6.5	
Qualifications of squatter population	Nonqualified	Semiqualified	Secondary	College	N.A.	
Percentage	7.5	55.5	12.7	4.6	19.7	
Employment of squatter heads of households	Social	Private	Employer	Farmer	Other	
Percentage	73.0	4.7	7.3	2.3	12.7	

Source: Krietmajer (1974).
[a]Average income per capita for the city was 872 dinars (about $5,800) in 1971.
N.A. = Not available.

private sector. The survey also showed that most squatters were either nonqualified (7.5 percent) or semiqualified (55.5 percent) workers. Very few squatters had higher qualifications; however, such persons were well represented in the group that built illegal secondary (weekend) homes. Characteristically for Yugoslavia, many squatters or their relatives were highly skilled in construction fields (plumbers, bricklayers, electricians, etc.), which greatly facilitated the construction of their houses. The average age of the squatters was between thirty and forty years, which meant that most of them had been employed for several years but were unable to solve their housing problems through available legal opportunities (Ravbar, 1974).

Geographic Characteristics

In contrast to the experience of other developing countries, where large slums usually appear in the center of the city, only one black house has been registered in the city center. One explanation of this fact is that urban inspection is frequent and thorough in city centers. Another explanation is that, as in most European cities, the center of Ljubljana has been historically and traditionally occupied by the middle- and upper-income population. There is also limited vacant land available in the center of the city.

The 1974 survey showed that 24 percent of the squatters in Ljubljana built in areas approved for residential development in 1971 but that the owners did not bother to ask for official documentation, that is, for location and building permits. Eight percent of the squatter buildings were in areas where housing development plans had been completed but construction had not yet begun; some squatters built at the location of a future school, park, or local road. Eighteen percent of the squatter buildings were in areas where land-use plans were under preparation, and where construction was prohibited by law until the completion of the plan (Krietmajer, 1974). These data indicate that many squatter buildings are semilegal because they are built on land zoned for future residential development.

More than 22 percent (480) of the remaining squatter buildings were in areas reserved for infrastructure corridors, such as underground water reservoirs, parks, recreational areas, highways, and energy corridors. The rest of the black houses (28 percent) were constructed on farmland and in woods. Contrary to expectations, only 128 buildings were located at the border of existing urban settlements. It was also expected that squatter housing would appear in large groups, but the survey showed that most dwellings were dispersed, with the exception of three areas where 50 to 100 buildings appeared together.

Building Materials and Construction

In contrast to other developing countries and some Yugoslavian regions, the construction quality of black housing is relatively high in Slovenia, especially in Ljubljana. In general, squatters use the same construction materials as official housing construction companies—brick and reinforced concrete (Photo 13.3).[5] Squatters tend to overbuild in terms of size of structure and number of rooms. Part of the reason is that squatters do not build only for themselves but also for their children. They also rent out rooms, which helps them financially, especially during the early years of construction (Klemencic, 1979).

Many squatters tend to be overambitious in terms of quality of construction materials, as well as size of buildings, leaving the completion of the house to the next generation. As in other developing countries, there is enormous flexibility in terms of time and financial constraints. Squatters build in phases, using their spare time over weekends and the help of friends and relatives (Pleskovic et al., 1976a). Many supplement their incomes through home gardening on adjacent plots (Photo 13.4). There is also extreme solidarity among squatter inhabitants. They help one an-

Photo 13.3 Ljubljana. Unfinished squatter buildings. Note the quality of construction and typical construction materials used (here, brick and reinforced concrete).

Photo 13.4 Ljubljana. Typical squatter houses. Adjacent vegetable gardens are owned and cultivated by the squatters.

other by lending tools for construction, and neighbors share manual work as well as water, electricity, and sanitary facilities. In addition, if any building is singled out for demolition, the squatters join forces to protect the structure from the authorities.

Major Reasons for Squatting

The reasons for black housing in Yugoslavia are numerous and complex. Many of them are similar to those that can be found in other developing countries. Among the primary reasons, the most important is the housing shortage, which resulted from the discrepancy between the rate of urbanization and industrialization and the rate of housing construction. During the 1960s and 1970s Yugoslavia achieved one of the highest industrialization growth rates among fourteen European countries. Its GDP growth rate was between 6 and 7 percent a year (World Bank, 1985). But its rate of housing construction was next to the lowest in Europe.

Other important factors contributing to squatting have been uncoordinated land-use planning and inadequate land-management policies. Housing development plans take years to prepare. In Ljubljana, it takes five to seven years from plan preparation to actual construction (Urban Inspectorate, 1984). The city usually lacks funds for prior land expropriation and buys the land at below-market prices. This induces landowners to sell their property to potential squatters at a higher price in advance of expropriation or before the land is prohibited for sale (Aganovic, 1972).

There is also a great shortage of sites planned for individual house construction. No construction area can be officially opened without first building all the necessary high-standard infrastructure. Although approximately 60 percent of existing and new housing stock consists of private individual dwellings, nearly all the organized financing schemes (mortgages), research, and construction are concentrated on high-rise, relatively high-standard housing construction projects (Pleskovic et al., 1976b). The goals of urban (master) plans are uniformly set with the objective of building a mix of about 80 percent high-rise dewllings and 20 percent individual dwellings: goals that run counter to past and present housing trends. The main argument of urban planners is that building high-rise, high-standard structures and constructing infrastructure is cheaper than any alternative because of economies of scale. But there are great shortages and delays in high-rise construction. Apartments in these buildings are also too expensive for the low-income population, which therefore builds squatter housing.

As indicated, housing reform since 1965 has given responsibility for housing construction to the enterprises. However, these enterprises have had insufficient funds to solve the housing situation of their workers. In order to satisfy as many employees as possible, they have divided their funds into numerous small loans (Finci, 1972). These loans, although too small to purchase an apartment, have become a welcome starting point for many squatters.

There are also several secondary causes of squatting in Yugoslavia. The process of obtaining legal papers and permits for construction is time-consuming and exasperating; it can take at least a year in Ljubljana and close to a year in other Yugoslavian cities (Aganovic, 1972). Equally long and complicated are legal procedures for identification and clearance of black housing. Clearance of squatter buildings is not only an expensive procedure but is also resisted very effectively by concerned owners, their friends and neighbors, and sometimes even by workers at agencies given the task of demolition (Contala, 1985).

Legal sanctions against squatters are extremely low, typically involving a very small fine or up to thirty days of imprisonment. On appeal, the penalties are often lowered or canceled because of inadequate or unclear land-use plans and legislation (Ravbar, 1978). Under these conditions, many squatters choose legal penalties rather than obtain the required permits and documentation (Urban Inspectorate, 1984). Therefore, ineffective sanctions contribute to the lack of respect for urban legislation.

Finally, there are important socioeconomic reasons for the appearance of squatter housing. Among them, squatters ranked as the most important the possibility for construction in stages, according to available finances, the use of their own work and free time, cheaper land, and protection against inflation (Pozenel, 1977). It has been estimated that a house built illegally costs 30 to 37 percent less than a house built by official construction companies (Ravbar, 1974). Squatters also said that tolerance of existing black housing represents a very strong stimulus for potential squatters (Bjelajac, 1972).

Consequences of Squatting

The costs and benefits of extensive squatting in Yugoslavia are similar to those found in any developing country. The most important benefits include mobilization of people's energies in terms of investment of their skills, own work, and financial resources toward self-help construction (Pleskovic et al., 1976a). But disregard for the future needs of the city, and the chaotic distribution of squatter housing, leads to several negative consequences, which may prove very costly in the medium and long term.

Some of the negative effects include pollution of underground water reservoirs, the demolition costs of squatter housing that lies in the middle of future road and infrastructure corridors, and more expensive construction of primary and secondary infrastructure because of dispersed, low-density illegal buildings. Another consequence, which is very often quoted by architects and urban planners in Yugoslavia, is the aesthetic degradation of the environment. This factor may be important, especially in tourist areas, but it is probably the one that could be dealt with most easily, if more positive policies toward improving squatter housing were adopted.

Policy Recommendations of the 1974 Survey

The major task of the 1974 survey was to recommend solutions that could eliminate the basic causes of squatting and prevent the future appearance of the problem. The survey identified 862 buildings that should be demolished in order to satisfy current urban legislation and prevent future squatting (Kreitmajer, 1974). Lack of funds for supplementary housing and the enormous financial and sociopolitical costs of clearance postponed the demolition indefinitely.

Medium-term solutions, recommended to prevent future squatting, included integration of socioeconomic and spatial planning, the introduction of industrialized housing construction with shorter amortization periods, development of financing schemes for primary infrastructure, and an increase in rents for subsidized housing. The primary objective of these recommendations was to make organized public housing construction cheaper than individual, private construction. The study also recommended an increase in the availability of land and basic infrastructure for private housing construction, along the lines of sites and services programs.

Although many of the recommendations were sound, they were never fully implemented. There was some improvement in land-use planning and urban legislation, but little progress in the improvement of housing policies and construction, with the exception of the introduction of solidarity housing in 1974. The problem was left largely to urban inspection, which has been unable to stop the growth of black housing.

Recent Developments: The 1984 Survey

The 1974 survey was repeated ten years later, although on a smaller scale. The 1984 survey showed that in spite of all the efforts of urban inspection, 2,370 new illegal buildings were constructed in Ljubljana between 1976 and 1980, of which approximately half (1,068) were black houses. Excluding previously legalized buildings, urban inspection identified 4,800 illegal buildings in 1980, an increase of 50 percent over the number reported in the previous survey. These illegal buildings were registered, and some of them were recommended for legalization. Many squatters are not interested in formal legalization, however, because required documentation and infrastructure fees are costly, whereas economic sanctions are either nonexistent or extremely low (Urban Inspectorate, 1984).

The 1984 survey analyzed several reasons for the continuous appearance of squatter dwellings. Most of the reasons were similar to the ones reported in the previous survey. Of these, the continuous shortage of housing was singled out as the most important factor responsible for the current situation. Table 13.6 shows that a correlation exists between the shortage of housing and the growth of squatter building in Ljubljana. There is a close relationship between the recent slight decline in the number of newly constructed black houses and the decline in the nominal housing shortage. The data also show that the gap between planned and actual housing construction had been closed to a great extent by squatter construction.

For example, from 1976 to 1980, Ljubljana planned an 87 percent increase in public housing construction (high-rise apartments) of 13,000 units and a 13 percent increase in private housing of 2,000 units. Al-

Table 13.6. Relationship between the Nominal Housing Shortage and Construction of Illegal Housing in Ljubljana

	1976	*1977*	*1978*	*1979*	*1980*
Growth of population					
Natural	2,730	2,655	2,864	2,943	2,815
Migration	4,548	4,497	2,585	3,829	3,529
Nominal housing shortage	8,686	8,429	6,095	6,360	6,464
Percentage of households	8.6	8.1	5.8	5.9	5.9
Increase in black houses	431	233	156	153	105
Percentage of nominal shortage	4.9	2.6	2.5	2.4	1.6

Source: Urban Inspectorate (1984).

though public housing construction was close to target at 78 percent, private construction at 38 percent exceeded the target. Instead of the planned total of 15,000 housing units, 2,115 fewer units were built. Approximately half of this shortage (1,068 buildings) was filled by black housing construction.

Other reasons identified as important factors contributing to squatting include inadequate land-use plans, lack of discipline with respect to urban law, low sanctions, public opposition to clearance, and continuing changes in urban legislation, which includes many loopholes. Formal legislation against squatters is very strict, but it is usually not enforced. For example, cities and communes responsible by law for clearance decide instead to change their urban plans and legalize squatter buildings, whether or not the investor provides the necessary documentation (Urban Inspectorate, 1984). In most cases responsible authorities do not react in time to head off squatting but respond when the building is completed and when intervention becomes more difficult.

Major recommendations of the 1984 survey focused on the improvement of urban plans and urban legislation. The same appeal was repeated by the most recent report on the squatter problem in Slovenia (Contala, 1985), which identified 15,000 illegal buildings in a region of 2 million inhabitants. The latter report recognized that current restrictive policies have been unable to alleviate the black housing problem.[6] Surprisingly, all the recommendations of the report, which included a republicwide urban inspectorate, focused on the need for improved urban plans, effective urban inspection, and better information systems as the most important factors in bringing about an end to the squatter problem. Changes in housing and financial policies were simply ignored.

Conclusion

In spite of the restrictive policies toward squatter buildings, Yugoslavian authorities have shown a great deal of flexibility in dealing with the problem. Very few, and then only the worst, black houses have been demolished, and some positive policies have emerged as a consequence of squatting. Of these, the most important was the establishment of the Solidarity Housing Fund in 1974, which has taken care of most of the poorest and most underprivileged households. Other limited but positive changes in housing policy include improvement in the speed and quality of urban documentation, legislation, and upgrading of existing squatters through infrastructure connections.

Where Yugoslavia has been least flexible is in the acceptance of lower housing standards and sites and services programs. Past experience proves that the process of squatting is very difficult to reverse, whereas the accommodation of squatters in terms of legalization has been feasible, partially because of the relatively low density of land use in Yugoslavian cities. Even a large increase in squatter dwellings during the last ten years, perhaps up to 50 percent, would have caused little or no damaging effects, including aesthetic ones, if the potential squatters had been channeled onto prepared sites, provided with minimum infrastructure facilities, and integrated into the urban fabric.

There have been only two such sites and services attempts, one in Zagreb[7] and the other in Novi Sad. While these attempts have been welcomed by some urban planners, others have argued that in both cities, and especially in Novi Sad, migration to the city increased four times as a consequence of this policy (Finci, 1972). Accordingly, such solutions have been rejected as harmful in terms of increased migration. The second obstacle against sites and services is related to the fact that city administrators and urban planners who have been designing housing policies view the problems of squatters from their personal perspectives (Ponzenel, 1977). Most of them have solved their housing problems by acquiring small apartments and do not see any rationality in a solution that would give the lower-income population the opportunity to obtain a higher housing standard by owning their own houses. Although the squatters are prepared to sacrifice time and resources to construct their housing units, the administrators and planners are not. The third reason for the resistance to sites and services programs is common to most developing countries and involves the reluctance to reduce housing quality standards (Grimes, 1976).

Yugoslavia seems to have two basic needs with respect to future housing policy; one is much cheaper than the other, but both need to be addressed simultaneously. The more expensive government action would be to increase direct construction of public housing and improve mortgage financing, especially for low-income families. This would, however, require substantial new investment in housing. By international comparisons (Burns and Grebler, 1976), Yugoslavia already devotes the same ratio of GDP (4 to 5 percent) to housing investment as do most other countries at the same stage of development. Therefore, an increase in housing investment may be resisted because of the current emphasis on the growth of GDP, and because of the perception that such expenditures on social overhead are a waste of valuable investment capital, even though it has been proven otherwise (Strassman, 1976).

The other option, which might be less costly in the medium term, is to lower housing standards and provide self-help sites along the peripheries of cities, where squatting occurs regardless. Such a policy would take into account positive aspects of squatting, in particular, the self-help contribution that reduces the cost of construction. In addition, the negative effects of black housing, including disorganized land-use patterns and the high cost of infrastructure caused by the low density of squatter buildings, could be prevented.

The present policy of applying relatively high standards to housing and infrastructure construction significantly contributes to the phenomenon of illegal housing and limits the production of public housing. Therefore, it seems unreasonable to insist on maintaining present levels of housing standards. The self-help, low-cost approach to housing, and the use of traditional materials, could significantly improve the employment situation, as well as the housing, health conditions, and labor productivity in less developed regions (Pleskovic, 1979).

Most of the literature and experience argue that a low-cost housing approach is highly recommendable for Third World countries. Nonetheless, some authors claim that this approach treats the symptom—inadequate housing—rather than the cause—poverty (Leeds, 1974); and it co-opts the savings and labor of the poor to help pay for what Marx has termed "the reproduction cost of labor," costs that otherwise would have to be borne by employers (Rivas, 1977). On these grounds, some authors suggest that attention should be paid more to the source of low incomes than to the amelioration of housing.[8] It should be noted that this chapter recognizes the validity of this argument. The low-cost approach to housing is recommended here as only one viable alternative, along with an emphasis on adequate financing and other diversified but consistent housing policies, including the provision of employment through low-cost, labor-intensive housing construction. Within the context of present economic, social, and institutional constraints in Yugoslavia—where inadequate financing through self-managed (worker-owned) enterprises cannot provide sufficient housing for low-income households, where the additional flow of resources to the housing sector is constrained by political emphasis on the growth of the GDP, and where the income distribution within the public sector of the economy can hardly be more equalized without affecting the overall economic incentive system—the low-cost approach to housing may certainly represent an important policy option in order to improve the housing situation of low-income groups. This will be true, at least in the medium term, until the more severe housing shortages are ameliorated.

At present, the housing situation in Yugoslavia, and especially in Ljubljana, is not as critical as in some large cities in developing countries. This reflects relatively low land-use densities, availability of open space, and the laissez-faire attitude of the government, which has been expressed in a wide tolerance of self-help black housing on the peripheries of cities. In general, the experience of Yugoslavia shows that squatter buildings may not disappear when the country reaches a higher level of development, as some governments hope. The experience also shows that reluctance to include positive aspects of self-help housing as part of a housing policy may bring more negative than positive effects because, in spite of all restrictions, squatting continues at its own pace, which includes its economic, environmental, and social costs.

Acknowledgments

The author is grateful to Marko Kranjec, Branko Milanovic, Karen Polenske, Michael Romanos, and Lojze Socan for their useful comments and suggestions.

Notes

1. The gross material product (GMP) concept differs from the gross national product (GNP) concept in its treatment of services, such as education, health, and government, which are excluded in the GMP as "nonproductive" sectors of the economy.
2. According to the 1958 Act of Nationalization of Urban Dwellings and Buildings Plots, no Yugoslavian is entitled to own, in principle, more than two dwellings.
3. Note that in Yugoslavia this term does not have a racial connotation.
4. The economy is divided into private and social sectors. The private sector consists of private agriculture (approximately 80 percent of land ownership) and businesses employing fewer than five to ten workers. The remainder is the social sector.
5. Greece provides an example of another country in which high-quality unauthorized construction is taking place (Patton and Sophoulis, 1983).
6. There are currently 1,273 illegal buildings designated in Slovenia for clearance; however, only about 7 percent of the "critical" buildings have been demolished in previous periods (Contala, 1985).
7. In Zagreb, 12,000 parcels were provided in 1970 for the "squatter" population.

8. It is interesting that these points have not been raised by Yugoslavian authors, some of whom recommended self-help and sites and services programs and other restrictive policies (see Finci, 1972).

References

Aganovic, M. 1972. "Uslovi Razvoja, Osnovne Technicko-Ekonomske i Socioloske Karakteristike Bespravne Stambene Izgradenje u Sarajevu." In *Bespravna Stambena Izgradnja u BIH,* ed. Jakhel Finci, pp. 163–86. Sarajevo: Akademija Nauka i Umjetnosti.

Anojuic, I. 1986. "Bespravno u Svojoj Kuci." *Politika,* March 23, p. 8.

Bassin, Peter. 1984. "Yugoslavia." In *Housing in Europe,* ed. Martin Wynn, pp. 155–76. London and Canberra: St. Martin's Press.

Bjelajac, Slobodan. 1972. *Bespravna Stambena Izgradnja u Splitu.* Split: UZD.

Burns, L., and L. Grebler. 1977. *The Housing of Nations.* New York: Wiley.

Contala, B. 1985. "Crne Gradnje v Sloveniji: Ukrepati je Treba Pred Buldozerji." *Delo,* December 14, p. 21.

Doebele, W. 1977. "The Pirate Market and Low Income Urbanization: The Private Subdivisions of Bogotá." *American Journal of Comparative Law* 25(3), 531–64.

Dubey, V. 1975. *Yugoslavia: Development with Decentralization.* Baltimore: Johns Hopkins University Press.

Dzankic, Fikret. 1972. "Drustveno-Politicki Aspekti Bespravne Stambena Izgradnje u Gradovima BIH." In *Bespravna Stambena Izgradnja u BIH,* ed. Jakhel Finci, pp. 61–73. Sarajevo: Akademija Nauka i Umjetnosti.

Federalni Institut za Statistiku. 1985. *Statisticki Godisnjak Jugoslavije.* Beograd: Sekretarijat za Planiranje.

Finci, Jakhel, ed. 1972. *Bespravna Stambena Izgradnja u BIH.* Sarajevo: Akademija Nauka i Umjetnosti.

Grimes, Orville F., Jr. 1976. *Housing for Low-Income Urban Families, Economics and Policy in the Developing World.* Baltimore: Johns Hopkins University Press.

Jankovic, Zivorad. 1972. "Uticaj Drustvenog Razvoja na Pojavu Bespravne Izgradnje Porodicnih Stambenih Zgrada." In *Bespravna Stambena Izgradnja u BIH,* ed. Jakhel Finci, pp. 119–34. Sarajevo: Akademija Nauka i Umjetnosti.

Klemencic, Bojana, 1979. *Opredelitev Stanovanjsko Bivalnih Tipov za Tiplologijo Samoiniciative in Sodelovanja Uporabnikov.* Ljubljana: Urbanisticni Institut SRS.

Kobe, Jurij, Dare Pozenel, and Vinko Torkar. 1973. "Crne Gradnje." School of Architecture, Ljubljana. Mimeo.

Kreitmajer, Katja. 1974. "Opredelitev Nedovoljenih Gradenj v Ljubljanskem Prostoru." Luz, Ljubljana. Mimeo.

Leeds, Anthony. 1974. "Housing Settlement Types, Arrangement for Living, Proletarization and the Social Structure of the City." *Latin American Urban Research,* 4, pp. 67–99.

Patton, Carl V., and Costas M. Sophoulis. 1983. "Great Expectations: Illegal Land Development in Modern Greece." *Ekistics* 50(301) (July/August), 259–64.

Pleskovic, Boris. 1979. *Low-Cost Approach to Housing in Yugoslavia.* Cambridge: MIT, Department of Urban Studies and Planning.

Pleskovic, Boris, and Marjan Dolenc. 1982. "Regional Development in a Socialist, Developing and Multinational Country: The Case of Yugoslavia." *International Regional Science Review* 7(1) (May), 1–24.

Pleskovic, Boris, Tomaz Souvan, and Darko Strajn. 1976a. "Yugoslav Planning System and Illegally Built Housing." Proceedings, IYF Symposium: Planning for Future Growth Alternatives, Lund University and Alnarp Institute, Stockholm, April 17–24.

———. 1976b. "Problem Crnih Gradenj v Jugoslaviji." *Arhitektov Bilten* 6(5) (September), 24–25.

Pozenel, Dare. 1977. "Cre gradnje." *Casopis za Kritiko Znanosti,* October, 70–74.

Ravbar, Marjan. 1974. "Preobrazba Obmestij Slovenskih Mest s Crno Gradnjo." Institut za Geografijo, Ljubljana.

———. 1978. "Varstvo Pokrajine v Luci Preobrazbe Naselij s Crno Gradnjo." Master's thesis, Institute za Geografijo, Ljubljana.

Rivas, D. R. 1977. "Development Alternatives for the Peruvian Barriada." In *Third World Urbanization,* ed. Janet Abu-Lughod and Richard Hay, pp. 321–29. New York: Methuen.

Stalna Konferencija Gradova. 1985. *Godisnjak Stalne Konferencije Gradova.* Beograd: Institut za Statistiku.

Strassman, P. 1976. "Measuring the Employment Effects of Housing Policies in Developing Countries." *Economic Development and Cultural Change,* 24 (3), (April), 623–32.

Urban Inspectorate. 1984. *Report on Illegal Buildings in Ljubljana.* Ljubljana: Ministry of Urban Planning.

World Bank. 1985. *World Development Report 1985.* Oxford: Oxford University Press.

IV

Policies and Prospects

Chapter 14

Economic Issues and the Progressive Housing Development Model

ERIC HANSEN AND JUSTIN WILLIAMS

Housing the nearly 1 billion inhabitants who will be added to cities in developing countries over the next fifteen years (United Nations, 1980) represents an enormous challenge for the new urban dwellers and their respective governments. After several decades of attempting to solve the shelter problem by trying to eradicate slums and squatter settlements and by providing public housing, many governments, including most of those discussed in earlier chapters, have recognized that it would be better to act in concert with the strong forces motivating the urban poor to build their own housing.

The work of Charles Abrams, John Turner, and others that described the processes by which the urban poor have provided their own housing laid the foundation for this major shift in the public approach to low-income housing. Turner's main contention was that householders must be able to make their own housing decisions and that most housing problems can be solved through self-help, mutual aid, core housing, and progressive development (Turner, 1967, 1972). Many of these concepts have become fully integrated into the basic housing policies recommended by the World Bank and other international development agencies. In addition, low-income housing research evaluating the experience in the last decade or so has focused on tenure choice, housing finance, and the determinants of housing demand. This research has led to considerable refinement of the original Turner self-help hypothesis, and from this has emerged the currently reigning hypothesis: the progressive development model.[1]

This chapter provides an overview of the major elements of housing demand and supply and reviews the economic evidence that has given shape and empirical substance to the progressive development model over the past decade. The chapter also discusses the limitations of this model and the orientation of basic housing programs toward owner-occupied housing, with attention focused on how rental opportunities can be expanded rapidly. The chapter concludes by suggesting how lessons learned from implementing basic housing projects during the past two decades might be most usefully applied in accommodating present and future housing needs in large and secondary cities in developing countries.

Approaches to Basic Housing in Developing Countries

Over the past quarter century, housing improvement programs in developing countries have evolved considerably from their earlier reliance on urban renewal and public housing construction. Instead of solving housing problems, squatter eradication and urban renewal exacerbated the housing shortage because resettlement schemes almost invariably were unable to accommodate the number of households displaced. Every shanty destroyed reduced the stock of housing and typically meant a substantial loss to a poor family that had invested in the dwelling and, to the extent that the dwelling served both as housing and workplace, caused a reduction in informal-sector jobs.

With squatter eradication programs came the predominant response of governments to the housing problem: subsidized public housing. With the exception of such cities as Hong Kong and Singapore (Yeh and Laquian, 1979), however, public housing has been an inadequate response. These programs are too expensive to represent a realistic supply response to housing needs, and they do not benefit the group that is most in need of housing: the poor. Indeed, the typical beneficiaries of subsidized housing programs are households that have the resources to acquire housing on the open market—often civil servants or other higher-income groups who, by one means or another, have acquired subsidized public housing.

By the 1960s squatter eradication and public housing approaches began to give way to two basic housing approaches that had evolved with the growing recognition that squatters and slum dwellers could solve their own housing problems: sites and services and settlement upgrading. The lessons learned in implementing these approaches to basic housing are discussed after we review the main supply-and-demand elements in spontaneous housing markets and the progressive development model.

Supply and Demand in Urban Housing Markets

The urban housing market in developing countries has been characterized as a three-tiered market (Renaud, 1982). At the top are households able to afford housing of high quality in fully serviced neighborhoods of low density. In the middle is a relatively narrow stratum of middle-income, middle-class households that occupy public and private institutional housing. At the bottom lies the largest and most rapidly growing tier in housing markets: low-income households whose housing is provided by the householders or by the informal sector. This low-income sector is the focus of our discussion of housing demand and supply.

Demand. The demand for housing depends on what households are willing to pay. Essentially, this is a function of their preferences for housing relative to other goods and services and their income. In terms of preferences, Linn (1983) has identified five key attributes of housing demand: access, space, security of tenure, on-site services, and shelter.

First, access to employment opportunities, community contacts, health and education facilities, and so on, is an important element of housing demand. Household location decisions by migrants and low-income families reflect the basic tradeoff between transportation costs and rents (or site costs).

Second, space, in terms of lot size, is a key element of demand reflecting the basic tradeoff between the size of the shelter structure and other commercial or agricultural activities that can take place on the lot (Linn, 1983).[2]

Third, an extremely important aspect of housing demand is security of tenure. As Turner (1967) observed, households assured security of tenure will invest substantially more in their housing than those who are unsure of their rights to the property. Also, households with secure tenure can enjoy the capital gains of increases in property value, the ability to use the property as collateral, and supplemental income from renting part of the house and from using the property for commercial activities.

Fourth, households derive direct and indirect benefits from the availability of on-site services such as water, drainage, electricity, and waste disposal (Laquian, 1983). The direct benefit is the service itself; the indirect benefit is the resultant increase in property value.

Finally, the structure itself provides basic shelter from the elements, privacy, and, for many households, a space to rent or a place to carry out commercial activities.[3]

The demand for housing services can be broadly characterized in terms of these five elements. Household preferences for these elements will vary considerably with household income, as well as other factors. In general, the poorest households are mainly interested in location and accessibility to employment opportunities. Their primary concern is to minimize transportation costs. Since their meager incomes allow only for food and other essentials for survival, their demand for housing space seldom extends beyond a place to sleep. Households with slightly higher and more stable incomes are interested in security of tenure and are willing to trade location for tenure. They are also more interested in space than in on-site services. The top group of low-income households is mostly concerned with amenities. Electricity, plumbing, well-designed houses, and recreation then become important and will be demanded by this group (Mohan, 1977).

Supply. The supply side of low-income housing consists of three primary components: urban land, on-site services, and shelter construction. These components are supplied by both public- and private-sector agents.

Urban land for housing is typically supplied in three ways: lots in subdivisions sold by private developers, land invasion and squatting, and subdivided land provided by government agencies (sites and services). Private lots are often affordable to low-income groups because they do not meet local zoning requirements with respect to lot size, access to roads, or provision of services. Nevertheless, this form of illegal land supply usually offers the household a reasonable degree of security of tenure and is popular in cities that effectively prohibit land invasion. In Bogotá, for example, over half of all households live in these "pirate" subdivisions (Doebele, 1977).

Land invasions, sometimes the only option for the poorest households, are becoming less prevalent in the large cities where undeveloped land is scarce. In Bogotá, for instance, with its population of over 4.5 million, squatters make up only 1 percent of all households as a result of strict legal enforcement, geographic factors, and an efficient, though illegal, process of private land subdivision (Doebele, 1977). In smaller but rapidly growing cities, however, land invasion can be widespread. In Valencia, with a population of roughly 1 million, nearly half of all residential land was occupied through invasions (Gilbert, 1983).

Economies of scale generally make the provision of on-site services by the public sector more efficient than by the private sector (Linn, 1983). Nevertheless, because service provision is increasing at a slower rate than the growth of housing stock (Beier et al., 1976), and a widespread absence of public services in low-income settlements exists, it is not uncommon to find on-site services such as water and sewerage provided by private land developers or, more often, by the inhabitants themselves.

Linn (1983) has indicated that the supply of dwelling units in developing countries is severely constrained. Rough estimates suggest that the aggregate supply of dwellings in developing countries is expanding by less than 3 percent a year (Grimes, 1976), while the demand for housing is expected to grow at 8 to 10 percent a year. Consequently, real housing prices are rising rapidly. This results in more overcrowding, lower-quality housing, and worse access to services than would be the case if the housing supply were growing more rapidly. The low-income housing that is built is done in incremental stages by owner–occupants or squatters as their resources permit.

These three components of housing supply—land, services, and construction—can be found in both owner and rental markets. But, as we argue, growth in the supply of rental housing often depends on the growth of owner-occupied housing. The interaction between supply and demand in urban housing markets can be perhaps most succinctly characterized by the following conceptualization of the progressive development model.

The Progressive Development Model

The progressive development model essentially describes the process by which low-income households make incremental investments in housing as their income permits. The conceptual underpinnings of the model stem primarily from recent evaluations of World Bank urban shelter programs conducted by Keare and Parris (1982), Struyk and Lynn (1983), and others. These evaluations focus on two types of housing development. Keare and Parris base their observations on evaluations of sites and services projects, while Struyk and Lynn focus on the settlement upgrading process. The following section extends and generalizes previous descriptions of progressive housing development by combining the evidence on sites and services and upgrading projects and by including evidence on housing investment in illegal subdivisions and squatter settlements. We also broaden the framework by explicitly recognizing the rental housing sector.[4]

Progressive housing development can be characterized as a path of low-income households as they move through four different stages of housing development (Figure 14.1).

Stage Zero: preownership
Stage One: initial settlement
Stage Two: self-motivated upgrading
Stage Three: external-shock-motivated upgrading

This path is highly stylized because, obviously, not all households move through these stages. Indeed, many households never become homeowners. Initially, migrants and newly formed urban households enter Stage Zero when they rent a room or house or are guests of or share space with another household. If they have sufficient resources to buy land or have a no-cost opportunity to occupy land (invasion), households can enter directly into Stage One. In Stage One, households acquire a plot in a squatter settlement or illegal housing subdivision and begin to build a structure. In Stage Two, some upgrading of the initial dwelling

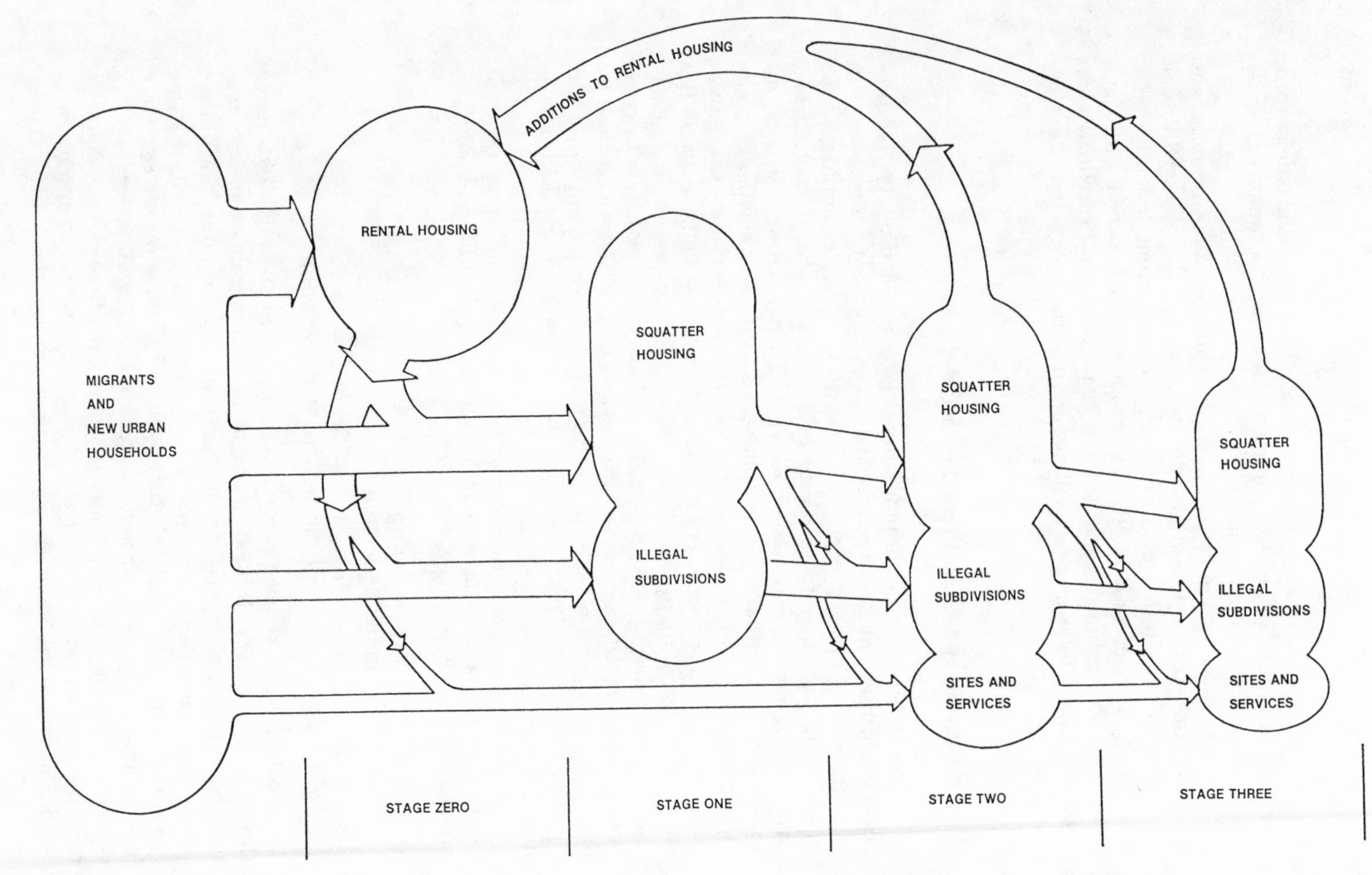
ADDITIONS TO RENTAL HOUSING
MIGRANTS
AND
NEW URBAN
HOUSEHOLDS
RENTAL HOUSING
SQUATTER
HOUSING
ILLEGAL
SUBDIVISIONS
SQUATTER
HOUSING
ILLEGAL
SUBDIVISIONS
SITES AND
SERVICES
SQUATTER
HOUSING
ILLEGAL
SUBDIVISIONS
SITES AND
SERVICES
STAGE ZERO
STAGE ONE
STAGE TWO
STAGE THREE

and services occurs. In Stages Two and Three, the security of tenure typically increases, as does the degree to which on- and off-site services exist. The condition of the structure improves through the stages. During each stage of the model, as households add space to their dwelling, the supply of rental housing also increases (represented by a feedback loop from Stages Two and Three back to Stage Zero).

Stage Zero: The Period Before Ownership. Before low-income urban households become homeowners, they typically fall into one of three situations that, collectively, we will call Stage Zero: renting; sharing living space with family or friends; or itinerant squatting after arriving in the urban area.[5]

Migrants often choose to rent until their family and occupational situations enable them to own. Renting is a transition stage in the progressive development model because the motivation to own a home is so great. For the urban poor, land and home ownership represents the main avenue to economic security, since it is an inflation-proof investment which can often provide access to credit and supplemental income through renting and commercial activity.[6] Because of these strong motivations, the renting-to-ownership pattern tends to be a one-way process (Gilbert, 1983).

Stage One: Initial Settlement. Stage One is achieved when the household has acquired both land and a rudimentary structure. The land may be acquired by legal or illegal purchase or by squatting. The structure is likely to be built by the family using scavenged or purchased materials. At this stage, the dwelling is usually large enough for the immediate family only and has no piped water or other services.

Family income is the most crucial factor influencing the level and pace of housing investment at Stage One. Expenditures for basic needs use up most or all of family income, and so the ability to invest in housing is low. Because households have difficulty raising initial investment sums, upgrading occurs incrementally, in accordance with their irregular income streams.

At this stage, household income comes from informal-sector earnings, from interhousehold transfers, and, to a lesser extent, from formal-sector wages. The kinds of income that tend to be most readily invested in housing are interhousehold transfers, savings, and income earned from persons other than the household head (Kaufmann and Bamberger, 1985; Keare and Jimenez, 1983). Windfall gains are also likely to be invested in housing.

Figure 14.1 Stages of the progressive development model. (Illustration by Justin Williams and Paul Olsen)

At Stage One, households are more inclined to invest their own "sweat" equity in construction because the opportunity cost of doing this is relatively low and the cost of paying hired labor is high relative to income. In El Salvador, for example, housing costs could be reduced by an estimated 30 percent by using one's own labor rather than hired contractors (Bamberger and Kaufmann, 1984).

The importance of security of tenure on housing investment is well established. But it is least important at this initial phase of the incremental housing process when households are more concerned with establishing a "beachhead" than they are about consolidation. Nonetheless, if the threat of eviction is great, households will be very reluctant to erect anything more than a basic shelter or to invest in upgrading.

Stage Two: Self-Motivated Upgrading. A household enters Stage Two of the progressive development model when it has upgraded its dwelling above minimum squatter levels (Stage One) and has the ability to raise additional income through renting or otherwise has the necessary long-term income to support upkeep; *or,* it buys into Stage Two directly from Stage Zero by purchasing an upgraded lot or sites and services lot after having accumulated sufficient savings. In contrast with Stage One, households in Stage Two are both more able and, if reasonably secure about their property tenure rights, more willing to invest in housing.

At Stage Two, households often supplement their wage and informal labor income with rental income. In a Zambia sites and services project, rental income amounted to about 25 percent of total household income for low-income households (Keare and Parris, 1982); in Manila's Tondo project, 40 percent of owner–occupants had renters (Struyk and Lynn, 1983). Rental income is typically used for both consumption and investment. Although research has not assessed what percentage of rental income is channeled for further investment, rental income represents a substantial portion of total income and can boost the ability of households to finance incremental investment. Ownership and upgrading would be more difficult without it.

Interhousehold transfer income remains an important source of income at Stage Two. As total household income increases, however, the amount of net transfers the household receives tends to decline. Evidence from El Salvador, Colombia, and the Philippines indicates that transfers are given to help households maintain their current level of housing or make key housing investments, but not for shelter upgrading if this is viewed as preferred consumption rather than an investment (Kaufmann and Bamberger, 1985).

By Stage Two, households tend to substitute hired labor for own or friendly labor. In many World Bank sites and services and upgrading projects, a high percentage of households preferred to hire laborers or small contractors to aid in building. In Tondo, for example, nearly a third of all households relied exclusively on hired labor, while another half hired workers to supplement their own labor inputs (Keare and Parris, 1982).

Stage Three: External-Shock-Motivated Consolidation. Stage Three is marked by the progression of the household to a higher and more stable level of income and to a relatively satisfied feeling about the dwelling condition. Housing investments are fewer, but much larger than in previous stages. The major impetus for additional housing investments becomes less self-motivated and stems more from external shocks, such as local service and infrastructure projects, or from the sudden need for additional dwelling space.

By Stage Three, household preferences shift from making marginal improvements in the dwelling to increasing their access to on- and off-site services. In general, demand for water, sewerage, electricity, roads, and other transportation services increases with income level and the extent of household consolidation.[7] In addition to the direct user benefits households receive from on- and off-site services, the provision of services in a neighborhood will be capitalized in the value of homes benefiting from these services. Generally, any investment made to a serviced dwelling will increase the dwelling's value proportionally more than investment made in the absence of the service. Consequently, the upgrading or installation of services or infrastructure can stimulate significant housing investment. Nevertheless, the actual degree of investment that is leveraged this way may be overstated in depictions of the progressive development model because of the existence of substantial subsidies in the infrastructure projects.

In sum, the progressive development model serves to characterize the process by which low-income urban households acquire and upgrade housing in developing countries. On the one hand, the resources that households are able to marshall—wage income, informal-sector earnings, rental income, and interhousehold transfers, as well as their own labor—are what drives this process of incremental investment in owner-occupied housing. On the other hand, the process is constrained by the cost and availability of land (with varying degrees of tenure rights), construction materials, on-site services, labor, and credit. Interactions between supply and demand at each stage of the progressive development model identify important areas for strategic policy intervention to stimulate housing investment. At Stage One, the critical issue is access to affordable land. At Stage Two, security of tenure is the main way to leverage increased investment. At Stage Three, housing investment is stimulated by external provision of on- and off-site services. Of course, at all stages the importance of increasing household income is critical. Before we discuss the policy implications of this model, some of its potential weaknesses must be recognized.

Subsidies, Affordability, and Replicability in Basic Housing Projects

Overall, there have been few objections to, or attacks made against, the progressive development model. Yet the model may depict a more optimistic picture of participation by the urban poor and of the housing consolidation rate in basic housing projects than is warranted. This distorted picture is attributable to the prevalence of subsidies in most of the projects from which observations about the model have been made.

The data base for the progressive model consists of evaluations of World Bank sites and services and squatter upgrading projects. In particular, Keare and Parris (1982) base their remarks on World Bank projects in Zambia, Senegal, El Salvador, and the Philippines. Struyk and Lynn (1983) have based their work on an analysis of the World Bank settlement upgrading project in Manila (the Tondo project). Much of Jimenez's work is based on evaluations of the Tondo project (Jimenez, 1983) and El Salvador (Jimenez, 1982). In each instance, careful analysis was conducted. Nevertheless, the lingering concern is that the investment behavior of project participants was greatly influenced by subsidies in these projects.

Subsidies are present any time a household acquires land, building materials, credit, or infrastructure below the market value. In many instances, subsidies are intentionally included in the project, usually with the purpose of making it more affordable for lower-income families, to increase the pace of consolidation, or to ensure the appearance of project success. Often subsidies are hidden—that is, they are not explicitly recognized in project design and implementation. These subsidies usually enter a project, intentionally or unintentionally, in the forms of low-cost government land, free administration or project management, or credit subsidies related to the term of the loan.

These World Bank projects invariably have some kind of subsidy. The most common subsidy is an interest rate subsidy on project loans. Mayo and Gross (1987) estimate that median interest charges in World Bank sites and services projects were roughly 45 to 80 percent lower than the then current market interest rates. Over half of these World Bank projects appear to have had negative real interest rates at the time of project appraisal. Mayo and Gross examined subsidies in six World Bank sites and services projects and found that all six projects charged less than the market price for their land, building materials, or completed dwellings, and had subsidized interest rates. The median subsidy, estimated conservatively, was about two-thirds of the project resource cost.[8]

Because subsidies exist, our contention is that the willingness of homeowners to upgrade their dwellings or to contribute to self-help or mutual aid programs perhaps would be substantially less if a project did not have a subsidy element. The level of investment by households in subsidized projects is considerable. For example, within the first five years of the highly subsidized Tondo project, 97.5 percent of the households surveyed had improved their dwellings, and there was heavy reliance on self-help, mutual aid, and involvement in decision making pertaining to the project (Laquian, 1983). It is questionable whether this degree of investment activity would occur in nonsubsidized projects, although it is expected that the provision of greater tenure security, legality, better services, and the like stimulates investment and participation by homeowners. Nevertheless, subsidies probably contribute substantially to the very high rates of activity found in the Tondo and other shelter projects with high subsidies. How much is largely an empirical question that has yet to be answered. Clearly, research on housing investment behavior in urban shelter projects without subsidies is necessary to test the robustness of the progressive development model as presented here.

Subsidies are advocated in urban shelter projects for two main reasons. First, subsidies are considered necessary in order to meet the difference between true development costs and what the poor can afford. But since affordability is closely linked to the design standards of the project, subsidies can be reduced or eliminated in many projects if standards are lowered to what people can afford. Second, it is also frequently argued that subsidies cannot be denied to the poor when the rich enjoy substantial subsidies in housing and other services. This issue of social justice is perhaps the most compelling argument for subsidies; since subsidies are present, they should be distributed fairly.

Despite the merits of these arguments, subsidies in urban shelter projects lie in direct conflict with full-cost-recovery and replicability objectives. Project replicability depends on the extent to which costs are recovered from project beneficiaries. Consequently, subsidies in shelter projects tend to limit the number of such projects. The argument against subsidies is based on the conviction that more urban shelter projects will increase housing supply more effectively and ultimately more equitably than fewer subsidized projects. To the extent that subsidies can be reduced or eliminated in sites and services and settlement upgrading projects, the projects may be more easily replicated.

At least three other factors affect the replicability of shelter projects. First, successful cost recovery depends on the levels and rates of repayment imposed on project participants and on the effectiveness of the collection machinery and procedures. In order to assure that project participants are able to repay their loans, most experience suggests the need for considerable flexibility in repayment scheduling, provision of accurate information to project participants, and clear repayment procedures.

A second problem concerns the availability of land for sites and services projects reasonably close to employment opportunities. The higher land costs of these sites will constrain affordability of the project by the poor; locations distant from employment opportunities will reduce the attractiveness of the project.

Finally, the problem of limited availability of capital often hinders the replicability of shelter projects in the short run. To the extent that scarce public resources are allocated to high-cost housing and public infrastructure programs, the availability of capital resources for basic shelter is limited. Beyond these issues about how basic shelter programs can be replicated, concerns about sites and services and upgrading projects themselves should be raised.

Problems With Sites and Services and Upgrading Projects

While it is generally acknowledged that the sites and services approach is a more effective investment of limited resources for low-cost housing than conventional housing programs, considerable criticism has been leveled at the sites and services approach. This criticism can be summarized along four main lines.

First, sites and services projects are too expensive to reach the poorest households, as they are typically large-scale projects that require organizational, managerial, and bureaucratic inputs. Such administration is expensive and thereby raises the costs to project participants. Shelter costs per plot in World Bank sites and services projects, for instance, seldom fall under the $750 to $1,000 range and consequently rarely reach the lowest 20 percentile income group (Linn, 1983). Therefore, the poor who lack the resources for initial entry and the income stability to make a fixed housing investment do not have access to sites and services projects. Indeed, the mismatch between housing cost and incomes has often resulted in massive defaults on monthly payments, or the original poor project participants have sold off their participation to more well-off families. Consequently, the intended beneficiaries often do not ultimately participate in the project.

Second, because only the more established working-class families can afford them, sites and services projects have the effect of "creaming" the wealthier families from squatter settlements, thus removing customers of the poorer families engaged in informal-sector economic activities (Peattie, 1982, p. 134).

Third, as mentioned regarding replicability, sites and services projects are typically located far from jobs and central marketplaces because large tracts of cheap, unoccupied land are found only on the periphery of cities.

Finally, sites and services have been criticized because they take from the homeowner the higher-status functions of being one's own architect, contractor, and supervisor of construction (Peattie, 1982).

Settlement upgrading projects avoid most of the problems identified with sites and services projects. But upgrading projects face their own set of problems. Because of the diversity of households and housing conditions in most slum and squatter areas, upgrading can be very difficult to coordinate. Usually, households are at various stages of the upgrading process, and their willingness to participate in mutual aid efforts varies. Within any community, differing priorities among households about community investments can lead to a lack of commitment for projects that can ultimately result in project delays and cost-recovery problems. In addition, the job of retrofitting neighborhoods with pathways, sewers, and roads imposes severe costs on certain households that must relocate temporarily or permanently.

Although settlement upgrading projects are able to penetrate to the lower-income-group percentiles, this positive equity aspect of upgrading projects is offset because these projects also provide benefits for the higher-income households living in slum and squatter areas. Sites and services projects, in contrast, can achieve greater equity because affordability criteria can be enforced more effectively. Nevertheless, because sites and services do not reach the very poor, whereas upgrading projects do, a joint approach is advantageous in order to reap the complementary benefits of the two approaches.

Rental Housing as a Possible Option for Low-Income Urban Households

Many low-income urban households in developing countries will never have the option of homeownership because the price of urban land exceeds their means. Thus the focus by governments and international development agencies on programs to increase owner-occupied housing among low-income families may be ill placed, if the ultimate goal is to provide as much shelter as possible with limited resources.

The literature on spontaneous shelter has also had an emphasis on ownership; very limited attention has been given to the rental market. Despite the strong motivations for low-income households to own rather than rent, rental housing accounts for a substantial proportion of the total housing market in most Third World cities, particularly in large cities. For example, more than half of urban households rent in Egypt, El Salvador, Thailand, Hong Kong, Bogotá, Abidjan, and Mexico City.[9] There is good reason to believe that as most Third World cities double or triple in size over the next twenty to thirty years, rental markets will assume an increasing share of the housing supply.

This contention can be supported by examining the constraints on homeownership opportunities for the urban poor. Much of the literature characterizes housing tenure choice as the outcome of preferences expressed by households. But tenure status also depends on the availability and cost of ownership opportunities. As Gilbert (1983) has shown, renters do not always choose to rent because it is suitable to their needs, cheaper, or of better quality; in most cases, they rent because of limited ownership opportunities.

Constraints to ownership are increasing in most developing cities. Access to land for the poor is becoming more difficult, as land prices are rising in real terms in many locales, including Bogotá (Carroll, 1980), Cali (Mohan and Villamizar, 1982), São Paulo (Haddad, 1982), South Korean cities (Mills and Song, 1979), and Singapore (Lim, 1982). Lot sizes also appear to be falling. In addition, land invasions by squatters have become less widespread because of land scarcity within city limits, and illegal purchases of land are becoming more commonplace (Doebele, 1977). The result is that where land costs rise, the proportion of households that can afford to become homeowners must diminish.

Because homeownership is becoming more difficult and renting is likely to become the predominant form of housing in most large Third World cities, housing policy might well focus more on promoting rental markets. Efforts should be made to stimulate the production of rental housing, including both informal housing, such as the rental of rooms in a small house, and more formal rental units, such as apartments.

At Stages One and Two of the progressive model, homeowners are inclined to add a room or two in order to generate rental income. At these stages of the housing investment process, rental opportunities can be expanded most significantly without any policy intervention. The symbiotic relationship between owners and renters reflects the coming together of powerful market forces. Poor households are striving desperately to obtain shelter and establish a foothold in the community. At the same time, low-income homeowners, who have either scraped together the means to own land and construct their own shelters (Stage One) or are in the process of consolidating their houses (Stage Two), are typically eager to increase total household income by renting.

Increasing the supply of rental units by encouraging homeowners to rent out rooms and add rental units may be the most efficient way to increase shelter in Third World cities. Two factors underlie this argument. First, adding rental units to existing housing means that no additional land costs, which can account for 50 percent of total dwelling costs, are incurred. Labor and materials are the only major inputs. Second, as a result of higher-density development, homeowners and renters combined on the same lot can better afford basic services such as water. Thus, the prospects for cost recovery of infrastructure investment are greater than in less dense, low-income communities.

Among the policies appropriate to expand the supply of rental housing are credit programs targeted to owners who add on rental units and the inclusion of rental components within sites and services and upgrading projects. In addition, homeowners should be guided in the design of their houses so that rental units can be added on later as family income permits.

Another way to stimulate rental housing supply lies in the reform of rent-control policy. Many developing countries with rent controls have experienced little or no new construction and noticeable deterioration of existing stock. In addition, recent evidence suggests that tenants as well as landlords can lose from rent controls (Malpezzi, 1986). Tenants in controlled units often suffer more than they gain because they may live in suboptimal units in terms of space, quality, or location. Rent-control reforms vary by country, but the reforms most needed include exempting new units from controls, decontrolling units as they become vacant, and improving the enforcement of maintenance requirements.

Housing Finance for Low-Income Shelter

Housing finance often has been identified as the major constraint on a more rapid expansion of low-income housing supply. Even though financing is a critical input for low-income housing, low-income households throughout the Third World finance their shelter without access to formal housing finance institutions. Indeed, the role of such institutions in providing housing finance is limited to less than 20 percent of annual housing investment in even the best cases (Renaud, 1984). There are three main reasons for this limitation.

First, the demand for mortgage credit by low-income households is constrained because their demand for housing does not rise in proportion to their increase in income (Mayo and Malpezzi, 1984), and their irregular income flows tend to reduce housing consumption. Second, the access of poor households to mortgage credit is severely constrained by a variety of factors that affect their capacity to borrow. Without secure land title, and unable to afford to comply with high official construction and land development standards, the poor are viewed as unacceptable credit risks. Third, very few viable formal housing finance institutions currently exist. In many cases, this is the result of the reluctance of national governments to encourage resource mobilization for housing because it is viewed as a consumption good and because the potential macroeconomic linkages between housing and other sectors of the economy are overlooked. In addition, the economic climate in Third World countries with high inflation rates and economic stagnation has hindered the performance and development of housing finance institutions.

Consequently, the informal housing sector largely operates without formal financial institutions. This is not to say that low-income housing markets function without financing. As indicated earlier, considerable informal financing takes place through the direct channeling of funds from savers to borrowers. In the spontaneous shelter sector, financial transfers between relatives, friends, and neighbors is virtually the only method of housing finance. But this method is insufficient to meet the credit demands of the sector. Low-income families are forced by poor regulations and lack of financing to build their housing in an inefficient piecemeal fashion.

It is frequently argued that a key priority of housing policy should be to increase the access of low-income households to formal financial institutions (Jorgenson, 1977). Experience has shown, however, that building down from existing financial intermediaries is problematic for a variety of reasons. All too often, governments fall into the trap of increasing access to credit by subsidizing interest rates. Interest rate subsidies invariably lead to some degree of credit rationing and often weaken the viability of the financial institutions themselves. The excess demand for credit created by subsidized interest rates gives financial institutions a wide choice of who receives loans. Usually, those households perceived to present the lowest risk of default—the better-off households and civil servants—receive the subsidized mortgage credit. Thus, although this approach may improve access to credit by the poor to some degree, overall, subsidized mortgages have negative implications for equity.

Subsidized interest rates also make housing finance institutions less viable as financial entities because, as seen in many countries, mortgage lending has occurred at rates of interest below the inflation rate. Such negative real interest rates can lead to severe decapitalization and render the financial institution at the mercy of central government funds. Clearly, the viability of housing finance institutions is closely related to the mortgage interest rate. This rate should be kept close to the market cost of funds so that the lending institutions can pay appropriate rates on deposits and mobilize funds.

The directions for housing finance for low-income shelter that appear most promising are twofold. One strategy entails the creation of new institutional forms for mobilizing resources for low-income housing by expanding the existing informal housing finance networks. The other strategy involves the deepening of formal financial institutions so that they may reach the upper part of the informal housing sector.

The first strategy calls for the development of new housing finance mechanisms that "build up" from the informal finance system—which is essentially a one-shot financing deal by family or friends—to institutional financing. Renaud (1984) argues that a step in this direction could be achieved by encouraging the growth of credit associations and other cooperative forms from the present interpersonal networks. These cooperative institutions could be based on common trade, religion, family, community, and so on. This approach is problematic, however, because it is extremely difficult for the public sector to take a lead in their formation. The creation of such cooperative finance associations may be assisted by establishing a system of incentives for organizers and participants. The growth of grass-roots finance institutions may also be encouraged if government housing banks operate as apex lending institutions for them.

A second strategy calls for the development of viable institutions that can reach the better-off households of the informal sector. New and improved financial services for middle- and low-income families might include the development of mortgage insurance, new deposit methods, and mortgage loans to the self-employed. In addition, these institutions should expand the range of financial services for all phases of residential investment.

These innovations in housing finance institutions will have an important impact on low-income families. The major beneficiaries of the second strategy are limited primarily to households at Stage Three. The first strategy, however, would serve households at Stages One, Two, and Three. In attempting to serve the poor, it makes more sense to pursue the first strategy rather than further develop formal financial institutions because the poor have limited capacity to borrow. Separate programs for the worse-off people in the informal sector, who cannot obtain ordinary housing finance, will have the greatest impact. Among these, as we have argued earlier, is a policy for mobilizing resources and developing specific programs for urban public infrastructure.

Future Directions for Low-Cost Shelter Policy

In pursuing a "learning-by-doing" approach during recent years, the World Bank and other agencies have made significant improvements in shelter policy in developing countries. In particular, experience with basic shelter programs has demonstrated that governments can intervene effectively in housing markets if, instead of imposing an inflated notion of "housing needs," they are sensitive to the level of housing and services that households want and can afford.

Despite efforts to reduce costs through lower standards, basic shelter programs remain beyond the reach of most poor urban dwellers.

Rapidly increasing land prices brought about by rapid urbanization and land speculation severely constrain access to affordable land by the poor. Sufficient amounts of serviced urban land are simply not available in most large cities because, despite some improvement in public policy, high standards and subsidies quickly devour scarce public resources and thus limit the expansion of services.

Problems with access to land suggest two future directions for shelter policy. One obvious direction is to wrestle with urban land markets directly. Much has been written on land issues (e.g., Dunkerley, 1983), therefore they will not be addressed here. A second direction is to give greater attention to rental housing markets in large cities and to owner-occupied housing markets in secondary cities and towns. Both markets offer distinct opportunities for rapidly expanding low-income housing in spite of the existence of constrained land markets in the large metropolitan areas and capital cities. Housing policy research clearly needs to focus greater attention on how to increase the supply of rental housing. Rent-control reforms and housing programs that recognize the importance of rental income to early stage owner–occupiers are especially promising options.

The scope for increasing the housing supply in secondary cities and towns of developing countries is considerable. The number of Third World cities with populations of 500,000 to 2 million is estimated to increase from 204 in 1980 to 293 in 1990, with the total population in these cities rising from 184 million to 281 million during the decade (United Nations, 1980). The potential for owner-occupied housing is much greater in secondary cities than large cities because land costs are considerably less, the demand for land is lower, undeveloped land is more abundant, and the opportunities for squatting and illegal land development are greater.[10]

There are distinct advantages to targeting a housing strategy for secondary cities. Many of the lessons learned so far in developing policy and executing projects in owner-occupied housing are directly applicable in secondary cities. In these smaller cities basic housing projects tend to be smaller and easier to manage than in large cities. Early intervention in the housing and urban land markets in growing secondary cities will help to prevent major problems from occurring as these cities grow into metropolises. Furthermore, a housing policy for secondary cities would avoid the general tendency for housing programs to concentrate on very large and capital cities and would help to accomplish regional equity objectives. It is also possible that by assisting families in these cities, they may be encouraged to stay there, thus reducing population pressures on the largest cities. Finally, by focusing on medium-size cities, where there is still considerable potential for ownership, developing countries stand to gain from the positive macroeconomic advantages of domestic savings and resource mobilization of owner-occupied housing investment.

In sum, the policies and programs for the large cities should differ from those for secondary cities. In large cities, housing policy should focus on improving the access of existing and new settlements to basic services and infrastructure, regularizing land title, settlement upgrading, increasing the supply of rental housing, and eliminating rent control. Housing policy in secondary cities and towns, in contrast, should concentrate on keeping land affordable for the poor, increasing the supply of serviced plots, and instituting settlement upgrading and sites and services projects.

Notes

1. The process of incremental investment in housing has been called "progressive development" (Keare and Parris, 1982), "the upgrading process" (Struyk and Lynn, 1983), and "incremental housing investment" (Hamer, 1985).
2. In Manila's Tondo area the mean lot size was 66 square meters (Jimenez, 1983). In the *kampung* of Indonesia, 73 percent of building plots were less than 100 square meters (Silas, 1984). In Nairobi (Chana, 1984) and Ismailia (Davidson, 1984), sites and services project lots typically exceed 100 square meters.
3. Dwelling sizes vary considerably. In Indonsia's Kampung Improvement Projects, 50 percent of the dwellings have less than 45 square meters of floor space, and 27 percent have between 45 and 75 square meters (Silas, 1984). The built areas in the Dandora sites and services project are slightly larger, averaging 60 square meters (Chana, 1984).
4. Our overview of the progressive development model uses the Struyk and Lynn (1983) framework as a point of departure to develop a more generalized version of the model. Struyk and Lynn termed the states as (*a*) initial settlement; (*b*) savings accumulation–internal upgrading; and (*c*) complacency–external upgrading.
5. Many poor urban migrants do not rent housing on arrival at the urban area (Strassman, 1982). Rather, they squat temporarily in low- or no-cost situations such as under a bridge or near a railroad right-of-way until they are able to obtain more stable housing, often rental housing.
6. According to Doebele (1977), households prefer to own for five reasons:

a. Land and housing are assets which are inflation-proof and almost surely to rise in value.
b. Ownership enables self-capitalization to take place by converting labor into capital, at a time of one's own choosing.
c. Ownership frequently provides access to income through renting and commercial activity.
d. Ownership provides access to a system of credit.

e. Ownership provides respectability and stature in a social order which offers the low-income class very little of either.

7. This is not to say that the poor households in earlier stages do not demand services. Such households are willing to pay for service installation if implementation is efficient and if payment schedules are flexible (Doebele, Grimes, and Linn, 1979). This suggests that service shortage in low-income communities is largely a supply-side problem.

8. Project resource cost comprises the financial costs of the project (land, material, labor, finance, and administration) as well as opportunity costs.

9. Mayo et al. (1982) find that in Cairo about 70 percent of households rent. Keare and Parris (1982) report that 53 percent of all urban families choose to rent. In Hong Kong, 40 percent of the population rents state-built apartments (*Urban Edge,* 1984). In Abidjan, 80 percent of households rent their accommodations (Grootaert and Dubois, 1986). Gilbert and Ward (1982) report that over half of the population of Bogotá and Mexico City rent.

10. In larger cities of developing countries, land prices have risen by an estimated 10 to 20 percent more than consumer price indexes (Lubell, 1979).

References

Bamberger, Michael, and Daniel Kaufmann. 1984. *Patterns of Income Formation and Expenditures among the Urban Poor of Cartagena.* Water Supply and Urban Development Department Discussion Paper no. 63. Washington, D.C.: World Bank.

Beier, G., A. Churchill, M. Cohen, and B. Renaud. 1976. "The Task Ahead for Cities of Developing Countries." *World Development* 4(5), 363–409.

Carroll, Alan. 1980. *Pirate Subdivisions and the Market for Residential Lots in Bogotá.* World Bank Staff Working Paper no. 435. Washington, D.C.: World Bank.

Chana, T. S. 1984. "Nairobi: Dandora and Other Projects." In *Low-Income Housing in the Developing World,* ed. Geoffrey K. Payne, pp. 17–36. New York: Wiley.

Davidson, Forbes. 1984. "Ismailia: Combined Upgrading and Site and Services Projects in Egypt." In *Low-Income Housing in the Developing World,* ed. Geoffrey K. Payne, pp. 125–48. New York: Wiley.

Doebele, William A. 1977. "The Private Market and Low Income Urbanization: The Pirate Subdivisions of Bogotá." *American Journal of Comparative Law* 25(3), 531–64.

Doebele, William A., Orville F. Grimes, Jr., and Johannis Linn. 1979. "Participation of Beneficiaries in Financing Urban Services: Valorization Charges in Bogotá, Colombia." *Land Economics* 55(1), 73–92.

Dunkerley, Harold B., et al. 1983. *Urban Land Policy: Issues and Opportunities.* New York: Oxford University Press.

Gilbert, Alan. 1983. "The Tenants of Self-Help Housing: Choice and Constraint in Housing Markets of Less Developed Countries." *Development and Change* 14(3), 449–77.

Gilbert, Alan, and Peter M. Ward. 1982. "Low Income Housing and the State." In *Urbanization in Contemporary Latin America: Critical Approaches to the Study of Urban Issues,* ed. Alan Gilbert, pp. 79–127. London: Wiley.

Grimes, Orville F., Jr. 1976. *Housing for Low-Income Urban Families.* Baltimore: Johns Hopkins University Press.

Grootaert, Christiaan, and Jean-Luc Dubois. 1986. *The Demand for Urban Housing in the Ivory Coast.* LSMS Working Paper no. 25. Washington, D.C.: World Bank.

Haddad, Emilio. 1982. "Report on Urban Land-Market Research in São Paulo, Brazil." In *World Congress on Land Policy 1980,* ed. M. Cullin and S. Woolery, pp. 201–16. Lexington, Mass.: Lexington.

Hamer, Andrew M. 1985. *Bogotá's Unregulated Subdivisions: The Myths and Realities of Incremental Housing Construction.* World Bank Staff Working Paper no. 734, Washington, D.C.: World Bank.

Jimenez, Emmanuel. 1982. "The Economics of Self-Help Housing: Theory and Some Evidence from a Developing Country." *Journal of Urban Economics* 11, 205–28.

———. 1983. "The Magnitude and Determinants of Home Improvements in Self-Help Housing: Manila's Tondo Project." *Land Economics* 59(1), 70–83.

Jorgenson, N. D. 1977. *Housing Finance for Low-Income Groups.* Nairobi, Kenya: General Printers.

Kaufmann, Daniel, and Michael Bamberger. 1985. *Income Transfers and Urban Projects: Research Findings and Policy Issues from Cartagena, Colombia.* Water Supply and Urban Development Discussion Paper no. 56. Washington, D.C.: World Bank.

Keare, Douglas H., and Scott Parris. 1982. *Evaluation of Shelter Programs for the Urban Poor.* World Bank Staff Working Paper no. 547. Washington, D.C.: World Bank.

Keare, Douglas H., and Emmanuel Jimenez. 1983. *Progressive Development and Affordability in the Design of Urban Shelter Projects.* World Bank Staff Working Paper no. 560, Washington, D.C.: World Bank.

Laquian, Aprodicio A. 1983. *Basic Housing: Policies for Urban Sites, Services, and Shelter in Developing Countries.* Ottawa: International Development Research Centre.

Lim, W. S. W. 1982. "Major Differences between Developed and Developing Countries in Application of Land Policy Instruments." In

World Congress on Land Policy 1980, ed. M. Cullen and S. Woolery, pp. 59–71. Lexington, Mass.: Lexington.

Linn, Johannis. 1983. *Cities in the Developing World: Policies for Their Equitable and Efficient Growth.* New York: Oxford University Press.

Lubell, Harold. 1979. Urban Development Policies and Programs. Working paper. Washington, D.C.: U.S. Agency for International Development, Economic Development Division.

Malpezzi, Stephen J. 1986. "Rent Control and Housing Market Equilibrium: Theory and Evidence from Cairo, Egypt." Doctoral dissertation, George Washington University, Washington, D.C.

Mayo, Stephen K., and David J. Gross. 1987. "Sites and Services—and Subsidies: The Economics of Low Cost Housing in Developing Countries." *The World Bank Economic Review* 1(2), 301–35.

Mayo, Stephen K., and Stephen J. Malpezzi. 1984. *A Comparative Analysis of Housing Demand in Developing Countries.* Water Supply and Urban Development Discussion Paper no. 41. Washington. D.C.: World Bank.

Mayo, Stephen K., et al. 1982. *Informal Housing in Egypt.* Cambridge: Abt Associates.

Mills, Edwin, and B. N. Song. 1979. *Urbanization and Urban Problems: The Republic of Korea 1945–75.* Cambridge: Harvard University Press.

Mohan, Rakesh. 1977. "Urban Land Policy, Income Distribution and the Urban Poor." In *Income Distribution and Growth in the Less-Developed Countries,* ed. Charles R. Frank, Jr., and Richard C. Webb, pp. 435–90. Washington, D.C.: Brookings Institution.

Mohan, Rakesh, and R. Villamizar, 1982. "The Evolution of Land Values in the Context of Rapid Urban Growth: A Case Study of Bogotá and Cali, Colombia." In *World Congress on Land Policy 1980,* ed. M. Cullen and S. Woolery, pp. 217–54. Lexington, Mass: Lexington.

Peattie, Lisa. 1982. "Some Second Thoughts on Sites and Services." *Habitat International* 6(1/2), 131–39.

Renaud, Bertrand. 1982. *Housing and Financial Institutions in Developing Countries.* Urban Development Department Discussion Paper no. 19, Washington, D.C.: World Bank.

———. 1984. *Housing and Financial Institutions in Developing Countries.* World Bank Staff Working Paper no. 648. Washington, D.C.: World Bank.

Silas, Johan. 1984. "The Kampung Improvement Programme of Indonesia: A Comparative Case Study of Jakarta and Surabaya." In *Low-Income Housing in the Developing World,* ed. Geoffrey K. Payne, pp. 69–87. New York: Wiley.

Strassman, W. Paul. 1982. *The Transformation of Urban Housing.* Baltimore: Johns Hopkins University Press.

Struyk, Raymond, and Robert Lynn. 1983. "Determinants of Housing Investment in Slum Areas." *Land Economics* 59(4), 444–54.

Turner, John F. C. 1967. "Barriers and Channels for Housing Development in Modernizing Countries." *Journal of the American Institute of Planners,* May, 167–81.

Turner, John F. C., and Robert Fichter, eds. 1972. *Freedom to Build: Dweller Control of the Housing Process.* New York: Macmillan.

United Nations. 1980. *Patterns of Urban and Rural Population Growth,* table 22, p. 55. New York: United Nations.

Urban Edge. 1984. "Rental Housing: A Rediscovered Priority." *Urban Edge* 8(2) (February), 1–5.

Yeh, S. H. K., and A. A. Laquian, eds. 1979. *Housing Asia's Millions: Problems, Policies, and Prospects for Low-Cost Housing in Southeast Asia.* IDRC-104e. Ottawa, Canada: International Development Research Centre.

Chapter 15

The Role of the State in Sheltering the Urban Poor

HOWARD HANDELMAN

Development specialists have long held that state programs should respond to the basic shelter needs of the urban poor, especially when those needs are not being met by the private sector. After decades of state efforts, however, there is a growing belief among urban policy scholars that public housing programs have generally not served well the needs of the urban poor in Third World countries. Today, virtually all Latin American governments have a state housing agency and at least a verbal commitment to the construction of shelter for low-income people. This situation provides an opportunity to assess the various effects of direct state involvement in housing the urban poor under alternative political systems and to suggest how their policies might be improved. While certainly not representative of the entire Third World, the Latin American experience provides a view of the state role under democratic, rightist authoritarian, and revolutionary regimes, all facing demands to shelter increasing numbers of the urban poor.

During the past four decades in Latin America, a combination of high birthrates and extensive rural–urban migration has produced a level of urban population growth unmatched in any region of the world. In 1940 the entire region was 19.6 percent urban. By 1975 that figure had increased to 40.5 percent, far exceeding the levels of other developing areas (23.7 percent in East Asia, 18.1 percent in Africa, and 17.4 percent in South Asia) and nearly approaching Europe's rate of 48.2 percent (Roberts, 1978, p. 7).[1]

User-Built versus State Shelter

Because of Latin America's underdeveloped economy and the limited purchasing power of most migrants, the commercial housing market has not grown rapidly enough to accommodate the vastly expanded population of the region's cities. Consequently, the burgeoning numbers of urban poor have found shelter primarily through housing units they have built themselves. In the sandy tracts surrounding Lima, on the hills overlooking Rio de Janeiro and Caracas, and in the outskirts of most Latin American capitals, some 20,000 to 30,000 squatter settlements have sprung up. In some cases, the squatter communities are no more than a series of individually built homes. In others, such as Lima's *pueblos jóvenes* (new towns), settlements resulted from coordinated group land invasions. Research conducted in the 1960s suggested that squatter settlements constituted 25 percent of the total populations of Lima and Santiago, 33 to 35 percent of Caracas and Rio de Janeiro, and 45 percent of Mexico City (Perlman, 1979, p. 12; Portes and Walton, 1976, pp. 38–43).

Another potential source of shelter for Latin America's urban poor has been government housing or state-provided sites and services. In some countries the government has been involved in this area for many years. Only in recent decades, however, have government programs begun to contribute significantly to the housing needs of many of the region's nations. This expansion of state activity has resulted from a combination of international and domestic pressures. During the 1960s, as the United States became concerned with the potential spread of revolutionary unrest from Cuba to other parts of Latin America, foreign aid programs such as the Alliance for Progress sought to contribute to basic needs, including housing, for Latin America's urban poor. The first fruit of that emphasis, Bogotá's Ciudad Kennedy, an Alliance-supported project housing some 18,000 families, was completed in 1965. At the same time, the growing number of urban squatters, with their increased influence as voters and their potential for creating political unrest, convinced many political leaders of the need to promote government housing programs.

Public housing has played a particularly strong role in the political agenda of reformist and revolutionary regimes. In 1964, for example, Chile's progressive Christian Democratic candidate, Eduardo Frei, was elected to the presidency on a platform pledging to construct government housing for 360,000 needy families. Six years later, the newly elected Socialist administration of President Salvador Allende criticized the shortcomings of the Christian Democratic program and promised that it would do more to satisfy the shelter requirements of the urban lower class (Lozano, 1975, pp. 177–94; Sanders, 1985, p. 2). In revolutionary Cuba, the regime promoted prefabricated apartment houses, assembled by volunteer "microbrigades," and reduced pressure on urban housing through rural development and the construction of apartment dwellings on state farms and in provincial cities (Eckstein, 1981; Gugler, 1980). But even rightist military–authoritarian regimes have sought to attain some popular support through the provision of low-cost shelter. In Venezuela during the 1950s, for example, the dictatorship of Marcos Pérez Jiménez began construction of a 10,000-unit apartment complex. Ironically, Pérez Jiménez was overthrown shortly before the project's completion, and the complex was occupied by invading residents from the neighboring shantytowns (Handelman, 1975, pp. 14–15). More recently, Brazil's military–authoritarian regime (1964 to 1985), shortly after seizing power, created the National Housing Bank and the Brazilian Housing Finance System, designed "to attract voluntary and contractual savings for the benefit of low-income lenders and borrowers for housing purposes" (Reynolds and Carpenter, 1975, p. 149).

The Critique of State Housing

At present, there is hardly a single Latin American government, regardless of its ideological stripe or constituent base, that has not developed a state housing agency and a verbal commitment to provide shelter for low-income groups. Such programs conform to the current notion, popular among development experts and agencies such as the World Bank, that the state should contribute to the basic needs of the poor, particularly those not met by economic growth within the private sector. But, after numerous state efforts, many urban policy scholars feel that most public housing programs in Latin America and in other parts of the Third World have not met the needs of the urban poor. Spontaneous shelter, they argue, has been a much more effective and satisfying means of providing housing for that sector (e.g., Fichter, Turner, and Grenell, 1972; Turner, 1967, 1976).

All too often, public housing projects lack the churches, bars, and neighborhood stores that help create a sense of community. An atmosphere of anomie may erode neighborhood pride. When visiting the giant Alomar housing project outside Havana (proudly described by government guides as a major accomplishment of revolutionary Cuba), I was struck by the weed-covered lots between the high-rises. The lots were clearly in disuse, despite their obvious potential as soccer fields, garden plots, or the like. At their worst, government projects have become vandalized, crime-infested eyesores. Caracas's 23 de Enero and parts of Bogotá's Ciudad Kennedy are but two examples of high-rise housing projects that have become monuments to poor planning and urban decay (Handelman, 1979; Turner, 1976, pp. 46–47).

Perhaps the most salient criticism of state housing, however, is that it usually does not benefit Latin America's urban poor. La Unidad is Mexico City's largest housing complex, its 10,000 homes built by the government in 1968. Unlike Ciudad Kennedy, it is well planned with a central plaza, church, school, zoo, children's hospital, sports and social centers, swimming pool, movie theater, and funeral home. A close inspection of La Unidad, however, reveals that its residents are primarily not the urban poor but the middle class and upper working class. While government spokespersons insist that the project was originally designed to house lower-class inner-city residents and squatters, other state planners admit that they never believed that the poor could afford to live there. The project's statutes require residents to earn the legal minimum wage, a level higher than Mexico City's poor attain. In fact, the government allocates a large number of the complex's houses to municipal employees, functionaries of various political parties (particularly the ruling PRI), army officers, and skilled industrial workers. Since 1968, houses built in La Unidad have sold for $10,000 to $16,000—far beyond the means of the urban poor—and an increasing percentage is allocated to municipal employees, members of elite labor unions, and even professionals such as doctors (Eckstein, 1977, pp. 64–67). While this Mexican example is particularly well documented, studies of state housing programs in Brazil, Colombia, Peru, Venezuela, and other Latin American nations reveal similar patterns. In-kind housing units (i.e., those ready for occupancy without the need for significant additional construction by the tenant) usually are sold or rented to the middle class or the better paid of the working class and rarely serve the poor (Dietz, 1980, p. 41; Handelman, 1975; Reynolds and Carpenter, 1975; Vernez, 1973).

Who Serves the Poor?

A study of low-income housing in Bogotá showed that, as of 1970, the poorest stratum of the city's population—those with monthly family incomes of under 500 pesos—constituted 7.4 percent of the total population, but only 4.0 percent of the residents of public housing (Vernez, 1973, p. 25). Ernest R. Alexander, in Chapter 6, argues that even government sites and services are still substantially more expensive than true informal housing, and are thus out of reach of the really poor. It is by no means clear, however, that spontaneous shelter serves the needs of the "really poor" much better. Most of Bogotá's user-built squatter settlements are not cost-free to their inhabitants. Land invasions are far less common in that city than so-called pirate settlements (referred to by Alexander as "clandestine developments"), in which residents purchase plots from speculators. But since the land has not been legally approved for urban development, the plots lack basic services such as water, sewerage, and electricity. These zones, ringing the city, may shelter some 50 percent of Bogotá's entire population and more than two-thirds of the city's lower class (Handelman, 1979, p. 3).

Speculators often sell pirate plots above their commercial value, but low-income purchasers may prefer them to less expensive lots because no down payment is required, costs are extended over a long period, and inhabitants are not evicted for missing one or two payments.

Still, the poorest of the poor can no more afford pirate lots than they can government shelter. Vernez (1973) notes that the poorest 7.4 percent of the population owned only 4.6 percent of the pirate housing, a figure scarcely different from the percentage (4.0) in government units.

In other countries, such as Peru, squatters are more prone to live on invaded land. But these invasions often involve negotiating with officials or bribing local authorities, hiring lawyers, and considerable organizing. Consequently, squatters usually are not the poorest of the urban poor (Butterworth and Chance, 1981, p. 155; Dietz, 1980, p. 37).

A Constructive Role for the State

Despite the faults of many public housing programs, it would be erroneous to propose a laissez-faire attitude by the state toward sheltering the poor. There is sometimes a tendency to romanticize squatter settlements when contrasting them to state efforts. Cheleen Mahar (n.d.) charges that Turner and other scholars imply that squatter settlements are little more than impoverished middle-class neighborhoods. That view, Mahar believes, "merely disguises the agonizing poverty of most true social conditions and provides a further barrier to their amelioration." Rather than leave the development of squatter communities totally in the hands of their inhabitants, the state should regulate and aid user-built housing in a way that would encourage and improve such spontaneous efforts. In the absence of governmental standards, spontaneous housing can be unhealthy and unsafe. In Caracas during the late 1970s, some 600,000 people lived in "shantytowns . . . precariously built on steep and eroded hillsides . . . and creek beds that were extremely dangerous in the rainy season" (Handelman, 1979, pp. 6–7).

Obviously state programs are also necessary to provide squatter communities with water, electricity, sewerage, paved streets, and other basic urban services. In Colombia and elsewhere, the government, when pressured, has offered squatters low-interest loans or low-cost construction materials for the improvement of their homes. Government technical aid and credit could also help establish local cottage industries that would both sell construction materials to the community and provide a source of employment and capital accumulation for the residents. In short, government programs can nurture and complement spontaneous efforts. Furthermore, while user-built housing must continue to be a primary source of shelter for the urban poor, sites and services programs can supplement that housing stock.

Although state sites and services lots are beyond the means of the poorest urban dwellers, they are within the reach of many workers in the bottom 30 to 40 percent of the income ladder. As noted earlier, most Latin American nations have some state housing programs that primarily provide in-kind housing for the middle class and skilled working class. Consequently, the issue should not be spontaneous shelter versus governmental programs, but how the urban poor can appropriate a larger share of state housing resources for low-cost sites and services projects. Similarly, the state must make sure spontaneous shelter is safe and has adequate urban services.

Thus, state housing policy is not determined solely by urban planners. The quality and quantity of state-initiated low-income housing obviously will be constrained by the availability of economic resources and the degree of competition for them. How much of those state resources will be devoted to housing, however, and what portion of that allocation will serve low-income dwellers will largely depend on the political environment. The urban poor will receive more state aid (services for squatter communities, sites and services programs, or in-kind housing) only if they are effectively able to mobilize politically and if the political system is responsive to lower-class demands. Three factors are critical. First, what capacity do the urban poor have to articulate their demands to the political system? Second, how strong are the other groups—such as middle-class government employees—competing for state housing resources? Finally, based on its ideological orientation and its base of political support, how receptive is the government to the demands of the urban poor? In the remaining portion of this chapter, I consider a range of political environments in order to examine the record of different Latin American regimes in the area of low-income housing. The kinds of regimes discussed are meant to be illustrative and not exhaustive.

Democratic Regimes with Competitive Party Systems

Although democratic institutions are still fragile in Latin America, and many electoral systems are a facade masking elite control, the growth of competitive party systems in Colombia, Costa Rica, Venezuela, and, before 1973, in Chile and Uruguay, has facilitated varying degrees of political input from Latin America's lower classes. In recent years, democratic competitive elections have been restored to Argentina, Ecuador, Peru, Uruguay and—in a more limited sense—Bolivia and Brazil. From the 1950s into the 1970s, a number of factors increased the political influence of the urban poor within these multiparty democracies. Heavy migration swelled the ranks of the urban lower class. Higher literacy rates increased their eligibility for suffrage and contributed to a greater level of political awareness. To the extent that competing political parties sought the support of lower-class voters, the poor in Latin America's cities used their electoral weight to negotiate for improved housing.

Nowhere was that more true than in Chile in the 1960s and early 1970s. In the *campamentos* (squatter settlements arising from organized land invasions) ringing Santiago, a network of grass-roots political organizations arose spontaneously or with the cooperation of outside organizers from the reformist Christian Democratic party, the various Marxist parties of the Popular Unity (UP) Front, or the more radical MIR (Leftist Revolutionary Movement) (Castells, 1972; Handelman, 1975; Petras, 1973; Vanderschueren, 1971). The intense political competition between Christian Democrats and the UP during that period, and the resulting mass politicization, enabled squatter settlements to petition the government successfully for home construction materials and social services. Under the governments of Christian Democrat Eduardo Frei (1964 to 1970) and the UP's Salvador Allende (1970 to 1973), low-income urban housing was a major concern of state policy.

Government aid was provided either as assistance to spontaneous housing settlements, as sites and services programs, or in the form of public housing projects. Particularly during the Allende administration, radicalized shantytown dwellers capitalized on the regime's redistributive ideological commitment and its dependence on working-class support to press forcefully their demands for state aid.

While the ability of the urban lower class to manipulate their political environment was particularly marked in Allende's Chile, other democratic regimes also provided the poor with some sort of housing benefits. Prior to the 1973 collapse of Uruguayan democracy, reformist factions of the major parties actively sought the support of Montevideo's lower class through patronage networks. One reward for party followers was access to public housing (Benton, 1986, p. 46).

In Venezuela, the first state construction of low-income urban housing dates from 1928. Before the establishment of a sustained democratic regime in 1958, however, the number of dwellings constructed by that agency was minimal. From 1928 to 1958, an average of only 1,350 units was constructed annually (Handelman, 1979, p. 15). Almost 75 percent of these units were built in Caracas, the center of political power. With the introduction of democracy came a dramatic increase in the number of dwellings constructed by the National Institute of Housing (INAVI) and a shift of activity to outside the nation's capital. The latter change reflected the fact that the ruling Acción Democrática (AD) party had received only a small portion of its electoral support from Caracas and based its strength in the provincial cities and the countryside. From 1959 to 1963, an average of 6,600 units were built annually, with over 93 percent of those dwellings outside the capital.

Government construction rose to 34,000 units annually from 1969 to 1973 when the COPEI Christian Democrats replaced the AD Social Democrats. Projects continued to be built primarily in the provinces, but in response to COPEI's electoral constituency, there was a slight increase in the proportion of housing built in Caracas (from 13 percent to 16 percent). More important, COPEI reached out to the poor of Caracas by instituting various programs to rejuvenate the user-built housing of the low-income *barrios.* The Barrio Urbanizing Project brought water, sewerage lines, and electricity to spontaneously built *rancho* (shantytown) areas. The Popular Urbanization Project was a sites and services program designed for families among the poorest 25 percent of Caracas's population (Handelman, 1975, p. 16). When the AD returned to office in 1974, there was yet another shift in the locus of state-constructed housing. The percentage of units built in the capital dropped below 10 percent and COPEI's *barrio* and popular urbanization programs were abandoned. In all these decisions, electoral constituencies seemed to play a greater role than urban planning.

Electoral politics may also influence state policy toward squatter invasions by the urban poor. In Lima, Peru, a vast influx of rural migrants swelled that city's population by some 400 percent from 1950 to 1975. Inner-city slum dwellers (including both migrants and those born in Lima) frequently organized group invasions of the sandy hills outside the capital (often marginal public lands), where they built *barriadas.* By the late 1960s, perhaps 25 percent of the city's population lived in these squatter settlements. Although technically illegal, many of these invasions were carefully coordinated with government authorities and political leaders, who were cultivating electoral support (Collier, 1976). Once settled, the squatters skillfully established clientelistic relations with government officials as a means of securing urban services. After Peru's 1968 coup, many shantytown leaders established a new set of linkages with the country's reform-oriented military government in order to secure legal title to the lots on which they had built their homes (Dietz, 1980).

An overview of state housing policy in democratic regimes suggests that the degree to which the urban poor benefit from either the provision of urban services for spontaneously constructed communities or from low-cost sites and services programs varies according to four factors: (1) the resources available to the state; (2) the level of lower-class political mobilization and the ability of the urban poor to press their demands on the political system; (3) the degree to which political parties cultivate urban lower-class electoral support; and (4) the extent of competition for state housing resources coming from the urban middle class.

Under the Socialist government of Salvadore Allende (1970–73) and, to a lesser extent, under the preceding Christian Democratic administration (1964–70), the vigorous party competition for mass support contributed to a high level of organization and politicization of Chile's urban poor. The Frei administration substantially expanded the number of state-constructed low-income dwellings and improved services to the spontaneous squatter settlements. Yet, state programs fell far below the level Frei had promised in his 1964 campaign (Lozano, 1975). Two factors constrained government efforts: limits on resources and strong competition for those resources from the Christian Democrat's major electoral constituency, the urban middle class. Under the succeeding Allende administration, there was an increase in mass political mobilization and an ideological shift by the government toward serving the needs of the urban poor. Frei's sites and services projects were criticized for allegedly having failed to provide the lower classes with housing of sufficient quality. Though seriously hampered by a deteriorating economy that constricted state resources, the UP government shifted the emphasis in state programs toward providing the *campamentos* with basic services and toward constructing in-kind low-income housing. From 1971 to 1973, the Socialist government constructed 39,000 housing units annually, the highest yearly output of state housing in Chilean history (Sanders, 1985, p. 3). Most of those units were provided to the lower class.

In Colombia, the political environment has been far less propitious for the interests of the urban poor. During the 1950s and 1960s, a political accord between the Conservative and Liberal parties effectively eliminated electoral competition. Even when competitive elections were restored, the two dominant parties were oligarchically controlled. Political attitudes among the urban poor in the 1970s and 1980s have been characterized by a high degree of apathy and a growing level of electoral abstention. Consequently, there has been neither sufficient popular pressure on the government nor an ideological inclination by the regime to allocate significant resources for low-income housing or for assisting spontaneous communities. From 1942 to 1970, the Institute of Territorial Credit (ICT), the state housing agency, built on average fewer than 6,000 units annually (Handelman, 1979, p. 8). This was insufficient to make even a dent in the urban housing shortage. Moreover, state housing efforts were clearly more beneficial to the middle class than to the poor. In Bogotá, lower-income residents (those in the bottom 34 percent of the income ladder) were the recipients of only 21.8 percent of public housing, while those in the middle-income stratum, representing only 27 percent of the city's population, received 44 percent of the public housing (Vernez, 1973, p. 25).

From 1970 to 1976, as the country returned to competitive electoral politics, the rate of ICT construction tripled to an annual rate of 20,000 units. At the same time, a shift in emphasis away from in-kind units and toward sites and services programs sharply reduced the cost of much ICT housing. In this way, the ICT was able to reach a clientele farther down the economic ladder. Yet even these cheaper units were sold at a price designed for persons making one to two times the minimum wage. In addition, the government continued to sell in-kind apartment units to middle-class and upper-middle-class purchasers earning two to ten times the minimum wage. Since those units were sold at 35 to 50 percent below their market value, the state was effectively subsidizing the middle class. While middle-class dwellings constituted only 16 percent of ICT-constructed units, they accounted for 40 percent of the agency's budget. One scholar observed in the late 1970s that, despite the increase in sites and services programs, "the ICT, with few exceptions, has not reached . . . the lowest strata despite its rhetorical claims to do so" (Laun, 1977, p. 331). In the late 1970s, as the price of middle-class and upper-middle-class housing in Bogotá's private-sector market spiraled, those groups increasingly competed with the urban poor for state housing resources. Given the oligarchical nature of Colombian politics, there is reason to believe that their housing needs will continue to have priority over those of the urban poor.

Rightist Authoritarian Military Regimes

During the 1960s and early 1970s, in the southern countries of South America, a combination of rampant inflation, growing trade union militancy, increased support for populist movements (Brazil and Argentina) or Marxist political parties (Chile and Uruguay), revolutionary guerrilla activity (Argentina, Brazil, Chile, and Uruguay), increased class conflict, and political polarization led the armed forces to overthrow democratically elected governments and create a series of military dictatorships. The Brazilian coup of 1964 established a pattern of bureaucratic–authoritarian rule that spread to Argentina, Chile, and Uruguay and predominated in the region until recently. These regimes sought to contain the mass political mobilization, particularly the growing militancy of the urban working class, that had developed during the preceding decade (Collier, 1979; O'Donnell, 1973). Obviously, the rise of bureaucratic–authoritarian regimes sharply reduced the ability of the urban poor to press the state for public housing or urban services for spontaneous housing settlements.

In the most extreme cases, inhabitants of squatter settlements found themselves in a fight for survival. Chile's 1973 military coup was followed by an assault on *campamentos* with leftist (particularly MIR) affiliations. Thousands of young men in these communities were rounded up and detained for various periods of time, and hundreds died during their internment. The *campamento* of New Havana was subjected to aerial bombing. From 1974 to 1978, state housing construction fell to the lowest per capita rate since the 1950s and to less than half the level of the Allende administration (Sanders, 1985, p. 3). Low-income squatters in other bureaucratic–authoritarian regimes found themselves under less extreme forms of siege. Janice Perlman describes the Brazilian military regime's forced relocation of residents of the Rio de Janeiro *favela* Praia do Pinto in the 1960s. When the inhabitants withstood the arrests, random gunshots, and beatings that had successfully ousted *favelados* in Jardim America, Morro do Pasmado, and Vila Kennedy at earlier dates,

Praia do Pinto was burned to the ground so that subsidized high-rise housing for the military could be constructed in its place. Although the urban poor might not have received much aid from the state under the earlier democratic regime, at least they had the capacity to block forced relocations by voting out local officials who contemplated such actions (Perlman, 1979, pp. 205–11).

In Uruguay, Montevideo's poor have generally lived in central city tenements (*conventillos*), roominghouses, or other deteriorating dwellings rather than in spontaneous shelter (Benton, 1986). Before the 1973 collapse of Uruguayan democracy, central-city residents, like all tenants, were protected by very favorable rent legislation. By 1974, it had become "nearly impossible for a landlord to evict a tenant or to raise rents in keeping with the pace of inflation" (Benton, 1986, pp. 36–37). In that year, the civil–military dictatorship enacted a new rent law that authorized the phasing out of all rent control. Protection against eviction was also loosened. Many of the urban poor, either evicted from their residences or unable to pay higher rents, moved into abandoned or condemned central-city buildings. Although these buildings generally lacked electricity or water, squatters still preferred them to expensive rental housing or outlying dwellings. From 1978 to 1981, when the regime promoted Montevideo as an international banking center and the central city experienced a brief Argentine-financed construction boom, the government permitted or even mandated the demolition of a large number of *conventillos* in the area. Throughout this period, the inner-city poor fell victim to the regime's free market policies. Benton notes that the "political climate offered residents of [the condemned *conventillos*] few avenues for organized political protest" (Benton, 1986, p. 46).

In general, the Chilean, Brazilian, and Uruguayan rightist regimes' commitments to reduced state spending, their lack of concern for support of the urban poor, and their restrictions on political protest served to reduce state aid to low-income housing. Only on rare occasions did such regimes respond to lower-class demands in this area. At the same time, inhabitants of the informal housing sector found themselves at the mercy of the market or of the needs of more powerful constituencies, with little or no protection.

Revolutionary Regimes

The January 1959 victory of Fidel Castro's revolutionary forces set in motion a far-reaching economic and political transformation of Cuban society. Twenty years later, Nicaragua experienced a similar revolutionary upheaval, although so far change has been more politically pluralistic and economically diverse. In both nations the revolutionary process dramatically reduced or eliminated the power of previously influential groups such as multinational corporations, the landed elite, and the urban bourgeoisie, and at the same time reoriented state policy toward meeting the basic needs of the nation's poor. One of the first needs to be addressed by the powerful revolutionary state was housing for the urban poor and working class.

The Cuban government's initial intervention in housing involved no new construction programs nor an extension of urban services, but an alteration of the terms of tenancy for renters. Less than three months after coming to power, the revolutionary regime lowered rents by 30 to 50 percent, with the greatest reductions going to families that had been paying under $100 monthly. Subsequently, the Urban Reform Law of October 1960 prohibited private rental and turned over to the state all rental housing units, with limited compensation for the former owners. The law stipulated that tenants would have to pay no more than 10 percent of their income toward rent. Families with per capita incomes of less than 25 pesos (then roughly $25) per month were freed of any rent, while retired or sick persons paid only 8 pesos monthly. The net result of these changes was to reduce sharply the cost of shelter for the urban poor. Alternatively, tenants could acquire the homes they had been inhabiting by paying the state, for a period of five to twenty years (depending on individual circumstances), the amount of rent that they had previously paid. By 1969, when the government suspended tenants' rights to buy their homes, 268,089 Cuban families had taken advantage of the purchasing plan. As of 1972, 75 percent of all Cuban families owned their own homes (67 percent in urban areas), 10 percent were in the process of buying them, 8 percent paid rent, and 6 percent lived rent free (4 percent in urban areas) (Acosta and Hardoy, 1971; Domínguez, 1978, p. 186; Eckstein, 1981, pp. 128–29; Mesa-Lago, 1981, p. 172). Since that time, the percentage of renters has increased as the right to purchase was phased out (although it was restored in 1985) and the state constructed more than 180,000 new rental units.

In Nicaragua, the new Sandinista government inherited a far more serious housing deficit than existed in most of Latin America. The devastating earthquake of 1972 had destroyed much of downtown Managua, including 40,000 housing units. Rather than rebuild the center of the capital, the Somoza regime consciously neglected it and banned squatter settlements in the area. This forced new construction to take place in the city's outskirts, where Somoza and his allies held huge tracts of land for speculative purposes (Booth, 1985; Williams, 1985, p. 384). Thus, seven years later, when the Sandinistas toppled the Somoza dynasty, a large part of Managua's central core remained blighted. The revolutionary struggle resulted in the destruction of 4,000 additional urban homes. Finally, in late 1979 (only months after the Sandinistas took power), a tropical storm destroyed several thousand urban and rural dwellings.

On July 18, 1979, the day before its triumph, the revolutionary junta announced its intention to create a new Ministry of Housing and Human Settlement (MINVAH), an urban reform program, and an emergency plan for marginal urban neighborhoods. Having inherited a totally bankrupt national treasury, the regime lacked the resources for substantial new construction. Consequently, as in Cuba, initial urban housing policy focused less on construction of new housing than on regulation of the existing market. During its first year in power, the new government addressed the problem of the 400 illegal subdivisions in Managua (with over 50,000 houses). Housing conditions in these areas varied widely, from well-constructed homes built by developers to poor squatter settlements. Private real estate developers were stripped of control of these areas, and the residents' outstanding land payments were paid thereafter to MINVAH. Rent was set aside in an account for each subdivision, to be used for infrastructure and neighborhood improvements. In 1980–81 the government responded to petitions from residents that costs were too high by first reducing and subsequently terminating all payments.

From 1981 to 1984, nearly 13,000 resident families received title to their lots, and more than 7,000 additional titles were awarded to nonresidents for vacant plots in the subdivisions. Also, a 1980 rental law, closely modeled on the Cuban example, set the maximum annual rent for tenants at 5 percent of the dwelling's assessed value, thereby reducing most rent outlays by 40 to 50 percent. By 1984, the government proposed legislation to eliminate private rentals (Williams, 1985, pp. 388–90).

Urban reform laws in Cuba and Nicaragua were followed by construction of state housing designed to serve the urban poor. During the 1960s, the Cuban government concentrated its housing efforts in rural areas and provincial cities, reflecting the regime's commitment to reducing Havana's long-standing disproportionate share of national resources. New urban housing consisted primarily of large apartment complexes built on the outskirts of major cities. The biggest development of this kind in the 1960s was the José Martí project, built outside Santiago (the city's reward for being "the cradle of Cuba's revolution"). Begun with Soviet aid and techniques in 1967, José Martí was originally designed to house 40,000 people (one-sixth of Santiago's population), but did not quite reach that figure (Ward, 1978, pp. 36–38). In Havana, two complexes were built in the 1960s: El Cotorro, in the city's southeast working-class neighborhood, and East Havana. During the 1970s, the capital began to receive an increased proportion of state housing resources as the regime sought to counter Havana's resentment over its inferior status since the revolution. The immense Alomar project was begun outside the city in 1971 and by 1976 housed some 25,000 persons. Construction was still going on when I visited Alomar in 1980, and plans called for an eventual population of 130,000 to 150,000 people (although that figure seems unrealistically high).

These complexes reveal several important aspects of the regime's attitude toward housing. The beneficiaries of state housing were not the middle class—as has often been true in both authoritarian and bourgeois democratic regimes—but workers and the urban poor. Santiago's José Martí project was begun in 1967 to replace the Marimón slum region destroyed by a hurricane. East Havana was built outside the city on a beautiful site overlooking the ocean that, before the revolution, had been chosen by real estate speculators for luxury housing. The initial inhabitants of that project were impoverished squatters, many of whom were not accustomed to apartment living. Some abused the facilities and eventually moved away. The sharp contrast between the upper-class clientele whom the private-sector developers had in mind when they planned luxury units for East Havana and the very poor recipients of the government housing eventually built there dramatically illustrates the effect of the revolution on housing priorities.

Early housing policies also reflected Fidel Castro's belief that nothing was too good for the working class. José Martí and Alomar were supposed to provide all of the amenities of life. Not only was in-kind housing preferred over sites and services projects, but José Martí was provided with schools, day-care centers, theaters, clinics, commercial centers, grocery stores, and meeting halls for political organization. Plans for Havana's Alomar called for eighteen semi-boarding schools, six theaters, thirty-two day-care centers, and new industries to employ many of the residents (Eckstein, 1981, p. 131; Ward, 1978, p. 36). East Havana and El Cotorro were characterized by one sympathetic observer as "costly and premised . . . on Western 'middle class' design ideas" (Eckstein, 1981, p. 129). Indeed, Eckstein argues that most of the early revolutionary architecture was "modern and innovative in design, but elitist in conceptualization and costly." What this meant, of course, was that the number of units built was far below both the country's need and government projections. East Havana, an extreme if atypical example, was supposed to consist of 100,000 dwelling units, but ultimately contained only 1,500.

In Nicaragua, the grave economic crisis facing the Sandinista regime has precluded construction of massive public housing projects such as exist in Cuba. From 1980 to 1983, MINVAH built only 10,162 housing units, with annual completions increasing from 1,146 in 1980 to 3,895 in 1983. On an annual per capita basis, this was less than half of Cuba's rate for the first four years of its revolution.[2] In 1980 Managua received 60.8 percent of the new units, but by 1983 that figure fell to 17.4 percent as the government shifted resources to rural areas and provincial cities (Williams, 1985, pp. 392–93). Early state projects, like those in Cuba, stressed in-kind housing with emphasis on "community support and interaction, such as apartment units . . . with communal social and recreational areas" (Williams, 1985, p. 392). The cost of construction exceeded initial estimates, thereby reducing the number of units built and inducing the government to rent some of the Managua dwellings to more middle-class government employees (an obvious violation of revolutionary principles of equity that was subsequently rectified as state construction shifted from the capital to the provinces). MINVAH first rejected sites and services programs, largely because officials felt that "the inherent potential of such programs to promote individualism and discourage community participation ran counter to the government's general policies of . . . community cooperation" (Williams, 1985, p. 391). Economic necessity and pragmatism, however, soon overtook ideological fervor. From 1981 to 1982, the number of sites and services lots allocated rose from 854 to 8,810, with the latter figure more than twice the number of in-kind units completed that year.

In Cuba the sites and services approach has been introduced in recent years on rural farming cooperatives. But in urban areas, in-kind housing remains the rule. In the late 1960s the government introduced what it hoped would be a less costly means of construction. Prefabricated apartment complexes were built for workers from specific workplaces by volunteer units called *microbrigades.* These consisted of employees selected from the workplace who had no particular background in construction. After a brief training period, they built the apartments under the guidance of Cuban or Soviet bloc technicians. Since co-workers back at the workplace were supposed to compensate for the production lost by the absence of the microbrigade volunteers (while the volunteers drew their normal wage), the housing was theoretically being built with minimal labor costs, thereby introducing one of the advantages of spontaneous shelter. In fact, amateur construction units proved to be inefficient, and in 1978 the government abandoned microbrigades and returned to the use of professional crews and more mechanized equipment (Mesa-Lago, 1981, p. 174).

In both Cuba and Nicaragua, allocation of housing reflects revolutionary principles. To begin with, unlike capitalist societies, where access to most housing in the private sector is determined by the marketplace, distribution takes place through the collective decisions of potential beneficiaries. Cuban workers decide at the workplace who will receive new apartment units. When microbrigade construction was still employed, construction volunteers were not necessarily recipients. In Nicaragua, neighborhood revolutionary support organizations (called Sandinista Defense Committees, or CDS) decide who is to receive new state housing for their areas. Obviously there is some potential for abuse in such decision making, and the process may not be as democratic as government spokespersons suggest. Nevertheless, my conversations with Cuban workers indicated that, while they were unhappy about the general shortage of new housing, they felt the distributional process was fair.

Collective decisions are supposed to be made in accordance with revolutionary criteria that include need, work performance, and political commitment. Said Castro, "In the case of two workers with equal need, the one with the greatest sense of social responsibility and merit should have priority" (Eckstein, 1981, p. 131). Cubans returning from voluntary military duty in Africa have priority status in securing new housing. Similarly, in Nicaragua the first housing projects built after the revolutionary victory served those neighborhoods that had been most actively involved in the insurrection and that consequently had suffered from aerial bombings by Somoza's National Guard. Sandinista Defense Committees, like Cuba's neighborhood Committees for the Defense of the Revolution, are charged with delivering many local social services, carrying out neighborhood cleanups and other maintenance activities, and communicating between the neighborhood and the state bureaucracy. Citizens who are active in CDS neighborhood projects and who attend rallies and other mass mobilization activities are more likely to get state housing.

Even the architectural style of state housing is influenced by ideological criteria. "As in Cuba, state housing projects [in Nicaragua] that reinforced community support and interaction, such as apartments . . . and individual units with communal social and recreational areas, were . . . given preference over those that followed the traditional patterns of separation and individuality of residences" (Williams, 1985, p. 392). One of the first housing complexes built after the revolution in Managua—involving the replacement of a slum with 463 families—was built in an open pattern with minimal space on the sides and front and an open common area to the rear. As Turner would have predicted, the communal goals of state planners were not in tune with residents' desires. Inhabitants built fences around their houses (although they were discouraged from doing so) in order to protect their gardens and property and to create privacy. Experiences such as these, as well as many of the earliest residents' inability to afford the rent for in-kind housing, made MINVAH planners more receptive to sites and services programs.

In all, revolutionary societies have been most successful in introducing greater equity to the distribution of urban housing. Even strong critics of Cuban policy such as Jorge Domínguez concede that "Cuba has made significant progress . . . in the distribution of housing. Government allocation . . . and the lowering of rents have eliminated income discrimination in access to housing as well as making it cheaper overall" (Domínguez, 1978, p. 188). But the Cuban regime has not provided large quantities of new housing. While the government brings foreign visitors to Alomar and other huge complexes so as to impress them with the magnitude of state efforts, Carmelo Mesa-Lago observes that "of all social services, housing is the worst in terms of revolutionary performance" (1981, p. 172). Indeed, construction of housing since the 1959 revolution has not kept pace with the rate in the decade before Fidel

Castro's victory. From 1946 to 1953, an average of 26,827 units were built annually. From 1953 to 1958, precise figures are unavailable, but Mesa-Lago estimates annual construction at about 28,000. By contrast, the highest annual rate of construction from 1959 to 1980 was 20,710 units in 1973. Output reached a low of 4,004 in 1970. For the 1970s, average annual production was 15,071. Overall, new construction has not kept up with the need, and the country's housing deficit has increased significantly (Mesa-Lago, 1981, pp. 172–73). During the 1960s, the housing shortage in Havana was partially alleviated by the emigration of large numbers of upper- and middle-class families, most of whose homes were turned over to applicants from the lower classes. "A few lucky recipients picked up keys and opened fully furnished luxury apartments high above the city [of Havana]" (Ward, 1978, p. 39). In all, 139,256 émigré homes shifted to needy families from 1960 to 1974, for an annual average of 9,284 (Domínguez, 1978, p. 187). During the late 1960s, émigré homes were a more important source of improved housing for Havana's lower class than was state construction.

Cuba's weak record of supplying new housing can be attributed to several factors. During the late 1960s, the country faced a serious economic crisis. From that period onward (even during the economic recovery of the 1970s), there has been a shortage of construction material. Consequently, the government has given low priority to housing, relative to other national construction needs. State expenditures for housing have been lower than each of the construction budgets for roads, dams, industrial plants, agriculture, schools, or hospitals. In 1970 only 5 percent of total construction expenditure went to housing, with that figure rising to 16 percent in 1972 and falling to 10 percent in 1976 (Mesa-Lago, 1981, p. 172). Finally, the regime's insistence on building in-kind housing (often accompanied by expensive social service facilities), and its rejection of both sites and services and spontaneous shelter, has made the unit cost of housing unnecessarily high. Since 1978, the government has tried to deal with this problem by reducing the size of newly constructed units, raising rents for new tenants, and increasing allocations for the repair and upkeep of existing housing (Mesa-Lago, 1981, p. 174). In 1985 the government announced that tenants could once again purchase their own homes (to encourage them to maintain those dwellings) and that private owners could rent parts of their homes.

Conclusion

For the foreseeable future, it is likely that a combination of "push factors" (the inability of small farmers to compete under existing market conditions and parcelization of peasant plots through inheritance) and "pull factors" (the greater level of services and the hope of economic improvement in urban areas) will continue to bring large numbers of rural migrants to Latin America's cities and to urban areas in other developing nations. Most of these migrants will find shelter either in spontaneous settlements or in inner-city slums. Past experience suggests that the extent to which the state supplements and improves spontaneous housing efforts will depend on the nature of the political regime.

The urban lower class in Latin America has generally fared most poorly under rightist bureaucratic–authoritarian governments. Because such regimes often have come to power in order to impose austerity programs, they have allocated minimal funds for low-income housing or for aid to squatter settlements. They have no ideological predisposition toward serving the poor, nor have they been subject to pressures from lower-class political mobilization. Spontaneous shelter has been permitted. But when squatter settlements have stood in the way of real estate development by influential private-sector interests or have conflicted with state plans, their inhabitants have sometimes been ruthlessly displaced.

Democratic–reformist regimes have been more supportive of spontaneous shelter efforts and more likely to provide sites and services for the urban lower class. The quantity of state funding allocated by democratic governments to poor city dwellers varies and appears proportional to the level of mass political organization and the extent to which major political parties have contended for lower-class votes. Thus, more resources were allocated to squatter settlements and to sites and services in Chile before the 1973 coup than in contemporary Colombia, a far less mobilized society. Even in fairly mobilized and responsive democracies such as Venezuela, however, the lower classes may find themselves at a disadvantage in the battle for government aid. When the middle class has needed state housing because the private market was too expensive, it has competed more effectively than the poor for limited government resources.

Revolutionary societies have clearly redistributed the largest proportion of new housing resources toward lower-income groups, and rents have also been reduced for those in existing housing. Like reformist democracies, revolutionary governments also have employed political criteria in the allocation of housing. But the nature of those criteria has been different. The middle class not only has lacked the competitive advantage it enjoyed in bourgeois democracies, but often it has been viewed by the revolutionary leadership as something of a pariah. At the individual level, the nature of political activity valued by the two kinds of regimes has differed. In Venezuela, working for a winning presidential or congressional candidate has been a useful way of securing the *palanca* (political influence) a person needs to move to the top of the waiting list for state housing. In Cuba and Nicaragua, revolutionary fervor (as demonstrated by volunteer labor, attendance at political rallies, etc.) has been a criterion in the selection of housing applicants.

Revolutionary governments have not provided large quantities of low-cost housing. The Cuban regime's generally poor economic growth performance, its elimination (until very recently) of almost all private building initiatives, its low priority for housing (as opposed to schools, hospitals, and roads), and its commitment to providing in-kind housing (often with extensive community facilities) have limited the number of housing units completed. While the government has recently allowed citizens to build additions to their own houses and to rent out rooms in their homes, its ideological objections to both spontaneous shelter and sites and services programs continue to present real obstacles to the expansion of low-income housing. Nicaragua seems to have learned from Cuba's mistakes, having recently shifted state resources from in-kind housing to sites and services, but it is too early to assess that nation's record.

In recent years Latin American politics has been marked by a transition from rightist authoritarian regimes to more pluralistic democracies. The most notable examples of this have been Argentina, Bolivia, Brazil, and Uruguay. Similar trends may now be under way in Guatemala and Haiti, and nonrepressive military regimes have been replaced by elected governments in Ecuador and Peru. The movement from military authoritarianism to competitive democracy—often led by reformist social democratic or Christian democratic parties—suggests that we might expect a gradually increasing role for the state in providing shelter for the urban poor or improving services to squatter settlements. The ability of either reformist or revolutionary governments to provide such aid, however, will be constrained by their economies. Heavily indebted nations such as Brazil, those further debilitated by low petroleum prices (Ecuador, Mexico, and Venezuela), or those ravaged by war (Nicaragua and El Salvador) will have to limit the role of the state in the near future. Difficult economic conditions will lead, one hopes, to a more prudent allocation of government resources.

The experiences of both revolutionary and democratic–reformist regimes clearly demonstrate that sites and services projects are preferable to in-kind housing. In democracies such as Colombia and Venezuela, not only are in-kind units too expensive for the poor, but middle-class constituencies are able to appropriate subsidized state housing for themselves because of their greater political influence. In revolutionary regimes, in-kind housing usually does reach the lower classes (although even in Nicaragua some projects served government bureaucrats), but the unit cost is too high for an adequate number of dwellings to be built.

In addition to providing sites and services, state programs can help the poor by offering loans and providing water, sewerage, and electricity to spontaneous settlements. Yet caution must be taken not to impose the planners' values on the recipients. During the 1960s and early 1970s, for example, Peru's civilian and military reformist governments introduced basic urban services to many of the squatter settlements outside Lima. Well-intentioned urban planners insisted that, before installing these services, the settlement had to have an orderly street plan. In imposing these plans from the outside, technocrats often overrode the inhabitants' preferences and contradicted the logic of the apparently chaotic layout of houses (Lobo, 1982). Government programs must supplement spontaneous efforts by the urban poor with state planning that is closely coordinated with the desires of the people it purports to serve.

Notes

1. These percentages are based on a definition of *urban* as a place of 20,000 people or more. Figures on the size and percentage of the urban population for a given country or region vary widely among sources, depending on where they establish their cutoff for defining an urban center. Thus, using a broader definition, another authority states that urban areas accounted for 47.3 percent of Latin America's population in 1960 and 61 percent in 1975 (*Latin America: Economic Report,* 1978, p. 3). While no single cutoff point is correct, the critical factor is to maintain consistency in any comparison.
2. From 1959 to 1963, Cuba's population grew from 6,977,000 to 7,512,000; an annual average of 17,089 dwelling units was constructed during this period. That average dropped slightly from 1964 to 1967 (15,209), fell sharply from 1968 to 1971 (5,095), and rose sharply again from 1972 to 1979 (27,700) (Mesa-Lago, 1981, pp. 41, 173). Nicaragua's population in the early 1980s was approximately 2,500,000.

References

Acosta, Maruja, and Jorge E. Hardoy. 1971. *Reforma Urbana en Cuba Revolucionaria.* Caracas, Venezuela: Sintesis Dosmil.

Benton, Lauren A. 1986. "Reshaping the Urban Core: The Politics of Housing in Authoritarian Uruguay." *Latin American Research Review* 21(2), 33–52.

Booth, John. 1985. *The End and the Beginning.* 2d ed. Boulder, Colo.: Westview Press.

Butterworth, Douglas, and John K. Chance. 1981. *Latin American Urbanization.* New York: Cambridge University Press.

Castells, Manuel, et al. 1972. *Los Campamentos de Santiago: Mobilización Urbana.* Santiago: Siglo XXI.

Collier, David. 1976. *Squatters and Oligarchs.* Baltimore: Johns Hopkins University Press.

———, ed. 1979. *The New Authoritarianism in Latin America.* Princeton: Princeton University Press.

Dietz, Henry. 1980. *Poverty and Problem-Solving under Military Rule: The Urban Poor in Lima, Peru.* Austin: University of Texas Press.

Domínguez, Jorge I. 1978. *Cuba: Order and Revolution.* Cambridge: Harvard University Press.

Eckstein, Susan. 1977. *The Poverty of Revolution: The State and the Urban Poor in Mexico.* Princeton: Princeton University Press.

———. 1981. "The Debourgeoisement of Cuban Cities." In *Cuban Communism,* ed. Irving Louis Horowitz, pp. 91–112. 4th ed. New Brunswick, N.J.: Transaction Press.

Fichter, Robert, John F. C. Turner, and Peter Grenell. 1972. "The Meaning of Autonomy." In *Freedom to Build,* ed. John F. C. Turner and Robert Fichter, pp. 241–54. New York: Macmillan.

Gugler, Josef. 1980. "A Minimum of Urbanism and a Maximum of Ruralism: The Cuban Experience." *International Journal of Urban and Regional Research,* no. 4, 516–34.

Handelman, Howard. 1975. "The Political Mobilization of Urban Squatter Settlements." *Latin American Research Review* 10(2), 35–72.

———. 1979. *High-Rises and Shantytowns: Housing the Poor in Bogotá and Caracas.* Hanover, N.H.: American Universities Field Staff.

Latin America: Economic Report. 1978. Data from the Latin American Demographic Center (CEDALE): 6, no. 8 (February 24), p. 3.

Laun, John. 1977. "El Estado y la Vivienda en Colombia. Analisis de Urbanizaciones del ICT." In *Urbanismo y Vida Urbana,* ed. Carlos Castillo, pp. 295–334. Bogotá: Instituto Colombiano de Cultura.

Lobo, Susan. 1982. *A House of My Own.* Tucson: University of Arizona Press.

Lozano, Eduardo E. 1975. "Housing the Urban Poor in Chile: Contrasting Experiences under Christian Democracy and Unidad Popular." In *Latin American Urban Research,* vol. 5, ed. Wayne A. Cornelius and Felicity M. Trueblood, pp. 177–94. Beverly Hills: Sage.

Mahar, Cheleen. n.d. "Squatter Settlements in Latin America: The Case of Oaxaca, Mexico." Unpublished manuscript cited in *Latin American Urbanization* by Douglas Butterworth and John K. Chance. New York: Cambridge University Press, 1981.

Mesa-Lago, Carmelo. 1981. *The Economy of Socialist Cuba: A Two Decade Appraisal.* Albuquerque: University of New Mexico Press.

O'Donnell, Guillermo A. 1973. *Modernization and Bureaucratic Authoritarianism.* Berkeley: Institute of International Studies, University of California.

Perlman, Janice E. 1979. *The Myth of Marginality: Urban Poverty and Politics in Rio de Janeiro.* Berkeley: University of California Press.

Petras, Elizabeth. 1973. *Social Organization of the Urban Housing Movement in Chile.* Council on International Studies, Special Studies, no. 39. Buffalo: State University of New York.

Portes, Alejandro, and John Walton. 1976. *Urban Latin America.* Austin: University of Texas Press.

Reynolds, Clark W., and Robert T. Carpenter. 1975. "Housing Finance in Brazil: Toward a New Distribution of Wealth." In *Latin American Urban Research,* vol. 5, ed. Wayne A. Cornelius and Felicity M. Trueblood, pp. 147–74. Beverly Hills: Sage.

Roberts, Bryan. 1978. *Cities of Peasants: The Political Economy of Urbanization in the Third World.* London: Edward Arnold.

Sanders, Thomas G. 1985. *Housing the Poor in Chile.* Indianapolis, Ind.: Universities Field Staff International.

Turner, John F. C. 1967. "Barriers and Channels for Housing Development in Modernizing Countries." *Journal of the American Institute of Planners* 33(3) (May), 167–81.

———. 1976. *Housing by People: Toward Autonomy in Building Environments.* London: Marion Boyars.

Vanderschueren, Franz. 1971. "Significado Politico de las Juntas de Vecinos de Santiago." *Revista Latinoamericana de Estudios Urbano-Regionales* 1, pp. 67–90.

Vernez, Georges. 1973. "Bogotá's Pirate Settlements: Opportunity for Urban Development." Doctoral dissertation, University of California, Berkeley.

Ward, Fred. 1978. *Inside Cuba Today.* New York: Crown.

Williams, Harvey. 1985. "Housing Policy." In *Nicaragua: The First Five Years,* ed. Thomas W. Walker, pp. 383–97. New York: Praeger.

Chapter 16

Prospects for the Future

CARL V. PATTON

Contributors to this book have shown that a shelter deficit exists, but it may well be one more of quality than quantity. Granted that substantial numbers of Third World inhabitants have no shelter, save what temporary relief they can find in abandoned structures, under bridges, in doorways, and elsewhere, even greater numbers are housed in low-quality structures that are threats to safe and sanitary living. Much can be done to improve the quality of these living conditions, both in terms of the structure itself and access to community facilities and places of employment.

The shelter situation differs widely, depending on the part of the world being examined, the size of city, form of government, and cultural setting. In some locales, such as Indonesia, substantial amounts of spontaneous shelter have existed for decades. In other places, such as Ecuador, it is a relatively recent occurrence. As McTaggart described, spontaneous housing is primarily a phenomenon of Third World countries with a market economy and as such is related to the structure of the urban economy. It reflects differences between the formal and informal sectors and their spatial relationships as expressed in the city landscape.

The influence of culture on the quality of spontaneous settlements can be seen clearly. What makes many of these places livable is not the quality of materials used, but the ways in which materials are combined to respond to cultural beliefs, practices, and social needs. In too many housing replacement schemes, these cultural factors have been ignored, with predictable negative results. In instances where people have been able to provide their own shelter, a remarkably high design quality has often been produced. In fact, Rapoport concluded that spontaneous settlements work more effectively culturally and aesthetically as residential environments than the "high style" solutions of formally trained designers.

In most instances, large-scale, government-provided housing projects have not proven effective, their solutions being too expensive and usually not responsive to the social and cultural values of the users. Smaller-scale projects are both more livable and more affordable. Furthermore, the housing unit cannot be viewed in isolation. Required also are community facilities, recreation space, infrastructure, transportation, and other services that make urban living safe and beneficial.

Lacey and Owusu illustrated the inability of large-scale projects to resolve the shelter shortage in Liberia. Early strategies failed to provide ample numbers of units and were expensive. This resulted in a change in policy, and several self-help projects for low-income families were initiated. The main difficulty was in benefiting sufficient numbers of people and providing substantial funds for community improvement services. Because of a lack of adequate funding, governments are seeking ways to share costs with the citizens they intend to help.

Sites and services and settlement upgrading efforts are more likely to provide better-quality, more culturally responsive shelter for greater numbers of people than high-tech solutions. Yet even the better approaches have met with difficulty. Sites and services projects have often resettled people too far from employment sources. Upgrading schemes have been criticized both as being mere "facelifting" and as having standards that tax the economic ability of residents. But relocation efforts have been even less successful. Even in Hong Kong, with its relatively effective public housing program, relocation housing has sometimes been too far from employment opportunities and friends. Taylor warned us not merely to exchange one set of problems for another. Rather than attempt to relocate all of Hong Kong's boat people on land, he suggests that a more viable solution might be to provide better anchorage and social services within the gradually shrinking floating communities.

In a number of instances, the poor have used sites and services projects and upgrading schemes to move themselves out of low-quality areas by selling their rights in those projects or by selling or renting their improved unit. This practice has been criticized, but it may not be ill advised as a way for people to move out of poverty.

Given the opportunity, poor migrants and urban residents cannot only house themselves but can improve their shelter conditions over time. Dubbed the progressive housing model, this incremental process enables Third World residents to improve their shelter conditions gradually as means allow. Even so, housing finance has long been a problem and remains one in Third World countries. For most people, building a home is a cash proposition, and relatives must be relied on as a source of both capital and donated labor. This has been an effective way to acquire shelter, but it becomes less so when construction standards are raised or rigidly enforced or when other attempts at regularization increase the cost of construction.

Even with the substantial evidence toward the value of self-help efforts, in some locales governments are still trying to provide larger-scale comprehensive projects. In Ecuador, Glasser concluded, user construction is the most productive investment available to the nation. In the present political climate, however, he believes support favors the formal rather than the informal sector of the economy.

Political settings have an impact on the shelter conditions of the poor. Handelman concluded that in Latin America the urban lower class fares most poorly under rightist bureaucratic–authoritarian regimes, receives more support for spontaneous shelter and provision of sites and services under democratic–reformist regimes, and has experienced the most redistribution of housing resources under revolutionary regimes. The recent transition in Latin America from rightist authoritarian regimes to more pluralistic democracies suggests a gradually increasing state role in providing shelter or improving services to the urban poor.

Unauthorized development and squatting are no longer restricted to the poorest residents but have expanded to include middle-income people seeking a lower-cost way to acquire shelter or obtain more housing from their funds. Experiences in such places as Italy and Yugoslavia demonstrate the adoption of the spontaneous shelter process by the middle class and call attention to possible future problems as middle-class households outbid the poor for conveniently located sites and efforts to prevent such unauthorized housing prove ineffective.

Uniform standards, approaches, and policies should not be applied without regard to city size and location. Hansen and Williams pointed out that policies for large cities should be different from those for smaller towns. In large cities, policies should concentrate on improving infrastructure, regularizing land titles, upgrading settlements, increasing the amount of rental housing, and eliminating rent control. For smaller cities and towns, they stressed the need to keep land affordable to low-income families, increase the supply of serviced plots, and initiate settlement improvement and sites and services projects. In addition, building standards might be raised in the more densely populated cities, but be completely revised and reconsidered for other locales.

Appropriate construction technology is an important related policy issue. Western standards and building practices have long been proposed for, and admired by, Third World citizens. While these building methods have come into question, and their inappropriateness in some instances has been recognized, many Third World residents are not aware of useful alternative technologies. Local construction techniques, sometimes long ignored, may provide clues to more cost-effective approaches to upgrading.

Glasser concluded that self-help constructors are invaluable in responding to shortages of low-cost housing in Third World countries, and he believes governments should encourage and assist these builders. High-tech methods simply will not work. They tend to harm much more than help through draining of necessary funds; increasing debt; destroying job opportunities; replacing traditional, naturally cheap, and abundant resource materials; and discouraging traditionally culture-rich design. Government assistance programs designed to tap the skill and imagination of self-help builders are seen as the best solution to this problem.

The question of appropriate technologies and standards is not easily resolved. In socialist Yugoslavia, Pleskovic pointed out, the present policy of maintaining high building standards only contributes to more illegal housing, while self-help efforts and lowered standards could assist in solving unemployment, housing, and productivity problems. But governments must be very careful when revising shelter design standards. Lowering them may increase the number of households that can afford shelter, but it may also result in lower-quality housing that will soon be abandoned.

The area most ignored by government policy is that of the environmental impact of spontaneous settlements. Ecologically sensitive lands have been destroyed and shelters have been built in earthquake and mudslide areas and near pollution sources. Residents continue practices that expose them to hazardous chemicals, disease from improper sanitation, and other threats to healthful living.

According to Page's analysis, the environment and the welfare of the economy, as well as human lives, are inseparably related. In the long run, economies cannot prosper without a healthy environment. There is an irrefutable need for direct action to help protect the environments of Third World countries. If spontaneous settlements are not controlled positively, environmental decline will continue. People must be educated about the real dangers of disease and disaster, and governments should provide decent sites for future user-built housing. Third World country leaders must foresee and prevent environmental problems.

Good sites on which to build spontaneous shelters are becoming increasingly scarce, and fewer poor people are able to obtain land, especially in larger cities. One response has been to suggest policies that would direct potential migrants to secondary or smaller cities; another approach might be the purchase of land by the government to be allocated to the poor, on which they can construct their own housing.

Such was the finding of Subanu and myself in our examination of the Indonesian Kampung Improvement Program (KIP). The concern for squatters settling on environmentally sensitive lands and the problems resulting from this can be addressed through a governmental land-demarcation policy and other efforts to steer settlers to areas that will be provided with urban services. Governments must find a way to set boundaries for spontaneous settlements before sensitive lands are encroached upon. Nationwide policies for improving conditions in smaller cities to check the flow of migrants into the overcrowded urban areas should be formed. This kind of policy could work along with the national development goals of Indonesia and the KIP strategy, for example, and would very likely have applicability in other developing countries.

The high cost of capital has resulted in rental housing playing a growing role in Third World shelter. In virtually all locales, increasing numbers of households are sharing or renting out portions of their homes and building additional rooms or units on their property to rent for supplemental income. There are even instances where people are building numerous unauthorized structures for rental income.

The rental market must be recognized as a source of affordable shelter for the many households that may never have the capital to purchase their own homes. Sharing of dwelling units, as well as sites, should not be overlooked as a possible way to increase shelter availability. Hansen and Williams concluded that rental housing is a viable way to increase the shelter supply, and they argue for policies to increase the amount of rental housing and eliminate rent control. Nevertheless, caution must be exercised in regard to the promotion of rental housing. Amis pointed out that, in Kenya, the government policy of acceptance of spontaneous shelter resulted in the securing of lands for private rental purposes. Outside investors have transformed formerly squatter-occupied land into extremely profitable rental areas and have forced out the squatters, who must now pay exorbitant prices for shelter.

No matter the setting, financing urban improvements is expected to remain a problem. Sites and services and upgrading schemes have been demonstrated to be preferable to in-kind housing, but funding for these efforts remains woefully inadequate. Alexander proposes that resource allocation policies be reoriented to investment in construction credits, assistance to craftworkers and materials suppliers, technical advice for self-management, and the planning and design of infrastructure. He goes further to propose that legalization be given a higher priority than sites and services programming. To aid in financing, he suggests implementation of a model used in Mexico for regularization. A *fideicomiso* would take charge of prospective and retrospective land sales in the informal sector and would, through money made by land sales, provide land titles, infrastructure, and services. Similarly, a cooperative is being used in Monrovia, Liberia, to provide, maintain, and expand community facilities while recovering costs.

Broader economic changes are also called for. Glasser concluded, in regard to Ecuador, that until major shifts in the mechanisms of economic distribution occur, incremental development of existing communities represents the most effective means of achieving housing progress. A similar conclusion was reached by Guttenberg in regard to Italy. He believes that prevention of unauthorized development must wait until alternative sources of wealth can be discovered and the social attitude of the offenders is given time to mature.

An overriding question is whether the shelter situation would be helped by more or less planning. Direct efforts to provide housing and regularize development have met with mixed success, and in some instances have caused even more illegal development. Subsidies have not always reached the target groups, especially the poorest, and the trickle-down process has not worked well. Instead, bubble-up or gradual improvement has tended to provide more available housing than formal approaches.

Alexander took this position even further to argue that in Latin America planning and administration has been more of a problem than a solution, since it does not provide a framework for development and incurs direct costs, indirect social costs, and delays. Other authors are not as sure about the abandonment of planning, although the question nags several of them when future policies are considered.

What the future holds is not clear, but a number of trends suggest several plausible developments. Palmer and I pointed out the tremendous growth of urban populations that will inevitably occur between now and the year 2000 in developing areas and in their megacities. The case studies clearly show that there is a shortage of good urban building sites in major Third World cities. Conveniently located, developable land is becoming scarce and expensive, which in turn has caused people to squat on even more marginal land, to subdivide small plots even further, and to increase densities substantially. Mounting pressures are being placed on already limited infrastructure, transportation costs are growing, and living and conducting business in Third World urban areas is generally getting more expensive. All these factors suggest that future policies may favor regional or metropolitan decentralization of workplaces, more migration to secondary cities, and even population growth control. There is the distinct possibility for another round of spontaneous development in secondary cities and remote locations. At the same time, governments may be well advised to provide land near employment opportunities to the poor for shelter construction so as to forestall development on environmentally sensitive lands, to prevent excessive crowding in older areas, and to avoid overloading of infrastructure.

The major specific policy proposals mentioned above and discussed in detail in the preceding chapters would include the following:

- Do not raze usable spontaneous shelter.
- Do not penalize people who attempt to resolve their own shelter problems.

- Help settlers secure tenure of their building sites.
- Place priority on upgrading efforts and infrastructure improvement rather than on in-kind housing provision.
- Facilitate credit mechanisms where households have the ability to repay loans.
- Find ways to subsidize cost recovery for the poorest residents.
- Make land near employment opportunities available for self-help efforts for low-income households.
- Steer settlers away from environmentally sensitive areas and possibly to secondary cities.
- Do not set minimum standards that are beyond the economic and technical reach of the poor or that are so low as to cause early abandonment of units.
- Allow households to select the components of improvement projects they desire.
- Incorporate other community services into shelter provision strategies.
- Control speculation in upgraded sites and building plots.
- Recognize the value of the rental sector as a potential source of affordable shelter.
- Eliminate rent control.
- Permit settlers to rent out portions of their shelters and sites and to use them for income-generating activities.
- Support the use of indigenous materials, traditional settlement patterns and technologies, and informal construction systems.
- Address the larger questions of economic development and population growth.
- Educate residents, builders, planners, and officials about the full dimension of the shelter problem.

Listing policy proposals is easy; executing them is not. But all the authors have provided specific implementation suggestions in their chapters. In most instances, the contributors also call for attention to be given to poverty and resource constraints—as well as to their result, unauthorized housing. Shelter improvement in the Third World is clearly linked to the improvement of general economic conditions. Although government efforts such as land acquisition, legalization, settlement upgrading, and improved credit mechanisms will help more households obtain shelter, the longer-term answer may well lie in broader economic reform and progress.

No matter which policy approach is attempted, it is important to heed Rapoport's call for solutions that respect and build on history, culture, and tradition.

Political ideology and stability will also have a great bearing on future prospects. Under more stable conditions, lower-income populations will have a better chance to earn a decent income, to acquire capital, to obtain land tenure, to secure their shelter investment, and to look toward the future.

Although contributors to this book would approach the shelter shortage in developing areas in different ways, they all agree that the challenge to provide adequate shelter is not impossible and that culturally responsive, environmentally sound, and economically feasible policy initiatives can be forged.

About the Contributors

Index

About the Contributors

Carl V. Patton is a professor of architecture and urban planning and dean of the School of Architecture and Urban Planning at the University of Wisconsin–Milwaukee. He has conducted research in Greece and Indonesia and has acted as consultant to various planning and development organizations. He is the author of *Academia in Transition,* co-editor of *The Metropolitan Midwest: Policy Problems and Prospects for Change,* and co-author of *Basic Methods of Policy Analysis and Planning.*

Ernest R. Alexander is a professor of urban planning at the University of Wisconsin–Milwaukee. He has practiced as an architect and planner in Britain, Ghana, Israel, and the United States. His research is in planning theory, decision making, and organizations. He is co-author of *Evaluating Plan Implementation: The National Statutory Planning System in Israel,* and author of *Approaches to Planning.*

Philip Amis is a human geographer at the Project Planning Centre, University of Bradford, Bradford, Britain. His interests are in housing and urban development in the Third World, and he has conducted research in Kenya, Tanzania, and Sri Lanka.

David Evan Glasser is an associate professor of architecture at the University of Wisconsin–Milwaukee. A specialist in self-help housing, he has twice been awarded Senior Fulbright Research and Teaching Grants in Latin America.

Albert Guttenberg is a professor of urban and regional planning at the University of Illinois at Urbana–Champaign and the author of numerous publications on urban structure and land use, and on the history of planning. He was recently a Fulbright Scholar in Rome, Italy, and is the editor of *Planning and Public Policy.*

Howard Handelman is a professor of political science at the University of Wisconsin–Milwaukee and director of the Latin American Certificate Program at the University's Center for Latin America. He was recently a Fulbright Scholar in Ecuador. He is the author or editor of three books on Latin American politics, as well as a number of journal articles and monographs.

Eric Hansen is an assistant professor of urban planning at the University of Wisconsin–Milwaukee. He has worked for the World Bank and in Iran, Brazil, and the Philippines conducting urban and regional research. *Justin Williams* has a B.S. in Architectural Studies with a minor in Economics from the University of Wisconsin–Milwaukee.

Linda Lacey is an assistant professor in the Department of City and Regional Planning at the University of North Carolina at Chapel Hill. She teaches Third World planning courses and is currently involved in several research projects related to population and development planning in Liberia and Nigeria.

W. Donald McTaggart has conducted fieldwork in Nouméa, New Caledonia, Malaysia, Borneo, Sumatra, Java, Bali, and Sulawesi. He is a professor of geography at Arizona State University.

Stephen Emanuel Owusu is an assistant professor and research fellow in the Regional Planning Program at the University of Science and Technology in Kumasi, Ghana. He teaches housing and environmental courses and has taken part in a number of housing and urban sanitation research projects in Liberia and Ghana.

G. William Page is an associate professor and chair in the Department of Urban Planning and associate scientist at the Center for Great Lakes Studies at the University of Wisconsin–Milwaukee. His research interests include environmental policy and public health issues including the options available to water utilities with contaminated groundwater sources.

Elizabeth Kubale Palmer is an assistant professor of psychology at Alverno College, Milwaukee. She has conducted research on spontaneous settlements and user-built housing in Mexico and is a consultant on cultural aspects of design.

Boris Pleskovic is an economist in the Tunisia Division of the World Bank's Europe, Middle East, and North Africa (EMENA) Regional Office. He is co-author of *Macroeconomic Effects of Efficiency Pricing in the Public Sector in Egypt* and *The Use of a Social Accounting Matrix Framework for Public Sector Analysis: The Case Study of Mexico* and a member of the Editorial Board of the *International Regional Science Review.*

Amos Rapoport, one of the founders of environment–behavior studies, is distinguished professor of architecture at the University of Wisconsin–Milwaukee. In addition to his more than one hundred articles, he is the editor or author of eight books, including *House Form and Culture, Human Aspects of Urban Form,* and *The Meaning of the Built Environment.*

Leksono Probo Subanu is a lecturer in city planning at the Department of Architecture, Gadjah Mada University, Yogyakarta, Indonesia. He is interested in promoting and establishing the appropriate format for participatory processes in urban planning and design in Indonesian cities. He also is a consultant to urban and regional governments in Indonesia.

Bruce Taylor is a lecturer in geography at the Chinese University of Hong Kong. His teaching and research interests include the consequences of transferring Western planning technologies and ideals to non-Western settings.

Index